BICENTENNIAL

1807

⊛WILEY

2007

BICENTENNIAL

THE WILEY BICENTENNIAL—KNOWLEDGE FOR GENERATIONS

*E*ach generation has its unique needs and aspirations. When Charles Wiley first opened his small printing shop in lower Manhattan in 1807, it was a generation of boundless potential searching for an identity. And we were there, helping to define a new American literary tradition. Over half a century later, in the midst of the Second Industrial Revolution, it was a generation focused on building the future. Once again, we were there, supplying the critical scientific, technical, and engineering knowledge that helped frame the world. Throughout the 20th Century, and into the new millennium, nations began to reach out beyond their own borders and a new international community was born. Wiley was there, expanding its operations around the world to enable a global exchange of ideas, opinions, and know-how.

For 200 years, Wiley has been an integral part of each generation's journey, enabling the flow of information and understanding necessary to meet their needs and fulfill their aspirations. Today, bold new technologies are changing the way we live and learn. Wiley will be there, providing you the must-have knowledge you need to imagine new worlds, new possibilities, and new opportunities.

Generations come and go, but you can always count on Wiley to provide you the knowledge you need, when and where you need it!

WILLIAM J. PESCE
PRESIDENT AND CHIEF EXECUTIVE OFFICER

PETER BOOTH WILEY
~~~~~ BOARD

Personal Finance

Vickie Bajtelsmit
Colorado State University

with Linda Rastelli

BICENTENNIAL
1807
WILEY
2007
BICENTENNIAL

Credits

PUBLISHER
Anne Smith

PROJECT EDITOR
Beth Tripmacher

MARKETING MANAGER
Jennifer Slomack

SENIOR EDITORIAL ASSISTANT
Tiara Kelly

PRODUCTION MANAGER
Kelly Tavares

PRODUCTION ASSISTANT
Courtney Leshko

PROJECT MANAGER
Shana Meyer

CREATIVE DIRECTOR
Harry Nolan

COVER DESIGNER
Hope Miller

COVER PHOTO
© George Doyle/Getty Images

Wiley 200th Anniversary Logo designed by: Richard J. Pacifico

This book was set in Times New Roman by Techbooks and printed and bound by R.R. Donnelley. The cover was printed by R.R. Donnelley.

This book is printed on acid free paper. ∞

To order books or for customer service please, call 1-800-CALL WILEY (225-5945).

ISBN-13 978-0-470-11123-9

Printed in the United States of America

10 9 8 7 6 5 4

PREFACE

College classrooms bring together learners from many backgrounds with a variety of aspirations. Although the students are in the same course, they are not necessarily on the same path. This diversity, coupled with the reality that these learners often have jobs, families, and other commitments, requires a flexibility that our nation's higher education system is addressing. Distance learning, shorter course terms, chunked curriculum, new disciplines, evening courses, and certification programs are some of the approaches that colleges employ to reach as many students as possible and help them clarify and achieve their goals.

Wiley Pathways books, a new line of texts from John Wiley & Sons, Inc., are designed to help you address this diversity and the need for flexibility. These books focus on the fundamentals, identify core competencies and skills, and promote independent learning. The focus on the fundamentals helps students grasp the subject, bringing them all to the same basic understanding. These books use clear, everyday language, presented in an uncluttered format, making the content more accessible and the reading experience more pleasurable. The core competencies and practical skills focus help students succeed in the classroom and beyond, whether in another course or in a professional setting. A variety of built-in learning resources promote independent learning and help instructors and students gauge students' understanding of the content. These resources enable students to think critically about their new knowledge, and apply their skills in any situation.

Our goal with *Wiley Pathways* books—with its brief, inviting format, clear language, and core competencies and skills focus—is to celebrate the many students in your courses, respect their needs, and help you guide them on their way.

Wiley Pathways Pedagogy

To meet the needs of working college students, all *Wiley Pathways* texts explicitly use an outcomes and assessment-based pedagogy for the books: students will review what they have learned, acquire new information and skills, and apply their new knowledge and skills to real-life situations. Based on the recently updated categories of Bloom's Taxonomy of Learning, *Wiley Pathways Personal Finance* presents key topics in personal finance (the content) in easy-to-follow chapters. The text then prompts analysis, synthesis, and evaluation with a variety of learning aids and assessment tools. Students move efficiently from reviewing what they have learned, to acquiring new information and skills, to applying their new knowledge and skills to real-life scenarios.

With *Wiley Pathways*, students not only achieve academic mastery of personal finance *topics*, but they master real-world *skills* related to that content. The books help students become independent learners, giving them a distinct advantage in the field, whether they are starting out or seek to advance in their careers.

Organization, Depth and Breadth of the Text

▲ **Modular format.** Research on college students shows that they access information from textbooks in a non-linear way. Instructors also often wish to reorder textbook content to suit the needs of a particular class. Therefore, although *Wiley Pathways Personal Finance* proceeds logically from the basics to increasingly more challenging material, chapters are further organized into sections that are self-contained for maximum teaching and learning flexibility.

▲ **Numeric system of headings.** *Wiley Pathways Personal Finance* uses a numeric system for headings (for example, 2.3.4 identifies the fourth sub-section of section 3 of chapter 2). With this system, students and teachers can quickly and easily pinpoint topics in the table of contents and the text, keeping class time and study sessions focused.

▲ **Core content.** Topics in the text are organized into fifteen chapters.

Part I: The Personal Financial Planning Process

Chapter 1, Personal Financial Planning in Action, provides an overview of the five steps in the personal financial planning process and the elements of a comprehensive financial plan that are developed throughout the text. How to make effective financial decisions is also explained.

Chapter 2, Money Management Strategies and Skills, looks at ways to collect and organize your financial information. Students learn how to compile and use personal financial statements to evaluate their financial conditions. Simple financial ratios are presented to determine where you need to save or to better allocate money.

Chapter 3, Managing Your Taxes, examines the United States tax system. Students are helped to understand their federal tax returns, including tax brackets, tax credits and exemptions, and calculating taxable income. How to file a return and avoid common filing errors is presented. Finally, effective tax planning strategies are offered.

Part II: Managing Your Personal Finances

Chapter 4, Managing Your Cash and Savings, explains the objectives and rules of cash management. Students are helped to understand the basic differences between financial institutions, and given guidance in choosing a financial provider. Cash management products and services are detailed. Tips are provided on how to resolve cash management problems, including bounced checks, fraudulent activity, and obtaining emergency cash.

Chapter 5, Consumer Credit, helps students make wise credit card and consumer loan decisions. It examines the benefits and costs of consumer credit, including credit cards. How to apply for consumer credit and correcting credit mistakes are presented. How to avoid identify theft is explained, as well as other pitfalls of credit card usage.

Chapter 6, Using Consumer Loans, outlines the characteristics and types of consumer loans. Student loans are covered in detail, as well as how interest is calculated on consumer loans and the role of credit reporting agencies. How to improve your creditworthiness is studied, including the five C's of credit. Managing your debt is explained, including how to reduce it, and as a last resort, filing for bankruptcy.

Chapter 7, Making Automobile and Housing Decisions, examines how to purchase and finance autos and homes. From determining how much you can afford to spend, to negotiating, to obtaining a mortgage or auto loan, all aspects of these important transactions are covered. Whether to lease or buy a car, mortgage financing, choosing a reputable real estate broker, and closing the real estate transaction are also part of this chapter.

Part III: Protecting Yourself with Insurance

Chapter 8, Insuring Your Home and Automobile, shows how to protect your car and home after you have purchased them. It explains how insurance works, including risk pooling, indemnity, liability, exclusions and deductibles. Which risks are covered is discussed, as well as which types of homeowner's and automobile coverages are available. Next, how to buy insurance, from finding agents to getting quotes, is explained. Making insurance claims is included in this chapter.

Chapter 9, Health and Disability Insurance, reviews why health insurance is an important employee benefit and component of a sound financial plan. The types of health insurance are described, including employer-sponsored and government sponsored plans. Finally, planning for disability income needs is discussed, together with the importance of understanding your chances of becoming disabled at some point.

Chapter 10, Financial Planning with Life Insurance, describes why life insurance may be useful in your financial plan. Topics covered include how to determine your life insurance needs, what types of companies sell life insurance, types of policies, and important provisions in a life insurance contract.

Part IV: Managing Your Investments and Your Future

Chapter 11, Investment Basics, outlines clearly how to develop realistic investment goals, as well as find the money for investing. Factors that reduce investment risk and your investment alternatives are offered. The need for a consistent investment strategy and how to establish one is explored.

Chapter 12, Investing in Stocks and Bonds, explains equity and debt investing in brief detail. Common and preferred stock, how common stock is classified, and buying and selling stock on exchanges are explained. Evaluating the performance of your stock is also presented. Then the advantages and disadvantages of bond investing are explored, including how to buy and sell bonds.

Chapter 13, Investing in Mutual Funds, describes mutual funds and why they may be preferred by the individual investor. Included in the discussion are mutual fund investment classifications. How to select a fund and how to evaluate a fund's performance are offered as well.

Chapter 14, Planning for Retirement, has information on estimating retirement income needs and sources of retirement income. Described here are IRAs and how to avoid paying more taxes in retirement than you need to. Employee-sponsored and government sponsored benefits are included in the discussion. Finally, preparing for retirement payouts is covered.

Chapter 15, Preserving Your Estate, outlines reasons why you probably need a will, and why estate planning is important for everyone. The key components of estate plans are presented, and how to avoid estate and gift taxes. The types and formats of wills, including how to establish a valid will, is included.

Pre-reading Learning Aids

Each chapter of *Wiley Pathways Personal Finance* features the following learning and study aids to activate students' prior knowledge of the topics and orient them to the material.

▲ **Pre-test.** This pre-reading assessment tool in multiple-choice format not only introduces chapter material, but it also helps students anticipate the chapter's learning outcomes. By focusing students' attention on what they do not know, the self-test provides students with a benchmark against which they can measure their own progress. The pre-test is available online at www.wiley.com/college/bajtelsmit.

▲ **What You'll Learn in this Chapter.** This bulleted list focuses on *subject matter* that will be taught. It tells students what they will be learning in this chapter and why it is significant for their careers. It will also help students understand why the chapter is important and how it relates to other chapters in the text.

▲ **After Studying this Chapter, You'll Be Able To.** This list emphasizes *capabilities and skills* students will learn as a result of reading the chapter. It focuses on *execution* of subject matter that shows the relationship between what students will learn in the chapter and how the information learned will be applied in an on-the-job situation.

Within-text Learning Aids

The following learning aids are designed to encourage analysis and synthesis of the material, support the learning process, and ensure success during the evaluation phase:

▲ **Introduction.** This section orients the student by introducing the chapter and explaining its practical value and relevance to the book as a whole. Short summaries of chapter sections preview the topics to follow.

▲ **"For Example" Boxes.** Found within each chapter, these boxes tie section content to real-world examples, scenarios, and applications.

▲ **Figures and tables.** Line art and photos have been carefully chosen to be truly instructional rather than filler. Tables distill and present information in a way that is easy to identify, access, and understand, enhancing the focus of the text on essential ideas.

▲ **Self-Check.** Related to the "What You'll Learn" bullets and found at the end of each section, this battery of short answer questions emphasizes student understanding of concepts and mastery of section content. Though the questions may either be discussed in class or studied by students outside of class, students should not go on before they can answer all questions correctly.

▲ **Key Terms and Glossary.** To help students develop a professional vocabulary, key terms are bolded in the introduction, summary, and when they first appear in the chapter. A complete list of key terms with brief definitions appears at the end of each chapter and again in a glossary at the end of the book. Knowledge of key terms is assessed by all assessment tools (see below).

▲ **Summary.** Each chapter concludes with a summary paragraph that reviews the major concepts in the chapter and links back to the "What You'll Learn" list.

Evaluation and Assessment Tools

Each *Wiley Pathways* text consists of a variety of within-chapter and end-of-chapter assessment tools that test how well students have learned the material. These tools also encourage students to extend their learning into different scenarios and higher levels of understanding and thinking. The following assessment tools appear in every chapter of *Wiley Pathways Personal Finance*:

▲ *Summary Questions* help students summarize the chapter's main points by asking a series of multiple choice and true/false questions that emphasize student understanding of concepts and mastery of chapter content. Students should be able to answer all of the Summary Questions correctly before moving on.

▲ *Applying this Chapter Questions* drive home key ideas by asking students to synthesize and apply chapter concepts to new, real-life situations and scenarios. Asks student to practice using the material they have learned in contrived situations that help reinforce their understanding, and may throw light on important considerations, advantages, or drawbacks to a specific methodology.

▲ *You Try It Questions* are designed to extend students' thinking, and so are ideal for discussion, writing assignments, or for use as case studies. Using an open-ended format and sometimes based on Web sources, they encourage students to draw conclusions using chapter material applied to real-world situations, which fosters both mastery and independent learning.

▲ *Post-test* should be taken after students have completed the chapter. It includes all of the questions in the pre-test, so that students can see how their learning has progressed and improved.

Instructor and Student Package

Wiley Pathways Personal Finance is available with the following teaching and learning supplements. All supplements are available online at the text's Book Companion Web site, located at www.wiley.com/college/bajtelsmit.

▲ **Instructor's Resource Guide.** Provides the following aids and supplements for teaching an Introduction to Personal Finance course:

- *Sample syllabus.* A convenient template that instructors may use for creating their own course syllabi.

- *Teaching suggestions.* For each chapter, these include a chapter summary, learning objectives, definitions of key terms, lecture notes, answers to select text question sets, and at least 3 suggestions for classroom activities, such as ideas for speakers to invite, videos to show, and other projects.

▲ **PowerPoints.** Key information is summarized in 15 to 20 PowerPoints per chapter. Instructors may use these in class or choose to share them with students for class presentations or to provide additional study support.

▲ **Test Bank.** One test per chapter, as well as a mid-term, and two finals: one cumulative, one non-cumulative. Each includes true/false, multiple choice, and open-ended questions. Answers and page references are provided for the true/false and multiple choice questions, and page references for the open-ended questions. Available in Microsoft Word and computerized formats.

ACKNOWLEDGMENTS

Taken together, the content, pedagogy, and assessment elements of *Wiley Pathways Personal Finance* offer the career-oriented student the most important aspects of personal finance as well as ways to develop the skills and capabilities that current and future employers seek in the individuals they hire and promote. Instructors will appreciate its practical focus, conciseness, and real-world emphasis. We would like to thank the reviewers for their feedback and suggestions during the text's development. Their advice on how to shape *Wiley Pathways Personal Finance* into a solid learning tool that meets both their needs and those of their busy students is deeply appreciated.

We would especially like to thank the following reviewers for their significant contributions:

Robert Vaughn Diamond, American River College
Christine Mooney, Queensborough Community College

BRIEF CONTENTS

CONTENTS

1

PERSONAL FINANCIAL PLANNING IN ACTION
Developing a Personal Financial Plan

Starting Point

Go to www.wiley.com/college/bajtelsmit to assess your knowledge of developing a personal financial plan.
Determine where you need to concentrate your effort.

What You'll Learn in This Chapter

▲ Personal financial planning and decision-making strategies
▲ Factors that influence financial planning
▲ The stages of successful financial planning

After Studying This Chapter, You'll Be Able To

▲ List the five steps in the personal financial planning process
▲ Examine the factors that influence personal financial planning decisions
▲ Begin to construct a comprehensive financial plan
▲ Consider opportunity costs and marginal effects in making personal finance decisions

INTRODUCTION

Knowing how to manage your finances can help you be more successful in life. In this chapter, we first look at the five-step financial planning process and then the factors that influence it, and we discuss the elements of a comprehensive financial plan. Finally, we explore strategies for making effective financial decisions. With this framework, you will be able to gain the tools for successful personal financial management.

1.1 The Personal Financial Planning Process

In your life, you've probably already faced some financial challenges. For example, maybe you've asked yourself one or more of the following questions:

▲ Should I take out a student loan to pay for college expenses?
▲ How can I get out from under my credit card debt?
▲ Can I afford to replace my car's transmission?
▲ Where should I buy my auto insurance?
▲ Would graduate school be a good investment for me?
▲ How much should I contribute to my 401(k) retirement plan?
▲ Should I start a savings plan to fund my child's college education?
▲ How do I decide among the employee benefit options that my employer offers?

These questions are all related to **personal finance**—a specialized area of study that focuses on individual and household financial decisions, such as budgeting, saving, spending, insurance, and investments. Understanding these topics will help you in many ways. For example, you'll make better decisions when you buy an auto, shop for a home mortgage, choose a career, and save for retirement. You may also be able to pay less in taxes and interest. **Personal financial planning** is the process of developing and implementing an integrated, comprehensive plan designed to meet financial goals, to improve financial well-being, and to prepare for financial emergencies.

The primary goal of personal financial planning is to develop and achieve financial goals, such as

▲ Buying a first home or a bigger home.
▲ Making a major consumer purchase.
▲ Supporting a growing family.
▲ Preparing financially for retirement.

People who have their finances in order gain important social and psychological benefits as well. Generally, they feel less stressed and experience improved

Figure 1-1

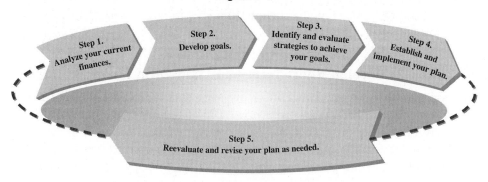

The five-step financial planning process.

relationships with friends, family members, and coworkers. As many couples know, financial difficulties are a major contributor to marital problems. Most people also find that the self-sufficiency that eventually results from good financial planning improves their self-esteem.

In this section, we introduce the five-step personal financial planning process (see Figure 1-1) and examine each step in detail. It's important as you read about the steps to recognize the circular flow of the planning process. Although you use the process to develop a personal financial plan, your plan won't ever be a finished product; you'll need to reevaluate and revise it continually as your life circumstances change. The process of personal financial planning is a lifelong activity.

1.1.1 Step 1: Analyze Your Current Financial Position

At the end of the month, many people struggle to meet their expenses. "Where did all the money go?" is a common lament. Before you can move forward with your financial plan, you need to determine where your money is coming from and where it is going.

Analyzing your current financial position requires that you take the following steps:

1. Collect and organize all your financial information.
2. Create personal financial statements.
3. Quantitatively evaluate your current financial position to establish a baseline against which you can measure improvement in the future.

This last step may involve hard work for those who are "organizationally challenged." Nevertheless, careful record keeping is vital to good financial planning, because it enables you to track actual expenditures and identify small financial problems before they turn into big ones. In Chapter 2, we explain how to analyze your current finances to determine your financial condition.

1.1.2 Step 2: Develop Short-Term and Long-Term Financial Goals

Everyone has a personal conception of "success." Have you thought about where you want to be 5 years from now? 10 years from now? For some, success may be defined in monetary terms and for others, in levels of personal satisfaction. However you define success, the second step in the personal financial planning process requires that you identify and prioritize specific goals and objectives.

The process of setting goals should involve some introspective assessment of why you have the goals you have. For example, are your objectives focused on your own needs or the needs of others? Are your objectives related to pressures from family members or peers?

Keep in mind that short-term and long-term goals change over time and may be influenced by changes in economic circumstances.

1.1.3 Step 3: Identify and Evaluate Alternative Strategies for Achieving Your Goals

Although every person's goals and objectives are unique to his or her circumstances, the strategies for achieving them are similar from person to person. In general, in order to have more money available to meet current or future goals, you either have to reduce spending or increase earnings. Step 3 in the personal financial planning process requires that you identify alternative strategies for achieving goals and compare the costs and benefits of each.

1.1.4 Step 4: Implement a Plan for Achieving Your Goals

Using the information developed in step 3, you are now prepared to decide on the best strategies for achieving your goals so that you can implement your plan. How do you make such decisions? How do you know which strategies are the best ones for achieving your goals? You acquire fundamental knowledge and master analytical tools that help you to make effective personal financial planning decisions. The result will be a personal financial plan that meets your basic household needs, builds wealth over time, and protects your income and assets.

1.1.5 Step 5: Regularly Reevaluate and Revise Your Plan

Many changes occur over the course of your life. Not only do changes in your personal circumstances (e.g., graduation, a new job, marriage, children) affect

FOR EXAMPLE

When Goals Must Change

In 2006, Jack Naughton was employed as a superintendent for a large residential construction firm. He and his wife lived comfortably on his $50,000 salary and felt lucky that he had been able to work his way up in the business, despite his lack of a college degree. They had recently stretched their finances to buy a larger house, and they planned to increase their retirement account contributions and to begin a college savings plan for their daughter.

Due to a real estate downturn, Jack was unexpectedly laid off from his job, and the Naughtons' goals had to change drastically. Instead of retirement and college savings, their new goals were to pay their bills and find a new job for Jack. After his layoff, Jack found a new job but had to take a significant pay cut, and his earnings no longer covered the family's expenses. To meet expenses, the Naughtons might use one or more of the following strategies:

▲ Mrs. Naughton could get a job.
▲ They could sell the house or possibly refinance it at a lower interest rate to reduce their monthly mortgage payments.
▲ They could sell other assets.
▲ They could dip into savings.
▲ They could borrow money.

Each of these strategies has costs and benefits that must be carefully identified and evaluated.

your financial planning objectives and strategies, but economic conditions may necessitate revision of the plan as well. An effective financial plan must be adaptable to changing circumstances. Thus, step 5 takes you continually back to steps 1 through 4.

SELF-CHECK

1. Define **personal finance** and **personal financial planning**.
2. List the five steps of the personal financial planning process.

1.2 Factors That Influence Personal Financial Planning

As you build your financial plan, you need to consider many factors that influence your spending and saving behavior. Some are unique to you, such as where you are in your life cycle, your family composition, your values, and your attitudes. Others, such as inflation and interest rates, affect everyone to some extent. Both types of factors can be expected to change over time, so your plan needs to continually adapt to new circumstances.

1.2.1 Changing Needs over the Life Cycle

Your household goes through several phases over your life cycle, and your financial situation changes as well. Figure 1-2 illustrates how a person's income and wealth might change over the life cycle. There are many different types of family situations. Although everyone's situation is unique, for everyone, there are significant differences in planning needs over the life cycle.

In general, your income level through your early 20s is lower than it is later, and your wealth may even be negative—that is, you may have more debts than assets at this point in your life. That's because you're making investments in your education that have not yet paid off.

Marriage, career development, the purchase of a home, and investments in your children's education will likely occur from your late 20s through your 40s.

Figure 1-2

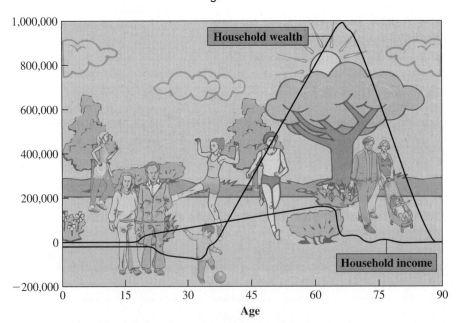

Household income and wealth over the life cycle.

During this time, your household will focus on setting goals, establishing savings, and protecting the family against unexpected negative events, such as premature death or job loss due to illness or disability. This is also the beginning of the wealth accumulation phase, which continues through your 50s to early 60s.

As retirement approaches, most people in their 50s and 60s pay closer attention to meeting retirement income and health needs and preserving wealth for their heirs. The earlier you plan for these needs, the better off you are when you get to that stage in the life cycle. During your retirement period, which generally begins at age 65, you decumulate, or spend, your accumulated wealth. Your goals during retirement may include maintaining an active lifestyle, including travel and leisure activities, and having sufficient income throughout your retirement period.

1.2.2 Values and Attitudes

People have different money styles—different values and attitudes regarding money and its use. A person's money style is generally the result of both learned behaviors and inherent tendencies. For example, if you were raised in a household where money was tight and consumer purchases were made with careful deliberation, you might carry the money skills learned from your parents' example into your adult life.

Whether your parents were spendthrifts or tightwads, however, your own genetic makeup also affects your personal money style. Individuals who are impulsive by nature often have difficulty controlling their spending, just as those with a tendency to orderliness are more likely to have their finances in order. Thus, both nature and nurture help to form your values and attitudes toward money. In fact, it is not uncommon to find that siblings raised in the same households have very different money styles. We explain here what we mean by values and attitudes:

▲ **Values** are fundamental beliefs about what is important in life. What do you think is most important: family, friends, things, education, religious faith, financial success, fame, health, self-sufficiency? The weight you place on each influences the goals you set and the strategies you develop to achieve your goals.

▲ **Attitudes** are opinions and psychological differences between people that affect their decisions. Are you an optimist or a pessimist? conservative or liberal? Do you like to have everything planned out in advance or just go with the flow?

Of particular importance to financial planning is your attitude toward risk, or uncertainty: Are you a risk-taker, or do you tend to avoid risk? What if you already know that you have a problem with money? Is it possible to overcome your biological makeup and your learned values and attitudes? Of course! You must first recognize what your values and attitudes are, particularly where they may run counter to achieving your goals. If you are a spender, you may need to approach your budget differently than someone who is naturally inclined to be more conservative in spending. Similarly, if you are a natural risk taker, you may need to learn to be more cautious, like someone who tends to avoid risk.

1.2.3 Life Situation

Family composition and demographic characteristics—such as age, marital status, income, and wealth—significantly affect financial planning. Households with children, for example, tend to have higher expenses and therefore less ability to save during their child-rearing years.

Children's college expenses can take a big bite out of family savings. Double-income couples, particularly those with no children, tend to be better off financially than singles. Those without children are also more able to focus on career goals and therefore can more quickly move up the employment ladder. However, the financial and social support provided by children to their parents in old age may eventually offset the increased earlier costs.

Also, education plays a critical role in financial success. College-educated people, particularly those with specialized skills (e.g., business, education, engineering), tend to receive higher starting salaries and larger wage increases over their careers. White-collar employees are also more likely to receive retirement plans and benefits packages.

Demographic factors such as gender, age, income, and education have also often been linked to risk attitudes. If you are male, childless, educated, and high income you are more likely to be a risk taker.

1.2.4 General Economic Conditions

A fundamental truth about the economy is that it is very unpredictable. Even experts cannot say with certainty what the future may hold. Nevertheless, some factors in the economy have a known influence on personal finances, and it's important for you to recognize these factors and incorporate them into your financial planning decisions. Many economic factors affect financial planning. Some factors that are highly likely to affect your future are

- ▲ Inflation.
- ▲ Interest rates.
- ▲ Employment conditions.
- ▲ Political unrest and global issues.

Everyone has at one time or another heard an older person say, "When I was a kid, it was a lot less expensive to . . . ." Such statements describe the effects of **inflation,** or the change in general price levels over time. Occasionally, we have a negative inflation rate—that is, the prices of goods and services actually decline over a given period. Generally, however, inflation refers to an increase in prices. As prices of goods and services go up, the spending power of your money goes down—a dollar will not purchase as much as it previously did.

Inflation affects nearly every aspect of your finances. Your grocery bills are probably higher this year than they were last year. You're likely paying more for gasoline now than in the past. Your monthly rent will probably go up next year, too. As prices of goods get higher over time, you can maintain your standard of living only if your income after taxes also rises by the same amount. For your standard of living to improve, your income must rise at a rate faster than the inflation rate. Inflation affects your investments as well. If the costs of goods rise at a rate of 4 percent, but your savings account is paying only 3 percent, then you are actually losing spending power.

For the overall U.S. market, inflation is measured by the change in the **consumer price index (CPI),** reported monthly by the Bureau of Labor Statistics. The CPI tracks prices of a representative basket of more than 400 goods and services used by urban households, including food, housing, consumer goods, gasoline, and clothing.

Whereas the price of a college education has tripled since 1980, that of gasoline has increased only 78 percent over the same period. Depending on various factors, you may experience a larger or smaller change in expenses than the price changes indicated by the CPI. For example, some areas of the country have higher rates of inflation than average, primarily because of higher fuel and housing costs. Housing in areas of the country that are in high demand can be extremely costly. According to the National Association of Realtors, at the end of 2005, the median price of a home in Indianapolis, Indiana was only $122,000, whereas the median resale price in San Francisco, California, was $718,700.

A person also has different demands for goods and services at different stages in the life cycle. For example, health care costs, which have risen at a much faster rate than other elements of the CPI, are a bigger component of a retiree's expenses—12.6 percent of total household expenses, compared with only 2.5 percent for those under age 25 and 4 percent for households aged 35 to 44. Housing costs, in contrast, have less importance for retirees because many retirees have paid off their home mortgages. Furthermore, inflation can be particularly problematic for people on fixed incomes. If your retirement income doesn't increase over time, but your expenses do, your standard of living gradually declines.

Although inflation has averaged 4.8 percent per year since 1970, the annual rates of inflation have ranged from 1.2 to 13.3 percent. Over that same period, the federal minimum wage rate has increased from $1.60 to $5.15, the equivalent of only 3.6 percent per year. Similarly, the average wage for production workers in private industry has increased 4.3 percent. These statistics illustrate an important economic reality—wages don't always keep up with prices—and this is particularly true during periods of high inflation. For example, in 1979, when inflation hit a high of 13.3 percent, production workers' average wages that year increased only 8.5 percent. Because 8.5 percent probably seemed like a good raise at the time, it's likely that the average worker didn't realize that his or her standard of living had actually declined.

Interest rates also affect general economic conditions. The **interest rate** is a measure of your earnings, or return, on an investment When you borrow money, the interest rate is a cost to you. Interest is usually expressed as a percentage of the amount lent or borrowed. Interest rates can also be thought of as a cost of spending money today instead of saving for tomorrow. How much additional money will you need to get in the future to be willing to delay spending that money on goods and services you can enjoy right now? For example, if your roommate asks you to lend him $1,000 and promises to pay you back exactly one year from now, how much will you require that he pay you at that time? If you have to take the money out of a savings account that pays you 4 percent interest per year, you'll probably want him to pay you at least the $1,000 plus 4 percent interest. But what if lending him the money means that you will have to forego a trip to Mexico over spring break? How much additional money in the future will it take to convince you to give up spending the money on the trip now?

What makes interest rates go up or down? Like the prices of goods and services, interest rates are driven by supply and demand. When there is a lot of demand for borrowing but not a lot of money available to borrow, interest rates go up. In recessions, when businesses do not need or want to invest in growth, the demand for borrowing is lower, and rates may go down.

Actions taken by the **Federal Reserve Bank** (referred to as "the Fed")—the central bank that controls the money supply in the United States—affect the

---

FOR EXAMPLE

How the Fed Moves Interest Rates

Between 2000 and 2003, the Federal Reserve several times took action to lower the **federal funds rate**—the rate that banks charge each other for short-term loans—in an attempt to stimulate the sluggish economy. By reducing the rate from 6.5 to 1.0 percent gradually over that time period, the Federal Reserve actions reduced short-term borrowing rates, which in turn resulted in lower commercial loan and mortgage loan rates. These actions helped to pull the country out of the recession. In June 2004, the Fed reversed this trend and began to increase rates. In addition to actions by the Federal Reserve, inflation and other economic conditions cause interest rates to go up and down over time, and, through a series of increases over the next two years, brought the rate back up to 5.25 percent by October 2006 in order to keep inflation in check.

finances of the average person, although they may not be aware of what the Fed is doing. Sometimes the Fed takes actions to increase or decrease the supply of money in the economy in order to manipulate the rate of interest on short-term, low-risk borrowed funds. When these rates go up, it becomes more expensive for people to obtain credit, to finance their mortgages, and to use credit cards. This slows down the economy. Conversely, lower rates increase economic activity by making it easier for people to obtain credit.

Although the ups and downs in interest rates tend to track each other, there are differences among interest rates on various types of loans at any given time. These differences are primarily due to differences in risk. For example, what is the chance that payments will not be made on time or that a loan will not be repaid? The higher the chances, the riskier the loan and the higher the rate charged by lenders. If the borrower does not pay the loan as agreed, does the lender have any way of recouping the loan? If not, the loan is riskier than it would otherwise be. Consumer loans and credit cards are riskier in that the borrower is an individual rather than a financial institution and might be unable to pay if his or her financial situation changes in the future. However, car loans have much lower rates than credit cards because the bank normally has the right to take back the car in the event of nonpayment. The riskier the investment or loan, the higher the interest rate because the lender or investor must be compensated for the risk of not being repaid.

Your personal finances are also affected by cyclical business and employment conditions, known as the **economic cycle**, or the historical pattern of ups and downs common to the U.S. economy:

▲ A low point in the cycle is called a **recession** (or, in the extreme, a depression), and is characterized by reduced business investment and high unemployment rates.

▲ Economic **expansion** periods are characterized by increased business investment and employment opportunities.

FOR EXAMPLE

Boom and Bust in Silicon Valley

During the technology boom of the 1990s, even undistinguished computer science majors had multiple job offers at graduation and were constantly bombarded by headhunters trying to entice them to different jobs for better pay and benefits. A few years later, new graduates in these fields were happy to get any job at all. Widespread layoffs at technology firms meant that new graduates were competing in the job market with individuals who had many more years of experience.

In times of growth and low unemployment, salaries tend to rise more quickly, and there are better opportunities for advancement. Your future will be less sensitive to changes in employment conditions if you choose an area of study that is likely to have continuing strong demand over time. You can also minimize the risk of layoff by keeping your skills up-to-date.

Political and global factors can also affect your personal finances. For some time following September 11, 2001, the looming threat of terrorism had a negative impact on the U.S. economy. The stock market, which had already seen substantial declines from its high of the previous year, continued to plummet, losing more than 20 percent of its value from September 2001 to September 2002; unemployment increased rapidly; and governmental spending on homeland security cut into state budgets.

SELF-CHECK

1. Define **inflation**, **CPI**, **interest rate**, and **federal funds rate**.
2. List the personal factors that affect financial planning.
3. What is a low point in the business cycle called?

1.3 Elements of a Comprehensive Financial Plan

There are four stages in developing a comprehensive financial plan, all of which are covered in various sections in this book:

1. **Establishing a firm foundation:** The first step to success in your personal finances is to establish the necessary foundations, including an understanding of the personal financial planning process, the necessary tools, and the tax effects of your financial decisions.
2. **Securing basic needs:** The second step is to secure your basic needs. This step includes meeting your consumption and housing needs, setting aside funds for financial emergencies, protecting your assets with insurance, establishing a career path, and making educated employee benefits decisions.
3. **Building wealth:** After you have secured your basic needs, you can begin to think about wealth building to meet future needs, such as retirement and college funding. With financial security comes the need to protect your wealth.

4. **Protecting wealth and dependents:** The final stage in the process of developing a comprehensive financial plan includes the protective elements of life insurance, long term care insurance, and estate planning.

SELF-CHECK

1. What are the basic needs you need to meet after you have a financial foundation?
2. What are four stages of a comprehensive financial plan?

1.4 Making Effective Decisions

As you work on your financial plan, you need to make many important decisions. After you identify your goals, you need to make decisions about consumption, savings, and investment alternatives. These decisions can more effectively help you achieve your goals if you use these decision-making strategies:

▲ **Base your decisions on reasonable assumptions:** Don't be unreasonably optimistic about your finances.

▲ **Apply marginal reasoning:** *Marginal* refers to the change in outcome or the additional benefit that will result from the decision you make.

▲ **Consider opportunity costs:** An opportunity cost is a measure of what you have to give up in order to take a particular action.

▲ **Use sensitivity analysis:** A sensitivity analysis asks the question "What effect would it have on my personal finances if my assumptions turned out to be wrong?"

Let's look at each of these strategies in more detail.

1.4.1 Making Reasonable Assumptions

Most financial decisions require you to forecast, or predict, future events and economic circumstances: What will your needs be 5 or 10 or even 20 years from now? What will your family circumstances require from you financially? When will you retire? How long will you live? Which investments will perform best over time? What will the rate of inflation be in the future? What rate will you earn on your investments? What kinds of risks will you face?

Life is, of course, unpredictable. But even if you don't know an outcome for certain, you can still use the information available to you to come up with a reasonable assumption. This is a critical component of successful decision making.

FOR EXAMPLE

Retirement Squeeze

Karen and Luke Amato were planning to retire in 2001, when both would reach the age of 65. They had invested all their retirement funds in the stock market over the 1990s, accumulating a total portfolio of about $1.5 million by the time the market reached its peak, an amount they thought would be more than adequate to meet their expected retirement needs. Unfortunately, one year later, they had to reconsider their plans because the value of their retirement nest egg had fallen by more than one-third, to less than $1 million. Although the Amatos might have limited their losses by moving their money to safer investments earlier, they, like many other investors, had unrealistically clung to the hope that the stock market would recover. In fact, they were lucky—some investors experienced much larger losses. If they had applied more realistic assumptions, based on a longer-term history of stock market returns, the Amatos and others might have avoided such extreme losses and been able to retire as they had planned.

One of the biggest mistakes people make in their finances is that they are too optimistic in their assumptions. During the 1990s, the stock market enjoyed a long period of strong growth. Investors who had never experienced a market downturn actually thought that stocks would continue to earn such high rates of return indefinitely. Unreasonably optimistic investors eventually lost a large percentage of their investment portfolios when the market declined.

1.4.2 Applying Marginal Reasoning

In choosing among potential strategies to achieve your financial goals, it is important to apply **marginal reasoning.** The term *marginal* refers to the change in outcome, or the additional benefit, that will result from the decision you make.

Suppose you and your spouse share a car and you're considering buying a second car. In applying marginal analysis, you need to consider only the additional benefits that the second car brings and not the general benefits of having a car in the first place. Similarly, if you're choosing between two possible cars, you need to consider how much extra benefit you would get from the more expensive of the two and balance that against the extra cost.

1.4.3 Considering Opportunity Costs

Every financial decision you make has an opportunity cost. An **opportunity cost** is a measure of what you have to give up in order to take a particular action. Opportunity costs can be personal costs, such as time and effort, but they are often financial costs, such as lost dollars or return on investment.

As explained in Section 1.2.4, your spending decisions often involve a trade-off because if you spend money, you are giving up the interest you could have earned on the money if you had invested it instead. When you invest, your money earns interest. If you leave your money invested for long periods of time, your money earns compound interest, or interest on interest. So, if you earn 10 percent interest on $1000 for one year, you will have $1100 at the end of the year. But if you leave the interest in the account, you will earn the 10 percent interest on the entire $1,100, so your interest the second year will be $110. This allows it to grow faster and is often referred to as the *time value of money*. The opportunity cost of missing out on earning compound interest is an important component of financial decision making.

For example, suppose you're faced with the decision of whether to take money from savings for your college education or to work while attending school to earn the money. If you choose to take money from savings, you give up what you could have earned on that investment—this is your opportunity cost. But if you otherwise would have to work 30 hours per week while you attend school, the lost investment earnings might be small relative to the personal costs you would incur—less time and energy to apply to your studies and extracurricular activities. Evaluating opportunity costs carefully results in better decisions.

1.4.4 Using Sensitivity Analysis

Suppose you are deciding on the purchase of a new home. Although the loan payment will be a bit of a stretch for you the first year, you anticipate that you

---

FOR EXAMPLE

The Power of Compound Interest

Marie receives a tax refund of $3,000. She wants to use the money for a college fund for her daughter who is three years old. If she invests this in an account that earns 5% interest and leaves it to earn compound interest for 15 years, she can calculate the amount she will have at the end using the equation: Future value = Present Value $\times (1 + r)^n$. So, in fifteen years, Marie will have $6,237 = $3,000 $\times (1.05)^{15}$. As a shortcut to figuring out how much difference interest will make to your decisions, you can use Figure 1-3. Find the column for the interest rate you expect to earn on your investment and look down to the number in the row corresponding to the number of years you plan to leave the money invested. That number is the amount you can multiply times your original investment to determine how much it will grow to. If Marie could earn 8 percent on her investment, the multiplier from the table is 3.17, so her $3,000 will grow to $3,000 $\times$ 3.17 = $9,510.

Figure 1-3

Years Invested	Interest Rate Earned on Investment							
	3%	4%	5%	6%	7%	8%	9%	10%
1	1.03	1.04	1.05	1.06	1.07	1.08	1.09	1.10
2	1.06	1.08	1.10	1.12	1.14	1.17	1.19	1.21
3	1.09	1.12	1.16	1.19	1.23	1.26	1.30	1.33
4	1.13	1.17	1.22	1.26	1.31	1.36	1.41	1.46
5	1.16	1.22	1.28	1.34	1.40	1.47	1.54	1.61
6	1.19	1.27	1.34	1.42	1.50	1.59	1.68	1.77
7	1.23	1.32	1.41	1.50	1.61	1.71	1.83	1.95
8	1.27	1.37	1.48	1.59	1.72	1.85	1.99	2.14
9	1.30	1.42	1.55	1.69	1.84	2.00	2.17	2.36
10	1.34	1.48	1.63	1.79	1.97	2.16	2.37	2.59
15	1.56	1.80	2.08	2.40	2.76	3.17	3.64	4.18
20	1.81	2.19	2.65	3.21	3.87	4.66	5.60	6.73
25	2.09	2.67	3.39	4.29	5.43	6.85	8.62	10.83
30	2.43	3.24	4.32	5.74	7.61	10.06	13.27	17.45

Future Value Multipliers

will get a good raise next year, which will make the payment affordable. But what if this assumption is wrong—what if you do not get the raise or, even worse, are laid off from your job?

Sensitivity analysis asks the question "What effect would it have on my personal finances if my assumptions turned out to be wrong?" By considering how the outcome might change with changes in other uncertain variables, you can reduce the risk that your plan will have an adverse impact on your finances.

Psychology research has shown that people exhibit different decision-making styles, many of which result in less-than-optimal outcomes. Even if you are naturally inclined to make decisions in a different way, you can still learn to apply the strategies and tools discussed in this chapter in order to make more effective decisions.

SELF-CHECK

1. List the decision-making strategies available to you for financial planning.
2. Define **opportunity cost** and **sensitivity analysis**.

SUMMARY

Personal financial planning can mean the difference between financial success in your life and problems down the road. The five-step planning process is a continuous cycle that helps you assess your position and get to where you want to be. Personal factors as well as general economic factors influence the planning process. The stages of a plan include laying a foundation, securing basic needs, building wealth, and protecting wealth and dependents.

KEY TERMS

Attitudes	Opinions and psychological differences between people that affect their decisions.
Consumer price index (CPI)	A U.S. government index that tracks prices of a representative basket of goods and services.
Economic cycle	A pattern of ups and downs experienced by the U.S. economy.
Expansion	Periods characterized by increased business investment and employment opportunities.
Federal Reserve Bank	The central bank that controls the money supply in the United States.
Federal funds rate	The rate banks charge each other for short-term loans.
Inflation	The change in general price levels over time.
Interest rate	A cost of money, expressed as a percentage.
Marginal reasoning	A strategy that takes into account the change in outcome or additional benefit resulting from a decision.
Opportunity cost	What you have to give up in order to do something.
Personal finance	A specialized area of study that focuses on individual and household financial decisions, such as budgeting, saving, spending, insurance, and investments.
Personal financial planning	The process of developing and implementing an integrated, comprehensive plan designed to meet financial goals, to improve financial well-being, and to prepare for financial emergencies.
Recession	A low point in the business cycle.
Sensitivity analysis	Consideration of how an outcome changes with changes in other variables.
Values	Fundamental beliefs about what is important in life.

ASSESS YOUR UNDERSTANDING

Go to www.wiley.com/college/bajtelsmit to assess your knowledge of developing your personal financial plan.
Measure your learning by comparing pre-test and post-test results.

Summary Questions

1. Which of the following is not normally considered an area of personal finance?
   (a) budgeting
   (b) investments
   (c) choice of a career
   (d) choice of a marriage partner
2. Personal financial planning skills are applicable only in the early years of a person's life. True or false?
3. Which of the following is the best definition of personal finance?
   (a) the study of individual and household financial decisions
   (b) the study of individual investment planning
   (c) the study of personal wealth
   (d) the study of personal money management
4. Which of the following is not one of the steps in the personal financial planning process?
   (a) developing short-term and long-term financial goals
   (b) identifying and evaluating alternative strategies for achieving goals
   (c) implementing a plan for achieving goals
   (d) determining the appropriate risk level of a participant
5. An effective financial plan should be inflexible in order to achieve the goals set. True or false?
6. A person's fundamental beliefs concerning what is important in life are referred to as:
   (a) values.
   (b) attitudes.
   (c) opinions.
   (d) judgments.
7. For a person's standard of living to improve, his or her:
   (a) income must be above the average standard of living.
   (b) expenses must decrease.

(c) assets must rise in value faster than his or her expenses

(d) income must rise faster than the inflation rate.

8. For the overall U.S. market, inflation is measured by the change in the:

(a) producer price index.

(b) consumer price index.

(c) gross domestic product.

(d) wholesale price index.

9. You are considering adding a wood shop to your home. You enjoy wood-working and could make items for sale. In considering this addition, you look only at the extra cost of the shop and the potential benefits of having the shop. This is an example of:

(a) opportunity cost decision making.

(b) sensitivity analysis.

(c) marginal analysis.

(d) reasonable assumptions.

10. When a person begins to spend his or her accumulated wealth, this is known as the distribution phase. True or false?

11. You decide to take a part-time job to help with your college expenses. The hours available for study are thus reduced. The reduction in study hours would be your:

(a) fixed cost.

(b) direct cost.

(c) variable cost.

(d) opportunity cost.

Applying This Chapter

1. Name three benefits of having a better understanding of personal finance.

2. Explain how your financial planning needs are likely to change over your life cycle.

3. Under what circumstances might the Federal Reserve take action to increase short-term interest rates?

4. Identify where each of the following fits into a comprehensive financial plan: career development, checking and savings accounts, stock investing, retirement planning, and life insurance.

5. Sanjay, an engineer at a major technology firm, earns $50,000 per year. He thinks that having an MBA degree will increase his chances of being promoted to a management position. He is trying to decide whether to

enroll in a part-time evening program that will take two years or in a one-year full-time MBA program. Identify the factors that Sanjay should consider in making this decision. What are the opportunity costs of each alternative?

6. How can marginal reasoning be applied to the analysis of Sanjay's situation in Question 5?

And Then There Were Three

Kenny and Ellen are married during their senior year in college. They plan and save $3,000 for a honeymoon trip to Europe after graduation. They both have offers for jobs that begin in July. Two months before graduation, they discover that Ellen is pregnant.

1. Should they change their honeymoon plans?
2. Explain why they should reevaluate their honeymoon decision based on the change in their life circumstances.
3. If they invest the $3,000 instead of spending it, how much will it be worth in 10 years if they earn 7 percent per year on their investment. (Hint: Use Figure 1-3)

What Happens if the Car Breaks Down?

Miranda is a single mother of two, struggling to make ends meet. Her salary of $40,000, after taxes and child-care expenses, doesn't go very far. Miranda is a careful budgeter, and she has been setting aside $40 per month for Christmas presents for her kids. By October, she is proud to have $400 in her savings account. But disaster strikes: Her car breaks down, and the mechanic tells her the cost of fixing it will be $350.

1. What are Miranda's options?
2. Taking Miranda's situation into consideration, at what stage is she in her comprehensive financial plan? Which elements do you think she needs to focus on in the short term (one year or less)? Which elements should she focus on over the next five years?

2

MONEY MANAGEMENT STRATEGIES AND SKILLS
Putting Your Financial House in Order

Starting Point

Go to www.wiley.com/college/bajtelsmit to assess your knowledge of money management strategies and skills.
Determine where you need to concentrate your effort.

What You'll Learn in This Chapter

▲ Document organization, storage, and safekeeping
▲ How to use personal balance sheets
▲ How to calculate personal financial ratios

After Studying This Chapter, You'll Be Able To

▲ Develop a system for organizing and maintaining your financial records
▲ Calculate your net worth by using a personal balance sheet
▲ Summarize your current inflows and outflows of cash by using a personal cash flow statement
▲ Use personal financial ratios to evaluate your current financial position

INTRODUCTION

The skills taught in this chapter provide the foundation for successful money management. You'll learn to organize and maintain your financial records and how to use personal financial statements to see how you're doing financially. You'll also learn how to calculate the financial ratios that determine your creditworthiness and how much you are saving. These tools will help you on your road to financial success.

2.1 Collecting and Organizing Your Financial Information

Although some people love to file and organize, most people do not. The older you get, the more stuff you accumulate, and it doesn't take long for a small pile of paperwork to grow to fill several file cabinets. The earlier you develop a system for organizing your financial records, the easier it is to maintain order as your life becomes more complex. The Personal Financial Planner that can be found in the Appendix and online includes a worksheet to help you get started organizing your records.

2.1.1 Why You Need to Save Bills and Documents

The first rule of organization is that there should be a particular purpose for everything you save and file. Although this list is not exhaustive, some possible reasons for keeping particular documents are

▲ Paying bills.
▲ Tracking your budget.
▲ Preparing for tax reports.
▲ Making investment decisions.
▲ Making insurance or warranty claims.
▲ Ensuring prompt access to essential records.

2.1.2 How Long You Should Save Documents

Of course, you need not keep all your documents forever. How long you should save each item depends on what you will use it for. Documents necessary for bill paying and budgeting have only short-term usefulness. Thus you need to save receipts for ATM withdrawals and deposits and for cash or credit purchases only until you receive a statement verifying that your account was correctly charged. You should keep bills for utilities, car expenses, and other irregular expenses that are not tax deductible for a full year so that you can accurately report the costs in your budget and personal cash flow statements.

You should file any documents that support tax deductions with your tax records. Although most Internal Revenue Service (IRS) audits occur within three years of the filing of a return, they can also occur later, so it's generally recommended that you keep tax records for seven years to be safe. The IRS audits about 1 out of every 174 returns, and most audits occur in the first year following filing. Audits in later years are usually the result of irregularities discovered in auditing earlier returns.

2.1.3 Where You Should Keep Documents

You can keep your personal financial documents anywhere, as long as you can easily access them when necessary. A system of file folders kept in a file cabinet or box is effective for most people. Although computer filing is also a possibility, most bills still exist on paper, so even if you can use your computer for some filing purposes, you still need to store paper copies as well.

You should keep important personal documents and valuables, particularly those that are difficult to replace—passports, birth and marriage certificates, Social Security cards, stock certificates, wills, and deeds—in a safe deposit box or fireproof lockbox. A safe deposit box is a secure private storage area (usually a small locking drawer) maintained at a remote location, often at a financial institution's place of business. A lockbox, which is a fireproof keyed safe that you keep in your home, is not as secure as a safe deposit box because it's usually movable, and any thieves that break into your house are likely to look for it right away. The primary purpose of a lockbox is to prevent loss or damage to the documents in the event of a fire.

If you use your home computer for managing your finances, you should be sure to regularly back up the information on a disk and store that disk in a separate location, such as a friend's house, your place of employment, or a safe deposit box. You need to ensure that your electronic records will be safe in the event of theft, fire, electrical outage, or water damage. The best way to do this is to back up your records immediately whenever you make any major changes to the files, such as when you pay bills or revise your budget.

SELF-CHECK

1. Explain the difference between a lockbox and a safe deposit box.
2. List the types of information you should store.

2.2 Using Personal Financial Statements

After you've collected and organized your financial information, you can use it to begin evaluating your financial condition. **Personal financial statements** summarize your financial information in a way that makes it easy to see where you stand and to plan for where you want to be in the future. Just as companies make regular reports on their financial status to their shareholders, you should make a financial report to yourself.

Others might request the information contained in your personal financial statements (e.g., financial companies considering your application for a loan, organizations evaluating your qualifications for a scholarship, financial advisors helping you with your personal financial plan). In this section, you'll learn how to develop a personal balance sheet to estimate your financial net worth and a personal cash flow statement to evaluate your cash inflows and outflows.

2.2.1 Preparing a Personal Balance Sheet

How much are you worth today? In other words, how wealthy are you? This calculation is a good starting point for financial planning. A **personal balance sheet** is a financial statement that details the value of everything you own and subtracts what you owe to others to arrive at your **net worth,** or the amount of wealth you would have left after paying all your outstanding debts. A personal balance sheet shows your assets and debts:

▲ **Assets** are the things you own. Assets include liquid assets (such as cash), personal property, real estate, and investments.

▲ **Debts,** or liabilities, are the amounts you owe. Debts include both short-term obligations, such as unpaid bills and credit card debt, and long-term debts, such as student loans, car loans, and home mortgages.

To prepare a personal balance sheet, you start by making a list of everything you own, beginning with the most **liquid assets**—cash and near-cash assets that can easily be converted to cash without loss of value—and ending with the least liquid. Checking and savings accounts are examples of liquid assets; your automobile and home are not liquid because it would take time to sell them, and you would incur transaction costs such as advertising fees and commissions. If you needed cash in a hurry, you would probably also have to discount the price to make a quick sale.

The next step in constructing your personal balance sheet is to make a list of your debts. As with your assets, you start with short-term debts, such as currently unpaid bills, and end with long-term debts, such as your student loans and home mortgage.

FOR EXAMPLE

A Personal Balance Sheet

Danelle, a senior at a large university in the Midwest, is graduating with a biology major. She says, "I'm also getting a teaching certificate so that I can be a high school biology teacher. My parents helped out with my first two years, but now I'm supporting myself with a part-time job, financial aid, and student loans. Although I think I'm in pretty good financial shape, I know I need to get better organized. My biggest problem is that I'm so busy—with my schoolwork and job responsibilities, it's sometimes hard to even find the time to pay my bills. To be totally honest, I also have a tendency to avoid financial matters because I've never particularly liked math. One of my financial downfalls is that I love to shop for clothes and can't resist a good sale. So my credit card balances have increased. I'm a little nervous about how I'll be able to pay them off, especially since I'll have to start paying my student loan once I graduate."

This section walks through how to create a balance sheet that itemizes Danelle's assets and debts, as shown in Figure 2-1. You can create your own personal balance sheet by using the worksheet provided in the Personal Financial Planner.

2.2.2 Valuing Your Assets and Debts

How do you go about assigning a dollar value to each asset and debt? Your most recent bank statements give you the value of your checking and savings accounts. For other assets, you can try to estimate the **market value**, or the price you could sell them for today.

The market value is not the same as what you paid for an asset. For example, if you just bought a new car, you won't be able to sell it now for what you paid for it. Similarly, the market value of your stereo system is much lower than what you paid for the system, even if it's practically new. In contrast, you might own some assets that have much higher market values than what you paid for them. A first-edition comic book that you paid $1 for 10 years ago may be worth $100 today. Also, normally, real estate increases in value over time, so your home probably has a higher market value now than when you purchased it.

For some of your assets, such as your car, there may be a corresponding debt. If you have outstanding debt on your car, you enter the market value of your vehicle on the asset side of your balance sheet and the loan balance on the debt side. Notice that Danelle has entered $5,000 as the value of her car and $3,000 as the remaining balance on her car loan. If you lease a car, your payment obligations are a debt, but you don't own the car, so you shouldn't include

Figure 2-1

Danelle Washington's Personal Balance Sheet, December 31, 2004

	Assets	
Checking accounts	$ 500	
Savings accounts	1,000	
Money market accounts		
Cash value of life insurance	———	
Total Liquid Assets		$ 1,500

List the values of your liquid assets (Chapter 5), household goods, and automobiles (Chapter 8).

Home furnishings	1,200	
Jewelry/art collectibles	500	
Clothing/personal assets	3,000	
Market value of automobiles	5,000	
Total Personal Property		$ 9,700

Market value of investments (stocks, bonds, mutual funds)		
Employer-sponsored retirement plan		
Individual Retirement Accounts (IRAs)		
Other retirement savings		
College savings plan		
Other savings or investments	———	
Total Investment Assets		

List the market value of assets, investments, and real property (Chapters 8, 11–15).

Market value of home		
Market value of investment real estate	———	
Total Real Property		
TOTAL ASSETS		$11,200

	Debts	
Rent or mortgage payment	$ 500	
Utillities and other bills	130	
Credit card minimum payments	150	
Total Current Bills		$ 780

Credit card balances		
1. Master Card	4,200	
2. JCPenney	1,000	
Personal Loans		
Car loans	3,000	
Alimony/child support owed		
Taxes owed (above withholding)	———	
Total Short-Term Debts		$ 8,200

List your short-term and long-term debts (Chapter 6–8).

Student loans	18,000	
Home mortgage balance		
Home equity loan		
Other real estate loans		
Other investment loans and liabilities	———	
Total Long-Term Debt		$18,000
TOTAL DEBTS		$26,980
Net Worth = Assets − Debts		−$15,780

Calculate your net worth by subtracting total debts from total assets.

Danelle Washington's personal balance sheet.

it as an asset. You can estimate the market value of your car by using a current automotive blue book, available in book form at most bookstores and libraries or online (e.g., www.edmunds.com). In some cases, your car's value may actually be less than what you still owe in car payments.

Although real property, including homes and other real estate, is not very liquid, it may be your largest investment. Real estate values are determined by the values of comparable properties in the area, so if you just enter what you paid for a property on your balance sheet, you will be understating your actual wealth. If you don't know of a recent sale of a similar property, you can consult a real estate professional to help determine the value of your home or other real estate investment. In general, real estate values increase over time, so you need to update this information regularly. Because Danelle is renting an apartment with some friends from school, she doesn't own any assets in this category.

An insurance policy is counted as an asset only if it's a policy that accumulates cash value over time. If you cancel an insurance policy that has a cash surrender value, the insurer returns that amount of money to you. Because this is an available source of cash, you should count it as an asset. Homeowner's, auto, and health insurance (discussed in Chapters 8 and 9) don't accumulate cash value, but some types of disability and life insurance policies (discussed in Chapters 9 and 10, respectively) may have cash value. This value is determined by the contract terms and is generally much smaller than the face value of the policy. In some cases, insurance policies also allow you to borrow against the cash value. If you have borrowed from one or more of your policies, you need to include the amount owed as a debt on your personal balance sheet. Danelle doesn't have any cash value insurance.

2.2.3 Calculating Your Net Worth

After you enter all the required information on your personal balance sheet, you can calculate your net worth by using the following equation:

$$\text{Net worth} = \text{Total assets} - \text{Total debts}$$

Notice in Figure 2-1 that Danelle's net worth is negative $15,780. What does this mean? If Danelle sold all her assets and used the money to repay her debts, she would still owe $15,780. In contrast, if your net worth is positive, it represents how much you would have left over after paying everything. Your net worth is thus a measure of your wealth.

There is no "magic number" that represents the ideal amount of net worth because it depends on an individual's life cycle stage and personal goals. However, in general, the larger your net worth, the better off you are financially.

What if you have negative net worth like Danelle? If you're like most students, you're in the accumulation phase of your life cycle. You're developing skills and abilities that will lead to greater income and wealth in the future. You may have student loans and car loans but little in the way of financial investments. This situation is not overly troubling at such an early stage of life. However, if it continues indefinitely, it will eventually result in **insolvency,** which is the inability to pay debts as they come due. Insolvency can lead to bankruptcy.

It's not uncommon for an individual's net worth to decline due to an unexpected change in life circumstances, such as an extended illness, the death of a spouse, or a divorce. One of the purposes of developing and evaluating personal financial statements is to identify ways to improve your situation so that you can be better prepared for such problems. As you proceed through the financial planning process, you should keep this in mind and conscientiously attempt to reduce your debt and increase your assets over time.

2.2.4 Preparing a Personal Cash Flow Statement

Your net worth is highly related to your spending and saving behavior. If you consistently spend more than you earn, you'll end up financing the extra consumption through borrowing. In contrast, if you're a regular saver, you'll accumulate more assets over time.

On average, Americans spend more than they earn and have very low savings rates. Not surprisingly, average household debt continues to rise over time. This problem has been exacerbated over the past few years, as increasing home values and low mortgage rates have encouraged many homeowners to access home equity lines of credit to pay for vacations and other non-investment expenses. When this happens, total debt goes up, and net worth declines, as you will see when you look at credit in more detail in Chapters 5 and 6.

A **personal cash flow statement** is a financial statement used to evaluate the relationship between your income and expenditures. Whereas your personal balance sheet is like a snapshot of your finances at a certain point in time, your personal cash flow statement shows inflows and outflows of cash over a period of time, often one month or one year.

You use a personal cash flow statement to carefully itemize the amounts of money that come into your household from various sources as well as all the money that goes out over the same period of time. You can utilize a worksheet such to record your cash inflows and outflows; for example, Figure 2-2 shows Danelle Washington's personal cash flow statement for 2004. A blank worksheet is included in your Personal Financial Planner; an alternative is to use the worksheets provided with a personal finance software package, such as Microsoft Money or Quicken.

When should you record cash flows? You prepare a cash flow statement on a "cash basis," which means you record cash flows when they are received or

Figure 2-2

Danelle Washington's Personal Cash Flow Statement, 2004

Cash Inflows			Cash Outflows		
	Monthly	January 1 to December 31, 2004		Monthly	January 1 to December 31, 2004
Salary/wage income (gross)	$792	$9,500	Income and payroll taxes	$71	$852
Interest/dividend income			Groceries	171	2,052
Other income (self employment)			Housing		
Rental income (after expenses)			Mortgage or rent	300	3,600
Cash from sale or assets			Property tax & insurance		
Student loans	500	6,000	Maintenance/repairs		
Scholarships	108	1,300	Utilities		
Other income			Heating	40	480
Gifts	17	200	Electric	25	300
			Water and sewer		
Total Cash Inflows	$1,417	$17,000	Cable/phone/satellite	15	180
			Car loan payments	113	1,356
			Car maintenance/gas	80	960
			Credit card payments	125	1,500
			Other loan payments		
			Other taxes		
			Insurance		
			Life		
			Health	42	504
			Auto	67	804
			Disability		
			Other insurance		
			Clothing	25	300
			Gifts	30	360
			Other consumables (TV's, etc.)		
			Child-care expenses		
			Sports-related expenses	13	156
			Health club dues		
			Uninsured medical expenses	17	204
			Education	333	3,996
			Vacations/travel	25	300
			Entertainment	84	1,008
			Alimony/child support		
			Charitable contributions		
			Required pension contributions		
			Magazine subscriptions/books		
			Other payments/expenses		
			Total Cash Outflows	$1,576	$18,912

Net Cash Flow = Cash Inflows − Cash Outflows =	−$159	−$1,912

Danelle Washington's personal cash flow statement.

paid. Thus, if you receive a bill on January 5 but don't pay it until February 1, you record it as an expense in February, not in January. If certain amounts are deposited directly to or withdrawn directly from your checking account, such as paycheck deposits or car payments, you record them when they occur.

Identifying Your Cash Inflows

You should include as cash inflows all amounts of money you receive during the period of time in question. You include any income you earn from a job—wages, salaries, tips, and commission. Other sources of income may include

- ▲ Scholarships.
- ▲ Cash allowances or gifts from your parents or others.
- ▲ Proceeds from the sale of assets.
- ▲ Alimony or child support.
- ▲ Government benefits, such as welfare, unemployment, or Social Security.
- ▲ Investment earnings (i.e., income from dividends and interest).
- ▲ Gambling winnings.

Notice that Danelle records her annual **gross income**—that is, income before taxes and expenses—and records the taxes she paid during the year as cash outflows. Last year, she earned $9,500 from a part-time job and received a $1,300 scholarship and gifts of $200. She also took out a student loan in the amount of $6,000. Her total cash inflows are therefore $17,000 for the year.

Detailing Your Expenditures

Whereas income is generally easy to identify and calculate, expenditures are more difficult to track accurately. You can probably easily determine the big **fixed expenses**—expenses that are a constant dollar amount each period, such as rent and car loan payments. But few people do a good job of keeping track of their **variable expenses**, which vary in amount from period to period, such as grocery bills and gas money, even though these can be a big portion of their total cash outflows.

You can see that on Danelle's personal cash flow statement, $2,052 for groceries was one of her largest annual expenditures, exceeded only by her rent, at $3,600, and her college expenses, at $3,996.

Small daily expenditures, such as money for parking meters or candy bars from vending machines, are especially easy to overlook, but often these expenditures can make the difference between achieving your financial goals and not achieving them. Even if you just buy a latté at the coffee shop every weekday afternoon on the way home from school or work, the seemingly small cost of $3 per day adds up to $780 per year—enough to take a nice vacation or to add to your investment portfolio.

If you spend money primarily by writing checks and using a debit card, it's a little easier to track your cash outflows because your bank statement and check register are useful sources of information. Alternatively, you can track your expenditures on a daily basis in a spending log in which you record all your cash outflows for a month or longer. Your Personal Financial Planner includes a spending log worksheet that you can use for this purpose. At the end of the time period you have chosen, you can then total the amounts entered in your spending log to put into your personal cash flow statement. You need to do this for at least a month to be sure that you've included even the irregular cash outflows.

You should be careful not to alter your normal spending behavior temporarily simply because you're recording everything. Suppose, for example, that you never realized how much money you spent on lattés until you began keeping your spending log. Even if you plan to reduce your latté spending, you need to incorporate this expense in your log so you can more realistically evaluate your current finances. If you quit your latté habit during your spending log period and decided to allocate the $780 per year to savings, what if you "fell off the wagon" and returned to your prior spending behavior? At this stage, it's better to be brutally honest and record all spending, regardless of whether you plan to make changes.

Calculating and Evaluating Net Cash Flow

After you enter and total your cash inflows and outflows on the personal cash flow statement, you can calculate your net cash flow. Danelle calculates hers as follows:

$$\text{Net cash flow} = \text{Total cash inflows} - \text{Total cash outflows}$$

$$= \$17,000 - \$18,912 = -\$1,912$$

Based on Danelle's personal cash flow statement, which shows a negative net cash flow, she has been spending more than her income during the past year. How did this happen? Her personal balance sheet gives some clues: Danelle has credit card debt totaling $5,200 and total student loan debt of $18,000. Because the personal balance sheet is cumulative, this amount represents debt she has accumulated over time, not just in the past year. For example, we know that she received $6,000 from a student loan this year, which means she must already have had $12,000 in student loan debt at the beginning of the year.

In addition to taking on more student loan debt, Danelle spent $1,912 more than she earned last year, so these expenditures must have been made using credit cards. The increased debt resulted in a decline in her net worth.

As you can see, Danelle's income and spending habits have had a big effect on her overall financial picture. We might be tempted to explain Danelle's financial position by pointing to her low income. However, an interesting economic truth is that those who have more tend to spend more. If you're struggling to make it on a student's budget, you likely eat ramen noodles at least once a week and make do with your current wardrobe. If you're a movie star earning millions of dollars each year, you probably have more than one extravagant home, entertain lavishly, and buy only designer clothes. But just because you have high income doesn't mean that your finances are in good shape. Many seemingly well-off people have gone bankrupt.

SELF-CHECK

1. Define **net worth, liquid assets, market value,** and **fixed expenses.**
2. List some of your variable expenses.
3. What type of statement helps you track your spending?

2.3 Using Financial Ratios

Financial ratios provide another important tool for evaluating your financial condition. You can calculate your financial ratios from the information you've collected on your personal financial statements, compare your ratios to recommended targets, and track your ratios over time as a measure of your progress toward achieving your financial goals. In this section, we examine ratios designed to measure three aspects of your finances:

▲ Liquidity.

▲ Debt management.

▲ Adequacy of savings.

The individual ratios and their calculations are explained in this section using Danelle Washington's financial information from Figures 2-1 and 2-2.

2.3.1 Measuring Liquidity

If you experience a total loss of income, if you're temporarily disabled or laid off, you might need to meet your expenses without having your regular income. The **liquidity ratio** tells you how many months you could pay your monthly expenses from your liquid assets. This ratio is calculated as follows:

$$\text{Liquidity ratio} = \text{Liquid assets/Monthly expenses}$$

FOR EXAMPLE

What if Danelle Loses Her Scholarship?

Danelle has liquid assets equal to $1,500, the total value of her checking and savings accounts (refer to Figure 2-1). Her annual expenses, from the cash flow statement in Figure 2-2, are $18,912, and her monthly expenses total $1,576. Thus, Danelle's liquidity ratio (rounded to one decimal place) is

$$\$1,500/\$1,576 = 1.0$$

This means that Danelle could meet her expenses for only one month without her regular income sources. Financial planners often recommend that you have liquid assets sufficient to cover your expenses for three to six months, so liquidity is a concern for Danelle, particularly at the end of the school year, when she has depleted her student loan and scholarship funds. However, a low liquidity ratio does not necessarily imply that she needs to increase her allocation of funds to liquid assets. She may have other sources of funds that can be tapped in an emergency, such as family loans or credit cards.

2.3.2 Measuring Debt Usage

Everywhere we turn, it seems there's someone inviting us to borrow money to buy something today instead of waiting until we've saved enough to pay cash. Small wonder that one of the biggest financial problems U.S. households face is that they have too much debt.

If your money style is to spend impulsively or if you tend to avoid financial matters altogether, you may already understand the problems associated with monthly payments on credit cards. Although debt is not inherently bad, payments made to lenders include interest charges and fees—funds that could be better used to build your financial wealth. You can use your personal financial statements to assess your debt management. Financial institutions such as banks and mortgage companies use a variety of debt ratios when they evaluate you for mortgage or car loans. We discuss three ratios in this section:

▲ The debt ratio.
▲ The debt payment ratio.
▲ The mortgage debt service ratio.

These are the ratios that financial institutions most commonly use in their mortgage lending process.

The **debt ratio** measures the percentage of your total assets that you've financed with debt. It is calculated as follows:

Debt ratio = Total debt/Total assets

As your credit card balances increase, so does your debt ratio because credit card purchases are usually for consumer goods that add little—if any—value to your assets. For example, suppose you use a credit card to pay for dinner and a movie for you and your significant other. This causes your debts to increase by, say, $50, but your assets don't increase at all. The end result is that your debt ratio goes up. However, the debt ratio generally declines as you get older because your financial assets and home equity increase in value.

The **debt payment ratio** estimates the percentage of your after-tax income that goes to paying required monthly minimum debt payments of all types, including mortgage loans, student loans, car loans, and credit card payments. The debt payment ratio is calculated as follows:

Debt payment ratio = Total monthly debt payments/After-tax monthly income

Note that we use after-tax income in the denominator of the equation because the purpose is to assess ability to pay. As you can see in Figure 2-2, Danelle's monthly after-tax income is $1,346 (calculated as monthly gross income of $1,417 less $71 in income and payroll taxes). Her monthly debt payments total $238 per month ($125 for credit cards plus $113 for her car loan). Using this information, we can calculate Danelle's debt payment ratio as follows:

$$\$238/\$1,346 = 0.177, \text{ or } 17.7 \text{ percent}$$

Bank lenders commonly require that total debt payments not exceed 33 percent to 38 percent of gross income, which implies that the debt payment ratio (based on after-tax income) could be even higher. By that measure, Danelle's 17.7 percent debt payment ratio is not very high, but she will have to begin paying her student loan a few months after graduation, so the ratio is likely to rise in the near future. In addition, this ratio tends to understate Danelle's actual financial obligations because it doesn't include her required monthly rent payments.

For most individuals, housing costs, either rent or mortgage payments, are the largest monthly expenditure. The total monthly cost of a mortgage, including the principal and interest paid to the lender, property taxes paid to the local municipality, and homeowner's insurance, is called the **mortgage debt service.** Mortgage lenders commonly require that borrowers make a single monthly payment to cover all these expenses. The **mortgage debt service ratio,** which measures the percentage of your gross income that you pay out in mortgage debt service alone, is calculated as follows:

Mortgage debt service ratio = (Principal + Interest + Taxes + Insurance)
/Gross monthly income

Both the debt payment ratio and the mortgage debt service ratio measure your ability to pay your financial obligations. In determining your creditworthiness, lenders commonly compare these or similar ratios to maximum values. For example, a mortgage lender might require that your total debt payments be no more than 35 percent of your gross income or that your total mortgage-related expenses be no more than 25 percent of your gross income.

2.3.3 Measuring Savings

You can assess how well you're implementing your savings goals by tracking your savings ratio over time. The **savings ratio** measures the percentage of your after-tax income that is being allocated to savings and is calculated as follows:

$$\text{Savings ratio} = \text{Monthly savings/After-tax monthly income}$$

Because the amount you have available for savings is what's left over from your income after you've paid all your expenses and taxes, it's quite possible to have negative savings. This happens whenever your cash outflows exceed your cash inflows. In that case, your savings ratio is negative as well. Danelle Washington's savings ratio is

$$-\$159/\$1,346 = -11.8 \text{ percent}$$

Because her negative savings ratio implies that, rather than saving, Danelle is accumulating more debt, this financial situation cannot continue for long. As she begins to develop her personal financial goals, Danelle will probably want to include goals related to improving some of the financial ratios described here. Financial advisors commonly recommend that households target at least a 10 percent savings ratio and that they attempt to increase this ratio over time.

SELF-CHECK

1. Define **gross income**.
2. What financial ratios measure your ability to pay your debt?
3. Where does the information for ratios come from?

SUMMARY

It's important that you develop a system for organizing and maintaining your financial records. You can use a personal balance sheet to figure out your net worth, which is the total value of your assets minus the total value of your debts. You can summarize your current inflows and outflows of cash by using a personal cash flow statement. This financial statement helps you calculate net cash flow. Personal financial ratios can help you evaluate your current financial position, based on your personal balance sheet and cash flow statements. By comparing your ratios over time, you can track your progress toward achieving your financial goals.

KEY TERMS

Assets	Everything you own, including liquid assets, real and personal property, and investments.
Debt payment ratio	A financial ratio that measures the percentage of disposable income required to make debt payments.
Debt ratio	Total debt divided by total assets.
Debts	Everything you owe to others, including unpaid bills, credit card balances, car loans, student loans, and mortgages. Also known as liabilities.
Fixed expenses	Expenses that are a constant dollar amount each period.
Gross income	Income before taxes and expenses.
Insolvency	The inability to pay debts as they come due.
Liquid assets	Cash and near-cash assets that can be easily converted to cash without loss of value.
Liquidity ratio	A financial ratio that measures the ability to pay household expenses out of liquid assets in the absence of regular income.
Market value	The price that something can be sold for today.
Mortgage debt service	The total dollar amount of monthly mortgage principal, interest, property taxes, and homeowner's insurance.
Mortgage debt service ratio	The ratio of mortgage debt service to gross income.
Net worth	The amount of wealth you would have left after paying all your outstanding debts.
Personal balance sheet	A statement that details the value of what you own and what you owe to others to arrive at an estimate of your net worth.
Personal cash flow statement	A summary of income and expenditures over a period of time.
Personal financial statement	A statement that summarizes your financial information.
Savings ratio	A financial ratio that measures the percentage of after-tax income going to savings.
Variable expenses	Expenses that vary in amount from period to period.

ASSESS YOUR UNDERSTANDING

Go to www.wiley.com/college/bajtelsmit to assess your knowledge of money management strategies and skills.
Measure your learning by comparing pre-test and post-test results

Summary Questions

1. Because most IRS audits occur within three years of when a return is filed, it is recommended that tax records be kept no more than five years. True or false?

2. When saving documents, it is recommended that you keep utility bills:
   (a) only until the next bill arrives.
   (b) six months.
   (c) one year.
   (d) three years.

3. A personal balance sheet shows assets and debts at a single point in time, and a personal cash flow statement reflects cash inflows and outflows that occur over a period of time. True or false?

4. Which of the following formulas is used to calculate personal net worth?
   (a) Total assets + Total debts
   (b) Total assets − Total debts
   (c) Total debts − Total assets
   (d) Liabilities − Unpaid bills

5. Which of the following would be the best definition of insolvency?
   (a) having more liabilities than assets
   (b) the inability to borrow any more funds
   (c) having no savings
   (d) the inability to pay bills on time

6. If you borrow money to buy a new car, which of the following items on the balance sheet are affected?
   (a) assets only
   (b) debts only
   (c) assets and debts
   (d) unable to determine

7. The savings ratio is negative if cash outflows exceed cash inflows. True or false?

8. If you have an insurance policy that has a cash surrender value:
   (a) this represents an asset for you.
   (b) this represents a debt for you.

    (c) you enter no value on the balance sheet unless the policy is surrendered.

    (d) the premiums still due are subtracted from the surrender value to arrive at market value.

9. You have estimated your total assets to be $10,000, your liquid assets to be $2,000, and your total debts to be $11,000. Your net worth is $2,000. True or false?

10. Don has assets of $5,000, of which $1,800 are in checking and savings accounts. His annual expenses are $15,000. Don's liquidity ratio is:

    (a) 0.333.

    (b) 3.00.

    (c) 0.12.

    (d) 1.44.

Applying This Chapter

1. Identify the purpose for saving each of the following documents, if any, and how long you should save it:

    (a) Visa bill

    (b) apartment rent receipt

    (c) bank checking account statement

    (d) tax return

2. Identify whether each of the following is an asset, a debt, or neither:

    (a) credit card balance

    (b) weekly employment earnings

    (c) car

    (d) rent paid to landlord

    (e) checking account

3. Use the following personal balance sheet to calculate the net worth:

Assets		Liabilities	
Bank accounts	$3,000	Current bills	$1,500
Car	$5,000	Student loan	$10,000
Personal assets	$2,000	Car loan	$3,000

4. Using the personal balance sheet from Question 3, calculate total liquid assets.

5. Using the personal balance sheet from Question 3, what is the debt ratio?

6. Using the personal balance sheet from Question 3, and assuming that monthly expenses total $1,200, calculate the liquidity ratio.

7. The Sandell family reports the following financial information:

Checking and savings account	$ 3,000
Monthly after-tax income	$ 2,500
Total monthly expenses	$ 2,000
Monthly savings	$ 500
Total debt	$10,000
Total assets	$40,000

Calculate the Sandells' liquidity ratio.

8. Calculate the Sandells' debt ratio.

9. Calculate the Sandells' savings ratio.

Can You Afford a New Car?

Suppose you have your eye on a new car, and your monthly after-tax income is $2,000. Your monthly expenses are as follows:

▲ Car insurance: $100
▲ Rent: 900
▲ Groceries: 300
▲ Entertainment: 200
▲ Utilities: 200
▲ Credit card payment: 100
▲ Other: 100

What is your net cash flow? Can you afford that new car? Why or why not?

What's Wrong with This Picture?

Melody and Charles Verona have been married for less than one year and currently live in a one-bedroom apartment. They would like a bigger place to live and, with two incomes, they think they could afford to make mortgage payments on a small home or condominium. Unfortunately, they don't have enough money for a down payment yet, so they want to begin saving for this purpose. Over the past few months, Melody has been dismayed to find that they always seem to be a little short on cash at the end of the month. She decides to sit down with Charles to look more carefully at their spending habits and begin making a plan that will enable them to buy a house. The Veronas have collected the following financial information in preparation for evaluating their current finances and determining how much to save:

Cash Inflows	Gross Income	After-Tax Income
Melody	$22,000	$18,000
Charles	28,000	22,400

Cash Outflows	Monthly
Groceries	$400
Eating out	200
Rent	950
Credit card payments	200
Telephone	50
Utilities	150
Car loan payments	360
Car expenses and fuel	160
Clothing	100
Entertainment	150
Health club membership	60
Travel and vacations	100

Assuming that these cash flows are accurate and complete, what is the Veronas' net monthly cash flow? If the Veronas allocate their net cash flow to savings each month and they can earn 4 percent after taxes, how much will they have in the account after two years? What is a possible explanation for why the Veronas are having cash flow problems each month? What would you suggest they do to identify the reasons for this problem?

Net Worth

Construct a personal balance sheet by itemizing your assets and debts. You can use the blank forms in the Personal Financial Planner to do this. If you aren't sure of an item's value, estimate as best as you can. What is your net worth as of today?

3

MANAGING YOUR TAXES
The Basics of the U.S. Tax System

Starting Point

Go to www.wiley.com/college/bajtelsmit to assess your knowledge of managing your taxes.
Determine where you need to concentrate your effort.

What You'll Learn in This Chapter

▲ The major features of the U.S. federal income tax system
▲ Tax basics
▲ How taxes are calculated
▲ How to file tax returns
▲ Tax planning strategies

After Studying This Chapter, You'll Be Able To

▲ File your taxes on time
▲ Calculate taxable income and determine your tax liability
▲ Select strategies to legally minimize the taxes you pay

INTRODUCTION

Taxes can take a big bite out of your budget, so your strategies for legally minimizing your taxes are crucial to your financial plan. It's important to consider the tax implications of your potential financial decisions and to be proactive in developing a plan to minimize tax payments. In this chapter, you'll first examine the main features of the federal income tax system and the requirements for filing, calculating, and paying taxes. Federal income taxes are the focus of this chapter because they take the biggest tax bite. Finally, this chapter discusses the most common tax planning strategies.

3.1 The Basics of Federal Income Tax

There's no question—the U.S. federal income tax system is complicated. The statutes and regulations that describe the tax laws fill literally thousands of pages, and it is estimated that the average taxpayer spends more than 10 hours per year filling out the required forms. It's a good idea to make one of your personal financial goals to learn more about the tax system so that you can keep adequate records and reduce what you owe. Your income tax is one of your household's largest cash outflows, and you work around four months out of the year just to pay your federal taxes.

3.1.1 The Progressive U.S. Tax System

Although there have been many changes in the tax law throughout our country's history, the United States has always maintained a **progressive tax,** one that imposes higher tax rates on taxpayers with higher incomes, requiring them to pay proportionately more in taxes, through either higher tax rates or other rules.

In its infancy, the United States had no income tax at all. It wasn't until the 16th amendment to the U.S. Constitution was passed in 1913 that Congress imposed a tax on income, which was necessary to pay national security expenses associated with World War I.

Since that time, tax rates have increased or decreased based on economic and political circumstances. Today, federal income taxes are used to finance many worthwhile government activities, including the national defense, education, social programs, drug safety, transportation, and road maintenance.

Because a progressive tax is based on each taxpayer's ability to pay, lower-income families do not bear a large tax burden. In fact, some people in the United States pay no federal income tax at all. If you earned less than $8,450 in 2006 ($16,900 if married and filing jointly), you didn't even need to file a tax return. As a result, high-income taxpayers account for the lion's share of all income tax revenues collected, and the poorest don't pay any taxes at all.

In contrast to a progressive tax, a **regressive tax** places a disproportionate burden on taxpayers with lower incomes. Any time the same tax rate is levied on all taxpayers—as in the case of payroll, consumption, and sales taxes—the tax is regressive. This type of tax takes a bigger bite out of low-income families' disposable incomes. Although rich people spend more on food, clothing, and other consumer purchases than poor people, the proportion of their income going to these categories is still lower, so the tax affects them less.

The tax that finances Social Security and Medicare, the federal systems for retirement income and retiree health care, is a classic example of a regressive tax. If you look at your pay stub, you'll probably see an amount withheld for FICA (Federal Insurance Contributions Act), the tax that finances Social Security and Medicare. The **FICA tax** is regressive not only because everyone pays the same rate but also because there is a maximum income on which the Social Security portion of the tax (6.2 percent) is imposed; earnings over the maximum are subject only to the 1.45 percent Medicare portion of the tax.

The U.S. income tax system maintains its progressive nature through increasing marginal tax rates, exemptions, credits, and deductions. (A **marginal tax rate** is the rate that applies to your next dollar of income.) These features of the tax system imply that not all your income is taxable and your taxable income is not all taxed at the same rate.

The current tax rules assess taxes on taxable income—the amount of income that is subject to taxes under the law—according to a table of marginal tax rates. Marginal tax rates today are low by historical standards. Not only is the bottom bracket lower than it's been in decades, but the current top marginal tax rate, which applied to any income above $336,550 in 2006, is only 35 percent. In comparison, the top bracket at the end of World War II was 94 percent on income over $1 million.

3.1.2 The Internal Revenue Service

The **Internal Revenue Service (IRS)** is the government agency responsible for collecting federal income taxes. Because there are sometimes ambiguities in the laws, the IRS also writes regulations and makes rulings that interpret laws, often giving specific taxpayer examples for clarification. When there are disputes about how to interpret and apply these laws and regulations fairly, the federal tax court sometimes hears cases and makes rulings. The **Internal Revenue Code**, a compilation of all tax laws passed by Congress, along with the IRS regulations and tax court judicial decisions, make up the totality of tax laws in the United States.

Although the IRS is often seen in a negative light—after all, nobody likes to pay taxes—it performs a truly amazing function, processing 130 million individual income tax returns each year, collecting more than $1.7 trillion in taxes, and issuing more than $200 billion in refunds, most within a few short months.

Figure 3-1

Schedule X: 2006 Tax Rate Schedule for Single Filers

If your taxable income is:

Over:	But not more than:	You will owe:	Taxable income over:
$0	$7,550	10% of	$0
$7,550	$30,650	$755 + 15% of	$7,550
$30,650	$74,200	$4,220 + 25% of	$30,650
$74,200	$154,800	$15,108 + 28% of	$74,200
$154,800	$336,550	$37,676 + 33% of	$154,800
$336,550	+	$97,653 + 35% of	$336,550

Schedule Y-1: 2006 Tax Rate Schedule for Married Filing Jointly

If your taxable income is:

Over:	But not more than:	You will owe:	Taxable income over:
$0	$15,100	10% of	$0
$15,100	$61,300	$1,510 + 15% of	$15,100
$61,300	$123,700	$8,440 + 25% of	$61,300
$123,700	$188,450	$24,040 + 28% of	$123,700
$188,450	$336,550	$42,170 + 33% of	$188,450
$336,550	+	$91,043 + 35% of	$336,550

Marginal tax rates in 2006.

Congress has provided funding to further automate the process, a trend that causes some taxpayers concern as they envision a futuristic government with electronic access to their most intimate financial information. More likely, though, honest taxpayers will benefit from further automation, and dishonest ones will be more easily forced to pay their fair share. The IRS also offers many free services to taxpayers at its Web site, www.irs.gov. Publications on most tax topics are available for download or by mail. The comprehensive tax preparation reference IRS Publication 17, "Your Federal Income Tax," is a must-have for individuals who prepare their own taxes.

3.1.3 Tax Rate Schedules

Tax rate schedules show how much income tax must be paid for particular ranges of income. There are separate schedules for different household types. Figure 3-1 shows two of these schedules—Schedule X, for single taxpayers, and Schedule Y-1, for married taxpayers filing jointly. Each schedule includes lists of income ranges and rates.

FOR EXAMPLE

Tax Brackets

Let's suppose that you're a single filer and your taxable income is $65,000 in 2006. Although this income puts you in the 25 percent tax bracket, the first $7,550 will be taxed at 10 percent, the income between $7,550 and $30,650 will be taxed at 15 percent, and the remainder will be taxed at 25 percent, for a total of $12,808 in taxes owed. Now what happens if you earn another $1,000? Because having taxable income of $66,000 wouldn't push you into a new tax bracket, the calculation of your taxes will be exactly the same except that you'll apply the 25 percent rate to an additional $1,000—resulting in an additional $250 in federal income taxes (25 percent of $1,000).

A **tax bracket** is the range of taxable income to which a particular marginal tax rate applies. Taxpayers sometimes use this term to describe the highest bracket that applies to their income. Thus, a single filer who, in 2006, told you that she was "in the 25 percent bracket," meant that her taxable income was between $30,650 and $74,200. As you can see, you pay lower tax rates on your first dollars of income and higher rates on later dollars of income.

For example, Schedule X indicates that the tax rate on the first $7,550 of taxable income in 2006 is only 10 percent. Thus, if you were a single filer with taxable income of $7,550 or less, you would be in the lowest tax bracket and pay only 10 percent of your taxable income in taxes. Unless your taxable income falls in the lowest tax bracket, the same marginal tax rate does not apply to your entire taxable income.

Because you can't do much about what tax bracket you fall in, much of tax planning is aimed at minimizing your **average tax rate,** or the proportion of total taxable income paid in taxes, for a given level of income.

Your average tax rate is calculated as follows:

$$\text{Average tax rate} = \text{Taxes paid/Taxable income}$$

For some purposes, it may be useful to consider the proportion of your total income paid in taxes (as opposed to taxable income as in the definition just provided). You may also see this ratio referred to as your average tax rate. Because of the progressive, or increasing, tax rate schedule, your average tax rate will always be less than your marginal tax rate.

Let's return to the previous scenario involving taxable income of $65,000 and taxes of $12,808. Although the marginal tax rate is 25 percent (your highest

Figure 3-2

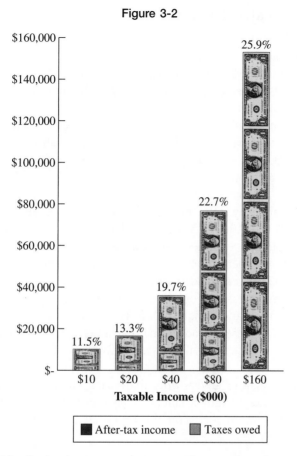

Taxes paid, after-tax income, and average tax rates for selected taxable income levels.

bracket), the average tax rate is only 19.7 percent: Figure 3-2 shows the proportion of taxable income paid in taxes and average tax rates for taxpayers at various income levels.

3.1.4 Inflation Indexing of Tax Brackets

The levels of income that trigger each successive increase in tax rate are automatically increased each year to account for inflation. This feature of the tax system has been in place since 1981—a year of double-digit inflation. This system banks on the fact that the income levels for each bracket will be higher next year than they are today. The fact that certain aspects of our tax law are indexed for inflation is an important protection for taxpayers in lower tax brackets. The government doesn't want households to have an extra tax burden unless they're actually experiencing a higher level of purchasing power.

3.1.5 The Marginal Tax Effect

The tax laws include many rules that can reduce your taxable income. For example, you can subtract contributions to certain employer-provided retirement plans from your gross income before you calculate your tax. When making decisions, you should always consider the **marginal tax effect**—the reduction in taxes owed as a result of a financial decision.

As discussed in Section 1.4, effective decision making requires that you evaluate your alternatives based on the effect on your finances. In estimating the marginal tax effect, you should apply a tax rate that includes all types of taxes that the income would otherwise be subject to—usually federal income tax, state income tax, Social Security, and Medicare tax.

Some people also pay state and local taxes on income. Suppose Jeremiah has a taxable income of $40,000 (25 percent federal tax bracket) and lives in a state with a 5 percent state income tax. His next dollar of taxable income will be subject to 25 percent + 5 percent + 7.65 percent Social Security and Medicare tax, for a total of 37.65 percent paid in taxes.

Suppose Jeremiah has the opportunity to work overtime for his employer and expects to earn an additional $2,000. How much better off will he be if he decides to do so? Because his additional earnings will be subject to the 37.65 percent marginal tax rate, he will net only $2,000 \times (1 - 0.3765) = $1,247 after taxes.

Although this chapter covers only the basics, there are many situations in which tax rules make certain financial decisions more attractive than others. It is always important to focus on the marginal tax effects when evaluating options.

SELF-CHECK

1. What is the purpose of the IRS?
2. Explain the difference between marginal tax rate and average tax rate.

3.2 Calculating Taxable Income and Taxes Owed

Although many people whine about filling out their tax forms as April 15 approaches, individuals who have their finances in order generally find that completing tax forms is fairly painless. The steps involved in calculating how much tax you owe are illustrated in Figure 3-3. In this section, we review terminology and rules and then look at how tax forms are filled out.

Figure 3-3

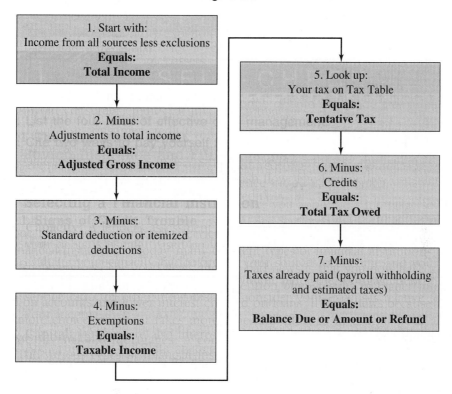

Steps in calculating federal income taxes owed.

3.2.1 Reporting Income

As indicated in Figure 3-3, the first step in doing your taxes is to calculate your income. The calculation of income for tax purposes requires that you report most types of income and then make certain allowed adjustments to that income:

▲ **Gross income** is your income from all sources. However, some categories of income are excluded to arrive at **total income** on your tax forms, an amount that can be thought of as gross taxable income.

▲ **Gross taxable income** is income from all sources, less allowed exclusions.

Table 3-1 details what is included and what is excluded in reporting total income. For example, you don't have to report scholarships used for tuition and course-related expenses or child support payments received from an ex-spouse. You do, however, have to report scholarships and grants applied to room and board expenses.

Table 3-1: What Is and What Is Not Included in Gross Taxable Income

Included

Alimony	Investment gains/losses
Business or partnership income	Moving expense reimbursement
Commissions, fees (if deducted)	Wages, salaries, tips, bonuses
Dividends	Pension income
Employer-paid disability income	Property rental income/loss
Gambling winnings and prizes	Royalties
Hobby income	Unemployment compensation
Interest	

Not Included

Annuities*	Long term care benefits
Child support	Military cost-of-living allowance
Disability payments*	Qualified benefits paid by employer*
Gifts	Required travel expenses paid by employer*
Inheritance	Scholarships and fellowships*
Insurance claim payments	State and local bond interest
Jury awards	Workers compensation payments
Life insurance proceeds	Welfare
Long-term capital gain on sale of primary residence*	

*Limitations apply to these categories.

For most people, the largest source of total income is **earned income** from employment—salaries, hourly wages, bonuses, tips, and commissions—all of which is included in gross taxable income. Other sources of gross taxable income include business income, investment income, alimony, unemployment compensation, and retirement benefits.

Unearned income may include interest and dividends from investments, net business income, rents, and royalties you received during the year, annuity and pension income, awards for scientific and charitable achievement, gambling and lottery winnings, and scholarships spent on room and board.

Employers and financial institutions must report the amounts they pay to you each year, and you generally receive a copy of this report in January following the tax year (Form W-2 for employment income and Form 1099 for other types of income), but you are also required to report other income (e.g., cash tips received by a waiter), even if these amounts do not appear on your W-2.

Your taxable income, as reported on your W-2, excludes any payments made on your behalf for tax-qualified health insurance and retirement plans—in other words, those amounts get taken off the top of your income and are not taxed. In addition to reporting profits from businesses, you may sometimes be able to subtract losses by entering a negative number in the business income category. However, the tax laws limit the deduction of losses to situations in which you actively participate in the management of the business.

Gross income also includes any **capital gain,** or increase in value, of taxable investments that you sold during the year. For example, if you sold a rental property during the year for $100,000 and you had only paid $80,000 for it, you owe tax on the $20,000 capital gain. Note that even though you may have received the whole $100,000 in cash flow that year, you report only the gain for tax purposes.

If you hold an investment longer than a year, the gain is subject to a special lower tax rate—5 percent for taxpayers in the 10 and 15 percent tax brackets and 15 percent for those in higher tax brackets. These rates also apply to certain dividend income. A special capital gain rule applies to profits on the sale of your primary residence, defined as where you lived for two of the five years before the sale. You can exclude up to $250,000 of the gain on the sale of your home ($500,000 for married couples) from your total income.

3.2.2 Adjusted Gross Income

Certain expenses are subtracted from total income to arrive at **adjusted gross income (AGI).** Although many of the allowed adjustments to total income are subject to income limitations, they can significantly reduce your taxes and may not require you to itemize deductions to qualify. Some of these adjustments include

▲ deduction for unreimbursed expenses up to $250 for teachers of kindergarten through grade 12.

▲ deductible individual retirement account contributions up to $4,000.

▲ interest paid on student loans during the year.

▲ tuition and fees for higher education up to $4,000.

▲ deduction for one-half of the Social Security taxes paid on business income.

▲ deduction for moving expenses, if required for a new job.

Without itemizing, you can also make adjustments for one-half of the Social Security taxes paid on business income and for moving expenses, if required for a new job. To see if you qualify for these or other adjustments to total income, you should consult the applicable IRS publications.

3.2.3 Standard vs. Itemized Deductions

You may deduct certain expenses from your AGI to arrive at the taxable amount: You can either claim a specified **standard deduction,** a dollar amount based on filing status that is subtracted from AGI in calculating taxable income, or itemize your deductions. With **itemized deductions,** you report and deduct actual expenses in certain allowed categories to arrive at taxable income. The amount of the standard deduction increases annually with inflation and depends on your filing status. For tax year 2006, the allowed standard deduction amounts were

- ▲ Single: $5,150.
- ▲ Married filing jointly: $10,300.
- ▲ Married filing separately: $5,150.
- ▲ Head of household: $7,550.
- ▲ Qualified widower: $10,300.

If your deductible expenses are greater than the standard deduction, and provided that you've kept careful records, you report itemized deductions on Schedule A. Although you don't have to provide supporting documentation when you file your return, you must be able to produce proof of the expense if the IRS requests it.

For example, if you've made charitable contributions during the year, you should have a statement or receipt that acknowledges your donation. But if you take the standard deduction, you don't have to keep this type of record. If you itemize, you must file the long form 1040 instead of the 1040A or 1040EZ. The categories for itemized deductions include medical and dental expenses, taxes, some types of interest, gifts to charity, casualty and theft losses, job expenses, and most other miscellaneous deductions.

The percentage of people who itemize deductions increases with income. This makes sense because people with greater income are likely to have greater expenses, most notably for mortgage interest and taxes, so the amount of their actual expenses is more likely to exceed the standard deduction. We discuss each category of itemized deductions in more detail next.

Medical and Dental Expenses

You can deduct out-of-pocket medical and dental expenditures for health insurance premiums, services (e.g., doctors, dentists, optometrists, nurses, hospitals), prescriptions, eyeglasses, hearing aids, travel for medical purposes, special schooling for disabled children, nursing homes, alternative medicine (e.g., chiropractors, acupuncturists), and other medical expenses if their sum is above 7.5 percent of your AGI. IRS Publication 502 lists legally deductible expenses.

If your expenses are paid by your health insurer or employer, you can't deduct them—you can deduct only unreimbursed expenses. To determine your deduction, you total your medical and dental expenses and then subtract 7.5 percent of your AGI. The remainder is your deduction.

Taxes You Paid

You may deduct state and local income taxes you paid during the tax year, real estate property taxes paid on your primary residence, and personal property taxes (imposed in some states on cars and other personal property). If you take a deduction for state taxes, you may have to make an adjustment to your income in a later year for state tax refunds.

Interest You Paid

Perhaps the most beneficial of all deductions is the mortgage interest deduction. You can deduct interest paid on your mortgage and home equity loans as well as certain charges, such as points or loan origination fees.

Sometimes, you can't deduct the full amount of points in the year paid but must spread them out over the life of the loan. Interest paid on credit cards, personal loans, and car loans is not deductible.

Gifts to Charity

The tax laws allow you to deduct contributions made to charitable organizations. There are separate lines on which to report cash donations and non-cash donations.

Noncash contributions include food donated to the local food bank or used clothing given to a local charity. You can deduct only the current market value of the items donated, however. If you're uncertain of an item's worth, you should consider what the item would sell for at a flea market, or, for a fee, you can get a list of fair market values for commonly donated items from www.taxsave.com.

People who are actively involved in volunteer organizations can also deduct expenses incurred in their volunteer work, including mileage expenses.

Casualty and Theft Losses

Suppose your car, which was worth $3,000, was stolen during the year, and you did not have theft insurance on it. For such an unreimbursed loss, the tax law allows you to deduct the amount of the loss that exceeds 10 percent of your AGI, less $100.

Job Expenses and Miscellaneous Deductions

Many people incur expenses required for their employment but are not reimbursed for them by their employer (e.g., union dues, licenses and fees, books and professional software, professional liability insurance, tools and supplies, job hunting costs, travel costs). Ordinary and necessary job-related expenses are deductible if they exceed 2 percent of your AGI.

Several special rules apply to the miscellaneous deductions category. Gambling losses up to the amount of reported gambling income can be deducted without regard to the 2 percent limitation. Disabled workers are also allowed to deduct all their job-related expenses.

Totaling Your Itemized Deductions

After calculating your deductions, you total them and compare the amount to the standard deduction. Note that although it's a good idea to claim all deductions to which you are entitled, unusually large deductions might subject your return to increased scrutiny by the IRS.

3.2.4 Exemptions

The last step in calculating your taxable income is to subtract the appropriate amount for your exemptions. An **exemption** is an amount of money that you're allowed to subtract for each qualifying person in your household. This usually means one exemption each for yourself, your spouse, and each of your dependents. A **dependent** is a member of a household who receives at least half of his or her support from the head of the household.

The allowed exemption amount was $3,300 in 2006, and it increases annually with inflation and is phased out for high-income taxpayers. A person can be claimed as an exemption on only one tax form. So if your daughter is being claimed as a dependent on your tax form, she can't take an exemption on her own tax form. Note that the marginal benefit to a family is higher if the exemption is claimed by the taxpayer in the highest tax bracket.

3.2.5 Final Calculation of Taxes Owed

Subtracting your deductions and exemptions from your AGI yields your taxable income. You use this amount to calculate your taxes. Figure 3-4 shows how each layer of income is taxed. In financial planning, you always consider the effects on the last layer of income.

You can find the appropriate tax amount easily by using the tax table provided in the instruction booklet that comes with your tax forms. Although Section 3.1.2 illustrates the increasing marginal tax rates by explaining how each layer of income is taxed, individual taxpayers are not expected to do that calculation themselves. Instead, the IRS has precalculated the tax. So all you have to know is your taxable income, and you can look up the tax amount that you must pay. When you've determined your tentative tax, you're almost done.

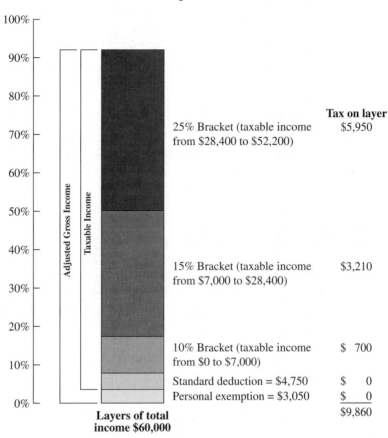

Figure 3-4

The taxation of your income, by layer.

Applying Available Credits

Tax credits directly reduce the taxes you owe. The currently available credits include credits for foreign taxes paid, child and dependent care expenses, elderly and disabled status, education expenses, retirement contributions, dependent children, and adoption.

Several of the available credits are particularly helpful for working parents and contribute to the progressive nature of the tax system. In addition to a flat credit per child under 17, you can take a credit for some of the costs of child care. For lower-income families in which both parents are employed, the Earned Income Credit can significantly reduce taxes paid. Some college students may also qualify for this tax credit. The Hope Scholarship Credit and the Lifetime Learning Credit are important for college students to be aware of. Contributions to retirement savings accounts may also qualify for credits.

Although many credits are fairly straightforward, some have specific income limitations or are phased out for higher-income families, so you may have to use an IRS worksheet to determine your eligibility for them. All credits except for the child tax credit require the filing of a special form (referenced on the appropriate line of Forms 1040 and 1040A). All the required forms and information on these credits are available on the IRS Web site, www.irs.gov.

Alternative Minimum Tax

Some taxpayers end up owing more in taxes than the calculation discussed so far would indicate because of the **alternative minimum tax (AMT).** This tax was originally designed to ensure that high-income people couldn't take advantage of too many special tax rules to avoid paying their fair share of taxes, but in recent years, it has also affected many middle-income taxpayers.

The AMT works this way: You recalculate your taxes under a different set of rules in which many of the current deductions, exemptions, and special tax breaks do not apply. If the tax calculated in that way is larger than the one calculated in the normal way, you must pay the AMT, a higher tax amount. Whether you should take the time to do this depends on whether your tax situation includes many of the AMT "triggers." Some of the triggers for AMT liability in a given year include

- ▲ a large number of exemptions claimed.
- ▲ exercise of incentive stock options.
- ▲ long-term capital gains.
- ▲ large itemized deductions, particularly for medical expenses or second home mortgage interest.

If any of these apply to you, you should follow the directions for calculation of the AMT to see whether it applies. Don't be surprised if it does—more than 2.7 million taxpayers were subject to it for tax year 2003, and the AMT is estimated to reach more than 35 million within the next decade. The IRS automatically calculates the AMT based on your submitted tax form, so if you neglect to do so and therefore underpay your taxes, you may end up paying additional interest and penalties. (Tax preparation software and tax professionals automatically calculate the AMT.)

3.2.6 Paying Taxes

Taxes are supposed to be paid on your income as you receive it. However, our tax system is complex enough that it isn't always easy to determine exactly how much you must pay until the year ends and you actually prepare your return. You must estimate this amount throughout the year to ensure that you pay enough.

For earned income from employment, the payment of estimated taxes is usually accomplished through **payroll withholding,** whereby the employer takes money out of your income for the government. The amount of tax withheld is based on expected income and your estimated number of exemptions, as indicated on a W-4 form, the Employee's Withholding Allowance Certificate. You complete a W-4 form whenever you begin a new job. The lower the number of exemptions claimed, the larger the amount withheld. Alternatively, if you don't expect to owe any taxes—if you have fairly low income—you can indicate that you are tax exempt so that no taxes will be withheld.

Most taxpayers have more withheld than they will owe and receive a refund (without interest). Even if an appropriate number of exemptions is claimed on the W-4, you may still end up overpaying in withholding because the amount withheld assumes that you'll take the standard deduction.

If you are self-employed or have investment income that hasn't been subject to withholding, you must still pay your taxes in advance of the April 15 due date. The law requires that you pay the tax in quarterly estimated tax installments during the tax year (on April 15, June 15, September 15, and January 15). If you underpay, you are subject to penalties. To avoid underpayment penalties, you should make sure that the total of your withholding plus estimated tax payments is at least as much as 100 percent of your prior year's tax owed.

If you're self-employed, you are likely to owe additional taxes beyond the federal income tax. Self-employed individuals report total business revenues and certain deductible expenses on Schedule C. The difference between their revenues and expenses is taxable and therefore must be reported as business income (or loss) on their 1040 form. Individuals who report self-employment income are also required to file a Schedule SE (for self-employment) with their federal tax forms. This worksheet determines the Social Security and Medicare payroll taxes owed on business income. Whereas wage and salary workers split the 15.3 percent tax with their employer (each paying 7.65 percent), self-employed people are their own employers and thus must pay both portions. The combined effect of federal and state income taxes plus the Social Security and Medicare tax is a hefty bite out of business income, sometimes more than 50 percent for those in the highest marginal income tax bracket.

If your total withholding and estimated taxes paid during the year are less than the amount of taxes you owe for the year, you must include a check for the remainder with your submitted form. If you've paid too much in withholding, you're entitled to a refund. You may receive a refund even when you didn't have sufficient income to require any payment of taxes. This occurs because Congress has made certain tax credits refundable—that is, you can get them even if you have no taxes owed to credit them against. The most important refundable tax credit is the additional child tax credit, which allows some households to receive the credit even if they owed no tax.

You should try to minimize the amount of refund you'll receive because overpaying taxes is essentially like giving the government a zero-interest loan. Some taxpayers like to overpay their taxes, although this strategy doesn't make good financial sense.

SELF-CHECK

1. Define **alternative minimum tax**, **payroll withholding**, and **capital gain**.
2. List some possible deductions a taxpayer may itemize.
3. What is the result when you subtract adjustments from total income?

3.3 Filing Your Federal Tax Return

Filing a tax return involves reporting income to the IRS on official tax forms and paying any outstanding taxes owed. In this section, we explain the requirements for filing.

3.3.1 Filing Status

Whether you must file a federal return depends primarily on your filing status, income, and age. Your **filing status** identifies your household type. Because your filing status may change, every year you must identify yourself as one of the following (based on your status as of the last day of the year):

▲ **Single:** Unmarried or legally separated from your spouse.
▲ **Married filing jointly:** Married couple filing a single tax return, even if only one spouse had income.
▲ **Married filing separately:** Married couple filing separate tax returns, each reporting his or her own income and allowed deductions from income.
▲ **Head of household:** Single person who lives with and pays more than half of the support for a dependent child or relative.
▲ **Qualifying widow(er) with dependent child:** Person whose spouse died within two years of the tax year and who lives with and pays more than half of the support for a dependent child.

3.3.2 Income

Your **taxable income** is a major determinant of whether you must file a tax return and, of course, also determines the amount of taxes you pay. The IRS defines your AGI as the total of your earned income (e.g., salaries, wages, tips, bonuses, commissions) plus **unearned income** (e.g., interest, dividends, capital gains, rents, royalties, net business income) minus certain allowed adjustments.

You are allowed to subtract certain amounts from your AGI to get your taxable income. The most important are called exemptions and deductions. You get a personal exemption of $3,300 (in 2006, indexed for inflation) for each qualifying person in your household, including yourself and each dependent, although this allowance is phased out for very high-income households.

Also, you receive a standard deduction for certain qualifying expenses on which you are not taxed. The standard deduction for single taxpayers in 2006 was $5,150, whereas married couples filing jointly were allowed to deduct $10,300, and heads of household could deduct $7,550. Standard deductions are higher for people who are age 65 and older and for people who are blind.

The allowed deductions are indexed for inflation so that the amount you can deduct increases annually. If your annual expenses in certain allowed categories exceed, in total, the standard deduction for your filing status, you should itemize instead of using the standard deduction. Itemizing deductions involves filing an additional form on which you detail all deductions. Whereas the standard deduction is available without proof of expenses, you must keep supporting documentation for all itemized deductions.

If your earned income is no more than the total of your exemptions and standard or itemized deductions, your taxable income is zero, and you need not file a return. For a single taxpayer, this means that you could have earned up to $3,330 + $5,150 = $8,450 in 2006 without having to file.

Married couples filing jointly had to file if they earned more than $6,600 + $10,300 = $16,900. Of course, if you made less than these amounts but had taxes withheld from your pay, you would need to file in order to get a refund.

In addition to exemptions and deductions, you can also use a tax credit to reduce the taxes you owe. Tax credits, unlike exemptions and deductions, do not represent adjustments to your income. Rather, they are subtracted directly from the taxes you owe.

3.3.3 Age

Age affects your obligation to file and pay taxes. For example, the larger standard deduction for individuals age 65 and older means that they can earn more income without being taxed. In certain circumstances, dependent children up to age 24 do not have to file. However, even if your parents claim you as a dependent, you still need to file a return if any of these apply:

▲ Your earned income was more than $5,150 (based on 2006 tax law).

▲ Your unearned income (such as earnings on investment accounts) was more than $750.

▲ Your gross income was more than the larger of $750 or your earned income (up to $5,150) plus $250.

In addition, you should file if you want to get a refund of taxes withheld from your income or if you qualify for a tax credit.

3.3.4 When and Where to File Taxes

There are very specific rules for when and where you file your taxes. Failure to meet these requirements is a violation of the tax law and may subject you to interest and penalties. It may also take longer to receive any refund.

Tax returns must be postmarked by midnight on April 15 of the year following the tax year. So for income you earned in 2005, you had to file your return by April 15, 2006. If April 15 falls on a day that the post office is closed, the due date is extended by one day. You can extend the deadline by four months, to August 15, by filing Form 4868, Application for Automatic Extension, on or before the April 15 deadline.

If four months is still not enough time, you can file another form to get an additional extension to October 15. About 9 million taxpayers request extensions each year. Although it might seem like a good way to avoid doing your taxes, extensions do not extend the deadline for paying the actual taxes, so you still have to include a check for any estimated amount you owe or be subject to penalties and interest. If you discover that you made a mistake on a prior year's taxes, you may file an amended return using Form 1040X for up to three years after the original tax year. The IRS receives about 4 million amended returns a year.

The IRS operates several service centers where tax returns are processed. When you get your tax forms in the mail, they include a preprinted address label that directs your return to the appropriate service center. Even if you file your taxes electronically, the IRS still sends you the label. You can also find out where to mail it by checking your zip code at www.irs.gov.

Many taxpayers choose to file their taxes electronically, either online, through their tax accountant, or by telephone. The **IRS e-file** uses online automation to replace many of the manual steps needed to process paper returns, resulting in faster processing with fewer errors (fewer than 1 percent of all electronic tax returns included errors in 2002). Most professional tax preparation services and software packages offer, and even encourage, electronic filing, but you can also do so on your own.

Although using e-file supposedly does not increase your chances of being audited, it does allow the IRS to better track the information contained in your forms—with paper forms, the IRS only inputs into its database certain data items from each return. If you have a very simple return, as is the case for college students, for example, you can even file electronically by telephone, entering the information by using your telephone keypad. A TeleFile package is automatically sent to any taxpayer who filed a Form 1040EZ in the previous tax year.

3.3.5 IRS Forms

You have a choice of three primary tax forms:

- ▲ Form 1040, known as the long form.
- ▲ Form 1040EZ.
- ▲ Form 1040A.

Which form to use depends on your filing status, your income (type and amount), and the deductions and credits you can claim.

Even if you qualify to use either of the short forms (1040EZ or 1040A), you can use the standard 1040 long form instead. Depending on your income, deductions, and credits, you may need to include additional forms. Your tax forms may be filled out by hand, typed, or completed electronically. You can also pay a professional tax preparer to complete your tax return, although you still need to collect the necessary documentation and give it to the preparer.

Software packages such as TurboTax and TaxCut can make completing your return and identifying the appropriate forms easier. These programs walk you through the entry of information by asking questions and then fill in the appropriate forms. After you use one of these programs, it remembers information from previous years, which makes it less likely that you'll forget potential deductions or credits. This can also help you avoid some common errors.

3.3.6 The Most Common Filing Errors

No one has ever argued that filing taxes is easy. Even people with advanced degrees make mistakes on their tax returns. But these mistakes can cost you money. Your refund might be delayed. Or, worse yet, you might have to pay additional taxes, interest, and penalties. According to the IRS, the most common mistakes are[1]:

- ▲ math errors, both addition and subtraction. Math errors are the number-one mistake. Don't forget to clearly indicate negative numbers, preferably by using parentheses.
- ▲ incorrect or missing Social Security numbers for members of the household.
- ▲ incorrect tax entered from the tables.
- ▲ withholding and estimated tax payments entered on the wrong lines.

▲ computation errors in figuring the child and dependent care credits and the Earned Income Credit. Also, missing or incorrect identification numbers for child-care providers.

Although somewhat less common than the preceding errors, the IRS also sees people make mistakes such as:

▲ not signing and dating the return. No signature, no refund!

▲ forgetting to report interest and dividend income. The IRS gets independent verification of this from your financial institution.

▲ not including all the required forms, especially those indicating taxes withheld (e.g., W-2, 1099).

▲ making out the check incorrectly (wrong amount, failure to sign). If your tax payment doesn't get to the IRS by the filing deadline because there is no signature, you are subject to penalties and interest.

▲ putting insufficient postage on the envelope. The post office then returns the envelope to you, and you could miss your filing deadline.

▲ giving the incorrect address for refunds. The IRS has refund checks totaling $80 million that came back as undeliverable.

▲ checking more than one filing status. For example, you can't be married and single at the same time.

SELF-CHECK

1. What are the three primary tax forms?
2. What are filing status options for married people?
3. List five of the most common filing errors.

3.4 Tax Planning Strategies

Understanding income taxation is important because it helps you anticipate the tax consequences of your financial decisions. The tax laws may often make one strategy clearly preferable to another—for example, one investment alternative may offer tax benefits, while another doesn't. Also, your tax knowledge will help you evaluate whether you need to consult a tax professional and to prepare the necessary information for your financial planner. If your taxes are simple, you should be able to handle them yourself. If your situation is more complex, you might benefit from a tax specialist's more detailed legal knowledge.

Tax planning strategies are those intended to:

▲ reduce taxable income.
▲ defer taxable income.
▲ receive income that is subject to lower tax rates.
▲ increase deductions and exemptions from income.
▲ maximize tax credits.

3.4.1 Tax Evasion vs. Tax Avoidance

Effective personal financial management requires minimizing unnecessary cash outflows—including any unnecessary taxes. Of course, you must pay taxes that you legally owe. **Tax evasion** is the deliberate failure to pay taxes that are legally owed, and it is against the law.

Examples of tax evasion include failure to report tip income or earnings received "under the table." Because waiters and waitresses usually earn more in tips than they earn in wages, the IRS regularly audits these jobs to estimate average tips and requires that employers withhold sufficient taxes from the employees' wage income, sometimes leaving them with very little in their paychecks. However, restaurant workers usually receive more in tips than what is reported by their employers in these audits, thus resulting in under-withholding.

Working under the table means working for someone who pays you in cash and doesn't withhold taxes. This is illegal. It is suspected that many farm and agricultural workers and their employers, particularly in areas near the U.S. borders, evade taxes in this way. Because these workers are often transient, it is difficult to catch them.

Although tax evasion is illegal and can have serious consequences, there is nothing illegal about **tax avoidance.** When you use your knowledge of the tax rules to make financial decisions that reduce the taxes you owe, you are ensuring that you do not pay more taxes than you legally owe. The money you save in taxes can be applied to achieving your financial goals.

Consider the example of tax-deductible versus nondeductible investment contributions. A tax-deductible investment allows you to invest without paying taxes on the money first. So, $1,000 of income results in $1,000 invested. If you invest instead in something without that tax benefit, then you pay taxes on the $1,000 in income first, leaving substantially less to actually invest. If your marginal federal income tax rate is 25 percent and your state tax is 5 percent, you will have only $700 left to invest after taxes.

Tax avoidance requires thoughtful planning. In general, tax planning is the ongoing process of using the provisions of the tax law to reduce your taxes or defer them to later years. As you begin to work toward long-term financial goals, you should consider not just the current year's taxes but the taxes in future years, too. Because tax laws frequently change, you should try to stay informed about new rules.

Tax evasion is a crime and can, sometimes, result in imprisonment. When a crime boss is successful in avoiding prosecution for murder and other mayhem, federal officials sometimes choose to prosecute for tax evasion instead because it's easier to prove. In 1930, for example, gangster Al Capone was sentenced to 11 years in prison for his failure to pay taxes for 4 years.

3.4.2 Reducing Taxable Income

You can reduce taxable income without reducing gross income. Many employers offer the opportunity to make pretax contributions to employee benefit and retirement plans, and they often match a portion or all of your contribution. This is a great benefit you should take advantage of if it is offered because the law allows you to use your pretax income to buy your benefits. Federal, state, and local income taxes as well as Social Security payroll taxes are calculated based on the income left after these expenditures have been made. You save whatever tax you would have paid on that income, and your employer saves its portion of the Social Security tax.

Many large employers also allow employees to take advantage of **flexible spending accounts,** reimbursement accounts for qualified medical and child-care expenses. Each pay period, the employer subtracts a certain amount from your paycheck and deposits it in your flexible spending account. The amount deposited is not part of your taxable income. However, these accounts may have restrictions on when you can spend the money, so you need to make sure you know how your plan works. You can obtain reimbursement from the account as you incur qualified expenses, such as child-care expenses. This allows you to pay

---

FOR EXAMPLE

Saving on Health Care

Suppose you work for an employer that offers you the opportunity to purchase your health insurance with pretax dollars at a cost of $300 per month. Your friend Jonah, who earns the same salary, has no health insurance through his employer and pays out of pocket, again for $300 monthly. How much better off are you than your friend if you are both subject to a marginal tax rate of 30 percent? Your taxable income will now be lower by the $300 amount, so you'll be able to avoid paying $90 per month in taxes ($300 × 0.30), or $1,080 per year. Jonah must pay taxes on his full earnings. In effect, the tax deductibility allows you to get a $1,080 discount on the cost of the health insurance (equal to your tax savings), money that you can apply to one of your financial goals.

for your child care with pretax dollars, substantially reducing your out-of-pocket cost because you save the amount in taxes you would have paid.

If your marginal tax rate is 20 percent (15 percent federal + 5 percent state tax) and you normally pay $5,000 per year for child care, you can save about $1,000 in taxes ($5,000 × 0.2) for the year with a flexible spending account. If you instead paid taxes on the $5,000 in taxable earnings, you'd have only $4,000 left after taxes [$5,000 × (1 − 0.2) = $4,000]—not enough to pay for your child care.

Investment real estate owners are allowed some deductions that aren't actually out-of-pocket expenses. A profitable investment property may produce a tax loss that can be applied against other income to reduce taxes. Therefore, taxpayers in high tax brackets often consider investing in real estate properties that will produce a tax loss after expenses.

3.4.3 Deferring Taxable Income

For some employer retirement plans, you can make investment contributions on a pretax basis and therefore avoid current income taxes on that income. (See Chapter 14 for more on retirement plans.) These plans also allow you to defer paying taxes on the investment earnings in the plan. If you earn $1,000 in investment income in a taxable account—such as interest on your bank savings account—you owe taxes on those earnings in the year received, with the actual amount owed being a function of your marginal tax rate (including state and federal income tax).

With a tax-deferred account, you don't pay tax on it until you withdraw it, which may be many years away. At that point, you may be in a lower marginal tax bracket. But even if you're not, you will benefit from the time value of money—it's always better to pay a given amount in the future than it is to pay the amount today because a dollar today is worth more than a dollar in the future.

Retirement plans can have great tax benefits. If you aren't fortunate enough to have a retirement plan option with your current employer, tax rules allow you to set up an **individual retirement account (IRA)**. There are two types of IRAs:

▲ A traditional IRA allows you to subtract your annual contribution to the account from income and to defer the payment of taxes until withdrawal. Note that this type of IRA has a tax effect similar to that of employment-based retirement plans.

▲ A **Roth IRA** does not allow you to take a current deduction, so you must make the contribution with after-tax dollars. However, assuming that you use the funds for retirement or other allowed purposes, you never have to pay tax on the money again—the account, including all accumulated investment earnings, can grow tax free, and you can withdraw the money at retirement without paying any taxes on it.

Another way to defer taxable income is to postpone receiving the income until a future tax year. Suppose a family friend hires you to build a deck in the fall of 2006. You know that your 2006 income is relatively high because you worked the whole year. Because you'll be attending college in 2007, you expect to be in a lower tax bracket that year. If you can delay the receipt of payment for your deck-building services until 2007—possibly by waiting to bill your friend—you won't have to pay the tax until 2007, and you'll reduce the overall tax owed (because you'll be in a lower tax bracket). Certain professions—small businesses and consulting practices, for example—can often take advantage of this type of tax strategy.

3.4.4 Receiving Income That Is Subject to Lower Tax Rates

Capital gains and certain dividends from long-term investments are taxed at a lower rate than ordinary income. For this reason, an important tax strategy is to avoid investments that pay you current income (interest or dividends) in favor of those that provide returns in the form of increased value. Because a capital gain is not reported on your taxes until you sell the asset, you can accumulate substantial wealth without incurring any current tax.

When you realize a gain on a qualifying investment, you pay at a lower tax rate, in most cases 15 percent. Your home has an even greater advantage in this respect because most capital gains from the sale of your primary residence are tax free.

Families can achieve lower taxes overall by shifting some income to household members who are in lower tax brackets. For example, you can give taxable investment accounts to your children. You are allowed to make gifts of up to $12,000 each per year tax free to as many people as you want without the receiver having to declare it as income. Children can earn up to $750 in investment income per year without paying any tax. If the child is under age 14, the next $750 in unearned income is taxed at the child's marginal tax rate (10 percent), and unearned income above $1,500 is taxed at the parent's marginal tax rate (under a rule commonly referred to as the "kiddie tax").

Children age 14 and over pay their own tax rate on all income over $750. So, if you have $12,000 in a taxable savings account earning 4 percent per year, or $480, you can avoid the taxes you would normally have to pay on the interest earnings by gifting the account to your child, who can receive the interest without any taxes being owed.

3.4.5 Increasing Deductions and Exemptions from Income

To maximize your tax deductions, you should plan ahead for the record keeping and timing of expenditures. Careful record keeping helps ensure that you are reporting all deductible expenses. When you have a choice as to when to incur an expense, you should consider how the timing will affect your taxes. To get an idea of how many people apply this rule to their finances, go to an office supply or computer store on New Year's Eve. The store will probably be packed because December 31 is the last day to make purchases that can be deducted for the tax year.

It's a good idea to roughly estimate your expected tax liability before December 31. Any deductible expenditures have a much lower effective cost than actual cost because you would otherwise be paying some of that money in taxes. Another example of strategic end-of-year expenditures involves the timing of uninsured medical procedures. Let's say that in tax year 2006, you've already incurred sufficient medical costs (greater than 7.5 percent of the AGI) to qualify for the medical expense deduction. Any additional uninsured medical expenses—including out-of-pocket premiums, deductibles and copays, doctor visits, surgery, vision care, and prescriptions—can all be itemized in 2006, reducing the effective cost by the amount of your marginal tax bracket. If you need a new pair of glasses, this is the time to get them. Making charitable contributions is another way to increase deductions. You should keep track of all the times you've taken clothing to Goodwill or donated food.

Although it's always a good idea to get receipts, they're only required by the IRS for large contributions of cash or goods. In high-tax years, you should consider making an end-of-year contribution to your favorite charity. If you donate a total of $400, it could save you $100 to $200 in taxes, depending on your tax bracket, substantially reducing the effective cost of making the contribution.

Your home also has some tax-sheltering value. In addition to its capital gain advantage, mortgage interest and property taxes are both deductible, so your home is an incredible tax shelter. You should also consider taking advantage of home equity loans. Not only do they usually have a lower interest rate than consumer loans, but the interest on up to $100,000 in home equity loans ($50,000 for single or married filing separately) is tax deductible, reducing the effective cost even more.

To see how home ownership can produce tax benefits, consider the difference between two taxpayers, each in the 25 percent marginal tax bracket. Assume that the first one is a renter and the second is a homeowner. Both have identical annual housing expenditures of $12,000 per year. The renter cannot deduct any of this; the homeowner, however, can deduct all the mortgage interest and property taxes. That's like cash in the pocket! Plus, the home can increase in value tax free.

Exemptions are another type of deduction from your income. For example, expectant parents have moved up the date of their Caesarian sections from January 1 to December 31 in order to gain a tax exemption on the surgery.

3.4.6 Maximizing Tax Credits

Many people are eligible for various tax credits but don't claim them. This generally happens when they either don't know about the credits or haven't kept adequate records to claim them. Your tax planning strategy should therefore include a careful review of available credits and evaluation of your eligibility for each.

SUMMARY

Your financial plan will benefit from your knowledge of the tax code and how to avoid overpaying your taxes. It's important to think about the tax implications of your financial decisions. The U.S. tax system is progressive, although less so today than it was originally. Keeping your finances in order can help you file your taxes on time and accurately. You should use tax planning strategies, such as pretax investing, to your advantage.

KEY TERMS

Adjusted gross income (AGI)	Earned income and unearned income minus certain allowed adjustments to income.
Alternative minimum tax (AMT)	A federal income tax designed to ensure that people who receive certain tax breaks pay their fair share of taxes.
Average tax rate	The proportion of a taxpayer's total taxable income that goes to paying taxes.
Capital gain	Profit on the sale of an investment. This profit is subject to a lower tax rate if the investment has been held for more than one year.
Dependent	A member of a household who receives at least half of his or her support from the head of the household.
Earned income	Income from salaries, wages, tips, bonuses, commissions, and other sources.
Exemption	The dollar amount per household member that is subtracted from adjusted gross income in calculating taxable income.
Federal Insurance Contributions Act (FICA) tax	A payroll tax levied on earned income by the U.S. government to fund Social Security

	and Medicare. Stands for Federal Insurance Contributions Act tax.
Filing status	The household type, for tax filing purposes.
Flexible spending account	An account maintained by an employer in which the pretax earnings of an employee are set aside and can be used for reimbursement of qualified medical and child-care expenses.
Gross income	Income from all sources, including earned income, investment income, alimony, unemployment compensation, and retirement benefits.
Gross taxable income	Income from all sources, less allowed exclusions.
Internal Revenue Code	A compilation of all statutes, regulations, and court decisions relating to U.S. income tax.
Individual retirement account (IRA)	A retirement account that allows the holder to subtract current contributions from taxable income and to defer income tax until withdrawal at retirement.
Internal Revenue Service (IRS)	The U.S. government agency that is responsible for collecting federal income taxes and enforcing tax laws and regulations.
IRS e-file	A system that enables the electronic filing of federal tax returns.
Itemized deductions	An alternative to the standard deduction in which the taxpayer reports and deducts actual expenses in certain allowed categories to arrive at taxable income.
Marginal tax effect	The change in taxes owed as a result of a financial decision.
Marginal tax rate	Tax rate imposed on a taxpayer's next dollar of income.
Payroll withholding	Money regularly withheld from employees' pay by employers for payment of the employees' taxes.
Progressive tax	A tax that requires higher-income taxpayers to pay proportionately more in taxes than other taxpayers, through either higher tax rates or other rules.

Regressive tax	A tax that places a disproportionate financial burden on low-income taxpayers.
Roth IRA	An individual retirement account to which contributions are made with after-tax dollars but in which investment earnings and withdrawals at retirement are tax free.
Standard deduction	A dollar amount based on filing status that is subtracted from adjusted gross income in calculating taxable income.
Tax avoidance	Strategic use of knowledge of tax rules to avoid overpayment of taxes.
Tax bracket	The range of income to which a particular marginal tax rate applies.
Tax credit	A reduction applied directly to taxes owed rather than to income that is subject to taxes.
Tax evasion	Deliberate nonpayment of taxes legally owed.
Taxable income	The amount of income that is subject to taxes under the law.
Total income	Gross income less certain exclusions allowed by the IRS.
Unearned income	Income from investments, interest, dividends, capital gains, net business income, rents, and royalties.

ASSESS YOUR UNDERSTANDING

Go to www.wiley.com/college/bajtelsmit to assess your knowledge of managing your taxes.
Measure your learning by comparing pre-test and post-test results.

Summary Questions

1. The current U.S. federal tax rates are considered to be the highest ever relative to historical rates. True or false?

2. A progressive tax is one in which:
   (a) you pay more if you earn more.
   (b) you pay less if you earn more.
   (c) you pay the same, regardless of earnings.
   (d) taxes are used for progressive services.

3. If your taxable income falls in the lowest tax bracket:
   (a) you pay no taxes.
   (b) your taxes are computed based on the AMT.
   (c) you receive the Earned Income Credit.
   (d) all your taxable income is taxed at the same rate.

4. Interest earned on bank deposits is classified as:
   (a) earned income.
   (b) an adjustment to income.
   (c) interest income.
   (d) capital gains.

5. Which of the following tax forms is known as the long form?
   (a) 1040A
   (b) 1040B
   (c) 1040C
   (d) 1040EZ

6. Tips you receive must be reported as income on your tax form. True or false?

7. Which of the following types of taxes paid is not an allowed itemized deduction?
   (a) property taxes on your home
   (b) personal property taxes
   (c) state income taxes
   (d) use taxes

8. A $1,000 tax credit would be more beneficial than a $1,000 tax deduction. True or false?

9. The amount of taxes withheld from your paycheck depends on your expected income and number of exemptions. True or false?

10. One reason to give investment accounts to children is that:
    (a) children pay no taxes.
    (b) accounts of children are not audited by the IRS.
    (c) their income would be subject to lower tax rates.
    (d) all of the above are correct.

11. Which of the following retirement accounts allows tax-free withdrawals at retirement?
    (a) 401(k) plans
    (b) traditional IRAs
    (c) Roth IRAs
    (d) 403(b) plans

Applying This Chapter

1. If you file a return as a single person with a taxable income of $25,000 in 2006, which tax bracket are you in?

2. If you are in the lowest tax bracket in 2006, how much income will be subject to that tax rate?

3. June's 85-year-old father has lived with her family for all of tax year 2006. June is receiving a stipend of $15,000 per year from her father's estate for taking care of him. His total expenses were $20,000. Can she claim him as a dependent for 2006?

4. Rashid has a total income of $21,000 in 2006 and tuition expenses of $1,000, resulting in an AGI of $20,000. He can claim an exemption for himself in the amount of $3,300, and he incurred the following expenses during the year: medical expenses, $500; property taxes, $1,500; mortgage interest, $5,000; state income taxes, $500. If the standard deduction for a single filer in 2006 is $5,150, should Rashid itemize deductions? Why or why not?

5. Tamika tore a knee ligament in 2006 and had to undergo arthroscopic surgery. Her total medical expenses were $8,000, but her health insurance covered all but $2,400. If her AGI is $20,000, how much of this out-of-pocket cost can she deduct on her taxes if she itemizes her deductions?

6. You earned less than $3,000 from your part-time job last year. Should you file an income tax return? Explain.

7. Explain why you would choose to itemize deductions, from a strategic standpoint.
8. Explain why capital gains are preferable to earned income, from a tax standpoint.
9. In what ways is a home a tax shelter?

You Be the Tax Advisor

For each of the following taxpayer characteristics, design potential strategies for minimizing taxes:

1. real estate investor in a high tax bracket
2. working parents with preschoolers
3. college student who is independent of parents

Capital Gains

Jack Spratt has an investment that gives him $1,000 per year in interest income. His friend Peter Pumpkineater has been telling Jack that he should invest in something that provides him with capital gains instead of interest. This year, for example, Peter sold some shares of a mutual fund (which he had held for more than one year) for a $1,000 profit. Assuming that Jack and Peter are both in the top marginal tax bracket (35 percent), how much difference did the type of income they received from these two investments make to the taxes owed on the income?

Calculating Your Withholding

How much should you have withheld from your paycheck? Go to the IRS Web site, www.irs.gov/individuals, and use the withholding calculator there to find out.

4

MANAGING YOUR CASH AND SAVINGS
Cash Management Strategies

Starting Point

Go to www.wiley.com/college/bajtelsmit to assess your knowledge of cash and savings management.
Determine where you need to concentrate your effort.

What You'll Learn in This Chapter

▲ Cash management
▲ Financial institutions
▲ Financial products and services

After Studying This Chapter, You'll Be Able To

▲ Assess your need for cash management products and services
▲ Evaluate the differences among providers of cash management products and services
▲ Choose cash management products and services that are important to your financial plan
▲ Compare cash management account options based on liquidity, safety, costs, and after-tax annual percentage yield
▲ Select appropriate tools for dealing with cash management errors

INTRODUCTION

Everyone manages cash. Your very first exposure to personal financial management was probably related to cash management. Perhaps you received a small allowance when you were a child and had to decide how to spend or save the money. Access to cash to meet transaction needs and emergencies is essential to your financial plan. A central part of your cash management strategies involves choosing cash management services, such as checking and savings accounts. This chapter helps you evaluate companies and the cash management services they offer. After you select the options that best meet your needs, you can implement your plan.

4.1 Objectives of Cash Management

Many people are guilty of occasionally, or not so occasionally, neglecting to balance their checkbooks or making bill payments after they are due. Keeping track of your cash and paying your bills are both important tasks associated with cash management. **Cash management** includes all your decisions related to cash payments and short-term liquid investments.

As discussed in Section 2.2, liquid investments are those that can easily be converted to cash without loss of value, such as the money in a checking or savings account. Although you can leave money in these accounts for longer periods, they are not generally the best choice for long-term savings, so we can also think of cash management as decisions related to investments of one year or less.

When you hold cash, whether it's in your pocket or in a bank checking or savings account, you incur certain costs. For one, you give up the opportunity to invest those dollars to earn a higher rate of return. Most people hold some of their money in a checking account. In some cases, this account might pay a small amount of interest, but in most cases, it does not. In fact, you may even pay for the privilege of holding money in certain types of accounts.

The lost interest is an important consideration. For example, if you carry an average balance of $1,000 in your checking account for a year, and you could instead have invested it to earn 10 percent interest, you've given up about $100 in interest (10 percent of $1,000). An additional cost of holding cash is psychological: If you have money sitting in your checking account, you can spend it very easily. It would be a shame if all your hard work in developing your budget went to waste because you couldn't resist the temptation of writing a check for an expensive item you hadn't planned to buy. In contrast, if you keep your cash in an account that's not as easily accessible, such as a savings account, you'll be more likely to stick to your plan.

Cash accounts pay less interest and increase the risk of overspending. So why are we willing to incur these costs? There are three general reasons for holding cash:

▲ Managing transactions

▲ Preparing for cash emergencies

▲ Making temporary investments

All these purposes are related to managing liquidity. Money held in less liquid investments, such as bonds, stocks, and real estate, provides a better investment return than money held in checking and saving accounts, but it's also more difficult to access on short notice.

4.1.1 Managing Transactions

Everyone has bills. To pay your bills easily, you need to have sufficient cash in a transaction account, commonly called a checking account, which is an account that allows you to regularly make deposits, write checks, withdraw funds, or make electronic payments in a timely fashion and at minimal cost.

Many people find it convenient to deposit their paychecks into a checking account and then to pay their bills from that account. There's a cost to using this banking service, in the form of lost interest earnings. So why not have your paycheck deposited in a savings account instead?

Although it's usually fairly easy to make transfers between accounts, the time and effort required to make multiple transfers each month as bills come due would probably outweigh the minimal interest that could be earned. Because the money is coming in and then promptly going out, the actual amount of time that it will earn interest is likely to be relatively short, and the interest you earn may not be enough to justify the time spent shifting money between accounts. However, if your paycheck is normally greater than the total monthly payments you make from the account, you should carefully estimate your needs and have the extra amount automatically transferred to an interest-earning account each month.

4.1.2 Preparing for Cash Emergencies

Life is full of unpredictable events. Maybe the car needs a new $2,000 transmission. Or your son breaks his arm playing football, and you have to pay $400 in doctors' bills. More serious emergencies might involve the loss of a job or temporary disability. To meet your emergency cash needs, you should manage your financial assets so that you can access cash when needed. For most households, this should include a **cash reserve**—an accumulation of liquid assets that you can turn to in an emergency.

In the past, a family might have had a few hundred dollars hidden in the bottom of a cookie jar or under a mattress. Today, in addition to traditional checking and savings accounts, you can arrange for credit cards and home equity lines of credit that can be accessed in an emergency but that otherwise incur no interest. Section 5.6 explains that you should avoid using credit cards as much as possible because of their high interest costs. However, they can be a source of short-term liquidity as long as you anticipate repaying the borrowed amounts in the future.

4.1.3 Making Temporary Investments

The third reason you might hold cash is in anticipation of a near-term need for the funds. Perhaps you're saving for a vacation or a new car, or maybe you're planning to buy a home. Or you might have sold some other assets recently and haven't yet decided how to reinvest the funds. During the recent ups and downs in the stock market, many investors used cash accounts to temporarily store funds as they bought and sold stocks.

4.1.4 How Much Should You Hold in Cash?

Financial experts disagree as to how much money a household should hold in cash. Very conservative advice suggests that you should have enough liquid assets to cover five to eight months of regular expenses. Others suggest that two months is more than enough and recommend investing the rest for higher returns.

For an average household with expenses of $2,000 per month, these rules of thumb would imply that the family should hold between $4,000 and $16,000 in cash or liquid assets. Even if the family split the difference and held $10,000 in liquid assets, these assets would greatly reduce the risk of cash shortfall in the event of a big shock to household income. But the cost can also be significant. You will forego the money you might have earned on an alternative investment—

FOR EXAMPLE

How Much Does It Cost to Be Safe?

Suppose you keep $4,000 in a checking account that earns 0 percent interest and $6,000 in a short-term savings account that earns 2 percent interest per year. Let's assume also that your alternative to holding cash would be an investment you expect to earn 8 percent per year. The opportunity cost of holding this much in cash is the average annual amount in cash multiplied by the difference between the interest you could earn on an alternative investment and the interest you earn on the cash account. The annual lost interest earnings are substantial: ($4,000 × 0.08) + ($6,000 × 0.06), or $680 per year. However, the reduced risk might more than make up for the lost interest earnings. You may not be willing or able to take much risk. You should assess your cash needs for transactions and emergencies and have sources you can tap into in an emergency.

likely involving some risk—with that cash. You have to decide if having the cash is worth it. The loss of interest earnings may be more than made up for by the reduction in risk.

If you have a high risk of job loss, you might consider holding a conservatively large amount in cash. But if you have a secure job and alternative sources of funds for emergencies, you might hold only enough to meet your needs. Each strategy has costs and benefits that you must carefully identify and evaluate.

SELF-CHECK

1. Define cash management.
2. Name the three general reasons for holding cash.

4.2 Rules of Effective Cash Management

Effective cash management minimizes the risk of bank charges for overdrafts and extra interest or penalties on overdue payments. Keeping track of cash flow is also necessary for budgeting so that you can achieve financial goals. In this section, we consider four practices that, if followed, result in better cash management outcomes.

4.2.1 Balancing Your Checkbook Every Month

Regularly balancing your checkbook is important. With the use of checks, debit cards, and automated teller machines (ATMs), it's very easy to lose track of how much you spend, particularly when more than one person is using the same account. If you don't balance your checkbook regularly, you're more likely to exceed your budget or, worse, bounce checks. Balancing your checkbook can be a daunting bookkeeping task if you write many checks or use your debit card often, particularly if you aren't careful about entering withdrawals and deposits. But the benefits to your finances far outweigh the costs.

The objective is to reconcile the balance your bank reports on its statement with the balance recorded in your checkbook register. To do this, you need to first adjust the bank balance for any additional checks and deposits that aren't reflected on the statement. Then you need to adjust your checkbook register to reflect checks and deposit transactions that aren't yet recorded, as well as any bank charges or interest.

If there's still a discrepancy between the checkbook balance and the bank statement balance, you should go over the withdrawals and deposits again to be sure you haven't missed any, and you should recheck your addition and subtraction.

Because a bank statement is based on computerized account records, it is highly unlikely that such a statement will contain any mathematical errors. There is, however, the possibility of errors in automatic withdrawals or ATM transactions. You may even find that someone has fraudulently accessed your account. You should try to discover any such problems promptly because delay in discovering and reporting an incident of abuse or error makes it more difficult to get the problem corrected.

4.2.2 Paying Your Bills on Time

Timely payment of bills not only reduces your costs but also minimizes the risk that your credit rating will be hurt. A history of late payments makes you a less attractive credit risk. If your credit rating is poor, you may not be able to qualify for loans, you may have to pay higher rates of interest, and you may have increased insurance premiums. By paying your bills on time, you also avoid getting annoying phone calls from your creditors.

Although many people use ATMs or check online to determine their checking account balances, doing only these things is a poor substitute for reconciling a checkbook. The balance shown on the ATM receipt is not an accurate reflection of the true account balance because it doesn't include transactions that have not yet posted.

4.2.3 Paying Yourself First

The single most common advice given by financial planners is "Pay yourself first." What this means is that you should set aside the money necessary for achieving personal goals before you do anything else. If you wait until the end of the month to see how much is left to put into savings, inevitably there will be none left. If, instead, you treat savings as a primary expenditure and take it off the top before paying any other expenses, you are more likely to stick to your financial plan and avoid casual erosion of your cash flow.

There are many convenient ways to pay yourself first. Most banks and financial institutions offer the option of automatic funds transfer, by which you arrange to have a certain amount automatically transferred from your checking to your savings or investment account after your paycheck is deposited.

Another useful tool is automatic bill paying. Not only can you arrange directly with your creditor or service provider for automatic payments each month, you can take advantage of online bill-paying services that electronically pay all your regular bills each month. This can be particularly helpful for busy individuals.

4.2.4 Evaluating Alternative Accounts and Providers

Effective cash management requires that you carefully evaluate your alternatives and select the services and service providers that best meet your needs. You have many providers and services to choose from, and they vary widely in interest paid, fees, safety, and customer service.

SELF-CHECK

1. List the four rules of effective cash management.
2. Cite two ways to pay yourself first.

4.3 Selecting a Financial Institution

At one time, cash management services could be obtained only at certain types of financial institutions. Today, many different types of financial institutions provide such services. The good news and the bad news is that you now have many choices. This is good news because competition often results in higher interest paid on accounts and lower interest charged on loans. It's bad news because having more choices means it takes more time and effort to investigate your alternatives thoroughly.

The various types of financial institutions are listed and defined in the following sections, but the differences between them are small and are becoming less important. In general, financial institutions are classified as depository or nondepository, based on where they primarily get their money to invest:

▲ **Depository institutions**—such as commercial banks, savings institutions, and credit unions—get their funds from customer deposits.
▲ **Nondepository institutions**—such as insurance companies, mortgage companies, and finance companies—get funds from other sources.

The different types of institutions in each of these categories are distinguished by what they primarily invest in.

4.3.1 Depository Institutions

Depository institutions include commercial banks, several types of savings institutions, and credit unions. All these types of firms are similar in two major ways:

▲ Their primary source of funds is customer deposits.
▲ Their primary source of income is interest earned on loans.

An important distinction between accounts held by banks and those held by mutual funds, brokerage funds, and insurance companies is insurance coverage against the organization going bankrupt. Most checking, savings, and certificate of deposit (CD) accounts in depository institutions are insured by the **Federal Deposit Insurance Corporation (FDIC),** a government-sponsored insurance agency, or a comparable federal agency, and thus are very safe places to put your money. Personal accounts held in commercial banks are insured for up to $100,000 per depositor by the FDIC. A common misconception is that this insurance covers accounts up to $100,000, but the guarantee is for $100,000 per depositor in a single institution. So, a good rule of thumb is to keep no more than $100,000 at any institution or to keep it in two different names (e.g., your name and your spouse's name).

On the other hand, checking and savings accounts offered by mutual funds, brokerage firms, and insurance companies are not insured. So, even if an uninsured account pays a little higher interest than an insured one, it might not be worth the risk.

Commercial Banks

Often simply called a "bank," a **commercial bank** is a depository institution that gets its funds from checking and savings account deposits and uses the money to provide a wide array of financial services, including business and personal loans, mortgages, and credit cards.

Savings Institutions

There are a number of types of savings institutions, including **savings and loan (S&L) associations,** depository institutions that receive funds primarily from household deposits and use most of their funds to make home mortgage loans), thrift institutions, and savings banks.

Savings institutions were originally designed to give individuals access to banking services previously available (through commercial banks) only to businesses. Thus, savings institutions were at first limited to offering savings accounts and making home and personal loans to individuals. Now, savings institutions offer a more competitive selection of checking and savings accounts; they can even offer credit cards, business loans, and financial planning services. However, savings institutions are still primarily home mortgage lenders. In fact, S&Ls are required to use at least 70 percent of their money to make home mortgage loans, as opposed to other types of loans.

As with commercial banks, accounts in S&Ls are insured for up to $100,000 per depositor. Although the various types of savings institutions are likely to offer similar products and services, one distinction among them is their form of ownership. A **stock-held savings institution** is owned by stockholders. A **mutual savings institution** is owned by its depositors. If you have an account in a mutual savings institution, even though the rates of return are competitive, the earnings you receive on your investments are called *dividends* rather than *interest*. If the mutual savings institution is very profitable in a given year, you receive a higher dividend that year because the dividend is the way the company passes on the profits to its owner-depositors.

Credit Unions

A **credit union** is a special form of mutual depository institution. It gets its funds from checking and savings deposits and makes loans to its depositors, who are also the owners of the institution.

An important distinction between credit unions and other depository institutions is that credit unions have nonprofit status and often use a partially volunteer labor force, allowing them a low-cost advantage. Their reduced costs often mean that credit unions can offer lower loan rates and higher interest. Depositors in credit unions are insured for up to $100,000 by the National Credit Union Association, which operates the National Credit Union Share Insurance Fund (NCUSIF).

Credit unions, which are a good choice for students, were originally designed to give individuals access to personal credit, which was not widely available at commercial banks and savings institutions. At that time, credit union members were supposed to have a common bond, such as a religious or employment affiliation. For example, the federal government has a credit union for government employees and their families. Similarly, most states have credit unions for public employees. The common bond requirement, particularly for smaller employers or organizations, necessarily limited the size of these institutions and the services they could provide.

Today, the common bond requirement of credit unions is defined fairly loosely. For example, some credit unions limit membership to people who live in a particular town or area. Credit unions can now be just as large as competing banks and offer a similar selection of products, including credit cards and mortgages. This is great news because credit unions can often beat the rates offered by other financial institutions because they pass on their profits to their owner-customers. The rates paid on savings are higher, and the rates charged on auto and other loans are lower. To find a credit union, you can go to the Credit Union National Association Web site, at www.cuna.org.

Web-Only Financial Institutions

Web-only financial institutions do not have physical locations but offer a menu of cash management accounts, loans, and investments. Presumably, web-only firms might have a cost advantage over traditional depository institutions, but consumers seeking higher interest and lower loan rates are cautioned to check out an institution's credentials before sending money.

For more information about online banks, you can visit several government regulator Web sites: www.fdic.gov (FDIC), www.occ.treas.gov (Office of the Comptroller of the Currency), and www.ots.treas.gov (Office of Thrift Supervision). At the FDIC Web site, you can find out whether a particular bank is legitimate and whether it is insured. If you have visited a bank Web site that appears fraudulent, you can report it there.

4.3.2 Nondepository Institutions

Nondepository institutions include

▲ mutual fund companies.
▲ life insurance companies.
▲ brokerage firms.
▲ other financial services firms.

Although nondepository institutions have always offered loans in competition with banks, savings institutions, and credit unions, only recently have they begun to provide cash management services. They now compete with depository institutions for their primary customers by offering a full range of cash management products and services. For consumers, this means more choices and potentially lower prices. Notably, however, none of the accounts offered by these firms are federally insured.

Mutual Fund Companies

A **mutual fund company** is an investment company that sells shares to investors and then invests the pool of funds in a selection of financial securities. Some mutual fund companies have low-risk mutual fund investment account options that also allow limited check writing. These accounts are not federally insured.

Life Insurance Companies

A **life insurance company** sells life insurance policies to provide financial security for dependents in the event of the death of the policy owner. Its primary source of funds is therefore the payments made to purchase the policies, usually called the policy *premiums*. These companies invest the collected premiums in stocks, bonds, and other financial assets. Many life insurance products include savings and investment features and thus can be considered an alternative to other savings accounts. In addition, life insurance companies are active lenders in the home mortgage market.

Brokerage Firms

A **brokerage firm** is a company that facilitates investors' purchases of stocks, bonds, and other investments. An investor generally keeps money in an account with a brokerage firm and authorizes an employee of the firm, called a *broker,* to take money out of the account to pay for new purchases for the investor and to deposit money received from sales of the investor's securities. A brokerage firm usually makes its money by charging a commission for each purchase and sale.

Today, more banks are competing for the brokerage business; in turn, traditional brokerage firms are offering a variety of cash management services and products.

Other Financial Services Firms

Many financial institutions that previously fit into one category or another have been trying to redefine themselves as multiservice financial institutions to provide one-stop shopping for their customers and to take advantage of their existing market penetration. For example, State Farm Insurance, previously a large insurance company, has added mutual funds and cash management products to its offerings. These firms offer a fairly complete menu of checking and savings accounts, insurance products, consumer and mortgage loans, and mutual fund investments.

4.3.3 Evaluating Financial Institutions

With so many different financial institutions to choose from, how should you decide which to use? You should base your decision on how each financial service provider rates on the "four P's":

▲ **Products:** The ideal financial institution has all the products you need to manage your cash effectively. Begin with a list of the products and services you'd like. Find out which institutions offer the greatest number of them and compare based on quality. For example, a savings account offered by a federally insured depository institution is obviously less risky than one offered by an uninsured financial institution.

▲ **Price:** Price includes both the interest you earn on liquid asset accounts and the fees you pay. The fees can make all the difference between one product and another. Many institutions offer similar products, but their pricing can vary dramatically. Interest rates on demand savings accounts—that is, accounts that allow you to withdraw your funds at any time "on demand"—are usually much lower than those for other types of saving. For example, the average annual rate paid on interest-earning checking was 1.5 percent in November 2006, whereas a 6-month CD, which required that you leave your money on deposit for 6 months, averaged 4.65 percent. Financial institutions also differ substantially in their fees. Some require that you maintain a minimum balance in your checking account. It's fairly common for an account to have a monthly fee if the balance drops below a stated minimum, which might be $100 or $1,000. Bounced check fees can range from $10 to $50. These fees can eat into your returns very easily. Retail banks make most of their profits on the fees they charge to retail customers.

▲ **People:** Customer service, although somewhat less important today than it used to be, thanks to the use of electronic transactions, should still count. Consider whether the main office and drive-up tellers are open during convenient times. Are the lines long? When you call, do you get to speak to a knowledgeable person? Are your phone calls returned promptly and courteously? In some instances, you may be choosing between smaller locally owned institutions that focus on relationship banking and larger multistate institutions that offer more services. A bank near your workplace may seem like a good choice, but it may be so understaffed over the lunch hour that you would have to wait 30 minutes just to get to a teller. You should make this decision based on your unique needs and preferences. You may be willing to live with a smaller selection of products for a more personal touch. If there are substantial differences in costs, you should also weigh these.

▲ **Place:** Where are the ATMs located? Where is the main office? In deciding between a nearby institution and one that is farther away but offers a slightly better interest rate or lower costs, you should consider whether the cost advantage will outweigh the inconvenience. It's a good idea to collect information from several financial institutions and see how they compare. Although you're not limited to using only one financial institution, it can be more cost-effective to do so. Not only do you save time through one-stop shopping, but you may be entitled, as a depositor, to receive better consumer and home loan rates.

SELF-CHECK

1. Define **depository institution, mutual savings institution,** and **credit union.**
2. Give four examples of nondepository institutions.
3. What type of financial service provider is a good choice for students?

4.4 Cash Management Products and Services

Financial institutions provide cash management services that include checking and savings accounts, loans, and asset management services. Each may play an important role in your financial plan, so you need to understand the available options, as well as the costs and benefits of various features.

4.4.1 Checking Accounts

One of the reasons for holding cash is to manage transaction needs. These needs are often best met with a checking account. Checking accounts allow you to make deposits and pay bills easily. Before opening one, you should get answers to the following questions:

▲ Will you earn interest on your balance? If so, at what rate?

▲ Will you be required to keep a minimum balance in the account? If so, how much is it, and what is the penalty for going below that minimum?

▲ Is there a monthly fee? If so, how much?

▲ Can you access the account with a debit card (i.e., a card that enables you to withdraw money from your account electronically)?

▲ Does the account offer overdraft protection?

▲ Are there any other fees?

All checking accounts are **demand deposit accounts** in that you have the right to "demand" withdrawal of your deposited funds with little or no notice to the bank. For cash management, the most important distinction between types of checking accounts is whether they pay interest:

▲ **Regular checking accounts:** Although your particular bank or savings institution may call it something different, such as "basic checking," the key feature of a **regular checking account** is that it pays no interest. A bank may advertise these accounts as "free checking" because it waives the monthly service charge if you keep a minimum balance—anywhere from $100 to $1,000 or more. Not all regular checking accounts require a minimum balance, however. Regular checking accounts usually also limit the number of checks you can write each month and are unlikely to offer additional services, such as debit cards, without assessing additional fees. Because of the generally low account balances and the high cost of processing transactions and maintaining records, financial institutions make very little money on regular checking accounts. Instead, institutions rely on this type of account to entice people to use other services—services on which they make more profit.

▲ **Interest-earning checking accounts:** Regular checking accounts offer minimal services. A checking account that pays interest and includes other features, such as debit cards and unlimited check writing, might better meet your needs. Such accounts usually have higher minimum balance requirements than regular checking accounts. If your balance falls below the minimum, your interest rate on the account is reduced or, in some cases, eliminated, and you may pay a fee—typically $3 to $7 per month. A checking account that pays interest is technically called a

negotiated order of withdrawal (NOW) account, but few institutions use this terminology. Your bank may call it "Gold Plus Checking" or "First Checking" or some other name that sounds attractive. In addition to paying interest, NOW accounts may include other services. For example, most financial institutions no longer include copies of written checks with monthly checking account statements, but this service may be available with NOW accounts.

If you plan to hold cash reserves in a checking account and will therefore be able to meet the minimum balance requirement, an interest-earning checking account is certainly a better choice than a regular checking account. However, because these accounts generally pay lower interest than savings account alternatives, you should consider the opportunity costs involved in keeping your cash reserves in checking rather than transferring them to a higher-interest savings alternative. Recall that the opportunity cost of a particular action is what you have to give up in order to take that action.

4.4.2 Savings Accounts

Whereas checking accounts vary in whether they pay interest, all savings accounts pay interest. It's not always better to have an interest-earning checking account. You need to compare the account's restrictions and fees to its non-interest-earning alternative before making that decision. Many interest-earning checking accounts have monthly service charges or other fees that more than offset the interest if your account balances are relatively low. The rate of interest depends on the type of account. Savings accounts can be either of the following:

▲ **Demand deposits:** Like a checking account, a demand deposit savings account allows you to withdraw your money any time. This makes these accounts more liquid than those that require you to leave your money deposited for a set period of time. Because demand deposits are easily converted to cash, they are less risky to you; because they're less risky, they pay a lower rate of interest on balances. (In general, the riskier the investment or loan, the higher the interest rate.)

▲ **Time deposits:** Whereas demand deposits can be withdrawn at any time, a **time deposit account** requires that you keep the money in for a minimum time and may require a waiting period before you can withdraw funds. When you deposit your money for a set time, the institution can more easily make profitable long-term investments, and it can, in turn, pay you a higher interest rate. Generally, the longer the time restriction, the higher the rate. Because a time deposit is less liquid than other cash management account alternatives, it exposes you to greater risk. You may not be able to withdraw your money in a hurry, or there may be a cost to doing so. However, the higher rates paid on these accounts make them preferable when the account is earmarked to meet a particular financial goal—perhaps a house down payment—and you are fairly certain you won't need the money sooner. The power of compound interest helps your savings grow faster.

4.4.3 Savings Alternatives

Recently, short-term savings options have increased markedly. To select the best type for your needs, you must understand the different types:

▲ **Regular savings accounts:** Regular savings accounts were once called *passbook accounts* because the account holder actually had a little book in which the financial institution would enter deposit and withdrawal information. Although these types of accounts still exist, account records are now kept electronically, and your bank sends you periodic statements, either monthly or quarterly, showing deposits, withdrawals, fees, and interest. In hopes of saving mailing and printing costs, financial institutions are developing online access tools that may eventually replace mailed statements. You may find it convenient to have a regular savings account in the same institution as your checking account. Generally, that makes it easy to move money between accounts. Sometimes, you can arrange for an automatic transfer to keep from bouncing a check.

▲ **CDs:** You get the highest interest rates on savings with time deposit accounts. A **CD** is a savings account that pays a stated rate of interest if you leave your money on deposit for a certain time. The end of that period is called the **maturity date.** Rates are higher for CDs of longer duration and for larger deposit amounts. For example, a 5-year CD can earn twice as much interest as a 1-year CD. It definitely pays to shop around. Even the rates paid on CDs with similar maturity dates can vary widely. CDs offered by depository institutions are very safe because they are federally insured, but CDs are not highly liquid because you may not be able to access funds immediately when you need them. If you need your funds before the end of the CD term, you can generally get them, but you incur a penalty—a sharply reduced interest rate, usually equivalent to a demand deposit rate. If you cash out a CD within a short time, you may even pay a penalty fee in addition to that. It makes sense to manage your money so as to minimize the likelihood that this kind of thing will happen. One way is to separate your investments into several smaller CDs that mature at different times, a strategy sometimes called "laddering." Instead of putting $10,000 in a CD that matures in 5 years, for example, you might put $5,000 in the 5-year CD, $3,000 in a 2-year CD, $1,000 in a 12-month CD, and $1,000 in a 6-month CD. Although you earn lower

---

FOR EXAMPLE

Watch Those Maturity Dates

Consider what happened to Joseph Gianetti, a retiree with three adult children. He decided to give a tax-free gift of $11,000 to each of his children in 2004 and was planning to take it from a $35,000 5-year CD that was maturing at the end of the year. Unfortunately, when he tried to withdraw the funds in December, he discovered that the CD had actually matured in October. Joseph had apparently overlooked the notice from his bank. Because he had not responded, the bank had rolled it into another 5-year CD; Joseph had to pay a penalty to cash it in. The moral of this story is that you should keep careful track of maturity dates and be sure to read any documentation from your bank.

---

rates on the shorter-term CDs, the reduced risk of incurring an early withdrawal penalty may outweigh the opportunity cost. When a CD matures, your financial institution usually automatically rolls over the funds into a comparable account unless you file the necessary paperwork. For example, if you have your money in a 1-year CD, the institution rolls it into another 1-year CD at maturity. Your financial institution may offer special types of CDs. With so many alternatives to consider, you need to make sure you fully understand the terms of a CD before you invest. The FDIC, Web site at www.fdic.gov, offers several tips for investors in CDs to consider.

▲ **Money market mutual funds:** As described in Section 4.3.2, mutual fund companies are financial companies that pool investors' funds and use the money to purchase a variety of financial assets. Most companies now offer one or more **money market mutual funds** with characteristics that make them alternatives to other liquid savings accounts (e.g., limited check-writing privileges). These funds invest in short-term, low-risk financial assets, such as short-term debt securities called money market securities, which is why the funds are called money market mutual funds. When you buy shares of a money market mutual fund, the interest depends on the interest that the mutual fund is earning on its investment portfolio. Generally, this is 1 to 2 percentage points higher than what you can earn on a regular savings account. Of course, these higher returns come with greater risk. Although money market mutual funds may be sold by your bank, they are not federally insured, nor is the rate guaranteed. If interest rates drop, you earn less than you originally expected; if the fund goes belly-up, you could lose everything.

▲ **Money market accounts:** A **money market account** is similar to a money market mutual fund in that it pays interest that fluctuates with market rates on money market securities. Again, the rate is generally higher than that on regular savings accounts. Like money market mutual funds, money market accounts usually allow some check-writing privileges. Today, you can sometimes get unlimited check writing. But, you must usually keep a fairly high minimum balance in a money market account, so, as with interest-earning checking accounts, you need to consider the opportunity cost of holding more in the account than you would otherwise. Finally, it's important to remember that money market accounts offered by depository institutions are usually federally insured, whereas those offered by insurance companies and brokerage firms are not.

▲ **Government savings bonds:** **U.S. savings bonds** provide short-term, low-risk investing. These bonds are exempt from state and local income taxes and pay interest that fluctuates with changes in market interest rates. There are several types:

- **Series EE bonds, renamed "Patriot bonds" after September 11, 2001:** These are bonds issued by the U.S. Treasury. Investors pay 50 percent of the face value, which may be as little as $50 or as much as $10,000, and can redeem the bonds for the original price plus interest earned over the holding period. To purchase a Series EE bond with a $50 face value, you'd pay $25. These bonds are called **discount bonds** because the purchase price is less than the face value of the bond. The bond is redeemable for the full $50 face value when it has accumulated $25 in interest. The maturity date is uncertain—it depends on the interest rate. When you know the interest rate, you can figure out how much time it will take for your bond investment to double in value by applying the **Rule of 72:** Divide the number 72 by the interest rate. The result is an approximation of the number of years it takes to double the money. You can use this rule of thumb with any investment. The interest, in addition to being exempt from state and local income taxation, is not subject to federal income tax until the bond is cashed in. For lower- and middle-income families, the interest income is exempt if it is used to pay for qualified higher education expenses. Because these bonds are very low risk, the interest paid is comparable to that for other types of cash accounts with similar maturities. If you live in an area with high state and local tax rates, though, the tax advantages may make this preferable to taxable cash accounts.

- **Series HH bonds:** If you have a Series EE bond that has accumulated enough interest to be redeemed at its face value and you'd like to receive regular interest income from your savings without having to pay federal income tax on the whole amount, you can use your Series

EE bonds to buy Series HH bonds. This is the only way to purchase Series HH bonds. These bonds pay interest to the holder semiannually, and this interest income is subject to federal income tax but exempt from state and local income tax.

- **Series I bonds:** In 1998, the U.S. Treasury began offering Series I savings bonds. These bonds are similar to EE bonds in their tax features but are designed to provide protection from inflation. The semi-annual interest rate is fixed when you purchase the bond, but the face value on which the interest is calculated adjusts semiannually with the consumer price index. Although individuals can buy up to $30,000 in Series I bonds each year, sales have been slow because inflation has been relatively low in the past decade.

4.4.4 Other Cash Management Products and Services

Financial institutions offer a wide variety of cash management services besides those described so far in this chapter, including electronic banking services and specialized checks. Your bank or savings institution may also offer credit cards, car loans, home mortgages, financial planning and investment management services, and insurance. Banking services today include the following:

▲ **Debit cards:** Many checking accounts allow you to use a debit card, a plastic card encoded with account information that enables you to withdraw funds electronically to pay for purchases. You need only swipe the card through the retailer's point-of-sale (POS) terminal and enter your personal identification number (PIN) to authorize the withdrawal. Consumers like the freedom from carrying cash or checkbooks and the ease of making transactions. Of course, the simplicity of paying with a debit card also means that you may be more likely to overspend. You need to be sure to record debit transactions as they occur so that your financial records are up-to-date. Note that using a debit card is identical to writing a check—the only real difference is that the debit, or withdrawal, occurs at the moment you use the card rather than when the check clears. Although debit cards look almost identical to credit cards, discussed in Chapter 5, they're quite different. When you use a debit card, you're paying with your own money rather than borrowing money. You should never keep your debit card PIN in written form in your wallet or purse. You should select a PIN that is something you can remember but that will not be too easy to guess. And you should not use numbers a thief would be likely to try, such as 1234 or 1111. And because many debit cards can be used to complete online or phone transactions without the entry of a PIN, you should guard your card carefully. For more information on identity theft and how to avoid it, see Section 5.6.2.

▲ **ATMs:** ATMs have reduced the demand for tellers, thus allowing financial institutions to cut their overhead costs. ATMs offer the convenience of 24-hour-a-day access, and they can be found at hundreds of locations. ATM transactions are free only when you use a terminal owned by your financial institution. If you withdraw money at a terminal owned by another bank, you have to pay a fee—anywhere from $1.50 to $4.00—and your own institution may charge you $1.00 to $2.00 as well. These small dollar amounts may not seem like much, but they can easily add up to more than the annual interest on your account!

▲ **Other electronic banking services:** Most financial institutions now accept automatic deposits of paychecks and allow you to authorize automatic electronic withdrawals for regular payments of everything from loan payments to monthly fees at retailers. Many people now make all their regular bill payments electronically, either through their financial institutions or private services. You should weigh the monthly costs against the convenience. An additional advantage of online banking is that many services let you download financial information to financial management and tax planning software packages. Some financial institutions also offer special asset management accounts (AMAs) that automatically transfer your account balances among different accounts and investments to get you the highest rate of return; however, these accounts often require high minimum balances.

▲ **Specialized checks:** Financial institutions also provide various kinds of specialized checks, including the following:

- **Traveler's checks:** Traveler's checks are checks issued in specific denominations (e.g., $10, $20, $50, $100) by large financial institutions that are accepted worldwide. The typical fee for issuance is 1 percent. The primary advantages are that, if traveler's checks are lost or stolen, you can't lose any money, and their replacement is guaranteed.

- **Certified checks:** A certified check is a personal check drawn on your own account and guaranteed by the financial institution in which you have the account. Because the institution certifies (i.e., guarantees) that the funds are actually available and places a freeze on those funds, a certified check is accepted as cash for many official transactions, such as when you are paying off a car loan or making a down payment on a new home. Fees for this service range from $2 to $10.

- **Cashier's checks:** A cashier's check is used similarly to a certified check, to make payments when the payee wants to be sure the funds are available. But instead of being drawn on your account, the check is drawn on the account of the financial institution itself and made out to the party the purchaser specifies. The person ordering the check pays the financial institution the amount of the check plus a fee between $2 and $10.

- **Money order:** A money order is a legal request for a company to pay a particular sum of money to a person or business. In effect, a money order is like a check drawn on the account of a business. If you don't have your own checking account, you can purchase money orders to pay your bills or other obligations. They're sold by financial institutions, by the U.S. Post Office, and by businesses such as convenience stores and grocery stores, for a small fee.

4.4.5 Evaluating Your Options

How do you decide which products and services are most appropriate for your needs? What are the most important factors to consider? Recall that the basic purposes of cash management are to meet transaction needs, to develop a cash reserve for emergencies, and to have a safe place to park money. Because all these needs require that the account have minimal risk and be easy to access, your primary concerns should be liquidity and safety. When you've narrowed your choices to those meeting this initial screen, you should consider costs and after-tax interest earnings:

▲ **Liquidity:** Can you withdraw money from the account without incurring fees or losing any of your original investment? In evaluating your account options, pay careful attention to features that limit the account's liquidity, such as minimum balance requirements, limitations on withdrawals, and number of transactions or checks allowed each month.

▲ **Safety:** Investment options differ in terms of level of risk, as do the institutions offering these options. Does a cash management account expose you to any risk of default by the financial institution? Is there any risk of losing your money? Is the interest rate paid on the account guaranteed, or does it fluctuate with market conditions? Because cash management accounts are earmarked as funds that you can't afford to risk, you should consider limiting your choices to insured deposits and federally guaranteed investments. Although FDIC-insured accounts are obviously less risky than uninsured accounts, the failure of your financial institution would still impose some costs. During the 1980s, numerous S&Ls failed, and many insured depositors were unable to access their funds for several months, although they were eventually repaid by the government insurance program.

▲ **Costs and after-tax interest:** When you're deciding between savings alternatives, you have to make trade-offs. Generally, the safer the investment and the institution, the lower the rate of interest paid. Accounts that are more liquid usually pay lower rates of interest and may have

FOR EXAMPLE

Inflation: The Hidden Risk of "Safe Accounts"

An often-overlooked risk of supposedly safe investments is inflation. Suppose you're planning to buy a new mountain bike one year from now. The cost of the bike is $1,000 today, so you set aside $1,000 in your FDIC-insured savings account at Safety First Bank, which pays 2 percent annual interest. At the end of the year, you'll have $1,020. But what if inflation this year turns out to be 4 percent? The cost of the bike, if we assume that it goes up only by the average increase in the cost of goods, will have risen by 4 percent, to $1,040. The spending power of your $1,000 will actually have declined over the one-year period because it would have been enough to buy the bike at the beginning, but it's not enough at the end of the year. Investors in "safe" accounts like this have practically zero risk of losing the nominal value of their invested money, but they still risk losing purchasing power through the eroding effects of inflation.

higher costs, such as monthly service charges, fees, and penalties. It's not uncommon for an account advertised as "free" to include many hidden costs that are very profitable for the institution, such as fees for check printing, overdrafts, stop payments, and debit cards. You may find that the accounts have different rules for when they calculate and pay you interest. The frequency with which interest is calculated and added to your account is called **compounding**. The more often the interest compounds—daily instead of monthly, for example—the more you get the advantage of interest paid on interest, which is discussed in Chapter 1. The difficulty in comparing accounts is that the stated, or nominal, interest rate is not directly comparable between accounts if the accounts have different rates of compounding. The interest may also be eroded by fees, so that the actual annual rate of return on your invested funds may be lower than the nominal quoted rate of return. Fortunately for consumers of financial services, the Truth in Savings law requires that financial institutions report the **annual percentage yield (APY)** on all interest-earning accounts, in addition to the nominal rate. This measure adjusts for different compounding periods and any interest-like fees to make it possible to compare "apples with apples." However, fees for specific services (e.g., debit cards, checks) aren't factored into this calculation, so you still need to consider them.

After finding the APY for each account, you shouldn't forget to consider tax effects. Because returns on liquid savings accounts are already low, the additional costs of federal, state, and local income taxes can erode your yield to very low levels. If your APY on a regular savings account is 2 percent, for example, and your marginal tax rate is 40 percent, your after-tax yield is only $2 \times (1 - 0.4) = 1.2$ percent after you pay the taxes on your interest earnings.

It's a good idea to consider having multiple accounts that vary in liquidity, cost, and interest to maximize your overall return. Most people have a transaction account for regular bill paying and a highly liquid savings account for short-term emergency needs. As they build their emergency fund to a desirable level, they may attempt to increase their interest earnings by spreading their funds among higher-yield savings options, such as U.S. savings bonds and CDs with varying maturities. This makes sense because, in most financial emergencies, you don't need the entire amount immediately. For example, if you lose your job, you need to cover only one month of expenses at a time.

SELF-CHECK

1. List five savings alternatives.
2. Define **compounding, APY,** and **certificate of deposit.**
3. What should be your primary concerns in evaluating your cash management alternatives?

4.5 Resolving Cash Management Problems

Unexpected cash management problems happen to everyone. It might be your own mistake, such as a bounced check or a seriously overdue bill. Or it could be someone else's fault, such as depositing a check that the check writer doesn't have the funds to cover. Worse yet, you may have your checkbook or debit card stolen. Here we consider some of these problems.

4.5.1 Bouncing a Check

The best way to avoid bouncing checks is to keep careful track of your cash flow. If the worst occurs, you can avoid hefty overdraft charges, often assessed by both your bank and the party to whom you wrote the bad check, by arranging for **overdraft protection** on your account.

Overdraft protection can involve an automatic transfer from a different account or automatic credit in the amount of the overdraft. Credit of this type is similar to a credit card loan and may have a relatively high rate of interest, so you need to pay it off promptly. If you bounce a check, this information will be reported to one or more check approval companies (e.g., TeleCheck, CheckRite). These companies provide two valuable services to businesses:

▲ They take care of the hassle of collecting the amount of your bounced check (usually requiring cash or a certified check) and assessing any penalties.

▲ They keep an electronic record of individuals who have bounced checks at any participating business. Thus, if you bounce a check at the grocery store, your checks will be refused at all establishments using the same check approval service the grocery store uses until you've paid the amount due plus any fees (often $20 to $30).

To maintain your ability to write checks, you should resolve an overdraft as quickly as possible. An additional cost of bouncing a check is that your depository institution also assesses a penalty, usually ranging from $20 to $30. Thus, your $50 bounced check to the local grocery store could end up costing you another $40 to $60 in penalties to the store and your bank.

4.5.2 Receiving a Bad Check

If you deposit a check and it bounces, your own institution often charges you a fee, even though you were not at fault. This fee is comparable to a bounced check fee ($20 to $30). If, as a result of the bad check, you bounce checks of your own, you pay penalties on those, too.

Although you can try to get the wrongdoer to pay you back, you're unlikely to be successful. Thus, the best way to avoid the problem is to take checks only from reliable sources and not to write checks against funds that have not yet been credited to your account.

4.5.3 Discovering Fraudulent Activity on Your Account

Suppose you are reconciling your bank statement and see a record of an electronic payment made to an internet retailer, but it's for a transaction you never made. The risk of unauthorized use of cash management accounts has jumped with the rise in electronic transactions. If this unfortunately common occurrence happens to you, you need to act promptly to correct this "mistake."

By law, a contact phone number for each company or person who received payments from your account must be provided on your bank statement, so you can simply call and ask a company to reverse the charges. Although erroneous charges can be the result of legitimate errors, such as when someone has input an account number incorrectly, more often, the charge is part of a larger scam in which a company requests electronic payments from numerous accounts, counting on careless consumers not checking their statements carefully.

When you call to contest a payment, the person who answers will likely say that you or another family member requested whatever you're being charged for, over the phone or on the internet. Legally, your financial institution is not supposed to make payments without your authorization. A signed check is one form of authorization, and your PIN is another. But as more transactions are being made electronically without these verification procedures, it is more difficult for a bank to be the gatekeeper to your account. Thus, the primary responsibility lies with you to safeguard the account number and access. We talk more about identity theft in Section 5.6.2.

4.5.4 Stopping Payment on a Check

Sometimes, you might want to keep a person or business from cashing your check. For example, you might have paid a contractor to work on your house but realized soon after he left that he hadn't actually finished the job. In this circumstance, you can have your bank issue a **stop payment order** on the check for a fee of $10 to $25. Although you can make this request by phone, you should follow up in writing to protect your rights in case the check slips through. Stop orders can be extended beyond their usual two-week period for an additional fee.

4.5.5 Getting Money in a Hurry

Nearly every college student has had to call home for money. Often, this can be handled by mailing a check. Suppose, though, that you're in a serious financial bind and need money more quickly. In such a case, you might need to arrange for a **wire transfer.** With a wire transfer, for a fee, a bank electronically transfers funds to your account at another institution, usually in 24 hours or less.

A faster but more expensive option than a wire transfer is to use a cash-delivery service such as Western Union, Money-gram, or American Express, which all have international branches and promise quick delivery of cash. If you're away from home and have your wallet stolen, you should consider using one of them.

SELF-CHECK

1. List the possible consequences of writing a bad check.
2. What are your options for getting cash quickly?

SUMMARY

Cash management involves many decisions related to cash payments and short-term liquid investments. Most types of financial institutions offer a diverse menu of products and services. You should evaluate cash management service providers based on the four P's (product, price, people, and place). After identifying which products you need, you should evaluate them based on liquidity, safety, costs, and APY.

KEY TERMS

Annual percentage yield (APY)	The amount of interest paid each year, given as a percentage of the investment. The APY makes it possible to compare interest rates across accounts that have different compounding periods.
Brokerage firm	A nondepository financial institution that helps its customers buy and sell financial securities.
Cash management	Management of cash payments and liquid investments.
Cash reserve	Liquid assets held to meet emergency cash needs.
Certificate of deposit (CD)	An account that pays a fixed rate of interest on funds left on deposit for a stated period of time.
Commercial bank	A depository institution that offers a wide variety of cash management services to business and individual customers.
Compounding	The frequency with which interest is calculated and added to an account.
Credit union	A nonprofit depository institution that is owned by its depositors.
Demand deposit accounts	Deposit accounts, such as checking accounts, from which money can be withdrawn with little or no notice to the financial institution.
Depository institutions	Financial institutions that obtain funds from customer deposits.
Discount bonds	Bonds that sell for less than their face value.

Federal Deposit Insurance Corporation (FDIC)	A government-sponsored agency that insures customer accounts in banks and savings institutions.
Life insurance company	A nondepository financial institution that obtains funds from premiums paid for life insurance, invests in stocks and bonds, and makes mortgage loans.
Maturity date	For a CD, the date on which the depositor can withdraw the invested amount and receive the stated interest.
Money market mutual fund	A mutual fund that holds a portfolio of short-term, low-risk securities issued by the federal government, its agencies, and large corporations and pays investors a rate of return that fluctuates with the interest earned on the portfolio.
Money market account	A savings account which pays interest that fluctuates with market rates on money market securities.
Mutual fund company	A nondepository financial institution that sells shares to investors and invests the money in financial assets.
Mutual savings institution	A savings institution that is owned by its depositors.
Nondepository institutions	Financial institutions that get funds from sources other than deposits.
Negotiated order of withdrawal (NOW) account	A type of checking account that pays interest.
Overdraft protection	An arrangement by which a financial institution places funds in a depositor's checking account to cover overdrafts.
Regular checking account	A checking account that does not pay interest and requires the payment of a monthly service charge unless a minimum balance is maintained in the account.
Rule of 72	A method of calculating the time it will take a sum of money to double that involves dividing 72 by the rate of interest earned on the funds.

Savings and loan (S&L) association	A depository institution that receives funds primarily from household deposits and uses most of its funds to make home mortgage loans.
Stock-held savings institution	A savings institution that is owned by stockholders.
Stop payment order	An order by which a financial institution promises not to honor a check that a depositor has written.
Time deposit account	A savings account from which the depositor may not withdraw money, without penalty, until after a certain amount of time has passed.
U.S. savings bonds	Bonds issued by the U.S. Treasury that pay interest that fluctuates with current Treasury security rates and that are exempt from state and local taxes.
Web-only financial institutions	Financial institutions that do not have physical locations but offer a menu of cash management accounts, loans, and investments.
Wire transfer	Electronic transmittal of cash from an account in another location. A wire transfer requires payment of a fee.

ASSESS YOUR UNDERSTANDING

Go to www.wiley.com/college/bajtelsmit to assess your knowledge of cash and savings management.

Measure your learning by comparing pre-test and post-test results.

Summary Questions

1. Which of the following is *not* one of the major reasons for holding cash?
   (a) avoiding unnecessary taxes
   (b) managing transactions needs
   (c) making temporary investments
   (d) preparing for cash emergencies

2. Which of the following would be considered a transaction account?
   (a) checking account
   (b) savings account
   (c) certificate of deposit
   (d) mutual fund account

3. Checking your balance at an ATM is now considered an effective alternative to balancing a checkbook. True or false?

4. Paying yourself first means:
   (a) buying items you desire before paying bills.
   (b) setting aside a reasonable sum for entertainment before paying bills.
   (c) putting money into savings before making other monthly expenditures.
   (d) keeping separate accounts from your spouse for personal needs.

5. Which of the following is a nondepository institution?
   (a) commercial bank
   (b) mutual fund company
   (c) savings and loan association
   (d) credit union

6. Checking accounts and savings accounts at commercial banks are both types of demand deposit accounts. True or false?

7. Which of the following is normally a disadvantage of a money market account?
   (a) no interest paid on balances
   (b) may impose higher fees for various services

(c) higher minimum balance required than other checking alternatives

(d) cannot be redeemed in the first six months.

8. Which of the following type of account is *not* federally insured?

(a) money market mutual fund

(b) CD

(c) regular savings account

(d) NOW account

9. An arrangement under which a bank places funds into a depositor's checking account if there are insufficient funds to cover all checks written is known as:

(a) check kiting.

(b) an insufficient fund charge.

(c) a check protection plan.

(d) overdraft protection.

10. Stop payment orders are usually good for a one-month period. True or false?

Applying This Chapter

1. Hanna is a college student who is working to pay for her own education. She has no savings and usually has no money left at the end of each pay period. She recently received an inheritance of $5,000. Why might it be a good idea for her to set aside some of that money in a cash account rather than use all of it for a down payment on a car?

2. Name the four rules of cash management and identify a consequence of not following each of them.

3. Under what circumstances might if be worthwhile to pay a monthly fee for a bill-paying service?

4. Zelda has just moved to a new state and needs to open a checking account. Which types of financial institutions would you recommend that she call for information?

5. Luis, a student at a large public university, opened his checking account at the largest bank in town because it offered free checking to students. He is planning to buy a car and will need a car loan. Explain why he might be able to get a lower interest rate at the university credit union than at the large bank. Which other factors should he consider?

6. Use the Rule of 72 to determine how long it will take for a $100 Series EE savings bond that you received as a wedding gift to mature if the average interest paid over the time you hold the bond is 4.25 percent?

7. Which savings account will have a greater APY: one that pays 2 percent interest compounded monthly or one that pays 2 percent interest compounded daily?

8. Suppose you're considering investing $1,000 in either a five-year CD that pays 5 percent compounded semiannually or a Series EE bond with an average interest of 5 percent. Your tax rate (including both state and federal income taxes) is 30 percent. What factors should you consider in deciding between the two investment options?

Bounced Checks

Erica White, a college junior, normally prides herself on keeping control of her finances. But the fall semester of 2004 was a disaster. She contracted West Nile virus and was very sick for months. It was an effort just to keep up with her classes, let alone balance her checkbook. Because she had to quit her part-time job, she knew her checking account balance was getting a little low, but she didn't realize quite how low until she got a bank notice indicating that she had bounced several checks. She had written four checks that were returned:

▲ Purpose Valley Electric Authority: $40.32 (electric bill).

▲ Safeway: $64.28 (groceries).

▲ Hot Wok Café: $8.54 (take-out Chinese).

▲ Papa John's: $13.68 (pizza).

Erica's current account balance is −$119.40.

1. Assuming that each retailer (but not the electric company) charges her a penalty of $20 and her bank charges $25 for each bounced check, how much will this cash management mistake cost her in total?

2. How much does she need to deposit in the account to have enough to make good on all her bills plus pay her penalties?

Liquidity or High Returns?

Phil and Kendra Gonzalez both work for the same high-tech company as software designers, and their combined take-home pay is $5,200 per month. With monthly expenses that average only $3,000, they've been able to accumulate $14,000 over the past year in a joint savings account that pays 3 percent interest. They also generally keep a little more than their $500 minimum balance in a checking account that pays no interest. If their checking account drops below the $500 minimum in any given month, the bank assesses a monthly fee of $10. This happens to them about once every three months.

Phil and Kendra have no investment accounts other than their savings account and their employment-based retirement funds. Phil is trying to talk Kendra into putting $5,000 of their savings into a higher-interest CD and another $5,000 into a stock mutual fund. He has found an online bank that is offering 6 percent interest on five-year CDs, and he has been investigating several stock funds. Kendra is not so sure. To investigate, she asks their current bank about cash management account alternatives that might provide them with better interest earnings. The bank officer suggests that they consider moving their checking to an interest-earning account that pays 2 percent per year and carries a $1,000 minimum balance. He suggests spreading their investments into several CDs with increasing maturities. The five-year CD at this institution pays 5.75 percent.

1. How much do you think the Gonzalezes should hold in liquid accounts? Explain your reasoning.

2. What are the risks of putting the money in CDs or in stocks instead of keeping it in regular savings?

3. Are Kendra and Phil exposed to any unusual liquidity risks because they work for the same company?

5

CONSUMER CREDIT
Credit Cards and Consumer Loans

Starting Point

Go to www.wiley.com/college/bajtelsmit to assess your knowledge of consumer credit.

Determine where you need to concentrate your effort.

What You'll Learn in This Chapter

▲ Consumer credit options
▲ Credit card types
▲ Credit card risks

After Studying This Chapter, You'll Be Able To

▲ Compare advantages and disadvantages of using consumer credit to make purchases
▲ Assess the various types of consumer credit
▲ Take steps to protect and establish good consumer credit
▲ Evaluate credit card alternatives, including terms and costs
▲ Predict the hazards of credit card use, including the risk of identity theft

INTRODUCTION

Learning how to manage consumer credit effectively by reducing reliance on high-cost borrowing is an important component of financial success. In this chapter, we first look at the types of consumer credit and then how to apply for credit. This chapter examines the advantages and disadvantages of credit and how to protect your credit and correct credit mistakes. Finally, it discusses credit cards in more detail, including their risks.

5.1 What Is Consumer Credit?

Any time you receive cash, goods, or services now and arrange to pay for them later, you are buying on **credit.** If you use credit for personal needs other than home purchases, you're using **consumer credit.** You can borrow from a friend or family member, a firm with which you do business, or a financial institution (e.g., bank, credit union, insurance company). The most common types of consumer credit are

▲ Credit card accounts.
▲ Automobile loans.
▲ Home equity loans.
▲ Student loans.

In each case, the lender lets you have the use of the money now and expects you to repay it with interest, often over a specified time period. Before you decide to borrow funds to make a purchase, whether through a credit card or a consumer loan, you should be careful to evaluate the short-term and long-term effects on your monthly cash flow.

The future payments, including the original purchase price and interest charges, will reduce your net monthly cash flow and thus your ability to make contributions to savings. Interest charges will increase the total cost of the product you are purchasing. Thus, in deciding whether to pay cash, take money from savings, or borrow the funds to make a purchase, you need to be sure to consider the trade-offs between the cost of borrowing and the lost earnings on savings.

Many types of consumer credit—most credit cards, for example—require that you pay interest rates that are much higher than what you can earn on your savings. If you have to pay 18 percent interest on your credit card and you're earning only 5 percent on a savings account, you'd be better off taking the money from savings than borrowing the funds for the purchase. Sometimes, though, consumer loan rates are lower than the rate you're earning on your invested dollars, making it preferable to borrow.

FOR EXAMPLE

Cash vs. Credit

Suppose you plan to purchase a car for $10,000. You have sufficient savings to make this purchase and are earning 5 percent interest per year on your savings account. If the car dealer is offering 3 percent interest on a car loan, you may be better off taking out the loan, making payments from the savings account, and earning the 2 percent difference. The advisability of this strategy depends on the terms of the loan (discussed in detail in Chapter 6) and any restrictions on your savings withdrawals.

5.1.1 Advantages of Consumer Credit

Consumer credit allows you to spread the cost of more expensive purchases over time. It can offer a convenient and safe alternative to carrying cash and also provides a source of emergency cash. Let's look more closely at the advantages of consumer credit:

▲ **Buy now, pay later:** Most people strive to improve their standard of living over time. The ability to purchase large-ticket items on credit—with borrowed funds—can sometimes make this dream a reality sooner. Being able to buy more expensive items now and pay for them over time makes it possible to fit purchases into your budget. You don't have to save up the entire purchase price of a car, for example, before buying one. Instead, you can essentially enjoy the use of the product while you are paying for it. This type of arrangement is advantageous as long as (1) you can afford the payments without sacrificing other worthy financial goals, and (2) the product you purchase lasts at least as long as the time period over which you make payments.

▲ **Convenience and safety:** Instead of carrying large amounts of cash, you can simply carry a credit card. It's convenient, and although a card can be stolen, it's not as easy as cash for a thief to use. If you pay off your balance monthly before the due date, you can take advantage of free credit offered by the card issuer and still have the convenience and safety of not carrying cash. It's important to note, however, that debit cards offer similar advantages.

▲ **Source of emergency cash:** Credit lines can be a source of funds to meet emergency needs (see Chapter 4). In deciding whether to use credit in this way, you need to consider whether you'll be able to repay the debt in accordance with the credit terms and how the payments will affect your household cash flow.

5.1.2 Disadvantages of Consumer Credit

The primary reasons for limiting your use of credit include the impact on your household financial health, the costs associated with borrowing, the potential for overspending, and the impact on your insurance premiums. Let's look more closely at these disadvantages:

▲ **Financial statement impact:** The more you borrow, relative to your total wealth, the worse your liquidity and debt ratios look. This means that you may limit your financial flexibility if you take on too much credit. You may also expose your household to too much risk because you're committing your family to greater fixed expenses; if you or your spouse were laid off, you might not be able to meet these expenses. In addition, if you're planning to buy a home, high levels of consumer debt may make it more difficult for you to qualify for a mortgage.

▲ **Increased costs:** When you use consumer credit as a means of spreading the cost of a purchase over time, you nearly always pay more for your purchase in the long run because of the financing costs of the loan. Credit is never free. Lenders charge interest for the use of their funds and commonly also charge additional fees and penalties, as discussed in more detail later. Even when retailers offer zero-interest financing, you can be sure that they're making money on fees or, alternatively, that you could get a better deal on the price if you didn't take the cheap financing.

▲ **Risk of overspending:** The availability of consumer credit increases the risk that you will overspend. Without credit cards, if you don't have enough cash in your pocket or your checking account, you can't make a purchase. If you have a credit card, you can more easily convince yourself to spend. Instead of buying one sweater at that great sale price, why not buy one in each of the three colors? Why make yourself choose between those two CDs, when you can buy both? Retailers even use advertising to reinforce the painlessness of making credit purchases. Next to the full price, you might see: "Only $25 per month if you take advantage of in-store credit."

▲ **Higher insurance premiums:** For the past several years, insurance companies have been using consumer credit history as a factor in pricing individual auto and homeowner's insurance policies. Thus, if you have a lot of outstanding debt or a history of making late credit card payments, you may pay a higher insurance premium than those with better credit.

5.1.3 Consumer Credit and the Economy

In addition to offering certain advantages to consumers, credit benefits the U.S. economy as a whole. When consumers spend more, businesses profit, employment increases, and the economic outlook improves. Yet, many experts believe

Figure 5-1

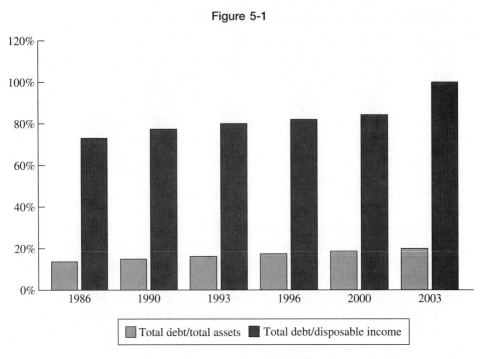

Household debt in the United States.

that the level of household debt in the United States, relative to income and wealth, may be cause for concern.

Because of easy credit and changing attitudes about debt, the average household is relying more on borrowed funds today than in the past. In 2003, for example, Americans added $30 billion to total revolving credit. Increasing levels of household debt have adversely affected personal balance sheets, particularly in conjunction with the decline in household wealth caused by the stock market decline in recent years.

Figure 5-1 shows aggregate U.S. household debt relative to aggregate household wealth and income over time. The trend is clear: The ratio of debt to assets has increased more than 30 percent over the past two decades, from 13.8 percent to 18.1 percent. Americans have been taking on more debt relative to total wealth. Interestingly, the home mortgage share of total debt has remained relatively stable over time—around 75 percent—so this implies that households have increased their use of all kinds of debt. Of more serious concern, though, is the even greater change in household debt relative to aggregate disposable income. The increase from 72 percent to 104 percent represents nearly a 50 percent increase in only 17 years. Households generally can achieve a higher standard of living in the short run by borrowing to finance current consumption, but in the long run, the bills must be paid. Because incomes are rising more slowly than debt, household budgets are likely to feel the strain very soon.

The average U.S. household has eight credit cards and owes more than $8,000 on them. About 50 percent report having difficulty making their minimum payments. The total amount of consumer credit outstanding in the United States increased 372 percent in the 20 years from 1983 to 2003, from $445 billion to $2.1 trillion.

Bad credit can hurt much more than your ability to get a loan. Prospective landlords and employers check your credit before doing business with you. Most insurers now use credit information in pricing auto and homeowner's insurance policies; this means that late payments on credit cards or large outstanding credit balances can now cause your premiums to increase or your policy to be canceled.

SELF-CHECK

1. Name the most common types of consumer credit.
2. List the advantages and disadvantages of using consumer credit.
3. How much credit does the typical U.S. household have?
4. In what ways can having bad credit hurt you?

5.2 Types of Consumer Credit

To buy something, you must do one of the following:

▲ Use current cash flow.
▲ Take money from savings.
▲ Borrow the money and repay it later.

Most people who choose to borrow for their consumer purchases use some type of consumer credit. Consumer credit is usually placed in different categories, based on the type of contractual arrangement. The two general types of credit arrangements are **closed-end credit** and **open-end credit:**

▲ **Closed-end credit:** This is credit that a lender approves for a specific purpose (e.g., the purchase of a television or a car). It must be paid back with interest either in a single payment or according to an installment agreement, with equal payments per period ending at a specific time. This type of credit is often called a *consumer loan.* The types of consumer loans and their unique characteristics are discussed in Chapter 7.

▲ **Open-end credit:** In contrast to closed-end credit, open-end credit, also called *revolving credit,* is generally not earmarked for a particular purchase, and the payment period is not specified in advance. Instead, the lender preapproves an amount of credit, called a **credit limit** or credit line, in advance of any purchase. You can then use this credit as you wish until you've reached your credit limit. Credit cards, such as Visa and Master-Card, are familiar examples of this type of credit. Personal loans, home equity lines of credit, and other delayed-payment arrangements offered by retail and government service providers (e.g., utility companies) are also open-end credit arrangements.

Table 5-1 provides examples of these two types of credit arrangements.

Table 5-1:   Types of Credit

CLOSED-END CREDIT		OPEN-END CREDIT	
Type	*Examples of Issuers*	*Type*	*Examples of Issuers*
Mortgages	Depository institutions, insurance companies	Credit cards Bank cards	Depository institutions (seviced by MasterCard, Visa)
Car loans	Depository institutions, auto manufacturers, such as General Motors and Ford	Retail cards	Sears, Foley's, Home Depot, Target, JCPenny's
Student loans	Depository institutions	Travel and entertainment cards	Americans Express, Diner's Club
Installment contracts	Consumer finance companies	Overdraft protection	Depository institutions
		Home equity line of credit	Depository institutions

SELF-CHECK

1. Define **open-end credit** and **closed-end credit.**
2. List some examples of closed-end credit.
3. List some examples of open-end credit.

5.3 Applying for Credit

You can apply for credit by filling out a credit application form or responding to an interview that requests information related to your creditworthiness—usually details about income, assets, and debts. If you've developed a personal income statement and balance sheet, the requested information will be easy to supply.

5.3.1 The Five C's of Credit

Although lenders use ratios in assessing your creditworthiness, they're concerned with much more than just your monthly cash flow. The factors they consider are often summarized using the "five C's of credit":

▲ **Capacity:** A lender's assessment of your ability, or capacity, to repay your debts is usually based on your household cash flow. Lenders may evaluate your capacity by looking at your sources of income and your expenses. They may use the debt payment ratio, the mortgage debt service ratio, or other measures that consider your expenses relative to your income.

▲ **Capital:** Lenders are also interested in your household's net worth, or capital. If total assets are greater than total debts, lenders consider that you could, if necessary, liquidate other assets to pay back the loan. In addition, lenders know that people who have more at stake are less likely to default on a loan because they don't want to risk their other assets being taken to repay the debt.

▲ **Collateral:** A loan protected by collateral (e.g., a car or home) is safer to the lender than one that is not. Therefore, the pledge of collateral makes you a better credit risk to the lender. The more valuable the collateral, the better the lender likes it.

▲ **Character:** Your previous credit, employment, and education history tell the lender about your character. Are you the type of person who honors an obligation? Do you have experience with making payments on debt? If you've previously borrowed money and repaid it on time, you're considered a better credit risk. Similarly, if you own a home, have held a job for a period of time, and have lived in the same area for a while, the lender assumes that you're less likely to default.

▲ **Conditions:** Every loan and every borrower represents a unique situation, and lenders sometimes take individual factors into consideration. Economic conditions, such as employment opportunities in the area, and special circumstances may make it more or less likely that you'll default on the loan. If you have insufficient credit history, a lender might still approve a loan to you if you have a **cosigner**—a person who agrees to take responsibility if you don't make your payments as agreed. This significantly reduces the lender's risk, but it's fairly risky for the person who cosigns because he or she is effectively taking responsibility for the debt. To ensure that cosigners recognize these risks, the Federal Trade Commission (FTC) requires lenders to provide the following notice: "You are being asked to guarantee this debt. Think carefully before you do. If the borrower doesn't pay the debt, you will have to. Be sure you can afford to pay if you have to, and that you want to accept this responsibility. You may have to pay up to the full amount of the debt if the borrower does not pay. You may also have to pay late fees or collection costs, which increase this amount. The creditor can collect this debt from you without first trying to collect from the borrower. The creditor can use the same collection methods against you that can be used against the borrower, such as suing you, garnishing your wages, etc. If this debt is ever in default, that fact may become a part of your credit record."

It may seem that some lenders do not carefully evaluate the creditworthiness of applicants. For example, college students are often inundated with credit card offers that ask for little more than their name, address, and signature. Although students may not seem to be the best credit risks, their rates are generally high, and lenders know that parents often step in to pay their children's debts. When credit offers are received over the telephone or through the mail, it's possible that the lender has already prescreened your income and credit, using credit bureau information.

In other cases, the lender checks your credit after receiving a signed application. On university campuses, students are commonly offered a free T-shirt or an entry in a prize drawing for filling out an application. Credit card lenders even offer student organizations the opportunity to use credit card applications as fundraisers; for example, an organization might be paid a $5 fee for each completed application it obtains. Even though you might be tempted to take the T-shirt and cancel the card later, it's a better idea to simply say no. It will be a lot harder to do so when your brand-new credit card arrives, with a $1,000 credit line. And if you don't cancel your card quickly enough, your application acceptance may obligate you to pay an annual fee.

Applications for consumer loans are usually more involved than those for credit cards. Because depository institutions prefer to make loans to the best credit risks, they ask for more detailed information on your income and assets. To streamline the application process, consumer lenders sometimes have online application forms or take your information over the phone. Again, the more organized your finances, the simpler it is to complete these forms.

5.3.1 If You Are Denied Credit

If you apply for a credit card or a consumer loan and are denied, you have the right to know why. Most lenders send a form letter that specifies the reason. These are the most common reasons:

▲ Adverse information in your credit report.

▲ Insufficient income relative to expenses.

▲ Insufficient collateral.

▲ Insufficient job history.

▲ Insufficient residency at current address.

Notice that each of these reasons is related to one or more of the five C's of credit. If you're denied on the basis of accurate information, such as a poor record of making credit payments on time, there's little you can do to immediately change this. Your only option is to apply to another lender.

The lenders that are most likely to overlook your past credit problems are also the ones that charge the highest rates of interest. It might, thus, be worthwhile to reconsider your financial situation and take steps to correct the problems noted by the lender before making additional applications. For example, if your credit record reflects late payments made within the past 12 months, you should resolve to pay your existing obligations on time so that you can show a 12-month history of on-time payments in the future. If you haven't worked at your current job for a long enough period of time, you should consider reapplying after the requisite time period has passed. If your current monthly payments are too large relative to your income, you could consider applying additional funds to debt reduction before seeking additional consumer financing.

SELF-CHECK

1. Define **cosigner.**
2. What are the five C's of credit?
3. Give an example of a common reason for being denied credit for each of the five C's.

5.4 Protecting Your Credit and Correcting Credit Mistakes

Because financial transactions are complex and many consumers don't understand them very well, Congress has passed many laws to protect consumers in credit transactions. These laws address consumers' rights to obtain credit, to receive full information about its cost, to have their credit information fairly and accurately reported, to be billed accurately, and to have their debts collected according to acceptable standards.

5.4.1 Rights in Obtaining Credit

In seeking credit, you have the following rights:

▲ **The right to full and accurate information:** Perhaps the most important consumer credit right is the requirement that creditors provide you with full and truthful information, written in plain English, including the true cost of consumer credit.

▲ **The right to freedom from discrimination:** Under the Equal Credit Opportunity Act, lenders can't discriminate against you based on certain protected characteristics—race, sex, marital status, religion, age, national origin, or receipt of public benefits. However, it's not against the law to deny credit based on income and credit history.

▲ **Special concerns for women:** Historically, it was common for women to be denied credit. Upon divorce or the death of a spouse, many women found themselves without access to credit at all. Today, lenders can't consider either marital status or gender. It's much easier for women to obtain credit and establish a credit history than it once was. It's important for a woman to develop a credit history in her own name. If a woman only has a history of joint credit with her spouse and she later divorces or is widowed, a lender could deny her credit based on having an insufficient credit history. However, if she has had credit in her own name, the Equal Credit Opportunity Act prohibits lenders from requiring her to reapply when her marital status changes.

5.4.2 Credit Reporting

Lenders evaluate your creditworthiness in part by checking your outstanding debt obligations and your history of making payments. This information is reported by your creditors and compiled by companies called **credit bureaus.**

Your consumer credit rights under the Fair Credit Reporting Act of 1971 include the right to know what is contained in your credit report, to have information reported fairly and accurately, and to dispute items on the report that you disagree with. To ensure that your credit report is correct, you need to take responsibility for regularly checking it for any errors.

What is included in your credit report? Many consumers are surprised to find that their credit report contains a lot more than just information on credit accounts. Typically, your report includes previous, current, and future credit history; specific information about average balances, late payments, and overlimit charges; employment and income history; and home mortgage amounts and payments.

The three major credit bureaus are Equifax Credit Information Services (www.econsumer.equifax.com), Experian (www.experian.com), and TransUnion (www.transunion.com). You can get a free credit report by contacting a credit bureau.

A credit report includes a list of every request for your credit report in the past two years. When you apply for new loans, credit cards, or insurance, the financial institution nearly always checks your credit with one or more of the major credit bureaus. If there have been too many recent requests for your credit report, lenders may be concerned that you're applying for a lot of other loans, an indication of potential future credit problems.

Based on the information in their files, credit bureaus classify individuals according to their credit risk, commonly using a credit scoring system such as the FICO system developed by Fair, Isaac and Company, Inc. This system and others use statistical models to calculate your probability of repayment. Each system weights factors differently, but the FICO system scores each person from 300 to 850, based on payment history (35 percent), debt (30 percent), length of credit history (15 percent), variety of debt sources (10 percent), and recent credit activity (10 percent). A score of 700 to 800 is considered good. If your credit score is too low, you can use one or more of these methods to raise it:

▲ Correct outdated and incorrect information in your credit report.

▲ Consistently make timely payments.

▲ Reduce your total debt.

▲ Develop a longer credit history.

▲ Include a mix of types of credit, not just credit cards.

▲ Close accounts that you haven't used recently.

5.4.3 Correcting Errors on a Credit Report

You have the right to view your credit report (for free if you've recently been turned down for credit because of information in the report), and a credit reporting agency must notify you whenever new negative information is added to your file. Negative credit information must be removed from your file after 7 years, with the exception of bankruptcies, which remain on record for 10 years. If there is incorrect information in your file, you can notify the credit bureau, and it will investigate and make corrections, if warranted.

The burden of proof for accuracy of credit information is placed on creditors rather than consumers. Lenders must certify that disputed information has been accurately reported. Even if the negative information is correct, you still have the right to add an explanatory statement. For example, if you're notified that your credit card issuer reported late payments during a specific period of time, you can request that a note be included on your report, explaining any extenuating circumstances, such as unemployment or illness.

Despite the extensive regulation of credit reporting, many reports contain some inaccurate, misleading, or outdated information, which isn't always easy to get corrected. If you have a common name, such as John Smith, your credit report may include negative information about a different John Smith's credit. If you divorce, you should notify credit bureaus so that your credit will not be affected by the possibly poor credit habits of your ex-spouse.

5.4.4 Billing Statements and Debt Collection

Lenders are required to provide you with full information related to all charges made to your account, and they must clearly explain any finance charges and how they are calculated. If you find an error on a bill, specific rules identify your right to contest the bill. Within 60 days of the billing error, you should do the following:

1. Send a written notice to the credit issuer, including copies of verifying documents, explaining why you believe the item to be incorrect. Under the Fair Credit Billing Act (FCBA), the company must immediately credit your account by that amount, pending resolution of the dispute.
2. Withhold payment for the disputed item. The issuer cannot charge you interest or penalties on this amount while it is in dispute.
3. Check your credit bureau file to see whether a notice has been sent relating to this item or your nonpayment.

When borrowers fall behind on their payments, lenders attempt to collect past-due amounts by using a variety of strategies, including sending past-due notices in the mail and making telephone calls. If you're extremely delinquent, your creditor might employ the services of a debt collection agency. The Fair Debt Collection Practices Act of 1978 gives you the right to be treated fairly and civilly by debt collectors. It specifically prohibits actions that would be considered abusive or deceptive and establishes acceptable procedures for debt collection.

SELF-CHECK

1. List ways to improve your credit score.
2. Define **credit bureau**.
3. What are your legal rights in obtaining credit?

5.5 Credit Cards

Credit cards are a familiar type of open-end credit. The term *credit card* is used to cover a variety of types of cards, some of which actually don't involve credit. In general, a credit card is a plastic card printed with an account number and identifying the holder as a person who has entered into a revolving credit agreement with a lender.

5.5.1 Types of Cards and Contract Terms

Some credit cards, in addition to allowing purchases, permit the holder to borrow cash in a transaction called a **cash advance.** You can get a cash advance at a participating financial institution, from an automated teller machine (ATM), or by writing a **convenience check,** a check supplied by the lender to make cash advances easier. The following are the common types of credit cards:

▲ **Bank credit cards:** A **bank credit card** allows the holder to make purchases anywhere the card is accepted. Although these cards carry a brand name from a particular service provider (e.g., Visa, MasterCard, Discover), the lender is usually a depository institution, such as a bank or credit union. Nearly all financial institutions offer credit cards, and they pay transaction fees to the service providers for managing payments to retailers and billing of account holders. Nonfinancial companies also offer these types of cards in collaboration with financial institutions to encourage spending on their products. Even alumni associations and other affinity groups (e.g., charitable organizations, political groups, fraternities, sororities) can issue credit cards. A retailer incurs a cost for accepting bank credit card purchases, usually ranging from 1.5 to 5 percent of the purchase, with the highest fees charged by American Express and Discover.

▲ **Retail credit cards:** Some businesses offer **retail credit cards** that can be used only at their own outlets. Retailers ranging from Home Depot to Neiman Marcus offer such cards. Issuing their own cards offers several advantages to retailers. The cards may encourage greater spending at their stores. They can be quite profitable because of their high rates of interest and annual fees. The cards also offer a marketing opportunity because cardholder mailing lists can be used to advertise special sales and discounts.

▲ **Travel and entertainment cards:** Some credit cards are designed primarily to allow business customers to delay payment of certain travel and entertainment expenses to coincide with their company's reimbursement system. These **travel and entertainment (T&E) cards** are thus a type of credit card, but they generally require that balances be paid in full each month. Diners Club and American Express are the best known.

▲ **Debit cards:** As discussed in Chapter 4, a debit card allows you to subtract the cost of your purchase from your checking or savings account electronically. Although these cards are a convenient substitute for cash and checks, they are not a means of borrowing—if you don't have enough money in your account, the transaction will be denied, and you may be required to pay a fee. Some debit card issuers offer overdraft protection, and others offer credit as an alternative.

▲ **Smart cards and other new technology:** A **smart card** is embedded with a computer chip that can store substantially more information than the magnetic strip on a traditional credit card. Smart cards actually store **electronic cash.** These funds have already been withdrawn from a bank account and are essentially "on deposit" in the card. During the 2003 holiday season, 6 out of 10 people received a gift card. Many experts believe smart cards will eventually replace the multitude of other cards and identification we now carry. The storage capacity of the chips used on these cards makes it possible for issuers to include additional security features and could permit recording of much information—driver's license, credit cards, checking and savings accounts, health club memberships—in one place.

Credit card agreements are legal contracts subject to numerous terms and conditions, which you effectively agree to when you apply for a card. These are some of the key contract terms you should be familiar with:

▲ **Annual fees:** Some credit cards charge an annual fee. Although competition has caused many lenders to eliminate these fees altogether, some cards charge as much as $300 per year. You should avoid cards that impose annual fees unless the cards offer other financial benefits that offset this cost. Suppose you have a card with a $1,000 balance, on which you pay 10 percent annual interest, or $100 per year. If you pay a $50 annual fee in addition to your interest charges, your total costs for the account are actually $150. The annual fee therefore increases your annual cost to 15 percent of your balance. Compensating features might include insurance, rebates, discounts, frequent flier miles, or other services. The value of these perks, however, usually doesn't come close to compensating for the fee.

▲ **APR:** The most important feature of a credit card is generally the interest rate charged on borrowed funds. In Chapter 4, you learned how to compare interest rates on investments by using annual percentage yield (APY). In the same way, you can compare the costs of borrowing by using the **annual percentage rate (APR).** Although lenders must report the APR on all types of loans and credit arrangements, credit card advertising normally emphasizes the nominal rate, which is generally lower than the APR. Therefore, you need to look carefully to ensure that you're comparing different types based on the APR. APR takes into account all the finance charges associated with the account, even if these are not technically called "interest"—annual fees and charges for credit reports, for example. The APR is calculated as follows:

$$\text{APR} = \text{Total annual finance charges} + \text{Annual fee/}$$
$$\text{Average loan balance over the year}$$

Finance charges can vary tremendously and may even be negotiable, so it pays to shop around. The average rate on a standard card in November 2006 was 14.8. Many issuers offer a below-market **teaser rate** to attract new customers and to encourage current cardholders to transfer balances from other cards. Although this might seem to make financial sense, the cards may also carry high annual fees and commonly have clauses that allow the rate to increase substantially if you make payments late, exceed your credit limit, or experience a change in credit status.

▲ **Credit limit:** The credit limit, or credit line, is the maximum amount you are allowed to borrow under the terms of your credit card agreement. Lenders usually start new cardholders with relatively low limits, such as $300, and then increase them with responsible card usage. Some people have credit limits of $50,000 or more, but the average is closer to $5,000 per card.

FOR EXAMPLE

When Low Rates Aren't Such Good Deals

A card issuer recently advertised an attractive 6.9 percent rate. But the low rate applied for only six months and did not apply to cash advances. Some other important conditions were buried in the fine print. At the end of the teaser period, the rate reverted to the issuer's "normal" rate of 18.9 percent. If any payments were late during the six-month low-rate period, the rate would immediately increase to 18.9 percent for the first offense and to 22.9 percent for the second late payment. In a case involving another credit card, an Illinois doctor was surprised to find that the interest rate on his MasterCard went from 6.2 percent to 16.99 percent in one month. When he checked with his financial institution, he was told that the change was due to a "change in his credit status." This surprised him because he had always paid his bills on time and stayed within his credit limit. It turned out that the change the lender was referring to was the fact that the doctor had obtained a new home mortgage.

▲ **Transaction, billing, and due dates:** Credit card statements are issued monthly. The date you use your credit card to make a purchase is called the **transaction date.** The lender closes off reporting of transactions on a predetermined **billing date,** and any new charges you make after that date appear on the next bill. Federal law requires that the bill be mailed to you at least 14 days before the **due date,** the date on which partial or full payment is due. This date is usually 20 to 25 days from the billing date. If you find it more convenient to have your payments due on a different date, you can ask the lender for a change in your billing cycle. Many credit cards do not calculate interest on new charges (other than cash advances) until the due date; this period of time is therefore called the **grace period.** When you make payments, the lender credits you as they are received. If you return purchases, these credits appear on the next month's statement as a reduction in the total amount owed. Most cards charge interest on new transactions beginning on the due date, so in this case, you could avoid all interest on the $100 by paying the bill by May 15. If you did that, you would have had the benefit of the credit for nearly two months without owing any interest. With some cards and with all cash advances, interest begins to accrue from the transaction date, so you must carefully read your agreement.

▲ **Minimum payment:** According to most credit card agreements, you must make a **minimum payment** each month to be in good credit standing. This amount is calculated according to the terms of your agreement with the lender, but it is the greater of $15 or a specific percentage of the outstanding balance. The minimum payment is always at least as great as the amount of interest due on the account for the period, but it isn't much more. Making only the minimum payment thus makes very little dent in your overall debt. If you have card debt of $1,000 at 16 percent interest, stop using the card, and pay the minimum payment of $15 a month, it will take almost 14 years to repay the debt!

▲ **Penalties and fees:** Credit card issuers generally assess penalties, including penalties for paying late and exceeding the credit limit. **Late payment penalties** range from $10 to $50. Although most credit card issuers charge the same fee to everyone who pays late, some have graduated fee schedules, based on the amount that is past due. If you make charges that cause your balance to exceed your credit limit, the lender assesses an **overlimit charge,** which can be as much as $50. Because both making a late payment and going over your credit limit violate the terms of your loan, these may affect your ability to get future credit. Fees for cash advances and for ATM usage are also relatively common. For example, some issuers charge as much as $70 per transaction for balance transfers, and many assess a $12 to $20 fee for making payments over the phone. It might be worth incurring that fee if you would otherwise be making your payment late and consequently paying a higher late payment penalty. Fees and penalties, although specified in the terms of your original agreement, can change, but your lender must give you written notification when they do.

5.5.2 Choosing Cards Based on APR

One of the big disadvantages of credit cards and other open-end credit accounts is the high interest rates commonly charged. In fact, credit cards generate more than $50 billion in finance charges a year for lenders. When you're comparing different credit card offers, you need to understand how finance charges are calculated and what factors increase your monthly costs. The **finance charge** is the dollar amount of interest charged by the lender in a particular billing cycle. It is calculated as follows:

$$\text{Finance charge} = \text{Periodic rate} \times \text{Account balance owed}$$

In this calculation, the **periodic rate** is equal to the stated rate of interest divided by the number of billing periods per year, usually 12. For example, if your nominal rate is 18 percent, then your periodic rate is $18/12 = 1.5$ percent per month. The periodic rate must be disclosed by the lender and specifically identified on your monthly bill.

Whereas the periodic rate is a known value, the account balance owed presents more of a problem because issuers use different methods to calculate this amount. The most common method for calculating the account balance owed is based on the average daily balance without a grace period—that is, including any new purchases. In this method, the lender calculates the balance owed on each day of the billing period, adding any new charges made and subtracting any payments received during the period. The lender adds these daily balances together, determines the average, and uses this value to calculate finance charges.

Although lenders are required to explain how finance charges are determined, the complexity of these calculations makes it easy for them to disguise differences between credit cards. Most people simply consider the nominal rate in making comparisons, and few read the fine print on their statements. Low-rate cards, and those that offer other perks, often employ a less favorable method for calculating interest so that the lender can make up for the lower rate in other ways. For example, the Discover Card, which advertises that it will "pay you cash" for each purchase—1 to 2 cents per dollar charged added back to your account—often uses a two-cycle method for calculating finance charges. For example, if you used your card to make a large purchase last month in order to get the 2 cent rebate, you would likely find that, unless you paid the balance fairly quickly after the purchase, your finance charges on those borrowed funds for the month of purchase and the month after would exceed the rebated amount.

There are two important rules to remember in comparing credit card terms:

▲ Always compare the rates based on APR rather than the nominal, or stated, rate.

▲ Read your credit agreement carefully to determine how finance charges are calculated.

In general, the best deals are on cards that calculate the finance charge using either the **average daily balance** with a grace period or an adjusted balance method, in which the finance charge is applied to the balance owed at the close of the last billing cycle minus a credit for payments made during the current billing cycle. Both of these methods give you access to short-term free borrowing.

If your credit card balances are gradually increasing, you'll have the highest monthly finance charge with the average daily balance without a grace period method. Because your personal financial plan probably includes a debt reduction goal, note that consumers who are gradually reducing their outstanding credit card debt should avoid cards that use the previous-balance method or the two-cycle method because both place more weight on your previous balance, which is always greater than your current balance as you continue to pay off the debt.

SELF-CHECK

1. List the types of credit cards available today.
2. Define **cash advance, APR, grace period,** and **finance charge.**
3. Cite the two important rules to remember when comparing credit card terms.

5.6 Advantages and Disadvantages of Credit Card Use

Section 5.1 notes that using consumer credit involves both advantages and disadvantages, both for individuals and for the economy. Although credit cards offer these same advantages, as well as some others discussed in this section, the high costs of interest and fees tend to outweigh the benefits of this form of borrowing, from the perspective of personal financial planning.

5.6.1 Advantages of Using Credit Cards

Like other forms of consumer credit, credit cards provide the opportunity to delay payment for purchases, the convenience and safety of not carrying cash, and a source of emergency funds. In addition, they may offer the following advantages:

▲ **Method of identification:** Most people use their driver's license for identification; a credit card is a secondary method for verifying your identity. Some cards now include photos to make them more useful for identification and to reduce the risk of fraudulent card use.

▲ **Means of record keeping for business expenses:** Credit cards provide a convenient way to organize business-related and tax-deductible expenses. Using a credit card for business expenses makes it easier to submit requests for payment to your employer. Similarly, if you have tax-deductible business expenses that you need to keep separate from household expenses, a credit card helps with record keeping. Some cards even provide an end-of-year summary that separates total annual expenditures into various categories, such as restaurants, hotels, and airfare.

▲ **Ability to make remote purchases:** Credit cards enable you to pay for purchases remotely—by phone, through a catalog, or over the internet. Today, it's practically impossible to get by without having a credit card. In fact, most airlines, car rental companies, and hotels will not accept reservations from you unless you have one. Many people worry about the safety of making purchases over the internet, but transaction verification—a feature offered by both MasterCard ("Shop Safe") and Visa ("Verified by Visa")—reduces the risk.

▲ **Ease of returning merchandise:** Some retailers let you return merchandise without a receipt if you paid by credit card because the record of a credit card purchase can be pulled up at a cash register terminal. If you received faulty merchandise, some credit card issuers promise they'll credit your account and deal with the seller directly on your behalf.

▲ **Free credit:** Some credit cards—those that calculate finance charges without including new charges during the billing cycle—allow you the opportunity to borrow without paying for the privilege. Of course, you must repay the borrowed funds by the end of the grace period to avoid the finance charge.

▲ **Other advantages:** Credit card issuers sometimes offer additional benefits, including travel insurance (if you are injured on a trip you paid for using the card), rebates (cash back for purchases made), frequent flier miles, and discounts on specific merchandise. Some features may require a one-time or monthly fee. Also, cards that have these features may charge higher interest rates than others.

5.6.2 Disadvantages of Using Credit Cards

Like other forms of credit, credit card debt can weaken your household financial statements and may enable you to overspend. The interest and fees on credit cards

FOR EXAMPLE

Consolidating Debt

Suppose your marginal tax bracket is 25 percent and you have $5,000 in credit card debt on which you're paying 15 percent interest, or $750 a year. If you take out a home equity loan at 6 percent interest to pay off that debt, your annual interest costs will be only $300, and because the interest is deductible, your effective after-tax interest cost will be $300 × (1 − 0.25) = $225. If you apply the annual $525 (= $750 − $225) savings to debt reduction, the net benefit will be even greater.

---

can significantly increase the cost of what you buy. Also, credit card ownership can increase the amount of junk mail you receive, expose you to the risk of loss of privacy, and increase the risk of identity theft. Let's look at the details of these disadvantages:

▲ **Most expensive way to borrow:** The rates of interest credit card users pay are higher than those most other types of borrowers pay, and they're higher than the rates earned on most investments. In addition, they're relatively insensitive to market interest rate movements, so as rates fall on auto loans and savings accounts, double-digit credit card rates continue. Also, credit card interest is not tax deductible. In contrast, the interest on certain types of consumer loans (e.g., home equity loans, some student loans) is tax deductible, which further increases the difference in cost between credit cards and other financing.

▲ **Negative effects of credit card marketing:** Financial institutions spend a lot of money attempting to entice you to add more cards to your wallet. This means more unsolicited mail, e-mail, and telephone calls. It also means more gimmicky attempts to get your attention, such as cards emblazoned with photos of famous people or your alma mater. Unfortunately, the latest target group is young teenagers. Some believe that this presents ethical issues similar to those raised in lawsuits against cigarette manufacturers. Here's another scary fact from the Consumer Credit Counseling Service: Within the first year of being a credit cardholder, one in five college freshmen owes more than $10,000. Credit card marketing also has a significant negative impact on the environment.

▲ **Loss of privacy:** Credit cards reduce the privacy of your financial information because your credit card provider may sell your credit and financial information to other companies that want to solicit you. Some legislation specifically prohibits telephone calls to the phone numbers on "do-not-call lists," which has significantly reduced unwanted calls. Telemarketing is still big business, though, and marketers are challenging the laws. To be added to the federal do-not-call list, you can log on to www.donotcall.gov. Many states have their own lists. Finally, some individuals have reduced the calls they receive by putting on their answering machines a message requesting removal from any telemarketer's list.

▲ **Fraud and identity theft:** Identity theft is the nation's fastest-growing crime, with an estimated 10 million victims per year, with most cases involving credit cards. Say that you receive your credit card billing statement and see one or more charges you didn't make. Or you check your credit bureau report after a credit denial and see a loan listed that you never applied for. Both scenarios are commonly referred to as *identity theft*. Fraudulent credit card charges often involve online or telephone orders because it's easier to use someone else's identity in a venue where no additional identification, such as a driver's license with a picture, is required. The negative outcomes of identity theft can be severe: Your credit may be damaged, and it takes time and effort to correct this. And it's not just credit card information that is at stake. It takes very little information to steal your identity. With your Social Security number, name, and address, a thief can apply for credit cards, mobile phones, loans, bank accounts, apartments, and utility accounts. You might even be the victim of someone you know. About 6 percent of the cases reported to the FTC involve family members. If your lender thinks you've been the victim of fraud, it temporarily puts a hold on the card, disallowing any credit purchases until the issue has been resolved. Although you certainly benefit from these antifraud mechanisms, sometimes your own behavior can trigger the antifraud system, such as using your card at the same retailer more than once on the same day (because that could be an indication that a store employee stole your number) or using a card that has been inactive for some time. Figure 5-2 provides some tips for avoiding identity theft.

SELF-CHECK

1. List the advantages of using credit cards.
2. List the disadvantages of using credit cards.

Figure 5-2

How to Avoid Identity Theft

▲ Don't give out your Social Security number, and don't print it on your checks.

▲ Check your credit report regularly.

▲ Shred old bank and credit statements before throwing them away.

▲ Notify credit bureaus to remove your name from marketing lists.

▲ Add your name to no-call lists.

▲ Do not carry extra credit cards and IDs.

▲ Keep a copy of your drivers license (both sides) and credit card numbers, expiration dates, and contact phone numbers in a secure location in case your wallet or purse is stolen.

▲ Mail bill payments at the post office or a locked mailbox.

▲ Examine the charges on your credit card statements before paying.

▲ Cancel unused credit card accounts.

▲ Never give your credit card number or personal information over the phone unless you have made the call and trust the business on the other end.

▲ Never give your credit card number or personal information over the Internet unless you have made the contact and the site has a high level of security.

Tips for avoiding identity theft.

SUMMARY

Consumer credit has many advantages, but it also has disadvantages. Types of consumer credit include open-end and closed-end credit. When applying for credit, it's important to remember the five C's of consumer credit that are used to evaluate your creditworthiness. You should protect your credit because it affects your future access to credit. Credit cards can be helpful but are tremendously profitable for lenders, so you need to be careful in choosing and using them. You can avoid identity theft by guarding your financial information and canceling unused accounts.

KEY TERMS

Annual percentage rate (APR) The standardized annual cost of credit, including all mandatory fees paid by the borrower, expressed as a percentage rate.

Average daily balance The average of the balances owed on each day of the billing cycle.

Bank credit card	A credit card issued by a depository institution
Billing date	The last day of a billing cycle. Credit card transactions made after the billing date appear on the next month's bill.
Cash advance	A cash loan from a credit card account.
Closed-end credit	Loans for a specific purpose paid back in a specified period of time, usually with monthly payments.
Consumer credit	Credit used for personal needs other than home purchases.
Convenience check	A check supplied by a credit card lender for the purpose of making a cash advance.
Cosigner	A person who agrees to take responsibility for repayment of a loan if the primary borrower defaults.
Credit	An arrangement to receive cash, goods, or services now and pay later.
Credit bureau	A company that collects credit information on individuals and provides reports to interested lenders.
Credit limit	The preapproved maximum amount of borrowing for an open-end credit account. Also known as a credit line.
Due date	The date by which payment must be received by the lender if the account holder is to avoid late penalties and, in some cases, interest on new transactions.
Electronic cash	Money in digitized format.
Finance charge	The dollar amount of periodic interest charged by a lender on a credit account.
Grace period	The time before interest begins to accrue on new transactions.
Late payment penalty	A penalty fee charged to an account for making a payment after the due date.
Minimum payment	The minimum amount that must be paid by the due date to maintain good credit standing and avoid late payment penalties.
Open-end credit	Preapproved continuous loans that can cover many purchases and usually requires monthly partial payments. Also known as revolving credit.

Overlimit charge	A penalty fee charged to an account for exceeding the credit limit.
Periodic rate	The stated rate divided by the number of billing periods per year.
Retail credit card	A credit card that can be used only at the sponsoring retailer's outlets.
Smart card	A card that stores identification and electronic cash in a computer chip.
Travel and entertainment (T&E) card	A credit card that requires payment of the full balance each billing cycle.
Teaser rate	A short-term below-market interest rate intended to encourage new customers to apply for a credit card.
Transaction date	The date on which you make a credit card purchase.

ASSESS YOUR UNDERSTANDING

Go to www.wiley.com/college/bajtelsmit to assess your knowledge of consumer credit.

Measure your learning by comparing pre-test and post-test results.

Summary Questions

1. A home equity loan is considered a type of consumer credit. True or false?

2. Credit cards should be compared based on APY. True or false?

3. If a bank loans you money for a new car, this is a type of:
   (a) closed-end credit.
   (b) open-end credit.
   (c) revolving credit.
   (d) cash advance.

4. Credit cards, such as MasterCard and Visa, are examples of:
   (a) closed-end credit.
   (b) open-end credit.
   (c) collateralized credit.
   (d) wholesale credit.

5. Which of the following is *not* one of the five C's of credit?
   (a) conditions
   (b) capacity
   (c) credibility
   (d) capital

6. When lenders evaluate your sources of income and your expenses, they are considering your:
   (a) capacity.
   (b) capital.
   (c) collateral.
   (d) character.

7. Under the Consumer Credit Reporting Reform Act of 1997, the burden of proof for accuracy of credit information is placed on consumers rather than creditors. True or false?

8. A credit card that calculates finance charges without including new charges during the billing cycle allows a cardholder to borrow without paying interest if he or she pays the entire bill by the end of the grace period. True or false?

9. Making the minimum payment on a credit card bill:
   (a) ensures that the bill will be repaid in the minimum time period.
   (b) ensures that late payment penalties will not be imposed.
   (c) does not reduce the overall debt significantly.
   (d) gives you the best credit standing available.
10. Which of the following is an advantage credit cards have over other forms of consumer credit?
   (a) buy now, pay later
   (b) source of emergency cash
   (c) safe alternative to cash
   (d) ease of returning merchandise

Applying This Chapter

1. Discuss the pros and cons of using consumer credit for purchases for your holiday shopping.
2. You have a $750 balance on your credit card. You want to purchase a new stereo system for your car. However, your credit limit is $1,000. What is the most you can finance on your card?
3. Suppose you get turned down by a lender for making late payments on your mortgage. How do you improve your credit history?
4. You have a FICO score of 300. Give some possible reasons and some possible solutions.
5. What is the potential problem with teaser rates for credit cards?
6. The total annual finance charges on your credit card account are $200. You also pay an annual fee of $50. If your average outstanding balance during the year is $1,000, what is the APR?
7. When might it be a good idea to do a balance transfer?
8. Carrie Chandler opens her June credit card bill and sees that her balance is a bit higher than she thought it would be. When she carefully examines the bill, she sees that there was a $75 payment to "Shoppers Cooperative" that she knows she did not authorize. Looking back at her May bill, which she unfortunately didn't look at very carefully the previous month, she sees a $75 payment to the same company that month, too. Explain the steps that Carrie should take to resolve this problem.

Calculating APR

You've just received a credit card solicitation in the mail that offers a 4 percent APR. Your current card, which has an outstanding balance of $5,000, has an APR of 14 percent. What factors should you consider in making the decision to transfer your balance? How much interest will you save the first month by switching cards, assuming that you make no additional charges and both cards calculate interest based on the average daily balance?

Comparing Cards

If you hold any credit cards, use your most recent statements to evaluate them. Make a table that compares their features, including annual fee, APR, method of finance charge calculation, and penalty fees. If you carry a balance forward on one or more cards, make a plan for paying off your cards, starting with the one with the highest costs and least desirable features.

Your Credit Score

Using the information in Section 5.4.2, contact a credit bureau and obtain a copy of your credit report. What can you do to improve or maintain your credit score?

6

USING CONSUMER LOANS
The Wise Use of Debt

Starting Point

Go to www.wiley.com/college/bajtelsmit to assess your knowledge of using consumer loans.
Determine where you need to concentrate your effort.

What You'll Learn in This Chapter

▲ Types and sources of consumer loans
▲ Warning signs of too much debt
▲ Bankruptcy and its alternatives

After Studying This Chapter, You'll Be Able To

▲ Compare types of consumer loans and lenders
▲ Assess the characteristics of different types of loans
▲ Manage your debts wisely
▲ Establish a plan for managing your consumer credit and reducing outstanding balances

INTRODUCTION

The most common types of consumer loans are home equity loans, student loans, and automobile loans. Consumer loan contract terms vary, depending on the lender and type, so you must be informed to make the best choices. As with credit cards, lenders offer better loan terms to more creditworthy borrowers. In this chapter, you'll learn how to challenge your credit information if it's incorrect and how to reduce your debt and get it under control before you get into financial trouble.

6.1 Characteristics of Consumer Loans

Consumer loans vary in the interest rates charged, payment arrangements, and collateral required. Typically, a lender charges lower interest rates if you meet contract terms that reduce the risk of your defaulting on the loan. In this section, you'll read about your options.

6.1.1 Interest Rates

Interest rates on consumer loans can be either fixed or variable. With a **fixed-rate** loan, the same interest rate applies throughout the life of the loan. With a **variable-rate** loan, the periodic rate fluctuates along with a predetermined measure, such as the prime rate or the Treasury bill (T-bill) rate. The **prime rate** is the rate banks charge to their most preferred customers, and it is commonly used as a base rate for variable-rate loans.

For example, suppose you took out a loan in February 2004, when the prime rate was 4 percent, and agreed to pay the prime rate plus 2 percentage points in interest. The interest rate on your loan would have started out at 6 percent, but you took the risk of unexpected increases in future payments. For example, by October 2006, the prime rate had more than doubled, to 8.25 percent, so your loan rate increased to 10.25 percent, resulting in a substantial increase in your monthly payment. In periods when interest rates are rising, especially when they rise rapidly, a variable-rate loan can subject you to unexpected increases in required payments. However, variable-rate loans generally carry lower initial interest rates than fixed-rate loans because the lender isn't facing the risk of having the interest rate fall behind market rates on comparable loans. Therefore, if the introductory rate is low enough, or if you don't expect to borrow the money for a long period of time, you might find it worthwhile to take out a variable-rate loan, despite the risk of increased payments.

Certain types of loans are more likely than others to have fixed rates. It's relatively common for rates on automobile loans to be fixed, whereas rates on home equity loans can be either fixed or variable. The interest rates on credit cards, discussed in Chapter 5, can be either fixed or variable. In practice, revolving credit agreements are most often classified as variable-rate loans because the issuer generally retains the right to change the rate at any time in the future.

6.1.2 Payment Arrangements

Loan agreements may be single-payment or, more commonly, installment arrangements. A **single-payment loan** requires that the balance be paid in full at some point in the future, including the **principal**—the original borrowed amount—and the interest owed on the borrowed funds. For example, many tax preparation firms offer to lend their customers money on the condition that it be repaid in full when the customers receive their income tax refunds.

An **installment loan** allows the borrower to repay over time, usually in monthly installments that include both principal and interest. An installment loan is said to be in **default** when a required payment is overdue. Loan agreements specify the consequences of defaulting, which may include late fees or even cancellation of the loan. Some loans include an **acceleration clause** that makes the entire balance due and payable in the event that the borrower falls behind in payments. A **prepayment penalty**—a fee charged for early repayment—can apply to certain loans.

6.1.3 Secured and Unsecured Loans

A **secured loan** gives the lender the right to take certain assets or property in the event that the loan is not repaid according to its terms. The pledged property—which can be any valuable asset, such as an automobile, a home, or business

---

FOR EXAMPLE

Comparing Interest Rates

There is often a large difference between the average rates on credit cards, which are unsecured, and the rates on automobile loans, which give the lender rights to your automobile if you don't pay the loan. The difference is often 10 percentage points or more. If you don't make your credit card payments, the lender has few options for recovering your bad debt, but if you don't make your automobile loan payments, the lender can repossess, or take back, your automobile, sell it, and keep the proceeds. If you don't make your automobile loan payments, the lender hires a repo firm to take your automobile back, usually by towing it away. The automobile is then sold at a wholesale auction to pay back your loan. Some loan agreements even include a deficiency judgment clause, giving lenders the right to bill you for the difference between what you owed and the value of the repossessed collateral.

property—is called the **collateral** for the loan. The right to take the **collateral** reduces the potential cost of default to the lender; thus, lenders usually charge lower rates of interest on secured loans than on unsecured loans.

When **real property** (i.e., land and anything attached to it, such as a home or commercial building) is used as collateral, as in the case of a home mortgage, the lender records a **lien** against the property at the county courthouse, putting the public on notice of its potential right to the property. This ensures that if you sell the home, the loan must be repaid before you can take any of the proceeds from the sale.

SELF-CHECK

1. Define **collateral, variable-rate loan,** and **lien.**
2. What types of loan payment arrangements are available?

6.2 Types of Consumer Loans

Although you can obtain a consumer loan for almost any consumer purchase, subject to your creditworthiness, certain very common consumer loans are designed to be used for specified purposes. Examples include home equity loans, automobile loans, and student loans.

6.2.1 Home Equity Loans

If you're like the majority of households, your family home is your most valuable asset. As your property value increases and your mortgage is repaid over time, you gradually build up home equity. **Home equity** is the difference between the market value of your home and the remaining balance on your mortgage loan (discussed in more detail in Section 7.5).

A home equity loan allows you to borrow against this valuable asset. Like your primary mortgage loan, a home equity loan is secured by your home. The lender's right to the home is secondary to that of the primary mortgage lender, however, so these loans are also referred to as second mortgages. In the event of default, the first mortgage must be repaid from the proceeds of the sale of the home before the second mortgage lender gets anything.

Depending on the lender, you may be able to borrow as much as 100 percent of your home equity, although most lenders limit your total mortgage debt to 80 to 90 percent of the market value of your home.

Suppose you own a home worth $150,000, and your mortgage balance is $100,000. Your home equity is $50,000 = $150,000 − $100,000. If you're approved for a home equity loan in the amount of $20,000, your total debt on the home is $120,000, which amounts to 80 percent of the market value. Home equity lenders commonly have maximum loan-to-value ratios of between 75 and 90 percent. This means that they do not allow your total debt on the home, including the first mortgage and the home equity loan, to exceed that percentage of the current market value of the home.

Home equity loans are usually installment loans payable over 5 to 15 years, in equal monthly payments. They are often established as lines of credit that you can access as needed. Generally, home equity loan proceeds can be used for any purpose. An important feature of home equity loans is that the interest is tax deductible up to a maximum of $100,000.

The tax benefits of home equity loans, particularly for households in higher tax brackets, can make this type of borrowing significantly less costly than other credit choices. If your marginal tax rate is 30 percent (including federal and state taxes), and the interest rate on your home equity loan is 6 percent, you are effectively paying only 70 percent of that amount in interest after your tax deduction, or 4.2 percent.

Recently, some lenders have begun offering loans that combine the characteristics of low-risk secured loans with those of high-risk unsecured credit. These types of loans, although they're called home equity loans, are more similar to credit cards and carry much higher rates of interest than typical secured loans. The rates are generally comparable to those of unsecured consumer loans and revolving credit accounts. This type of product is like a home equity loan and credit card in one, but you risk your house in the process of acquiring this type of loan because you are borrowing more than the value of your home. If you default, the lender can take your house *and* you may still owe money.

FOR EXAMPLE

Tax Benefits of Home Equity Borrowing

Suppose that your taxable income is $46,200 and your marginal tax rate is 30 percent. If you take out a home equity loan of $20,000 at 6 percent interest, the total interest for one year is $1,200 = 6% × $20,000. If you can deduct this interest on your taxes, you lower your taxable income by $1,200—to $45,000 instead of $46,200. At the 30 percent tax rate, this saves you $360 = $1,200 × 30%. Because you don't have to pay that tax, the actual cost of the loan is the $1,200 in interest less the $360 in tax savings, for a net marginal cost of $840. The effective after-tax cost of the loan is therefore $840 / $20,000, or 4.2 percent.

6.2.2 Automobile Loans

An automobile loan is a secured loan made specifically for the purpose of buying an automobile. Lenders typically limit the amount of an automobile loan to some percentage of the current market value of the automobile being purchased, and they require that the borrower pledge the automobile as collateral for the loan. In addition, the borrower must list the lender as an insured party on his or her auto collision insurance. See Chapter 8 for more details.

Because of the relatively short economic life of a car, automobile loan maturities are typically from two to six years. Both new car prices and rates on automobile loans have been unusually low in the past few years due to competition among auto dealers and generally low market interest rates. As a result, consumers have taken on significant automobile loan debt and monthly payments.

It's worth noting that getting a below-market interest rate from an auto dealer doesn't necessarily mean you've come out ahead. As discussed in Section 7.2, dealers generally make up the difference in higher prices and fees. Average automobile loan rates are lower than home equity loan rates, but home equity loan interest is tax deductible, and automobile loan interest is not. The after-tax cost of home equity loans is actually comparable to that of auto loans, although the difference depends on your marginal tax rate.

6.2.3 Student Loans

A student loan is a loan made for the purpose of paying educational expenses. Many people use borrowed funds to cover some or all of the costs of higher education. Understandably, as the costs of both public and private higher education continue to rise at a faster rate than inflation, student loan debt is also on the increase. Because your education is an investment you hope will pay off later in the form of increased income, borrowing for this purpose may make good financial sense.

Despite the advantages of student loans, as with other types of debt, it's much easier to get in debt than it is to get out. Consider how much it costs a typical student to repay a $17,000 student loan. If we assume that it's repaid over the average 10-year period offered by lenders, at an interest rate of 5 percent, payments are about $180 per month, which is a significant burden for most new college graduates living on entry-level salaries. (Section 6.4 shows how to estimate your expected loan payments and your repayment options.)

Rates on student loans tend to be more favorable than those on other forms of borrowing and in some cases are subsidized by the federal government. For this reason, it is generally better to borrow money for your education through student loan programs than it is to use other forms of consumer financing to pay for college. About two-thirds of all student financial aid comes from federal programs, including the loans discussed in this section. To be eligible for a federal student loan, you must

▲ Be a U.S. citizen with a high school diploma or the equivalent.

▲ Be taking courses to fulfill requirements for a degree or certificate.

▲ Meet satisfactory progress standards set by your school.

▲ Certify that you will use the funds only for educational purposes.

▲ Comply with Selective Service registration, if you're a male aged 18 through 25.

▲ Certify that you are not in default on any other federal student loan.

The Student Guide, a free Department of Education publication, describes federal student aid programs and how to apply for them. You can request a copy from Federal Student Aid Information Center, P.O. Box 84, Washington, DC 20044-0084, or by calling 800-433-3243. Student loans are available through campus-based aid programs and directly from financial institutions.

Loans made to students can be either subsidized or unsubsidized. Table 6-1 shows information on types and characteristics of student loans.

▲ **Subsidized loans** are awarded on the basis of need and do not require the payment of interest or repayment of principal until six months after graduation.

▲ **Unsubsidized loans** accrue interest from the time they are awarded, although it is sometimes possible to defer repayment until after graduation.

To qualify for subsidized student loans, you must demonstrate financial need by filling out the Free Application for Student Aid (FAFSA). Based on the financial information provided on that form, the federal government calculates an expected family contribution amount that is compared to your expected costs to determine any shortfall, which tells the government how much you need from other sources (e.g., grants, loans, work-study programs, scholarships).

The four major student loan programs are subsidized Stafford loans, unsubsidized Stafford loans, PLUS loans, and federal Perkins loans. The Department of Education also administers the Federal Family Education Loan (FFEL) program and the William D. Ford Federal Direct Loan (Direct Loan) program. Loans made through these programs directly to students are called Stafford loans, and those made to parents of dependent undergraduates are called PLUS loans. A federal Perkins loan is a low-interest (5 percent) loan for undergraduate and graduate students who have demonstrated financial need. The lender is the

Table 6-1: Student Loan Types and Characteristics[1]

	Subsidized Stafford Loan	Unsubsidized Stafford Loan	PLUS Loan	Federal Perkins Loan
Annual limits for dependent (independent) Students	Undergraduate: Yr 1: $2,625 Yr 2: $3,500 Yrs 3,4: $5,500 Graduate: $8,500	Undergraduate: Yr 1: $2,625 ($6,625) Yr 2: $3,500 ($7,500) Yrs 3,4: $5,500 ($10,500) Graduate: $18,500	Cost of attendance not covered by other financial aid.	Undergraduate; $4,000 Graduate: $6,000
Total maximum for dependent (independent) students	Undergraduate: $23,000 Graduate: $65,500	Undergraduate: $23,000 ($46,000) Graduate: $138,500	Cost of attendance not covered by other financial aid.	Undergraduate: $20,000 Graduate: $40,000
Disbursement	Direct loans from federal government go to school; loans from private lenders go to students.	Direct loans from federal government go to school; loans from private lenders go to students.	Direct loans from federal government go to school; loans from private lenders go to students	School disburses the funds to students.
Repayment begins	6 months after graduation	6 months after graduation	2 months after disbursement	9 months after graduation
Maximum schedule for payment	Several choices; 25 years if total loan > $30,000	Several choices; 25 years if total loan > $30,000	Several choices; 25 years if total loan > $30,000	10 years
Other terms	Department of Education pays interest while student is in school and during deferrals.	Borrower pays interest during the life of the loan.	Available to parents of dependent undergraduate students.	Lender is the school and federal government. Not all schools participate.
Interest rates	Adjusted annually Maximum: 8.25% 7/1/02–6/30/03: 4.06%	Adjusted annually Maximum: 8.25% 7/1/02–6/30/03: 6.8%	Adjusted annually Maximum; 9% 7/1/02–6/30/03: 8.5%	5%

Source: U.S. Department of Education.

educational institution, but the U.S. Department of Education contributes some of the funds used to make these loans.

In addition to their other benefits, student loans generally allow borrowers to defer loan payments under certain circumstances. Loan payments can be temporarily deferred for up to three years for economic hardship, postsecondary study (at least half-time), unemployment, or service in the military or the Peace Corps. Perkins loans have the added advantage of being forgiven in whole or in part if the borrower dies or is disabled or if the borrower takes permanent employment in certain professions (e.g., math and science teachers in inner-city schools, special education teachers, law enforcement, nursing).

SELF-CHECK

1. Define **home equity.**
2. List three types of consumer loans.
3. Name two types of student loans.

6.3 Sources of Consumer Loans

Most financial institutions offer one or more types of consumer loans. Figure 6-1 summarizes the loan types that various lenders offer. Many Web sites, such as www.lendingtree.com and www.bankrate.com, offer information and rates on consumer loans. For automobile loan rates, try http://finance.yahoo.com/loan.

6.3.1 Depository Institutions

Depository institutions, such as banks, savings and loans, and credit unions, are financial institutions that obtain funds from deposits into checking and savings accounts. These institutions offer the widest variety of consumer loans and, on average, the most favorable interest rates.

Figure 6–1

Types of Consumer Credit Products	Depository Institutions	Consumer and Sales Finance Companies	Brokerage Firms	Cash-value Life Insurance Policies	Retirement Plans	Pawn Shops
First mortgage	X					
Home equity loan	X				X	
Automobile loan	X	X				
Credit card	X	X				
Debit card	X					
Student loan	X					
Unsecured personal loan	X	X				
Secured personal loan	X	X	X	X	X	X

Sources for various types of consumer credit.

Depository institutions can offer low rates because they pay relatively low rates of return to their depositors, from whom they obtain the funds they lend out. In return for lower rates, however, they tend to be a bit picky about the risk characteristics of those to whom they lend. Thus, if you have very little experience with borrowing or have made payments late in the past, these lenders may not be willing to do business with you. They are also likely to require that you have funds on deposit at their institutions, such as in regular checking or savings accounts. Despite these restrictions, nearly half of all consumer lending is done through commercial banks.

6.3.2 Consumer and Sales Finance Companies

Consumers who cannot borrow from depository institutions, either due to poor credit or insufficient credit history, might consider borrowing from a **consumer finance company.** Consumer finance companies do not take deposits; instead, they obtain funds from their investors and from short-term borrowing. Because generally these companies make riskier loans and pay more for the funds they lend than do depository institutions, they tend to charge higher rates of interest to consumers.

The advantages of consumer finance companies include access and speed, with approvals often taking 24 hours or less. Many consumer finance companies specialize in debt consolidation loans and offer credit counseling services, but they may require home equity as collateral for such loans.

Most towns have several consumer finance companies. In addition, if you do an internet search on "installment loans," you'll find hundreds of lenders to choose from and may be able to complete an application through the mail or online. While many of these firms are legitimate businesses, some are not. You should never do business with an unfamiliar financial institution before checking on its status with appropriate authorities.

A **sales finance company** makes consumer loans to buyers of products offered through its parent company, usually a large retailer. For example, most major automakers have their own finance companies, as do large department stores, such as JCPenney and Sears. These companies usually require that the item being purchased be pledged as collateral for the loan. The rates charged by sales finance companies are likely to be lower than those charged by consumer finance companies.

6.3.3 Other Sources of Consumer Loans

You can obtain short-term consumer loans through investment accounts at brokerage firms (discussed in Chapter 12), cash-value life insurance policies (discussed in Chapter 10), and retirement plans (discussed in Chapter 14). Because these types of accounts are primarily designed for distant savings goals, however, borrowing from them may jeopardize your ability to achieve other financial goals.

FOR EXAMPLE

Short-Term Gain for Long-Term Pain

Suppose you borrow against a life insurance policy and then die before you've repaid the loan. The proceeds of your life insurance policy are then reduced by the amount of the outstanding loan. If you borrow from a retirement account, your investment returns are then earned on a smaller principal balance, and you may owe income taxes on the amount you withdraw. In both cases, you will be adversely affected down the road.

Certain types of businesses, known as pawnshops, regularly provide short-term loans to people who don't have other, less costly, options. A pawnshop makes the loan in return for holding something of value as collateral, such as jewelry, electronics equipment, or a musical instrument. The maximum loan amount is usually a percentage of the resale value of the item being held, often 50 percent or less, and the pawnshop has the right to sell your valuable if you don't repay the loan within the allowed period of time.

SELF-CHECK

1. List two types of companies that finance high-risk customers.
2. Name two advantages of loans from institutions other than banks.

6.4 Managing Your Debts

For many consumers, controlling the use of consumer credit is the most difficult aspect of their financial plan. An important advantage of consumer credit is to spread the cost of a purchase over time, allowing you to use the purchased item while making payments. Another good use of credit is to make investments that will earn a return later, such as investments in education or real estate.

Unfortunately, most consumer credit is used to finance assets that decline in value over time. When is the use of credit appropriate? Here are some guidelines:

▲ Don't borrow money to pay for items you can't afford to buy with cash unless you have a specific plan for repaying the debt.

▲ If possible, pay your credit card balance in full by the due date in order to avoid finance charges.

▲ Keep track of monthly expenditures to ensure that your net monthly cash flow is on target.

▲ Limit yourself to a small number of credit cards.

▲ Avoid high-interest consumer credit.

▲ Avoid consumer credit that involves annual fees.

▲ Don't use consumer credit to pay for regular expenditures unless you're doing so in order to take advantage of free frequent flier miles and discounts or because a credit card is required (e.g., internet purchases, car rentals) and you plan to pay the balance in full each month.

6.4.1 Signs of Credit Trouble

Consider the signs of credit trouble offered by consumer credit expert Greg Pahl, in his book *The Unofficial Guide to Beating Debt*. If you answer "yes" to many or most of the following questions, you definitely have a problem with credit and should seriously consider getting help[2]:

▲ Are you spending increasing amounts of your income to pay your bills?

▲ Are you paying bills late or juggling your bills because you don't have enough money to cover them?

▲ Are you at or over the limit on your credit account?

▲ Are you making only minimum payments on your bills?

▲ Are you paying your bills with money that was supposed to go for something else?

▲ Are you using credit cards to pay for normal living expenses?

▲ Are you using your savings to pay your bills?

▲ Are you paying off one loan with another one?

▲ Have you had any credit cards cancelled due to poor payment history?

▲ Are you getting letters or phone calls from creditors regarding overdue payments?

▲ Are you repeatedly overdrawn at the bank?

▲ Do you worry a lot about money?

▲ Do you and your spouse argue about money problems?

▲ Are you embarrassed to tell others about your financial situation?

If any of these apply to you, you need to develop a plan for reducing your debt. If your list of financial goals doesn't already include debt reduction, you should revisit it to include this objective as a short-term or intermediate-term financial goal. No matter what kinds of credit you now have, you should regularly evaluate your credit usage and, if necessary, take action to reduce your debt.

It's more difficult to pay back funds than it is to build up the debt in the first place, so the earlier you get things under control, the easier it will be. You can find advice for reducing debt at www.debtadvice.org.

6.4.2 Getting Out of Debt

To help approximate the impact of debt reduction on your budget, Figure 6-2 shows the monthly payments necessary to reduce specific amounts of total indebtedness. For example, if you currently owe $10,000 at 18 percent, you need to pay about $293.75 per month for 48 months to reduce that debt to zero.

Although debt reduction is the ideal outcome, some people get into so much debt that they have trouble meeting even their minimum payments out of their

Figure 6-2

Months	APR %	Amount of Total Indebtedness					
		$1,000	$2,500	$5,000	$7,500	$10,000	$15,000
12	15	90.26	225.65	451.29	676.94	902.58	1,353.87
	18	91.68	229.20	458.40	687.60	916.80	1,375.20
	21	93.11	232.78	465.57	698.35	931.14	1,396.71
24	15	48.49	121.22	242.43	363.63	484.87	727.30
	18	49.92	124.81	249.62	374.43	499.24	748.86
	21	51.39	128.46	256.93	385.39	513.86	770.78
36	15	34.67	86.66	173.33	259.99	346.65	519.98
	18	36.15	90.38	180.76	271.14	361.52	542.29
	21	37.68	94.19	188.38	282.56	376.75	565.13
48	15	27.83	69.58	139.15	208.73	278.31	417.46
	18	29.37	73.44	146.87	220.31	293.75	440.62
	21	30.97	77.41	154.83	232.24	309.66	464.49
60	15	23.79	59.47	118.95	178.42	237.90	356.85
	18	25.39	63.48	126.97	190.45	253.93	380.90
	21	27.05	67.63	135.27	202.90	270.53	405.80
72	15	21.15	52.86	105.73	158.59	211.45	317.18
	18	22.81	57.02	114.04	171.06	228.08	342.12
	21	24.54	61.34	122.68	184.02	245.36	368.04

Monthly payments necessary to achieve debt reduction goals.

current cash flow. Under these circumstances, it is necessary to take some intermediate steps to reduce monthly cash outflows or increase monthly cash inflows. Consumer credit counselors suggest the following for people who are having payment troubles:

▲ **Obtain a debt consolidation loan at a lower interest rate:** A debt consolidation loan is a loan earmarked for repayment of higher-interest debt. For example, if your credit card interest rate is 18 percent on your $10,000 balance, and you could get a home equity loan from your local financial institution at 6 percent, you could repay the loan in four years with a monthly payment of $234.85, a savings of almost $60 per month. Consolidating several individual credit card balances can save you even more because, if you cancel the credit cards, you eliminate all the fees as well. Sometimes just calling your credit card company and telling them you are going to close the account is enough to encourage the company to negotiate a lower rate with you to keep you as a customer. If you don't ask, you won't receive!

  If you decide to consolidate your debts to reduce your payments, you absolutely must refrain from running up your credit cards again. If you couldn't afford the payments before, you certainly won't be able to make payments on both the new loan and new debt. Another factor is the term of the loan. Obviously, your monthly payment will be lower if you stretch out the payment schedule, but that also means additional interest charges, and it will take you longer to get your finances on track. It's best to take the shortest loan that you can reasonably afford to pay.

▲ **Take a second job specifically earmarked to pay down the debt:** Although working two jobs may not sound like fun, it's often the fastest way to reduce your outstanding credit card debt. If you can work an extra 20 hours per week, at $6 per hour after taxes, you'll be able to get rid of your $10,000 debt in less than two years.

▲ **Develop a zero-based budget:** Zero-based budgeting is a strategy planners often recommend. To construct a zero-based budget, you start with absolute necessities and debt payments and then add expenditures until you run out of cash. Thus, fun money for entertainment, eating out, and clothes shopping would all have lower priority than debt reduction payments.

▲ **Live with your parents or other family members to cut your expenses:** Although this may not be ideal, it can be helpful in reducing the debt load that many people accrue during their education.

▲ **Sell assets:** Many families get into trouble by trying to finance a higher standard of living than they can afford. If you can't afford to maintain your standard of living, you must downsize. This might mean selling an expensive automobile or even downsizing your home. You might need to sell other marketable valuables, such as musical instruments, collectibles, or consumer electronics, but only if you will not need to replace them later at a much higher cost.

FOR EXAMPLE

Revisiting Danelle

When Danelle evaluated her finances in Chapter 2, she realized she was spending beyond her income, which is part of the reason her credit card debt is so high. She'll have to make some changes in her budget if she wants to balance it and, at the same time, work on debt reduction. Consider whether Danelle can apply any of the suggestions discussed here:

▲ **Obtain a debt consolidation loan:** Danelle's automobile loan carries a rate of 8 percent, which isn't too bad, but the rate on both of her credit cards is 18 percent. Her bank will give her a $5,200 three-year loan at 8 percent interest. The payments on this loan will be about $163 per month, a little more than the total minimum payments on her credit cards ($125), but a larger portion of the monthly payments will be going toward repaying the principal. With this loan and her automobile loan, her total debt payments will be $276 per month, which is $38 more than they were before the new loan. Also, Danelle plans to avoid the risk of running up her credit again by canceling her JCPenney and MasterCard accounts. She has a debit card, so she doesn't really need the other cards.

▲ **Take a second job:** So far, Danelle has only been working part-time in order to focus on her schoolwork. Her course load isn't too bad this semester, so she estimates that she can work 10 more hours per week, which will net an additional $80 per week. If she applies all this extra income to the debt consolidation, it will also help her net cash flow.

▲ **Create a zero-based budget:** After carefully evaluating her necessary expenditures, Danelle thinks she can cut her other expenses by about $50 per month.

▲ **Live with family members:** Her family does not live nearby, so this isn't an option.

▲ **Sell assets:** Danelle doesn't have anything that she can sell to raise money, so this isn't an option.

SELF-CHECK

SELF-CHECK

1. List eight signs of being in consumer credit trouble.
2. What are some guidelines for using credit appropriately?
3. Name five debt reduction strategies that financial counselors recommend for people in trouble.

6.5 Declaring Personal Bankruptcy

We've looked at strategies for getting your debt under control before you get into serious credit trouble. But what if it's too late—what if you've already gotten so far behind on your payments that you can't see any way out?

Probably the most common strategy of people experiencing this kind of financial distress is avoidance—throwing the past-due notices in a pile and refusing to answer the phone. This is *not* a good approach, and it increases the risk that your creditors will take more serious steps to collect your debts. The following are more responsible options:

▲ **Contact your creditors directly:** When you know you can't pay your debts, you should immediately contact your creditors. Consumers are often surprised to find out that, although accumulated interest and late fees still accrue, their creditors are often willing to make alternative arrangements. Creditors would much rather get something than nothing.

FOR EXAMPLE

Retiring in the Red

Picture this: Grandma and Grandpa are getting by on Social Security and a small pension from Grandpa's former employer; it's just enough to pay their necessary expenses. Grandpa gets sick and requires medication that costs several hundred dollars per month, and this isn't covered by their health insurance. Rather than take a chance with his health, Grandma responds to a couple of credit card offers and soon has a $10,000 credit line. Before they know it, the couple has several high-interest credit card balances. Many older Americans are struggling with rapidly increasing medical costs and prescription drug costs, eroded pension income, and reduced investment returns. Retirement savings have been siphoned off to pay for college and other family expenses. The number of elderly people who've declared bankruptcy in the past decade has increased more rapidly than for any other age group.

If your budget crunch is temporary, as in the case of a short period of unemployment, contacting your creditors immediately may help you get through it without becoming seriously delinquent.

▲ **Consumer credit counseling:** If you have serious financial problems, you should consider getting professional consumer credit counseling. There are many reputable sources of free help, so you should avoid organizations that charge fees. Some organizations that advertise credit counseling services prey on desperate people, making a profit by charging high fees to those who can least afford them or providing consolidation loans at unreasonably high interest rates. Many large employers offer financial counseling through their human resources departments, and you may be able to get free counseling through your bank, a county extension office, or an employee union. The National Foundation for Consumer Credit (NFCC), an organization sponsored by large creditor firms, offers free consumer credit counseling through local nonprofit branches called Consumer Credit Counseling Services (CCCS). In addition to providing educational materials on many financial matters, NFCC counselors help consumers develop realistic budgets, plan for debt reduction, and negotiate with creditors.

▲ **Bankruptcy:** Some people get so deeply in debt that repayment isn't really an option. In such a situation, it's sometimes necessary to declare bankruptcy as a last resort. **Bankruptcy** is the legal right to ask a court of law to relieve you of certain debts and obligations. If a court grants you bankruptcy, your creditors divide up your assets in a fair and equitable process overseen by a trustee. Although old law would have relieved you of further obligations to these creditors, the new Bankruptcy Abuse Prevention and Consumer Protection Act of 2005 makes it more difficult to walk away from your debts, instead forcing many into debt repayment plans. Bankruptcy appears on your credit record for 10 years and may affect your ability to obtain a home mortgage or other credit. This long-lasting impact may outweigh the benefits of debt reduction. Before considering bankruptcy, you should consider the costs associated with it: Court costs, attorneys' fees, and trustees' fees can add up to more than $1,000. For information on personal bankruptcy, go to www.bankruptcy.org.

According to the American Bankruptcy Institute, more than 2 million personal bankruptcies—those filed by individuals rather than businesses—were filed in 2005, a record number. Bankruptcies have been increasing at an average of 20 percent per year since the early 1990s but are expected to decline somewhat under the stricter new bankruptcy law.

What accounts for the rise in personal bankruptcies? When the economy slows, as it did at the beginning of the twenty-first century, layoffs and reductions in earnings are common, and families with too much debt and too little liquidity can't survive even brief periods of lost income.

You might be surprised at how common bankruptcy is among young people who, at least theoretically, haven't had much time to accumulate debt. Although baby boomers still account for the largest share of bankruptcies, about 120,000 people under age 25 declare bankruptcy each year, and that number is on the rise.

Most people who declare bankruptcy have low incomes, earning less than $20,000 per year, but even some celebrities—Kim Basinger and Burt Reynolds, for example—have declared bankruptcy. Even so, it is an extreme measure that should be your last alternative.

Bankruptcies take several forms, each named for the relevant section of the U.S. Bankruptcy Code, the federal statute governing bankruptcy. The debtor files an application for bankruptcy with the appropriate court, which may either accept the application or deny it. Here, we'll look at two major forms of personal bankruptcy:

▲ **Chapter 7 bankruptcy:** A Chapter 7 bankruptcy requires the liquidation, or sale, of most of the debtor's assets. Under current law, the debtor is allowed to keep a small amount of home equity, Social Security and unemployment insurance payments, a vehicle, household goods, trade tools, and books. The proceeds of the sale of the debtor's remaining assets are used to pay creditors to the extent possible, and most of the person's financial obligations are then cleared. However, certain obligations—alimony and child support, student loans, and debts that were not disclosed in court—are unaffected by a Chapter 7 bankruptcy, and the debtor must still pay them. In addition, a debtor is not allowed to repay certain preferred creditors (such as family members) in anticipation of a bankruptcy. Under the new bankruptcy law, most higher-income households are required to opt for Chapter 13 bankruptcy.

▲ **Chapter 13 bankruptcy:** A Chapter 13 bankruptcy is a method of protecting a debtor from creditors' claims while that person develops and implements a plan to repay his or her debts. The plan, which must be approved by the court, generally includes new payment arrangements with creditors for reduced balances and payments. In a Chapter 13 bankruptcy, the debtor generally can keep all of his or her assets. If the repayment plan fails, though, the debtor may eventually end up losing the assets in a Chapter 7 liquidation.

SELF-CHECK

1. Describe the first two steps you should take if you can't pay your debts.
2. What are the two types of personal bankruptcy?

SUMMARY

The most common types of consumer loans are home equity loans, student loans, and automobile loans, most of which are available from commercial banks and other depository institutions. It's important to shop around for loans. The interest rates charged for consumer loans can vary dramatically, depending on the type of loan and the type of lender. Lenders evaluate your creditworthiness in five areas, sometimes called the five C's of credit: capacity, capital, collateral, character, and conditions. Understand your consumer credit rights, including the right to have credit information reported truthfully. Before incurring debt, you should have a plan for repaying it.

KEY TERMS

Acceleration clause	A loan term that requires immediate repayment of the total amount due on an installment loan that is in default.
Bankruptcy	The legal right to ask a court of law for relief of certain debts and obligations.
Chapter 7 bankruptcy	Requires the liquidation, or sale, of most of the debtor's assets.
Chapter 13 bankruptcy	A method of protecting a debtor from creditors' claims while that person develops and implements a plan to repay his or her debts.
Collateral	Valuable assets or real property that can be taken by a lender in the event of loan default.
Consumer finance company	A nondepository institution that makes loans to risky consumers.
Default	Failure to meet the terms of a loan agreement, such as when payments are not made in a timely fashion.
Fixed-rate loan	A loan for which the rate of interest remains the same throughout the term of the loan.
Home equity	The market value of a home minus the remaining mortgage balance.
Installment loan	A loan that requires repayment in equal periodic installments that include both interest and principal.
Lien	Public notice of a right to real property.

Prepayment penalty	A fee charged to a borrower when he or she pays a loan balance before the end of the loan term. Not all loans are subject to prepayment penalties.
Prime rate	The interest rate that banks charge on loans to their most favored business customers.
Principal	The original amount borrowed or invested.
Real property	Land and anything attached to it, such as a home or commercial building.
Sales finance company	A nondepository institution that makes consumer loans to buyers of products offered through its parent company.
Secured loan	A loan that includes a pledge of collateral.
Single-payment loan	A loan that requires the repayment of interest and principal in a single payment at a specified date in the future.
Subsidized loans	Student loans awarded on the basis of need that do not require the payment of interest or repayment of principal until six months after graduation.
Unsubsidized loans	Student loans that accrue interest from the time they are awarded, although it is sometimes possible to defer the repayment until after graduation.
Variable-rate loan	A loan for which the rate of interest varies periodically with a changing market rate, such as the prime rate.

ASSESS YOUR UNDERSTANDING

Go to www.wiley.com/college/bajtelsmit to assess your knowledge of using consumer loans.

Measure your learning by comparing pre-test and post-test results.

Summary Questions

1. When real property is used as collateral to secure a loan, which of the following does the lender record against the property?

   (a) deed

   (b) judgment

   (c) lien

   (d) mortgage

2. Fixed-rate loans usually carry lower initial interest rates than do variable-rate loans. True or false?

3. Which of the following statements is true concerning home equity loans?

   (a) Home equity loan proceeds are generally restricted as to purpose.

   (b) Home equity loans are generally installment loans with a 1- to 10-year term.

   (c) Home equity loan interest is tax deductible up to a maximum of $100,000.

   (d) All of the above are true.

4. Which of the following is *not* a requirement to be eligible for a federal student loan?

   (a) Comply with Selective Service registration.

   (b) Be enrolled in a federally accredited college.

   (c) Be taking courses to fulfill degree or certificate requirements.

   (d) Be a U.S. citizen with a high school diploma or equivalent.

5. Ford Motor Credit, which finances Ford autos for customers, is an example of a:

   (a) consumer finance company.

   (b) sales finance company.

   (c) retail finance company.

   (d) wholesale finance company.

6. Borrowers who do not qualify for loans at commercial banks are often able to obtain loans at consumer finance companies. True or false?

7. Which of the following is *not* a recommended solution if you are having trouble making payments on your consumer credit?

   (a) Take a second job.

   (b) Live with your parents or other family members.

   (c) Transfer balances to another credit card.

   (d) Sell some assets to raise money to pay back the debt.

8. It is recommended that borrowers take the shortest loan they can afford to take when obtaining debt consolidation loans. True or false?

9. Which type of bankruptcy requires the liquidation of most of the debtor's assets?

   (a) Chapter 5

   (b) Chapter 7

   (c) Chapter 11

   (d) Chapter 13

10. Which type of bankruptcy implements a payment plan for the debtor and generally allows the debtor to keep all of his or her assets?

    (a) Chapter 5

    (b) Chapter 7

    (c) Chapter 11

    (d) Chapter 13

Applying This Chapter

1. You're considering taking out an unsecured loan at 7 percent interest from your local home improvement store for the purchase of new kitchen cabinets. Alternatively, you could take out a home equity loan at a rate of 8.5 percent. Assume that your marginal tax rate is 25 percent. What are the advantages and disadvantages of these different courses of action?

2. Al and Janet Fernandez have two alternatives for financing their son Joel's college costs—taking out an unsubsidized student loan with a variable rate that is currently at 6 percent or taking out a fixed-rate home equity loan at 7 percent. Assume that both loans will have 10-year terms for repayment. What factors should they consider in deciding between these two alternatives?

3. Use Figure 6-2 to estimate the monthly payments necessary to reduce a $1,000 debt to zero within 2 years, assuming simple interest at 15 percent.

4. Use Figure 6-2 to estimate the monthly payments necessary to reduce a $5,000 debt to zero within 5 years, assuming simple interest at 15 percent.

5. Why is it insufficient to simply make the minimum monthly payments required by your lender?

6. Trevor's online gambling debts have gotten out of control, so Trevor has gone to an agency that advertises it will help people get out of debt. He has $15,000 in credit card debt and is unable to make his minimum payments. The agency agrees to help Trevor take out another loan at 13 percent interest, for a $200 fee. Because he's now paying a rate of 18 percent, this sounds like a good deal. Explain the pros and cons of Trevor's decision.

A Home Equity Loan to Consolidate Debt

Jasmine currently has three credit cards with outstanding balances that total $15,000. Her minimum monthly payments on these cards total $350. Jasmine's home is currently worth $120,000 and she has a mortgage of $80,000.

1. How much can she borrow on her home if the lender is willing to lend a maximum of 80 percent of the market value?

2. How much will the monthly interest-only payment be on a home equity loan at 6 percent interest only?

3. If Jasmine decides to take a home equity loan, explain why she should make larger payments and pay both interest and principal.

The Effects of Debt on Your Financial Plan

Suppose you're currently saving $300 per month, in an account earning 5 percent interest, so that you can attend graduate school six years from now. You decide to buy an automobile and take out a six-year loan with payments of $150 per month. This decision means that you will have to reduce your monthly graduate school savings contributions by $150 per month. At the end of the six years, how much money would you have been able to save (not counting the interest you would have made on the money, had you deposited it in the account)?

7

MAKING AUTOMOBILE AND HOUSING DECISIONS
Buying a Car or a House

Starting Point

Go to www.wiley.com/college/bajtelsmit to assess your knowledge of automobile and housing decisions.
Determine where you need to concentrate your effort.

What You'll Learn in This Chapter

▲ The auto and housing decision process
▲ Auto insurance and auto financing options
▲ Home mortgages and real estate transactions

After Studying This Chapter, You'll Be Able To

▲ Assess your automobile needs and determine what you can afford
▲ Decide among automobile financing alternatives
▲ Be an informed automobile consumer
▲ Evaluate your housing needs and determine what you can afford
▲ Select a home that meets your needs and negotiate an acceptable price for it
▲ Choose among financing options and know how to apply for and qualify for a mortgage

INTRODUCTION

For most families, automobiles and homes make up a significant portion of household net worth. Also, the auto and home loans that finance these purchases represent the lion's share of household debt. Your decisions relating to the purchase or lease of automobiles and housing are therefore very important components of your financial plan. Deciding whether to buy or rent (lease, in the case of automobile decisions) requires an understanding of the financing options and the pros and cons of each.

7.1 Buying a Motor Vehicle

You might be surprised at how many people buy new cars on impulse. They stop in at a dealership "just to look" at the new models, and two hours later, they drive away with a new car and a big monthly payment. How can a person spend less time on a major financial decision like this than they'd spend buying a new television set? The answer is complex but is related to both the nature of the car sales experience and the nature of human beings. Fortunately, you can develop good purchasing skills and avoid situations where you might be influenced to make poorly thought-out decisions. Figure 7-1 shows the best process for making auto and housing decisions.

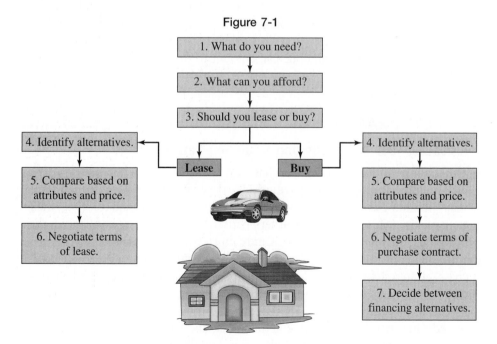

Figure 7-1

The auto and housing decision process.

7.1.1 Preparing to Shop

For all purchase decisions, the first question is whether you actually need the item. The fact that needs have higher priority in your goal setting than wants affects how you approach the problem.

Families can usually get by with fewer cars than they have, especially in urban areas where mass transportation is available. Nevertheless, 88 percent of all households in the United States own at least one vehicle, and the average household owns two. For most auto purchase decisions, then, and particularly for those related to second and third family vehicles, the truth is that the automobile really isn't needed. When a new vehicle is not a necessity, the purchase decision should be analyzed against other luxury and convenience expenditures.

If a car purchase will reduce or slow your ability to achieve more important goals, you might want to seriously consider alternative methods of meeting your transportation needs, such as car pooling, using mass transit, bicycling, walking, or renting a car for weekends and holidays. At $19.99 to $29.99 per day and with no maintenance obligations, occasional renting is a practical and often-overlooked alternative to owning a car, particularly for urban consumers.

Even if you need a vehicle, you may not be able to afford it. Therefore, the next step in the process is to evaluate your ability to meet your auto purchase goal in light of your budget. To illustrate this decision, we meet the Thompson family, who are considering the purchase of an additional vehicle.

Many people make the mistake of estimating the cost of automobile owner-ship based on their auto lease or loan payment. They should include many other costs in the decision process as well, however, because costs other than those related to financing the automobile can amount to thousands of additional dollars

---

FOR EXAMPLE

Assessing Your Car Needs and What You Can Afford

The Thompson family currently has two vehicles. They purchased Dave's pickup fairly recently and are paying $237.61 per month (with more than three years remaining on the loan). Cindy's older minivan is fully paid for. Kyle, their teenage son, will soon get his learner's permit, so the family is considering the purchase of a vehicle for his use. Cindy and Dave are particularly concerned with safety and want to purchase a vehicle with dual front air bags. The purchase of an additional vehicle will require reducing their other fixed or discretionary expenditures. They estimate they can put $2,000 from their savings toward a down payment and $300 per month toward a loan or lease payment by reducing spending on food, entertainment, and vacations. They must determine the car price this monthly allocation will allow them to buy or lease.

per year. It's a good idea to record your auto-related expenses, at least until you have a good estimate of your average monthly outflows. For example, you can keep a logbook in your car and regularly record mileage, gasoline, and maintenance expenditures. If some or all of your auto expenses are tax deductible for business, you need a written record to justify the deduction, so this type of log is necessary. A sample log that you can use is included in this book's Personal Financial Planner in the Appendix.

The costs of automobile ownership can be separated into two categories:

▲ **Fixed expenses:** These are expenses that stay the same, regardless of how much you use your car or how well you take care of it.

▲ **Variable operation expenses:** These are expenses that increase with your car usage.

Let's look more closely at each category. Fixed expenses of automobile ownership include the following:

▲ **Finance charges:** Whether you borrow money to buy a car or take the money from an investment or savings account, you incur an opportunity cost. You're paying the interest to one financial institution, or you're not getting the earnings on investment from another financial institution. You need to take this into account in making a car purchase or lease decision. This cost varies, depending on the market rates and the price of the vehicle.

▲ **Depreciation: Depreciation** is the decline in value of an asset over time. Automobiles depreciate due to wear and tear, obsolescence, and competitive factors. Businesses are allowed to deduct depreciation of business assets from their income, but individuals are not, so the declining value of your vehicle over time means that your net worth also declines, all else being equal. People often joke about the loss in new car value that occurs as soon as you drive off the dealer's lot. Within the first two years, a new car may lose 40 to 60 percent of its value. However, not all vehicles depreciate at the same rate, and you may want to consider this factor. The patterns of depreciation for particular makes and models are even a factor in the ratings of various vehicles. However, history is no guarantee that the future will be the same. Values of used cars in 2002 and 2003, for example, declined much more quickly than usual because of unusually stiff competition from the new car market. Stagnant new car pricing and low financing rates led to sharply reduced used car prices.

▲ **Incremental auto insurance premiums:** If you already have auto insurance, the relevant insurance cost to consider is not the total premium but, rather, the incremental increase in premium from the purchase of a car. In the case of the Thompsons, Kyle will presumably need to be covered by his parents' insurance, regardless of whether they have two cars or three. However, the premium increase for a third driver in a household with two cars is much lower than it is for a household with three cars because the insurer will rate the new driver in the latter case as a "primary" driver rather than an "occasional" driver. Another insurance-related factor is that some makes and models of cars require the payment of higher premiums than others. You should ask your insurance agent for an estimate of the incremental cost increase of adding a car and/or a driver to your policy. Automobile insurance is discussed in Chapter 8.

▲ **Other fixed costs:** Other fixed costs include automobile registration, licenses, and taxes. Some states charge a fixed price per vehicle for registration. Others use a sliding scale, with more expensive vehicles being more expensive. All automobile sales are taxed, and a few states impose personal property taxes, usually calculated annually based on a percentage of all personal property owned.

Variable expenses, as noted, depend on how much you use your vehicle. The more you use it, the more you spend on gas and maintenance. The more miles you drive, the more often you need to change the vehicle's oil and repair or replace parts such as belts, brakes, and tires. Additional variable expenses for commuters could include parking fees and tolls.

Your total operating costs depends primarily on miles driven and the age of the car, but it may also be related to the conditions under which you drive. New vehicles generally require less maintenance than older ones. Furthermore, larger vehicles can have much higher variable operating expenses, not only due to higher gasoline costs but also because replacement parts and maintenance tend to be more expensive. Regular maintenance can reduce your overall costs. Cars that are well maintained tend to depreciate less; that is, they have higher resale value and higher trade-in value. Regular tune-ups can put off or avert more expensive repairs.

You can compare the costs of different vehicles by considering the total annual cost or the cost per mile. Because a portion of the total cost is fixed, the cost per mile decreases with mileage driven as the fixed costs are spread over a larger number of miles. However, from a budgetary point of view, the total dollar cost is probably the more relevant number to consider.

7.1.2 Evaluating Alternatives

If cost were not a factor, you could purchase a new car with every option available. Most people, however, must make their purchase decisions based on predefined priorities. What are the key vehicle features that will meet your needs? Although price is usually a major factor, most people enter into the car-buying process with other objectives, too, whether safety and reliability, sufficient size for a growing family, or ruggedness for an avid off-roader.

There are many sources of information on vehicles, their features, and their costs. The following are some of the things to consider when selecting a vehicle:

▲ **Price:** Manufacturers provide printed forms for new cars that identify the manufacturer's suggested retail price (MSRP) for the car, with its accessories and options. This is usually referred to as the **sticker price,** but some dealers use this term to refer to a different sticker they place on the car that gives the total price as the MSRP plus additional charges for delivery, detailing, and other dealer-provided services, which add to their profit. The **dealer's invoice price** is the price the dealer paid to purchase the vehicle from the manufacturer and is an important piece of information to have during negotiations. Sometimes, automobile dealers advertise that they'll sell vehicles for a set amount—say, $200—over their invoice price. In essence, they're implying that this is the limit of their profit. Although this may be true, often, the "invoice" they're using is actually the dealer's invoice price plus all the dealer-installed options on which they'll also profit. Used cars are sold by used car dealers and private owners. An asking price may be advertised in the newspaper, on the internet, or on the vehicle itself. Both sticker prices for new vehicles and asking prices for used vehicles are negotiable, so the actual price depends on the motivation of the seller and the local market for the vehicle. The price range you can consider is directly related to your household budget and financial goals. If you know how much you have available for up-front costs and how much you can allocate to your total automobile costs each month, you can get a rough estimate of your price range. Although you may need to revise this estimate, you shouldn't waste your time with vehicles outside this ballpark price range.

▲ **New vs. used:** Based on your price range, you might find that you can't consider buying a new car. If you're interested in a used vehicle, there are many to choose from, through both private sale and dealerships. The market values of used cars have declined substantially in the past several years, so you may be able to get a low-mileage car that is one or two years old at a fraction of the cost of a new car. You take a risk buying a used vehicle that may have hidden defects, but you can minimize that risk by taking the car to a mechanic for a systems checkup prior to buying. In addition, dealerships usually offer a 30-day warranty. If you're buying from a private party, you should be sure to ask the seller why the car is being sold and what kind of maintenance has been done over the vehicle's life. Although there's no guarantee that you'll get an honest answer, you might learn something useful, so it's worth asking.

▲ **Equipment:** Depending on the make and model, vehicles can differ substantially in terms of standard equipment, options, and accessories. You should create a list of options that you require and a list of options that you'd like to have but don't absolutely need. (You can find a sample checklist in your Personal Financial Planner.) If you're buying a used car, you may not be able to be as picky as you would when buying a new car, but it's still a good idea to think about the most important features. As you consider different vehicles, you should keep track of which ones satisfy your requirements.

▲ **Size and fuel efficiency:** All new car dealers are required by federal law to report the estimated mileage per gallon (MPG) for city and highway driving. *Consumer Reports* also provides independent, and often lower, MPG results, based on its own tests. The larger and heavier the car, the less fuel efficient it is, and the greater the costs of operation. If you drive a lot, this may be a significant expense. For example, if Kyle drives 10,000 miles per year (about half the average for a male teenage driver), the additional gasoline costs to the family at $2.50 per gallon could range from about $625 per year for a fairly fuel-efficient car (40 MPG) to $2,500 for a gas guzzler (10 MPG). To estimate your annual gasoline costs, you divide the number of miles you drive by the MPG you think your vehicle will get on average to find the number of gallons the vehicle will consume per year. Then you multiply the gallons per year by the average price per gallon to get the annual fuel cost. This dollar cost could rise rapidly in the face of sudden oil price changes. In Europe, where the price of gasoline is two to three times that in the United States, consumers prefer to buy small, fuel-efficient cars and to use alternative modes of transportation, such as gasoline/electric hybrids.

▲ **Safety:** The odds of having a minor accident, or fender-bender, are fairly high, and increase with the number of miles you drive. Because there are at least 40,000 auto accident fatalities per year, safety should be a factor in any automobile purchase. Seatbelts and air bags are required in all new cars, and manufacturers are working to develop more ways to keep drivers safer. Small car manufacturers are particularly active in safety research because they know they could lose market share if buyers become wary of the risks of competing for road space with the many huge sport utility vehicles (SUVs) out there today.

▲ **Reliability:** Buying a new car doesn't guarantee that you'll have zero expenses for maintenance and repairs in the first several years. Some makes and models are notorious for their lack of reliability. *Consumer Reports* and other auto information providers usually report information on reliability based on customer surveys. The Insurance Institute for Highway Safety regularly conducts crash tests on new vehicles. Although big cars can easily crush little cars in a collision, that doesn't necessarily mean people are safer in SUVs. The results of front and side crash tests for vehicles are available at the Web site of the National Highway Traffic Safety Administration, www.nhtsa.dot.gov. Surprisingly good performers are the new Volkswagen Beetles, which, although small, have been redesigned to protect the driver and front passenger from collision injuries.

▲ **Warranties:** Most new vehicles and late-model used vehicles sold at dealerships come with both express and implied warranties. A **warranty** is a legal promise made by the seller, in this case with respect to the qualities of the vehicle being sold. An express warranty is a promise made by the seller verbally or in writing. Even without an express warranty, there is an implied warranty that a purchased vehicle is suitable for its intended use—unless it is explicitly sold "as is," which means the seller makes no warranties at all. Express warranties may include a promise to repair certain types of defects within a period of time after the sale. If the seller promises to fix any problems or, if a problem isn't fixable within a reasonable time, replace the vehicle, the warranty is a full warranty. Auto dealerships and manufacturers usually offer a limited warranty, labeled as such. Limited warranties are likely to cover parts and labor for certain types of repairs for some number of years or miles driven, whichever comes first. After a warranty has expired, most manufacturers still cover the costs of repairs that result from defects in workmanship or design if the owner complains loudly enough. In addition, most manufacturers and dealers offer the opportunity to purchase an extended warranty or service contract. This either extends the time that the car is covered by the original limited warranty or adds services or coverage to the existing warranty. It's important to read the fine print on this carefully because many extended warranties exclude coverage for the problems you're most likely to experience. Usually, the warranty contract price is greater than the expected costs of covered repairs.

▲ **Comfort and style:** Most buyers are interested in qualitative features, such as comfort, smoothness of ride, color, and attractiveness. When you research your alternatives, you should be sure to test drive vehicles under normal driving conditions so that you can judge these features. Several auto manufacturers (GM, Chrysler, and Ford, so far) are experimenting in some markets with allowing potential qualified buyers to take cars for overnight test drives. (And no, you don't have to take the salesperson.) Sellers hope that if you spend more time with a car, you'll get attached to that "new car smell." All new car manufacturers offer some type of bumper-to-bumper warranty, at a minimum for the first 2 years or 24,000 miles, whichever comes first.

7.1.3 Determining Purchase Price

Whether you lease or buy a vehicle, you should negotiate the best possible terms. A lower price reduces the amount to be financed in the case of a purchase and the depreciation charge for a lease. Very few people pay the price originally asked by the seller, and those who do pay too much.

You should go into any negotiation with as much information about the vehicle's value as possible. Although the negotiated price is very important, it's a mistake to focus on price alone because many factors count, including needed repairs, fuel efficiency, and finance charges.

You can negotiate most effectively if you understand how dealers make their profit. These are the main sources of dealer profit:

▲ The difference between what dealers pay for the car (dealer's invoice price) and what they sell it for.

▲ Profit on dealer-installed options, dealer delivery and preparation, and undercoating (a generally overpriced rustproofing process).

▲ Manufacturer incentives, such as rebates, allowances, and discounts.

▲ Extended warranties and service contracts.

▲ Finance charges and application fees

▲ Profit to be made on traded vehicle.

When car sales are slow, dealers often offer fairly good prices, with minimal mark-ups, to attract customers, but they make up this difference in other charges, which may vary widely. For example, the delivery and preparation charge, which covers the dealer's cost of getting the car to the lot and cleaning it up, can add as much as $1,000 to the originally contracted price. And you often don't see this until you're signing the paperwork.

An uninformed consumer could easily be fooled into thinking that he or she got a good deal on a car by paying only $100 over the dealer's invoice when the dealer is making several thousand dollars on other aspects of the deal. Trade-in values are usually significantly lower than resale values. Financing is quite profitable as well, particularly if borrowers fail to compare loans based on annual percentage rate (APR). You can research different makes and models of cars online at www.autosite.com and at the Kelley Blue Book Web site, www.kbb.com.

Darrell Parrish, an author and former car salesman, gives advice in his books for beating the car salesman at his own game. The following suggestions are based on ideas from Parrish's books *The Car Buyer's Art* and *Used Cars: How to Buy One*. In the shopping phase,

▲ Don't negotiate or go into a salesperson's office. You're only shopping.

▲ Test drive only the cars you are seriously considering.

▲ Write down car details and any "offers" made by salespersons on their business cards. These can be used in negotiation later and encourage competition for your business.

In the negotiation phase,

▲ Know what your bottom line is and don't make that offer first.
▲ Understand the car salesperson's objectives and the dealer's profit sources.
▲ Always act like you are willing to walk away, even when you have almost closed the deal.
▲ Plan to spend three hours negotiating.

7.1.4 Resolving Consumer Complaints

Although no one likes to think about what can go wrong, a car you've purchased may not live up to your expectations. Most problems with a new car should be covered by the warranty. If you don't get satisfaction at the service department, you should go to the service manager or owner.

The next level of complaint is the manufacturer, where you need to contact someone in the Consumer Affairs Department. If this fails, you can contact your state consumer protection office. You need to make all complaints in writing and provide adequate documentation of each attempt you've made to get the defect fixed. Sometimes, when a vehicle is clearly defective and repairs don't help, **lemon laws** may require that the dealer reimburse you for repair expenses or refund the price you paid for the vehicle. Because these laws vary, you should check your state's lemon law for requirements.

SELF-CHECK

1. Define **depreciation, sticker price,** and **dealer's invoice price.**
2. Name several sources of dealer profit other than price.
3. List the fixed expenses of automobile ownership.

7.2 Automobile Financing Alternatives

In deciding whether to lease or buy, you can use the worksheet in your Personal Financial Planner. Generally, the up-front and monthly costs of buying are higher than those costs with leasing. This tends to make leases attractive to consumers who don't have enough money for a down payment or who want to limit their monthly expenses. But the difference may be made up at the end of the lease. After two years, a buyer may have equity and owe less on the loan than the car is worth—but a person who leases will have nothing but the use of the vehicle.

7.2.1 Basics of Leasing an Auto

A **lease** is essentially a rental agreement between the owner of the car, the **lessor,** and you, the **lease,** in which you agree to pay money for the right to use the vehicle for the period of your contract. The newspapers are full of ads touting low monthly payments for new cars. Usually, these are lease payments as opposed to loan payments.

Why are lease payments so much lower than loan payments? The lessor can afford to charge a lower monthly payment during the lease term because it still owns the vehicle and will eventually make up the difference by selling it later. When you buy a used car instead of leasing, you're the one who can make money from selling it later. Leases are popular, with about one-third of all new cars being leased rather than bought, primarily because of the attractively low monthly payments and the ability to turn in your car for a new one every two or three years.

The cost of a lease is determined by the difference between the initial value of the car and the resale value at the end of the lease—or, in other words, how much the car will depreciate in value over the two- or three-year lease term. For example, if the car is worth $29,000 today and is expected to be worth $15,000 in two years, then your lease payments must compensate the lessor for the $14,000 depreciation plus finance charges.

In a closed-end lease, the lessor takes the risk that the resale value of the car will be less than what was originally assumed. This type of lease is also sometimes called a *walk-away lease* because you can return the car in good condition and simply walk away from any further responsibilities. In the preceding example, if you didn't exceed the mileage limitation on the lease but the resale value at the end of the two years turned out to be only $13,000 instead of the assumed $15,000, the $2,000 additional depreciation cost would be borne by the lessor.

However, if you exceeded the mileage limitations or if your car had too much wear and tear, you'd still be subject to a surcharge. Most auto leases are closed-end leases. A disadvantage of closed-end leases is that you are committed to the full term of the lease and may be subject to a large penalty for canceling prematurely. An open-end lease, which is not very common, requires you to bear the risk of greater-than-expected depreciation. The contract makes you responsible for any difference between the actual and estimated depreciation. However, the amount you may be charged is limited by the Consumer Leasing Act to three times the monthly lease payment.

7.2.3 Important Lease Terminology

If you don't understand your rights under a lease agreement, you may be taken advantage of. Under the Federal Consumer Leasing Act, lessors must tell you all the relevant information about your lease on a disclosure form; however, these forms can be confusing. Understanding the most important terminology and common contractual clauses can help you make sense of automobile lease agreements:

▲ **Gross capitalized cost:** The value of the vehicle is called the gross capitalized cost. You should negotiate this price before discussing leasing; statistics show that negotiated prices for leased vehicles are, on average, about 4 percent higher than prices for purchased vehicles.

▲ **Up-front fees:** You may be required to pay some up-front or acquisition fees, which cover the cost of obtaining your credit report and processing your application. Sometimes, these fees may be included in the capitalized cost of the vehicle.

▲ **Capitalized cost reduction:** If you make a down payment, benefit from a rebate, or trade in another vehicle, the gross capitalized cost is reduced by this amount.

▲ **Residual value:** The residual value is the expected depreciated value of the vehicle at the end of the lease term.

▲ **Rent charge:** The rent charge is the total dollar finance charges for the term of the lease. This is added to the expected depreciation of the vehicle to determine the payment.

▲ **Lease term:** The number of months in the lease is called the lease term.

▲ **Excess wear and mileage limits:** Automobile lessors commonly charge a penalty for excessive wear and use of a vehicle. This penalty can be assessed for physical damage to the vehicle (not usually defined clearly in the contract) and for mileage in excess of that specified in the contract, commonly 12,000 to 15,000 miles per year. Charges can range from 10 to 30 cents per mile. For example, if your contract specifies 12,000 miles per year and you drive 30,000 miles during your two-year lease, you are subject to a charge of at least $600 (6,000 extra miles × 10 cents per mile) when you return the vehicle.

▲ **Purchase option:** Most leases allow you to purchase your leased vehicle at the end of the lease term. The amount you for which you can purchase the vehicle is specified in the lease contract and may include a purchase option fee. This amount is often the same as the residual value used for calculation of the depreciation amount.

▲ **Early termination:** If you decide to terminate the contract early, you may be assessed a penalty for early termination, in addition to owing the balance on the lease. This penalty may also be imposed if the car is stolen or destroyed in an accident, although auto insurance may cover some or all of the loss.

▲ **Disposition fee:** The lessor may charge a disposition fee, to be paid at the end of the lease if you choose not to purchase the vehicle.

SELF-CHECK

1. Will the monthly payment be more if you buy or lease a car?
2. With a lease, who owns the car: the lessor or the lessee?

7.3 The Housing Decision

Spending more on housing necessarily involves a trade-off: The more you spend on any one thing, the less you have to meet your other needs or to achieve your financial goals. You should make this choice in light of your other household goals. For example, if reducing your credit card debt is a high priority, it would make sense to rent a smaller apartment and live with a roommate until you have achieved that goal.

7.3.1 The Rent vs. Buy Decision

The decision about whether to rent or buy housing depends on your preferences, your budget, and your creditworthiness. Although it usually costs more to buy than to rent equivalent space, homeowners generally experience long-term financial advantages from the growing value of their home and the tax deductibility of interest and property taxes.

   The advantages of renting include the following:

▲ **Lower monthly payments:** Rent is usually less expensive than the monthly costs for a comparably sized purchased house. Tenants don't generally pay property taxes or homeowner's insurance, and they avoid expenses for maintenance and repairs. Usually, renters don't have to provide appliances, such as a refrigerator, and the landlord may pay some or all utilities. These differences can add up to savings that you can apply to your financial plan.

▲ **Mobility:** Renting enables you to move on short notice. Leases are commonly made for one year, but many landlords reduce the term if they're given sufficient notice to find a replacement tenant. At worst, you might lose your security deposit. In comparison, it usually takes at least several months to find a buyer for a house.

▲ **Less responsibility:** Renters of apartments usually have no responsibility for maintenance of lawns and gardens, clearing of snow, or exterior cleaning and painting. However, if you rent a home, your lease is likely to include some of these responsibilities. As a renter, you also have less liability for injuries that occur on the property.

The disadvantages of renting include the following:

▲ **Increasing costs over time:** Rent usually increases with the rate of inflation over time, whereas mortgage payments are often fixed for the life of the loan.

▲ **No investment value:** Paying rent doesn't contribute to your wealth because you don't benefit from the increase in value of the property over time. In contrast, homeowners benefit from the investment and can borrow against their home equity.

▲ **No tax deduction:** Rent is not tax deductible, which makes it more expensive than a mortgage payment of the same amount, after taxes. Both the interest paid on a mortgage and property taxes are tax deductible. If you're in a low tax bracket and do not itemize, this doesn't matter to you. Usually, however, the annual expenses of home ownership exceed the standard deduction and therefore provide tax advantages.

▲ **Restrictions on use of the property:** Lease contracts often restrict the use of the property—how many people can live there, whether pets are allowed, how much noise will be tolerated, and the ability to upgrade and decorate the place. Although some subdivisions and most condominium complexes place restrictions on homeowners, these restrictions are generally limited to such matters as exterior color, fencing, and landscaping.

▲ **Uncertainty:** There are no guarantees that you'll be able to continue renting the property after the end of the lease term.

As you make a decision about whether to rent or buy, it's important to weigh the relative costs and benefits. You can use the worksheet provided in the Personal Financial Planner to help compare the financial costs. Note that in the short term, renting tends to have the cost advantage, but over time, the tax and investment benefits of home ownership make owning more attractive.

7.3.2 The Costs of Home Ownership

To calculate how much you can allocate to a mortgage, you need to take the total amount of monthly cash flow that you have available for housing expenses and subtract any additional costs of home ownership not related to the mortgage itself. In comparing renting and buying, it's easy to make the mistake of assuming that the mortgage payment is the total monthly cost of buying.

However, in addition to the financing costs, you also pay local property taxes, homeowner's insurance, and repairs and maintenance on the property. For condominiums and some residential developments, you may have an association fee for maintenance of common areas. (You should investigate whether a condominium association or co-op board is financially solvent before you buy, as well as whether there are any outstanding disputes that would affect you if you buy.) All these costs can vary substantially in different places and for different properties but are likely to constitute 20 to 25 percent of your total housing cost. Your total homeowner expenses include the following:

▲ **Principal and interest:** Your mortgage payment usually includes a level payment for the amortized loan, although other options are discussed in Section 7.5. This payment includes tax-deductible interest on the balance of the mortgage as well as some repayment of principal.

▲ **Property taxes:** Most local jurisdictions pay for community services such as roads, schools, fire, and police protection by levying a tax on real property. **Property taxes** are usually calculated by multiplying a property tax rate, often called the mil rate, by the assessed value of the property, in thousands. For example, a property assessed at $90,000 would pay the tax rate times 90, whereas a property assessed at $150,000 would pay the tax rate times 150. The more expensive the house, the more you pay. The assessed value is determined by a government official usually called the tax assessor. Periodically, the assessor estimates market values for every property in the town or city and then multiplies each by the applicable **assessment ratio,** a fraction less than 1, to determine the assessed value. You can call the local taxing authority to determine the applicable tax rate and assessment ratio. Depending on the values of properties in the area and demands on local services, tax rates may go up or down. Although homebuyers can use the previous owner's property taxes as an estimate, that amount may understate their property tax liability if the town has not recently reassessed. When a property is sold, most jurisdictions use the new sales price to reestimate the market value in calculating property taxes. When prices are rising rapidly, this can result in large tax increases for the new owners.

▲ **Homeowner's insurance:** All lenders require that borrowers carry homeowner's insurance on their property. For more about homeowner's insurance, see Chapter 8. You can include an estimate in your calculation of monthly costs. This type of insurance can range from $200 per year to much more, and the cost increases with the value of the property. A real estate broker can generally give you an estimate of costs in your area, or you can contact a local insurance agent.

▲ **Repairs and maintenance:** Buying a home may result in significant costs for repairs and maintenance, from lawn maintenance to repair of major systems, such as plumbing and electrical systems. In general, the older the house you buy, the more you can expect to spend.

FOR EXAMPLE

Estimating How Much You Can Afford for Your Mortgage

Let's assume that, based on your budget, you know that the maximum you have available to apply to housing is $1,000 per month. From this, you must subtract the additional costs of home ownership as identified in this section. You estimate that property taxes will be $150 per month, homeowner's insurance $30 per month, and repairs and maintenance $60 per month. You don't expect to pay any association dues. The amount you have available to pay the principal and interest on a mortgage is therefore $760 = $1,000 − $150 − $30 − $60.

▲ **Association dues:** Condominiums and some residential properties require that homeowners pay dues to a homeowners' association. These pay for the maintenance of common areas, such as gardens and sidewalks, and sometimes more expensive items, such as a swimming pool. Such fees can range from $100 to several thousand dollars annually. Although your mortgage costs are fixed, association dues are usually determined by a volunteer board made up of a few homeowners. If a major project is required (e.g., the pool needs to be resurfaced), homeowners can be hit with one-time special fees.

▲ **Offsetting tax benefits:** Although home ownership can cost quite a bit more than renting, the tax savings from deductibility of mortgage interest and property taxes provide an offsetting benefit. In addition, subject to some limitations, your home can appreciate in value without triggering any capital gains or tax liability upon sale.

The worksheet "Calculating Affordable Home Price" provided in the Personal Financial Planner walks you through the steps in determining what size mortgage fits your budget.

SELF-CHECK

1. List the advantages of renting.
2. What are the costs of being a homeowner?
3. How are roads, schools, and other services paid for?

7.4 Buying a Home

Although your decision of which house to buy involves many factors, including affordability and personal preference, it's important to remember that your home is also an investment. You should therefore consider each alternative property's potential for appreciation in value.

In the real estate business, it a common joke to ask, "What are the three determinants of real estate value?" The answer, as everyone knows, is (1) location, (2) location, and (3) location. Although not entirely true, in general, a home in a good location appreciates more quickly than one in a less desirable spot, and you'll have an easier time reselling it. If your house backs up to a large vacant lot zoned for commercial use, you might one day find a Wal-Mart in your backyard.

Other factors that influence the value of homes include the following:

▲ The type of structure (single- or multifamily).

▲ Age.

▲ Characteristics of the structure and land (e.g., condition, size, number of rooms/bathrooms, square footage, acreage, landscaping, outbuildings).

▲ Curb appeal (i.e., attractiveness from the street).

▲ Asking price relative to value.

Perhaps most importantly, real estate values are determined by what a reasonable buyer is willing to pay for the property, and this is highly dependent on market conditions and mortgage rates at a given time.

7.4.1 Choosing a Real Estate Broker

Although you're not legally required to use a broker, many homes are advertised and shown exclusively through real estate brokers, so you don't have the same selection if you don't use one. Brokers' familiarity with the properties for sale in the area and available financing terms and lenders, as well as the negotiation process, can be invaluable, and their fee is paid by the seller. When you sell, a broker can also help you price your home more realistically, since psychological factors may cause you to be unrealistic about your home's value.

In your first meeting with a broker, in addition to assessing whether you feel comfortable working with the person, you should consider asking the following questions:

▲ **How long have you been selling real estate?** An experienced agent who is very familiar with the area will be better able to assist you with finding a home and arranging financing.

▲ **Is real estate your primary profession?** You don't want a broker who is doing this as a second job. Not only is this type of person likely to give you lower-quality service, but this may be an indication that the person can't make a living selling real estate.

▲ **What is your sales track record, and what is the average price of the homes you have sold?** The answer to this question tells you how successful the agent is and whether he or she is familiar with homes in your price range.

▲ **Do you have references from former buyers or sellers you have worked with?** It's a good idea to follow up to find out about service, dependability, personality, and handling of paperwork.

▲ **How big is your office?** Larger offices may have more in-house listings. When the market is "hot," the best properties listed with large offices may all be sold before they are even advertised.

7.4.2 Your Legal Relationship with a Broker

Real estate sellers pay brokers on a commission basis; the commission is a percentage of the negotiated sale price of the house, commonly 6 to 7 percent.

A real estate broker is an **agent,** a person who is acting on behalf of another through a contractual agreement. An agent has a legal duty to act in the best interests of the **principal** for whom the broker works. The principal is the person who has delegated responsibility to an agent and to whom the agent has a duty.

FOR EXAMPLE

How a Broker Is Paid

Say that you buy a house for $100,000 and that two agents are involved in the sale—Pete and Sandra. Pete is the broker who originally contracted with the seller of the house you're buying. Pete is called the *listing broker,* and in a standard listing contract, he is entitled to one-half of the full commission, which he is to split with the supervising broker in his office. So if the full commission is 6 percent, Pete's commission is 1.5 percent of the sales price, and his boss gets 1.5 percent as well. Sandra is the broker who originally showed you the house and helped you negotiate the sales price. She is called a *cooperating broker* and is entitled to the other half of the 6 percent, to be shared with her office. Because the sales price is $100,000, the listing broker, the cooperating broker, and each of their managing offices will get $1,500, all paid for by the seller out of the money received from the sale of the home.

Although most buyers believe that their brokers are acting as their agents—after all, the brokers are taking them to look at houses and then shepherding them through the negotiation and transaction—this is not actually the case.

The seller pays the broker the commission and is thus the one to whom the broker has a primary legal duty. The relationship between the broker and the buyer is therefore a bit ambiguous because the broker has an obvious conflict of interest. The objective of the seller is to get the highest price possible for the house, and the objective of the buyer is to pay the lowest amount possible. The broker obviously cannot act in the best interests of both parties.

Some states have acted to create a "dual agency" rule under which the broker has legal duties (e.g., confidentiality, professionalism) to both the buyer and the seller, but this doesn't really remove the conflict inherent in the negotiation process. A good rule of thumb is to never reveal information to your broker (e.g., the highest price you're willing to pay) that you don't want relayed to the seller.

A relatively new development in the real estate brokerage business is the concept of the **buyer broker,** a real estate agent who works exclusively for the buyer and has no legal duty to the seller. These agents help buyers find suitable homes, negotiate the price, and facilitate the transaction without any of the conflicts of interest inherent in the usual real estate broker relationships. This sounds like a good thing; the problem is that these brokers need to be paid. Because the listing broker's contract is with the seller, a buyer who wants this type of service may have to pay for it separately, with fees ranging from hourly rates to 3.5 percent of the sales price. In some states, a buyer broker may be able to share the seller's commission as a cooperating broker.

SELF-CHECK

1. List some questions to ask a prospective broker.
2. Define **agent, principal,** and **buyer broker.**
3. What factors influence home value?

7.5 Mortgage Financing

A **mortgage** is a long-term amortized loan that is secured by real property. Remember that a secured loan carries a lower interest rate than an unsecured loan because the lender has less at risk. If you don't make your mortgage payments as promised, the lender has the right to foreclose—to take your home in satisfaction of the debt.

Mortgages are made by many different types of financial institutions, including depository institutions, such as commercial banks and savings and loans, and nondepository institutions, such as insurance companies. There are also mortgage brokers who, for a fee, shop around and arrange appropriate financing for buyers. Like other amortized loans, mortgages usually have level payments that include interest and some principal repayment.

At the end of the mortgage term, you will have completely paid back the original loan, with interest. During the early years of the mortgage, when the balance you owe is high, most of your payment goes toward paying interest. As you gradually pay back the loan, your payment stays the same, but the interest charge is a smaller proportion of the total payment because the balance on which the interest is computed is lower.

You should check your credit report before you apply for a mortgage so that you can negotiate a competitive interest rate. See Section 5.4.2 for more on credit reporting.

7.5.1 Types of Mortgages

Mortgages fall into a few general categories:

▲ **Conventional mortgages:** A **conventional mortgage** is a fixed-rate, fixed-term, fixed-payment loan. Rates vary with market conditions and borrower qualifications, but once contracted for, they are fixed for the life of the loan, which is commonly 15, 20, 25, or 30 years. Payments are fixed as well and made monthly. A portion of the monthly payment goes toward paying interest on the balance owed, and the remainder is applied to repayment of principal.

FOR EXAMPLE

Fixed-Rate Mortgages

A $100,000 30-year conventional mortgage at 6 percent interest will have fixed payments of $599.55 per month for 360 months. The first month, the interest amounts to 0.5 percent (6 percent divided by 12 months) of the mortgage amount of $100,000, or $500. The remaining $99.55 goes toward paying back the principal. The next month, you owe 0.5 percent interest of the new balance, $99,900.45 ($100,000 − $99.55), or $499.50. Because the monthly payment is fixed and the interest portion is declining over time (as you gradually reduce your loan amount through the repayment of principal), you apply more to the principal with each payment.

▲ **Insured mortgages:** To help certain homebuyers qualify for mortgages, the Veterans Administration (VA) and the Federal Housing Authority (FHA) offer insurance for conventional loans under certain circumstances. These agencies do not actually provide the mortgage financing money —they simply guarantee to pay lenders (usually banks and savings institutions) the promised interest and principal if the borrower defaults. This guarantee makes lenders more willing to provide favorable financing terms to buyers with higher loan-to-value ratios and less income. Minimum down payments range from 3 to 5 percent, and these loans commonly require the payment of points, as discussed later in this section.

▲ **ARMs):** An **adjustable-rate mortgage (ARM)** has an interest rate that changes with market conditions. Because the lender is less exposed to the risk that mortgage rates in the market will rise to exceed the rate being paid by the borrower, the initial rates on ARMs are generally from 1 to 3 percentage points lower than those on conventional mortgages. Usually, the rate adjusts based on changes in a defined index or market rate, such as the 10-year Treasury bond rate or the prime rate, every one or two years. The amount the rate can change is limited by **interest rate caps,** which apply to both the change per year and the total change over the life of the loan. You might, for example, have an ARM with an initial rate of 4 percent, an annual rate cap of 1 percent, and a lifetime rate cap of 5 percent. The most you will ever pay on that loan is 9 percent per year (the original rate plus the lifetime rate cap), and you will never see a larger increase than 1 percentage point annually. However, the payment might grow to be more than you can afford. If you borrow $100,000, your payment at 4 percent is only $477 per month, but if rates rise steadily over the next five years, the payment could increase to more than $700 by year 5. Some ARMs also have a payment cap, limiting the amount the payment can change during the loan. Although this protects you from large payment increases, a payment limit that is less than the amount of interest you owe for the period results in **negative amortization:** The unpaid interest is added to the balance owed on the loan. This may mean that, at the end of the loan term, you still owe some principal to the lender. Many variations on ARMs have been developed.

▲ **Balloon mortgages:** A balloon is a loan for which the final payment is much larger than the earlier, regular payments. The payments are calculated based on a long amortization schedule, as in conventional mortgages, but the payments don't continue for the full length of the schedule. Instead, the balance is due at a specified point, usually 5 to 10 years after the mortgage begins. This type of loan was popular in mid-1980s, when interest rates were high.

▲ **Graduated payment mortgage:** A graduated payment mortgage carries a fixed interest rate but allows payments to be lower in the early years and increase over the life of the loan. Because the costs are shifted to later years, with this type of mortgage, you may qualify for a larger loan balance. However, this produces negative amortization in the early years of the loan, so, as in the case of the payment caps on certain ARMs, your mortgage balance actually increases. If you think that home values will rise proportionately and that you'll have the income necessary to support the higher future payments, a graduated payment mortgage might be a good choice. A similar arrangement, called a *lender buy-down mortgage,* allows borrowers to have lower early-year costs but doesn't result in negative amortization. In this type of loan, the rate changes on a set schedule to produce gradual increases in the payment. Higher rates toward the end offset the slightly reduced rates in the early years.

▲ **Growing equity mortgage:** Payments on a growing equity mortgage increase over time, but the added amounts are applied to the principal so that the loan balance can be paid off more quickly. A common form of this type of loan is a bi-weekly mortgage, sometimes called a 26-pay mortgage. Here, you make payments every two weeks in an amount equal to half the amount you'd have paid per month on a conventional fixed-rate, fixed-payment loan. Because there are 52 weeks in the year, you make the equivalent of an extra monthly payment over each year, and this amount is applied to principal. Of course, you can generally accomplish the same effect on your own by making extra principal payments throughout the life of the loan.

▲ **Shared appreciation mortgage:** With this type of mortgage, the buyer shares the increase in value of the home with the lender when the home is sold. In return, the lender charges a much lower interest rate, often one-third or more lower than the going rate on conventional loans.

▲ **Reverse annuity mortgage:** If you have a lot of equity in your home and would like to take the cash out, you may be able to access this cash through a reverse annuity mortgage, also known as a home equity conversion mortgage. A financial company converts your home equity to a tax-free stream of payments, either for life (which generally results in a lower amount annually) or for a certain term. Older homeowners who need cash but don't want to sell their homes can use this to finance their retirement.

7.5.2 Factors Affecting Mortgage Payments

The following are the most important factors that affect mortgage payments:

▲ **The amount you borrow:** Because the mortgage payment consists of interest paid to the lender and some repayment of principal, the payment

Table 7-1: Monthly Principal and Interest Payments on a 30-Year Mortgage

Mortgage Amount	*Annual Fixed Rate (APR)*						
	5%	5.50%	6%	6.50%	7%	7.50%	8%
50,000	$ 268	$ 284	$ 300	$ 316	$ 333	$ 350	$ 367
75,000	$ 403	$ 426	$ 450	$ 474	$ 499	$ 524	$ 550
100,000	$ 537	$ 568	$ 600	$ 632	$ 665	$ 699	$ 734
125,000	$ 671	$ 710	$ 749	$ 790	$ 832	$ 874	$ 917
150,000	$ 805	$ 852	$ 899	$ 948	$ 998	$1,049	$1,101
175,000	$ 939	$ 994	$1,049	$1,106	$1,164	$1,224	$1,284
200,000	$1,074	$1,136	$1,199	$1,264	$1,331	$1,398	$1,468

is larger if you borrow more money. Table 7-1 gives a rough idea of the principal and interest component of the loan for various interest rates and loan amounts.

▲ **Interest rate:** As you can see in Table 7-1, the higher the annual percentage rate charged on a mortgage, the larger the mortgage payment. In general, for every percentage-point increase in the rate, you pay about 10 percent more per month in your mortgage payment. Although the increase is not proportional, this is still a good rule of thumb to use for a rough estimate.

▲ **Term:** All else being equal, the longer the term of the loan, the smaller the mortgage payment. Most lenders now offer both 15- and 30-year mortgages. The payment for a 15-year mortgage is generally 30 to 40 percent greater than that for a 30-year mortgage. Most lenders give you a lower interest rate for a 15-year mortgage than for a 30-year mortgage.

▲ **Points:** Lenders often let you pay **discount points** to reduce your loan interest rate. A point is 1 percent of the loan amount, so for a $70,000 mortgage, one point is equal to $700. The points required for a specific rate reduction vary over time with competition and market conditions.

▲ **Economic factors:** Mortgage rates vary widely over time with different economic conditions. In the past 25 years, the average annual mortgage rate has ranged from less than 5 percent to more than 18 percent. More recently, rates have been attractively low, allowing homebuyers to afford more expensive homes and homeowners to refinance their original mortgage loans to free up cash for other purposes. Most economic forecasters predict that mortgage rates will return to the 7 to 8 percent range in the future.

▲ **Location:** Although the mortgage market is increasingly national in scope, rates are still lower in some areas than in others. So you shouldn't limit your search for a lender to local companies. Although you might get more personal service locally, the local lender is going to sell your loan anyway, so it's probably more important to get the best deal.

▲ **Your default risk:** Your mortgage payment is affected by the risk that you represent to the lender. If your ratios are too high or if you have a less-than-perfect credit history, you'll end up paying higher interest and having fewer loan options. If you have a poor credit history—prior loan defaults, late payments, or too much debt—you won't be eligible for favorable mortgage terms.

▲ **The property:** Lenders evaluate the property that you're purchasing. Based on an independent appraisal, they try to ensure that the loan-to-value ratio is low enough to meet their requirements. Appraisers assign a value to a home most often based on recent sales prices of comparable homes in the area.

7.5.3 The Mortgage Application

After finalizing a purchase contract and shopping around to evaluate your mortgage options, you need to select a lender and make a formal loan application. You can use the four P's from Chapter 5 (price, product, people, and place) to help you evaluate potential lenders. Although you may be most concerned with the rates a lender offers, the lenders with the lowest rates may also be slower at processing loans. If your loan will be sold in the secondary market, the location of the lender is not very important.

Once you have applied for the loan, the lender by law must provide you with a **good faith estimate** of the costs associated with the transaction, including the APR, all fees, and all costs you will incur in closing the loan. The application can usually be processed within a few days but may take longer during very busy times (as when rates have recently fallen and many homeowners are refinancing).

Mortgage rates may change, favorably or unfavorably for you, between the time you apply for a loan and the time you complete the transaction. If rates are rising, you may want to get a **lock-in** from your lender, which guarantees you a particular rate even if rates rise before your closing date. Some lenders will lock in within 30 or 45 days of closing at no charge, but others may require that you pay a point or a portion of a point for a lock-in. What if rates fall? With most lock-in agreements, you won't be entitled to have your rate reduced when rates fall before the closing.

7.5.4 Refinancing a Mortgage

There are many circumstances in which you may want to consider obtaining a new mortgage to pay off your old mortgage, a process called **refinancing.** Suppose you bought a home and financed it with a 7 percent mortgage. Mortgage rates have now fallen to 6 percent. If you refinance, you'll be able to reduce your mortgage payment. Although it might seem like a simple problem—exchanging the old rate for the new rate and the higher payment for a lower payment—the many costs associated with refinancing might outweigh the benefits of refinancing.

As a result of large rate reductions in the past several years, about half of all existing mortgages have been refinanced. The following are some good reasons for refinancing:

▲ **To save money:** If you'll save money by doing so, it makes financial sense to refinance.

▲ **To access your home equity:** Although you can do this with a second mortgage, it's often less expensive to do so by refinancing your first mortgage for a larger amount. You should evaluate both choices to see which one is better for you.

▲ **To reduce the term of your mortgage:** If you have 25 years to go on your current mortgage and the lower rate will allow you to reduce the term to 15 years for a similar monthly payment, this might be a good financial move.

Because a refinance is a completely new mortgage, you incur most of the same mortgage-related charges as with an original mortgage. You may get a little break on the cost of an appraisal if the lender asks the same appraiser to do an update appraisal. Title insurance companies charge a slightly reduced rate relative to the original rate to transfer the insurance to the new loan. Also, some loans carry a prepayment penalty, which means that you will have to pay a fee if you cancel the loan early. You can get a rough estimate of whether refinancing is worthwhile with this calculation:

1. Estimate the change in monthly payment.
2. Estimate the closing costs for refinancing the loan.
3. Divide the non-escrow closing costs by the payment savings to determine the number of months it will take to recoup the closing costs.

Although you know your current payment, you'll need to know how much you're financing with the new loan to estimate the new payment. If you've been making mortgage payments for several years, you'll have paid off some of the original mortgage, so you can refinance a smaller amount. In some cases, lenders may allow you to add the closing costs to the loan balance so that you don't have to bring any cash to the closing. This may seem attractive but is not necessarily a good idea, since it means you'll be paying interest on these costs for years to come.

7.6 Completing a Real Estate Transaction

A home purchase and mortgage financing are finalized at the real estate closing or settlement. In this section, we outline what happens at this meeting and the costs you can expect.

7.6.1 The Closing

The date of the **closing**, a meeting to finalize a home purchase, is set by the mutual agreement of the buyer, seller, and lender. Beforehand, the lender gives you a detailed accounting of the mortgage-related costs as well as an accounting of the other purchase-related funds that will be collected and disbursed at the closing, such as property tax and insurance escrows, which are discussed in Section 7.6.2. Most importantly, the lender tells you the specific amount of funds (usually in the form of a certified check) that you must bring to the closing.

Before coming to the closing—usually earlier on the same day—you have an opportunity to inspect the property to be certain that the former owners have removed all their belongings and that it's in the agreed-upon condition. If you find any problems, you can negotiate them at the closing. The closing is usually conducted at the office of a title insurer, real estate broker, or lawyer who is involved in the transaction.

At the actual closing, which usually takes no more than an hour, you, the seller, and the lender or the lender's legal representative sign all the necessary legal documents to transfer property ownership to you, record the transaction, and finalize the mortgage. Although this can vary from state to state, usually, a title insurance agent collects and disburses the funds and ensures that all the closing costs are paid to the appropriate parties.

7.6.2 Closing Costs

You and the seller must pay a number of expenses at the closing. These closing or settlement costs are difficult to quantify because every purchase and financing transaction is unique. The following are some of the most important closing costs:

▲ **Mortgage costs:** Your good faith estimate from the lender identifies the mortgage-related costs fairly accurately. In addition, you bring the remainder of the down payment to the closing. With your down payment, the total cost of the mortgage, including applications fee, credit report, points, loan origination fee, and interest to the end of the month, can easily add up to a large dollar amount.

▲ **Escrows:** Lenders commonly agree to take responsibility for making sure your property tax and homeowner's insurance payments are made in a timely fashion. To make this possible, you include money for taxes and insurance in each monthly mortgage payment. The lender collects some amount in advance at the closing to hold in an **escrow account** and then uses the funds in the account, together with additions from your monthly payments, to pay your taxes and insurance premiums as they come due. Although two months' payment of each is usually collected at closing, your lender may require as many as six months' payment in advance, depending on when the tax and insurance bills are due. If your property taxes and homeowner's insurance total $1,200 per year, your monthly mortgage payment will be $100 = $1,200/12 more than your principal and interest alone, but you have to pay $200 to $600 at the closing to establish the escrow account. If these bills go up, your lender adjusts your payment amount.

▲ **Title insurance:** The seller has promised to give you ownership of the property you're buying. But what if the seller doesn't actually own it? The purpose of title insurance is to verify the seller's legal ownership of the property and to ensure that there aren't any other claims on the property that might interfere with the buyer's future ownership. The title insurance company researches this and identifies any problems so that they can be cleared up before closing. After you purchase, the title company protects you and the lender from any financial losses resulting from problems with the title. Rates for title insurance vary but are based on the value of the home.

SELF-CHECK

1. List some costs that you pay at a closing.
2. Define **closing** and **escrow account**.

SUMMARY

It's important to evaluate your home and auto needs and what you can afford before purchasing. You should consider your vehicle usage and then negotiate the best possible terms for your automobile. Similarly, you should decide on a home based on your financial goals and your present and future needs. You need to consider all the costs of homeownership before buying. It's important to shop around for the best terms and rates on your mortgage and to know how to qualify for the mortgage you want. If interest rates drop, you can consider refinancing.

KEY TERMS

Adjustable-rate mortgage (ARM)	mortgage loan with an interest rate that, by contract, varies over time with market conditions.
Agent	A person who is acting on behalf of another through a contractual agreement.
Assessment ratio	The proportion of market value used to calculate assessed value of real estate on which the property tax rate will be assessed.
Buyer broker	A real estate broker who works exclusively for the buyer and owes no legal duty to the seller.
Closing	A meeting to finalize a home purchase.
Commission	A percentage of the sales price paid to the brokers and agents who assist in the sale of a home.
Conventional mortgage	A fixed-rate, fixed term, fixed-payment mortgage loan.
Dealer's invoice price	The price that a dealer pays to purchase a new vehicle from a manufacturer.
Depreciation	The decline in value of an asset over time due to wear and tear, obsolescence, and competitive factors.
Discount points	Interest paid up front to a lender in return for a reduction in annual rate on a mortgage.
Escrow account	A reserve account held by a mortgage lender in which it collects a monthly prepayment of property taxes and insurance and then pays those bills as they come due.

Good faith estimate

An estimate of loan costs provided by the lender to the borrower.

Interest rate caps

Caps on annual and lifetime increases in an adjustable rate mortgage's interest rate.

Lease

A rental agreement between a lessor (i.e., the owner of a car or real property) and a lessee, in which the lessee agrees to pay money for the right to use the lessor's property for the period of the contract.

Lemon laws

State laws that protect consumers against chronically defective vehicles.

Lessee

A person who pays money for the privilege of using someone else's vehicle or real property for a period of time.

Lessor

An owner of an asset, commonly a vehicle or real property, who charges money for the use of that asset for a period of time.

Lock-in

Agreement with a lender that guarantees a particular mortgage interest rate at closing.

Mortgage

A long-term amortized loan that is secured by real property.

Negative amortization

An addition to a loan balance that occurs when the monthly payment is insufficient to cover the monthly interest cost.

Principal

A person who has delegated responsibility to an agent and to whom the agent has a duty.

Property tax

Local tax assessed on real estate that is proportional to value.

Refinancing

Obtaining a new mortgage to pay off a previous, usually higher-rate, mortgage.

Sticker price

The manufacturer's suggested retail price (MSRP) for a new vehicle, including manufacturer-installed accessories and options.

Warranty

A legal promise made by a seller, such as with respect to the qualities of a vehicle being sold.

ASSESS YOUR UNDERSTANDING

Go to www.wiley.com/college/bajtelsmit to assess your knowledge of automobile and housing decisions.

Measure your learning by comparing pre-test and post-test results.

Summary Questions

1. Which of the following is a variable operating expense of an automobile?
   (a) taxes
   (b) incremental insurance premiums
   (c) finance charges
   (d) toll fees

2. What is normally referred to as the sticker price on a new car is actually the:
   (a) manufacturer's suggested retail price.
   (b) dealer's invoice.
   (c) manufacturer's invoice.
   (d) dealer's retail price.

3. Which type of lease makes you responsible for any difference between the actual and estimated depreciation on the car you lease?
   (a) closed-end lease
   (b) open-end lease
   (c) contingent lease
   (d) depreciated lease

4. Which of the following is *not* a disadvantage of renting a home?
   (a) no tax deduction
   (b) no investment value
   (c) higher up-front fees
   (d) increasing costs over time

5. The square footage of a house is the most important determinant of its value. True or false?

6. The principal for whom a real estate broker works is the:
   (a) buyer.
   (b) seller.
   (c) agent.
   (d) intermediary.

7. Which of the following statements is true of adjustable-rate mortgages?
   (a) They generally carry higher initial interest rates than conventional mortgages.
   (b) They cannot be converted to fixed-rate loans.
   (c) The interest rate changes on ARMs are limited per year and per lifetime.
   (d) There is no limit on the amount of payment change on an ARM.
8. Which of the following mortgage loans does *not* have the possibility of negative amortization?
   (a) balloon mortgage
   (b) graduated payment mortgage
   (c) adjustable-rate mortgage
   (d) lender buy-down mortgage
9. A reserve account held by a lender used to pay property taxes and insurance as they come due is known as an escrow account. True or false?

Applying This Chapter

1. Joel looks up the value of his four-year-old vehicle and finds that the average resale value is $6,000. He paid $13,000 for the vehicle new. How much has it depreciated over the four years he has owned it, in percentage terms?
2. Explain to Joel (from Question 1) why it might have been a better idea to buy a one-year-old car than a new car.
3. All else being equal, do the following changes to an automobile lease contract increase or decrease your lease payment?
   (a) Increased gross capitalized cost
   (b) Increased residual value
   (c) Increased lease term
   (d) Increased finance charge
   (e) Increased mileage limitation
4. All else being equal, is each of the following likely to increase or decrease the price of the house you can afford to buy?
   (a) Increasing mortgage rates
   (b) Longer mortgage term
   (c) Higher gross income
   (d) Better credit history
   (e) Fixed-rate mortgage rather than adjustable
5. When interest rates are low but expected to increase in the future, is it better to take an ARM or a conventional mortgage? Explain.
6. Explain the effects of negative amortization and list the types of mortgages to which it applies.

Costs of Automobiles

Assume that you own a car that gets 20 miles per gallon on average. If you typically drive 16,000 miles per year and the price of gasoline goes up from $2.65 per gallon to $2.95 per gallon, what is your additional cost per year?

Rent vs. Buy

Maria is comparing two housing alternatives. She can rent an apartment for $800 per month, which equates to $9,600 per year. The security deposit is $1,200 (1[½] months' rent). Renter's insurance is $140 per year. Alternatively, she can buy a condominium and incur the following costs: annual mortgage payments, $7,200 (of which $5,966 is interest); property tax, $1,300; insurance and maintenance, $500; down payment and closing costs, $5,000; annual increase in value, $4,000.

She earns 2 percent on her savings account after tax, and her marginal tax rate is 25 percent.

1. Based on her first-year costs, which alternative will have a lower cost?
2. What would you recommend to Maria and why?

How Long to Recoup?

Go to the Bankrate.com Web site, at www.bankrate.com, and find the national average mortgage rates for a conventional 30-year mortgage loan with 1 point. Then go to the Lending Tree Web site, at www.interest.com, and click "Calculators" to find out how long it will take to recoup the cost of that 1 point, assuming that your loan is for $120,000.

8

INSURING YOUR HOME AND AUTOMOBILE
Managing Risk

Starting Point

Go to www.wiley.com/college/bajtelsmit to assess your knowledge of insuring your home and automobile.
Determine where you need to concentrate your effort.

What You'll Learn in This Chapter

▲ Homeowner's policies
▲ Insurance claims and features
▲ Auto insurance

After Studying This Chapter, You'll Be Able To

▲ Analyze how insurance works
▲ Assess your homeowner's or renter's property and liability risk exposures
▲ Select the right homeowner's or renter's insurance for you
▲ Compare your automobile insurance coverage requirements, options, and costs
▲ File claims for homeowner's or auto insurance

INTRODUCTION

Personal financial planning is all about risk management. Modern life is full of risks. Your house might be hit by lightning, or you might be the victim of a drunk driver. As many people learned in the stock market downturn of the early twenty-first century, you are also exposed to the risk of financial loss through your investments. When you buy insurance, you're paying a company to reimburse you for losses. You should shop around for both auto and homeowner's insurance, and you need to understand your risks.

8.1 How Insurance Works

Insurance companies are financial institutions that provide a valuable risk-spreading service by pooling premium dollars and using the money to pay losses incurred by policyholders during the policy period. In this section, we examine risk pooling and other basic insurance principles.

8.1.1 Risk Pooling and Insurance

The concept of risk pooling is based on the **law of large numbers,** which holds that, for large pools of identical risks, the risk that actual losses per person will be greater than predicted decreases as the size of the pool increases.

To better understand how an insurance pool works, consider a group of 1,000 homeowners, all in different cities in the United States. Each owns a home worth $150,000. Let's assume that each homeowner has the same risk of having his or her home destroyed by a fire: 1 in 1,000. On average, then, we can expect that 1 of these 1,000 homeowners will suffer the devastating loss of a home in the coming year. Now suppose all the homeowners got together at the beginning of the year, and each contributed an amount of money equal to his or her share of the pool's total expected loss of $150,000 (the value of one home). The cost to each would be only $150 ($150,000/1,000 = $150 per home). Then, at the end of the year, the person who experienced the loss could collect the money from the pool. If, however, two houses happened to burn down that year, the pool would not have enough funds to cover the $300,000 total loss. In that case, we could go back to the pool members and ask each of them to chip in another $150. Do you think everyone would pay up?

Suppose, instead, that the pool is even larger, perhaps 100,000 homeowners or more, as is the case with insurance company risk pools. The average individual share of the cost is still the same, $150. But the larger size of the pool means a reduced risk of deviations from the expected 100 claims per year. Furthermore, the insurer can charge each policyholder a little more than his or her share of the expected loss, enough to offset the small chance that losses in a given year will be greater than expected.

8.1.2 Insurance Premiums

The amount an insurer charges each policyholder for insurance protection is called a **premium.** In determining what premium to charge a policyholder, insurers estimate the expected loss by classifying policyholders according to their risk characteristics. Thus, for homeowner's insurance, people in rural mountain areas have a different **risk classification** than those whose homes are situated next to the local fire station. And homes with cedar shake siding are classified as riskier than those covered in fire-resistant stucco.

A riskier classification implies a higher expected loss and therefore normally results in a higher premium. If insurers can accurately classify policyholders and predict the losses of a pool, they can charge each policyholder a premium that is fairly close to that person's individual expected loss.

However, insurers also need to include charges for expenses and profit in the premiums they charge. Some insurers may be able to charge lower premiums than others because they are better at keeping their costs down. Sometimes, an insurer's premiums are lower because it has estimated expected loss differently than other insurers. In actual practice, it isn't always easy for insurers to estimate the average expected risk for a pool of policyholders.

FOR EXAMPLE

Insurers Cut Their Losses After Florida Hurricanes

Hurricane Andrew hit the Florida coast on August 24, 1992, and caused $26 billion in insured losses. More damage was caused by the terrorist attack of September 11, 2001 ($40 billion), and $30 billion was caused by Hurricane Katrina in 2005. The American insurance industry was ill prepared for Andrew, but by shifting its risk to reinsurers outside the country, minimized its losses for Katrina. According to the Los Angeles Times (April 5, 2006), during the 2004 hurricanes in Florida insurers covered roughly 50 percent, but by Katrina, they covered only about 30 percent, because of high flood damage, which private insurers don't cover. In 2004, the risk had not been factored into rates, and too many insurers had high concentrations of policyholders in coastal areas. In the wake of the Andrew, many insurers faced insolvency, others left the state, and rates increased sharply, although insurers claim rates are still too low. Major insurers such as Allstate have moved to limit their risk, including not approving homeowner policies in parts of the East and Gulf coasts.

Three types of risks are sometimes hard to insure because the nature of the risk makes it difficult to estimate expected losses, prevents the pooling mechanism from working, or limits how well the pooling mechanism works:

1. **Correlated risks:** These are risks that affect large numbers of policyholders at once in the same area (e.g., homes in floodplains, damage due to war or terrorism). The following example shows the extent to which this problem can be devastating to the insurance industry.
2. **Nonrandom risks:** These are risks that are within the control of the policyholder (e.g., intentional acts, suicide).
3. **Unpredictable risks:** These are risks that have potentially unlimited dollar losses and make it impossible to estimate the pool's expected loss with any certainty. Several categories of liability risk now fall into this category because of escalating jury verdicts for environmental damage (e.g., oil spills, chemical dumping, mold contamination) and certain types of liability.

8.1.3 Insurance Policies and Terminology

An insurance policy is a contract between you (the insured) and a financial institution (the insurer), in which you promise to pay a certain amount of money per period in return for the insurer's promise to pay for certain covered losses if they occur during the policy period.

An insurance policy explains all the rights and responsibilities of the parties to the contract. The law requires that insurance contracts be written clearly and in language that can be understood by people who don't have expertise in law or insurance. Nevertheless, these documents can be relatively complicated and difficult to comprehend. You need to read your insurance policies and understand your coverage. Many people put off doing this until they want to make a claim, only to find out that their loss isn't covered.

Insurance policies generally include terms intended to increase the predictability of the loss to the insurer and reduce premium costs to the insured. These include exclusions and limitations, incentives for hazard and loss reduction, and deductibles. An **exclusion** is a contract clause that specifically identifies losses that aren't covered under the policy at all. For example, your automobile insurance might exclude coverage for hail damage. Limitations may also be placed on specific categories of losses, such as a homeowner's insurance policy that covers a maximum of $1,000 for lost or stolen jewelry.

For an additional premium amount, most insurers offer supplemental coverage for limited or excluded items in the form of a contract addendum called a **rider.** The rates on this coverage can be substantially more expensive per dollar of coverage than on the rest of the policy. Property and liability policies commonly also include an upper limit on total losses, although you can usually increase the limit by paying an increased premium.

The basic purpose of insurance is to restore you to the financial condition you were in before a loss occurred. The **principle of indemnity,** which underlies insurance law, says that you should never be able to recover more from your insurance than what you've lost. Thus, even if you insure your $100,000 home for $120,000, the most you can recover from your insurance is $100,000. Similarly, if you have health insurance policies with two insurers, you can't collect for the same health expenses from both of them.

Insurers attempt to make premiums more affordable by incorporating elements in the insurance policy that reduce their expected losses. For example, your policy terms commonly include a **deductible,** which is an amount that you must pay out of pocket before the insurance company is obligated to pay anything. If your deductible is $250 and you have a $1,000 loss, you pay the first $250, and the insurer reimburses you for the rest. Policies with larger deductibles have lower premiums than those with small deductibles.

Some types of insurance (e.g., auto and homeowner's insurance) apply the deductible to each individual loss, and others (e.g., health insurance) require that you pay the deductible only once per year, after which the insurer compensates you for your losses. Some policies also place a cap on the total losses payable under the contract or on certain categories of losses. In general, the lower the cap, the lower the premium.

SELF-CHECK

1. Define **law of large numbers, deductible,** and **principle of indemnity.**
2. List the three types of risks that are uninsurable.

8.2 Managing Homeowners' and Renters' Risk

A home is the single largest asset that most families own. Home ownership has allowed U.S. households to benefit from steadily increasing real estate values. Home ownership is not risk free, however. Besides the financial risk of fluctuating real estate values (which can provide either loss or gain), homes are exposed to many risks of loss or damage (e.g., theft, fire, wind, rain) as well as the risks of financial losses arising from legal rules that hold homeowners responsible for injuries to visitors. Insurance can help homeowners pay the costs of both property risks and liability risks.

Homeowner's insurance generally protects the homeowner against property and liability risks. Even renters are subject to liability risk and to the risk of damage to or loss of personal property, neither of which is covered by the landlord's insurance policy, which insures only the building itself. For that reason, renters often purchase **renter's insurance,** which has coverage and terms that are similar to those of homeowner's insurance, except that the policies cover fewer risks.

Homeowner's insurance policies are designed to cover losses in one or more of the following risk categories:

▲ The risk that the physical building or its contents will be damaged by a covered event or peril, such as fire, rain, wind, hail, or other natural occurrence.

▲ The risk that personal property, either in the home or in another location, will be stolen or damaged by others.

▲ The risk of liability, or being held legally responsibility for another person's losses.

The first two categories are fairly clear-cut types of property risk exposures. In evaluating your exposure to property risks, the safety of the neighborhood you live in (e.g., crime rate, proximity to fire and police protection), your home's safety features (e.g., locks, alarm, smoke alarms, sprinklers), and your geographic location (e.g., wildfire area, hurricane zone, flood zone) are important.

In contrast, understanding your liability risk exposures requires that you have some additional knowledge about the law. What is liability risk? If a person or a person's property is injured on your premises, you may be held responsible for the loss. This usually occurs when the person sues you in a court of law to get you to pay for the injuries or losses.

The fact that you are sued, however, doesn't automatically mean you'll be held responsible. Generally, you're held financially responsible only when the loss was caused by your **negligence.** This requires that the injured person prove three things:

▲ You had a duty to that person.

▲ You didn't fulfill your duty.

▲ Your failure to fulfill your duty directly caused the other person or the person's property to suffer a loss.

If you're a homeowner, you have a duty to keep your property reasonably safe for people who come onto your property. For example, if you fail to clear your sidewalk of snow and your neighbor slips on an icy spot on the way to your front door, you may be responsible for the resulting medical costs. In a few rare situations, you may be held to an even higher duty. Most states have a special standard called **strict liability** that applies whenever children are injured by an "attractive nuisance" on your property—defined as a dangerous environment that might be attractive to children, such as a swimming pool or construction equipment. Strict liability holds you responsible for a child's injuries in this situation, even if you weren't negligent.

As in the snow shoveling example, pet owners are generally held strictly liable for injuries caused by pets that are known to be dangerous. In the past, dog owners often used the excuse that they didn't know their dog was dangerous because the dog had never bitten anyone before, but this doesn't always get people off the hook today. Many homeowner's insurance policies now exclude certain dog breeds from policies or deny coverage to dog owners.

Sometimes, you may be able to defend yourself against a negligence lawsuit by claiming that one of two legal rules applies:

▲ **Contributory negligence:** With **Contributory negligence,** the injured person actually contributed to his or her own injury. If the person is partly responsible, he or she may not be able to hold you financially responsible.

▲ **Assumption of risk:** If the injured person knew about the risk and voluntarily exposed him- or herself to it, you may be able to use the defense of **assumption of risk** to avoid legal liability.

Consider again the example in which you neglect to shovel your sidewalk after a snowstorm and your neighbor slips on the ice and is injured. The direct cause of the injury is your negligence in failing to clear the snow. But if your neighbor was running up the sidewalk in high-heeled shoes at the time, you could claim that she contributed to her own injury. And if the ice was clearly visible, you could argue that she had assumed the risk by stepping on the ice—in which case she wouldn't be able to hold you financially responsible.

If you understand these rules, you can protect yourself in advance from potential liability. For example, if you temporarily have a dangerous condition on your property, such as a pothole or a broken step on your porch, it's a good idea to warn your neighbors or put up a sign.

SELF-CHECK

1. Define **strict liability.**
2. What three things must be proven in a negligence action?
3. List two defenses against a negligence lawsuit.

8.3 Homeowner's Insurance Policies

All homeowners and renters are inevitably exposed to certain property and liability risks that could result in financial obligations to others. Although you can take certain actions (e.g., installing smoke alarms, clearing snow from your sidewalk) to reduce the potential frequency and severity of losses, you can't eliminate the risks entirely. Most homeowners and many renters choose to transfer some risk by buying insurance.

How do you choose the right insurance policy for you? How much insurance should you buy? How much does it cost? Homeowner's insurance contracts are standardized, making it easier to comparison shop. In this section, we compare different types of policies, explain the pricing of policies, and provide some guidelines to use in buying homeowner's insurance.

8.3.1 Homeowner's Insurance Forms and Coverages

In general, homeowner's insurance provides coverage for both property losses and liability losses, including damage to buildings, costs of additional living expenses while a home is being repaired, loss or damage to personal property, and financial losses due to liability for injuries to others or to their property.

There are six homeowner's policy forms (commonly labeled HO forms) that apply to different types of homes and cover different losses:

▲ **HO-1 Basic Form:** This type of insurance covers fire, lightning, windstorms, hail, explosions, riots, damage from aircraft or vehicles, smoke, vandalism, theft, glass breakage, and volcano damage. It is no longer sold in most areas.

▲ **HO-2 Broad Form:** This type of insurance covers all HO-1 perils, plus falling objects, weight of ice/snow/sleet, discharge of water/steam, pipes bursting from heat/cold, and electrical surge damage. It is no longer sold in most areas.

▲ **HO-3 All-Risk Form:** This type of insurance covers all perils except those excluded, including damage due to floods, earthquakes, war, and nuclear accidents.

▲ **HO-4 Renter's Contents:** This type of insurance covers all HO-2 perils but only covers contents, not buildings. The landlord's insurance covers the building and liability for the landlord's negligence.

▲ **HO-6 Condominium:** This type of insurance covers all HO-2 perils but only covers contents; it is similar to HO-4 for renters. The condominium association carries coverage for common areas and building.

▲ **HO-8 Older Home:** This type of insurance covers restoration but not necessarily with the same quality and detail as the original. It is designed for older or historic homes that have high replacement cost relative to market value.

All types of homeowner's insurance include coverage for personal liability, medical payments for guests, and additional living expenses during repairs. All the forms are divided into two parts: Section I, for property, and Section II, for liability.

Section I (Property Coverage)

When most people think of homeowners' risks, they tend to focus on the risk of fire because that's the most widely reported injury to homes. But homes are subject to damage from many other sources, and homeowner's insurance provides broad coverage for financial losses from most of these risks:

▲ **Buildings and structures:** The property coverage component of homeowner's insurance applies to financial losses due to damage or destruction of your property—most importantly, your house and any attached structures. Fire, lightning, windstorms, hail, explosions, and vandalism are examples of perils included under all policies. Also included is coverage for detached structures on your property and for landscaping, limited to 10 percent of the home's coverage. HO-4 Renter's Contents and HO-6 Condominium are the only forms that do not include this coverage. Usually, unless you pay an extra premium for replacement-cost insurance, your policy pays you the depreciated value of what you have lost. In places where home values are much lower than the cost of building new, this amount may be insufficient to rebuild. The HO-8 Older Home form is recommended if you have a historic home that would require much more expensive renovation to restore to its original value.

▲ **Personal property:** Personal property is covered regardless of where it was located at the time it was lost or stolen. Suppose you go to the bookstore to purchase textbooks, and you spend $500. Then your backpack, containing all your books, is stolen. Your homeowner's or renter's insurance would cover your loss, subject to the deductible. If your parents still claim you as a dependent, their homeowner's insurance is likely to cover the loss, even if you don't live with them. Personal property coverage is limited to 50 percent of the amount of insurance on the house, and specific categories of personal property may have individual limits. Pets are not considered personal property.

▲ **Living expenses:** If you're forced to leave your home due to an insured loss (e.g., fire or smoke damage), your policy covers reasonable living expenses during repairs, up to a limit of 20 percent of the insurance on the home. If you normally receive rental income from your property, the insurance also covers the lost rent.

Section II (Liability Coverage)

The United States has experienced an explosion of litigation recently, making it more important than ever before to purchase insurance protection to cover potential liability risks. Most homeowner's insurance policies provide $100,000 in basic personal liability coverage.

For minor injuries and accidents, policies include no-fault medical coverage in the amount of $1,000, as well as no-fault property coverage of $250. No-fault coverage, in this context, means the insurer pays the loss, without requiring that the injured party prove negligence. To see how the no-fault provision might apply, suppose your friend is visiting and trips on a rock in your driveway, breaking her arm and ripping her suit jacket, resulting in medical costs of $800 and property loss of $50. Your friend is reimbursed for her expenses without having to file a lawsuit. If your friend's injuries are more severe, perhaps resulting in the long-term loss of function of her arm, she may decide to sue you, in which case your policy covers the liability judgment up to the limit of $100,000. If your negligence causes someone to be severely injured on your property, it wouldn't be unusual for a jury verdict to be well in excess of the $100,000 liability limit. Then you would be held personally liable for the remaining amount.

It's often advisable to buy an **umbrella policy,** which comes with a limit of $1 million or more, to supplement your basic coverage, particularly if you have significant net worth. Umbrella coverage supplements your other liability coverage and also includes coverage for personal injury claims against you that wouldn't normally be covered under your homeowner's insurance, such as libel, slander, and invasion of privacy.

8.3.2 Pricing of Homeowner's Insurance

Insurers consider your risk factors in determining the base rate per $1,000 of insured property and then apply discounts, as appropriate. A separate (and much higher) rate per $1,000 of coverage is applied if you buy extra coverage for personal property such as jewelry or artwork.

The rate you are charged is primarily determined by characteristics of your home—its location, the amount of coverage (which usually depends on replacement cost or market value), the type of structure, and discounts. It's important to consider the relevant factors before buying a home. When you own a home with high risk factors, you can do little to change them. Insurers sometimes also consider your risk based on previous loss history and your credit rating.

This section looks at some of the risk factors you should consider.

Location

Your risk of property and liability loss is related to where your property is located. For example, wildfires are more common in the West than other places; wind damage is common in areas where tornadoes and hurricanes occur; and theft is common in certain urban areas. Even if you really love the idea of living in a rural mountain cabin, you may not be able to purchase property insurance at a reasonable price because if your house catches fire, it may be too far from

---

FOR EXAMPLE

The Risk of Mold

A recent development in homeowner's insurance is mold risk—the risk that mold contamination in a home, usually due to continued moisture and heat conditions, may cause damage to the structure and contents, as well as significant health problems for residents (e.g., asthma, migraines). Homes in high-humidity areas (e.g., Texas, Florida) have cost insurers millions of dollars in claims and litigation costs, resulting in increasing homeowner's premiums in those states. For this reason, more than half of all states have approved revised homeowner's policy forms that exclude coverage for mold.

---

available water sources and fire protection equipment. In May 2003, in anticipation of a drought-driven year of high wildfire risk, State Farm Insurance notified many of its rural customers in the Western part of the country that their insurance would not be renewed unless they took risk management steps suggested by fire authorities, including the clearing of land within a certain distance of the homes. Homeowners have similar problems obtaining coverage for beachfront properties in hurricane-prone areas.

Coverage Purchased

Insurance premiums are based on the **face amount** of coverage you select, which depends on the value of what you're insuring. Because the market value of your home includes both the building and the land (which can't be destroyed), your insurance should be based on the value of the structure alone (either replacement cost or market value, which are usually not equal). Although this can vary by geographic area, a common rule of thumb is that the land value is about one-fifth of the total market value of a home. For example, if you purchase a home for $150,000, you purchase less than $150,000 in coverage, perhaps $120,000, because you don't need to insure the land value. You shouldn't underinsure your home, however (e.g., buying $80,000 in coverage when you should buy $120,000). Most policies include a requirement that the face amount be at least 80 percent of the actual value. If not, the insurer proportionally reduces your loss reimbursement. For example, if you bought insurance that was two-thirds of the correct amount ($80,000/$120,000) and you incurred fire damage of $60,000 during the policy period, the insurer would only reimburse you for two-thirds of the damage, or $40,000. Your insurance agent can help you determine the amount of necessary coverage.

If you have a mortgage on your property, your lender requires that you carry coverage with a face amount at least equal to the amount of the mortgage.

A deductible is an amount that you must pay before the insurer will pay any losses. The higher the deductible chosen, the lower the premium. To keep your premium costs down, you should choose as high a deductible level as you can, retaining the risk of smaller losses that you can afford. Although the standard deductible is a fairly low $250, your premium is about 10 percent lower with a $500 deductible and about 30 percent lower with a $1,000 deductible. The reason that the premium drops so dramatically is that many claims on homeowner's insurance policies are for fairly small dollar losses. The deductible provision effectively removes these from coverage, so the insurer's estimate of expected losses on your policy is lower.

Limitations on Coverage

One of the ways insurers keep homeowner's insurance premiums affordable is to limit coverage for certain items—such as jewelry, collectibles, guns, and antique cars—and to allow additional coverage for those items, as desired. So people who need coverage can get it, but other policyholders don't share the cost unnecessarily. Most homeowner's policies provide coverage for jewelry and collectibles (e.g., artwork, comics, and antiques) up to a specified amount. For jewelry, the limit might be as low as $1,000, which is less than the value of many wedding rings. To get more insurance for your valuables, you pay a dollar amount per $1,000 value, and this rate is substantially higher than the rate on the rest of the policy. Also, you must usually make a specific list, or **schedule,** of the insured property; sometimes, you may need to get an appraisal to verify the value of the property.

In deciding whether to buy extra coverage for jewelry or other personal property, you should evaluate the probability of loss and the replacement cost to determine whether the cost is justified. Suppose it will cost $50 per year to insure your wedding ring; if you never take it off your finger, so the probability of loss is pretty low, the insurance may not be worth it. One of the factors to consider is that, if a loss occurs, the insurer reimburses only the item's resale value. Sentimental value isn't considered.

Characteristics of the Insured

Your own characteristics can affect your premium. If you are a nonsmoker, for example, you may get a lower rate because many house fires are caused by careless smokers.

Your previous loss history is also relevant. Your insurer can look up your loss history in a national electronic database for insurance claims, called the Comprehensive Loss Underwriting Exchange (CLUE), which can include all previous claims paid by auto and homeowner's insurers, as well as inquiries to insurers regarding losses that did not result in paid claims. If you have a clean record, the insurer considers you a better risk and may offer a lower premium. If you've had many losses, you may have difficulty getting insurance or at least have to pay more.

Also, a poor credit score affects the company's assessment of your risk and results in a higher premium.

Discounts

Insurers usually give discounts on insurance premiums for factors that are expected to reduce your losses. For example, if your home includes features such as smoke detectors, sprinklers, or fire extinguishers, it is judged to have a reduced risk of damage from fire. If your home has a security system, you may qualify for a discount because your risk of theft is reduced. Many insurers also give discounts to customers who have more than one type of insurance with the same company.

Characteristics of the Property

Your homeowner's insurance premium is affected by characteristics of your property. Your insurer considers factors that might increase its risk. An older home with expensive-to-replace moldings or a home that is in an obvious state of disrepair might be subject to higher premiums. Homes with pools and wood-burning stoves are considered higher, risks too. When you buy a home, you should ask the owner for a copy of the CLUE report to check for any problems with the home.

SELF-CHECK

1. Define **face amount** and **umbrella policy**.
2. List five risk factors that affect homeowner's insurance premiums.

8.4 Automobile Insurance

Unless you're into extreme sports, your riskiest behavior is probably driving. Although you may be a very good driver, each time you get behind the wheel, you're exposing yourself to others who are driving while talking on mobile phones, eating lunch, speeding, or—worst of all—driving while intoxicated. According to the National Highway Traffic Safety Administration, which tracks automobile accidents and encourages vehicle safety testing, auto accidents result in approximately 3 million injuries and 42,000 fatalities annually. With more than 200 million cars on the road, your risk of an accident resulting in injury is about 1.5 percent.

8.4.1 Managing Automobile Risks

When you're on the road, you risk injury to yourself, your passengers, and your vehicle, as well as injury to others resulting from your negligent driving. You can reduce your risk by owning a safe car, avoiding driving when intoxicated, and obeying traffic laws, but you should also protect yourself financially by carrying sufficient auto insurance.

All states have laws requiring car owners to carry at least a minimal amount of auto liability insurance. Most states have **compulsory automobile insurance laws,** which require proof of liability insurance to register your car, and all states have **financial responsibility laws,** which require drivers who have been in traffic accidents to show proof of insurance or the ability to pay a claim. The requirements vary by state; commonly, insurance must cover

▲ $20,000 or $25,000 per person in the accident
▲ $40,000 or $50,000 total for all people in the accident
▲ $10,000 or $15,000 for all property damage

Accordingly, insurers commonly quote rates by specified amounts of coverage for these three categories, as illustrated in Figure 8-1. Minimum insurance requirements differ significantly from one state to another and, usually, are insufficient to cover potential losses for serious traffic injuries.

For example, if you cause an accident that totals another person's car, the $10,000 minimum coverage applicable in more than half the states is not likely to be enough to cover the loss. In that situation, you are personally liable for the difference between the insurance coverage and the actual loss. Thus, when deciding on the coverage to buy, you need to consider your potential liability if an accident as well as the household resources that you put at risk if you underinsure.

Figure 8-1

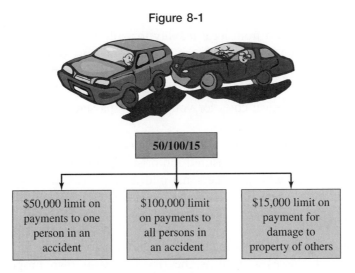

Automobile liability quotations.

Figure 8-2

Bodily injury coverage

Part A: Bodily injury liability
Part B: Medical expenses coverage
Part C: Uninsured motorist protection

Property damage coverage

Part A: Property damage liability coverage
Part D: Collision coverage
           Comprehensive physical damage
           coverage

Auto insurance coverage.

8.4.2 The Personal Automobile Policy (PAP)

Like homeowner's insurance, automobile insurance includes coverage for both property and liability risks. Each state has a standard automobile insurance contract form—the personal automobile policy (PAP) for individual coverage and the family automobile policy (FAP) for several people in a family who are driving the same car. The standardization of contracts helps make coverage comparable across companies. Figure 8-2 shows the components of coverage for these two types of policies under the categories of bodily injury coverage and property damage coverage.

Bodily Injury

Bodily injury coverage includes three types of protection:

▲ Part A protects you from legal liability for auto accidents by covering your financial costs (including the judgment against you, should you lose in court), your legal defense costs, and court costs. Part A covers liability losses for both bodily injury and damage to other people's property.

▲ Part B covers medical costs for you and any passengers injured in an accident.

▲ Part C, which is required in some states, covers injuries you incur in an accident caused by an uninsured motorist. Note that in most states, the costs associated with your personal injuries would be the responsibility of the at-fault driver (or that driver's insurer).

Property Damage

Your automobile property risk includes the risk that you will be liable for other people's property losses as well as the risk that your own property will be damaged or stolen. As noted, Part A of the PAP covers your liability for property damage to others. Coverage for loss or damage to your own property is optional under Part D of the PAP.

Part D includes both **collision coverage,** which insures you against loss or damage to your vehicle if you are in an accident, regardless of who is at fault, and **comprehensive physical damage coverage,** which covers loss or damage to your vehicle from any other peril (e.g., fire, theft, a falling object, hitting a deer on the road).

If you're in an accident caused by someone else, your collision coverage still pays you, but your insurer is entitled to recover the loss from the other driver's insurer. Under both collision and comprehensive coverage, the insurer's payment obligation is limited to the actual cash value of the vehicle and is usually subject to a deductible.

If the cost of repairing a vehicle exceeds its value, the insurer pays you the actual cash value and takes the vehicle (often referred to as "totaling the car"). It's not always smart to carry physical damage coverage on old reliable vehicles that have very low market value because any damage at all could result in the vehicle's being totaled.

Most lenders require property damage insurance coverage as a condition for a loan because they want to ensure that you'll maintain the value of the vehicle, which is collateral for their loan. They usually also require that they be named as an insured party on the policy.

8.4.3 No-Fault Auto Insurance

Suppose you're in an accident that was caused by the negligence of another driver. You sustain significant neck and back injuries, you miss work for several weeks, and your car is totaled. If the insurer for the other driver decides to contest the claim, how long do you think it will take to settle the dispute and get your losses paid?

If you have adequate health and disability insurance (or available sick days), your immediate medical costs and lost earnings may be covered, but you might spend years trying to get reimbursed for your other losses as the case moves through the overcrowded court system. For some people, particularly those with the most serious injuries and those without other sources of reimbursement, this can be a significant financial burden.

Beginning in the 1970s, many state legislatures attempted to help auto accident victims receive prompt compensation for their injuries by enacting **no-fault automobile insurance** laws, under which each driver looks to his or her own insurer to pay his or her economic losses, regardless of who was at fault in the accident. The intent of this type of insurance arrangement, commonly called personal injury protection (PIP), is twofold:

▲ Prompt (and adequate) compensation of accident victims.
▲ Reduced premiums for state residents for the reduction in litigation costs.

FOR EXAMPLE

Shopping for Auto Insurance Can Save You Money

Anna is a 21-year-old college senior. After getting notice of a premium increase in 2003, she decided to shop around before renewing. She requested quotes from six major insurers, specifying the minimum state insurance requirements with a $500 deductible and giving each insurer the same information on her car, her perfect driving record, and her good-student status. Monthly premium quotes ranged from $115 to $250. This shows something that has long been true: Auto insurance premiums vary widely for essentially the same product. Anna called only well-known companies with reputations for good service, but a nationwide survey by Progressive Insurance in 2000 found an average price variance of $586 per six months. Most of those surveyed said they were unwilling to shop around, although younger people and men were more likely to do so.

Unfortunately, no-fault laws have fallen short of the mark in achieving these objectives. Although allowed economic loss benefits generally include medical expenses and lost wages, subject to a maximum, the adequacy of the statutory benefit limit varies widely across states. Furthermore, health care costs have been rising at a much faster rate than inflation, which has translated into increasing premiums for the medical cost component of no-fault auto insurance.

No-fault insurance has also failed to significantly reduce litigation costs, mainly because state legislatures have left open the opportunity for an injured person to sue for damages in excess of the no-fault limits. In most no-fault states, if an injury exceeds a verbal threshold ("accidents resulting in death or dismemberment" or "serious bodily injury") or a monetary threshold ("economic loss in excess of $2,000" or some other dollar amount), the injured person can go to court to seek compensation for pain and suffering and other unreimbursed losses.

Because the largest cost savings under no-fault insurance are achieved when litigation is significantly reduced, the fact that most no-fault states still allow injured parties to collect from their own insurer and sue the other driver has limited the usefulness of the no-fault system. The problem, according to public policy experts, is not in the concept but rather in the implementation. Rising premiums and public dissatisfaction have led several states to modify their no-fault systems or scrap them altogether. Today, only 12 states and the District of Columbia have no-fault laws.

8.4.4 Auto Insurance Premiums

As with other types of insurance, premiums for auto insurance are intended to cover the insurer's expected losses and expenses and generate a reasonable amount of profit. Expected losses are determined by the company's assessment of each policyholder's risk level. The following are the factors that insurers most commonly use in measuring your risk:

▲ **How much you drive:** The more you drive, the higher your probability of being in an accident. If you drive only occasionally, you should pay a lower premium than if you're a salesperson who drives 30,000 miles annually. Although some vehicles are being tested with global positioning system (GPS) technology that can report this information to insurers, insurers currently don't have a perfect method for assessing how many miles you drive each year. They must use other factors that they know are correlated with miles driven. For example, you probably already know that young female drivers pay lower auto insurance rates than young males. What's less commonly known is that this isn't because women are better drivers—it's because teenage girls drive less, on average, than teenage boys. Because insurers can't accurately measure how much you drive (and people, if asked, are likely to underreport their actual mileage), gender acts as a proxy for miles driven for this age group. Similarly, most insurers give discounts for multiple cars in the same household, on the principle that you'll be driving each one less than if you only had one car.

▲ **How well you drive:** Having many accidents or tickets negatively affects your premium. The more serious the violation, the bigger the impact. For example, charges for driving under the influence (DUI) and driving while intoxicated (DWI) are treated very seriously. A second offense is likely to result in cancellation of your policy. In general, insurers consider only your recent driving record (the past three years), so you can eventually have lower premiums if you don't continue to break the law.

▲ **Your risk characteristics:** Insurers have found that people who are responsible in other areas of life are also better drivers. For years, they've given good-student discounts to students who have a B average or better and to new drivers who successfully complete a driver education course. Married couples often get lower rates than singles. Many insurers give better rates to nonsmokers, too. As with homeowner's insurance, credit reporting information is also a factor: The worse your credit rating, the higher your premium.

▲ **Where you drive:** Auto insurance rates depend on your address. If you live in New Jersey and regularly use congested roadways, you pay higher rates, on average, than if you're a rural customer in Wyoming, where there are few other cars on the road at the same time as yours. Drivers in Utah enjoy lower rates than other areas because of the low incidence of alcohol and substance abuse in that state.

▲ **What type of vehicle you drive:** Certain makes and models of cars are more subject to theft than others, so premiums for their coverage are higher than for other cars. Also, foreign cars and rare collectible cars are more expensive to repair than domestic ones, so they cost more to insure. On the other hand, you may be eligible for discounts if your vehicle has air bags, antilock brakes, or other safety features.

▲ **Who your insurer is:** Premiums for auto insurance vary widely. Some insurers charge as much as double what others do for the same policy terms and limits. This range exists partly because companies have different costs, but it also results from the fact that companies operate in a highly competitive market in which consumers are reluctant to switch insurers for small reductions in premiums. New companies entering an area must heavily undercut established firms to build their business. They know they'll lose money in the first few years, but they expect to make up the difference in investment returns and be able to charge higher premiums later on, without great risk of customer cancellation. Although such competition might seem to offer an opportunity to get a good deal on auto insurance, remember that any firm pricing its policies at a loss may go bankrupt before it can make it to the profitable years. The company is thus more likely to skimp on service and to deny otherwise payable claims to cut costs. It's important to consider reputation and financial solvency ratings when choosing an insurer.

8.4.5 What to Do If You Have an Auto Accident

Even if you have so far avoided having an auto accident, the odds are that eventually you'll have one. Taking the correct steps can save you trouble and make the process of filing an insurance claim run more smoothly. Immediately following the accident, you should take the following steps:

1. Stop your vehicle and wait at the scene of the accident for police officers.
2. If you or someone else on the scene has a mobile phone, call 911 to report the accident and seek medical assistance for anyone who is injured. Otherwise, send someone to the nearest phone to seek help.
3. Exchange names, addresses, phone numbers, and insurance information with the other driver or drivers.
4. Obtain contact information for any witnesses.
5. When police officers arrive, provide information that they request but do not admit fault.
6. Obtain a copy of the police report.

SELF-CHECK

1. Identify the difference between no-fault insurance and negligence.
2. Define **financial responsibility laws** and **comprehensive coverage**.
3. What are five factors that affect the price of auto insurance premiums?

8.5 Buying Insurance and Filing Claims

The following are the steps to follow in buying property and liability insurance:

1. Determine how much coverage you need (e.g., structure, personal property, potential liability, household resources at risk).
2. Identify the top insurers and agents in your area.
3. Call the top insurers and agents for price quotes on the coverage you need.
4. Choose the best package, considering the discounts offered.
5. Reevaluate at least annually and with changes in property owned, personal risk characteristics, or premium increases by your insurer.

Whether you're purchasing auto, homeowner's, or renter's insurance, you must choose an agent, get price quotes, and select the best policy.

8.5.1 Finding Agents and Insurers

You can buy auto insurance directly from an insurance company or through an insurance agent, who may also be called a *broker* or *producer*. An insurance agent can be an **exclusive** (or captive) **agent,** who works directly for a specific insurer and sells only that insurer's products, or an **independent agent,** who sells insurance products for a number of different insurers.

You should consider the trade-offs between service and cost. Selling insurance directly is less expensive for the company than selling through an agent, who must be paid a commission. But you may find that a commissioned agent provides you with better, more personalized, service, helping you through the claims process, and ensuring you maintain adequate insurance over time. In deciding between insurance agents, you should consider the recommendations of friends and relatives, as well as the agents' experience and certifications.

To evaluate insurance companies, you can consult A. M. Best's Key Rating Guide on Property and Casualty Insurers, available on the A. M. Best Web site, at www.ambest.com. A company that consistently has high ratings is unlikely to become insolvent in the near future and so will be around to pay your claims. You can check on an insurer's financial strength at www.moodys.com or www.ambest.com.

8.5.2 Getting Price Quotes

One way to get insurance price quotes is to call local agents and insurers. Also, you can contact the many internet sources for auto and homeowner's insurance. You need to be sure the price quotes you receive are all comparable, so you should make sure to provide all the companies with the same information and request quotes on policies that have the same limits and deductibles.

You can get insurance price quotes on the Web at www.insquote.com, www.insweb.com, and www.quotesmith.com. For insurers that don't use agents, such as Geico (www.geico.com), Erie (www.erieinsurance.com), and USAA (www.usaa.com), you can also go directly to the insurer's Web site for a quote. When you've collected all your information, you can weigh the price quotes against differences in quality and service. You can use Worksheet 19 in the Personal Financial Planner in the Appendix to compare quotes.

8.5.3 Making a Claim on Your Insurance

If you have suffered a loss that you think is covered by your insurance policy, you must decide whether you want to file a claim. Unless it's a very small loss, it's probably worthwhile to file, but you need to consider the impact the claim will have on your future insurance premiums.

If you decide to make a claim, you should take the following steps:

1. **Promptly notify your insurance agent or insurer and follow his or her directions:** This usually involves filling out forms, providing a copy of the police report in the case of an accident or theft, and taking steps to minimize further damage or loss.

2. **Document your losses:** Documentation can include photos, receipts for lost or stolen items, a written description of the event, names and addresses of witnesses, and other information that verifies your loss.

3. **Document the progress of the claim:** You should keep copies of all records, phone calls, letters, and other materials you submit to the insurer and anything that supports your claim.

4. **Don't sign anything:** You should refrain from signing anything that limits your ability to receive further payment from the insurer until you're satisfied that the entire claim has been paid. The insurer commonly designates a person, called a **claims adjuster,** to assess whether your loss is covered under your policy and to assign a dollar amount to the loss. If you disagree with that assessment, you may need to provide independent evidence of the value of your loss (e.g., a repair estimate from your local auto body shop). It's not uncommon for an insurance adjuster to offer to settle a homeowner's claim fairly promptly following a fire or theft loss by writing a check on the spot. Although it may be tempting to take the money and run, homeowners often later discover that additional items

have been damaged or stolen, so it's a good idea to let some time pass before agreeing to a final settlement.

SELF-CHECK

1. Differentiate between an exclusive agent and an independent agent.
2. Define **claims adjuster.**
3. List the steps to follow in filing a claim.

SUMMARY

When you buy insurance, you pay a premium in return for the insurance company's promise to reimburse you for covered losses that occur during the policy period. Insurance companies classify policyholders according to their risk characteristics and charge higher premiums to those with higher risks.

If you own or rent a home, you are exposed to both property and liability risks. Your homeowner's insurance is meant to reimburse you for financial losses that arise out of covered perils in the policy, such as theft, wind, rain, and fire, as well as the risk that someone who comes onto your property will sue you for injuries to person or property. The major determinants of homeowner's insurance premiums are the characteristics of the home, the insured person, and the policy coverage selected.

Driving a car exposes you to risks of bodily injury and loss of property, as well as liability risk for injuries you cause to the person and property of others. The major determinants of auto premium costs are how much you drive, your driving record, your risk characteristics, your geographic location, and the vehicle you're insuring.

KEY TERMS

Assumption of risk	A defense to a claim of negligence that is available when the injured party voluntarily took on the risk.
Claims adjuster	A person designated by an insurer to assess whether a loss is covered by the insured's policy and to assign a dollar value to the loss.
Collision coverage	Insurance that covers loss or damage to the insured's vehicle caused by an automobile accident.

Comprehensive physical damage coverage	Insurance that covers loss or damage to the insured's vehicle caused by a peril other than an automobile accident.
Compulsory automobile insurance laws	State laws that require proof of liability insurance as a prerequisite to auto registration.
Contributory negligence	A defense to a claim of negligence that is available when the injured party contributed to his or her own injury.
Deductible	The amount of a loss that must be paid by an insured before the insurance company will pay any insurance benefit.
Exclusion	A potential loss that is expressly excluded from coverage by an insurance policy.
Exclusive agent	An insurance agent who sells products for only one insurer. Also called a captive agent.
Face amount	The value of assets insured under a policy.
Financial responsibility laws	State laws that require proof of ability to cover the cost of injury to persons or property caused by an auto accident.
Homeowner's insurance	Insurance purchased by a homeowner to cover property and liability losses associated with a home.
Independent agent	An insurance agent who sells products for multiple insurers.
Law of large numbers	A principle which holds that, for large pools of identical risks, the risk that actual losses per person will be greater than predicted decreases as the size of the pool increases.
Negligence	A failure to fulfill a legal duty to another that causes injury to that person or to his or her property.
No-fault automobile insurance	A type of automobile insurance system in which each insured driver in an accident collects his or her claim from his or her own insurer, regardless of who is at fault.
Premium	The price an insurer charges a policyholder for insurance protection.
Principle of indemnity	The principle that insurance reimburse a policyholder only for actual losses.

Renter's insurance	Insurance purchased by a renter to cover personal property and liability losses but not damage to the building itself.
Rider	An addendum to an insurance policy that requires payment of an additional premium in return for additional specified insurance coverage.
Risk classification	The categorization of policyholders by characteristics that affect their expected losses; insurers use risk classification to price policies fairly.
Schedule	A list of otherwise excluded valuables that are to be covered under a homeowner's or renter's policy for an additional premium.
Strict liability	A rule of law that holds a person liable for damages without proof of negligence.
Umbrella policy	A supplemental personal liability insurance policy.

ASSESS YOUR UNDERSTANDING

Go to www.wiley.com/college/bajtelsmit to assess your knowledge of insuring your home and automobile.

Measure your learning by comparing pre-test and post-test results.

Summary Questions

1. The concept of risk pooling is based on:
   (a) the laws of probability.
   (b) the law of averages.
   (c) the law of large numbers.
   (d) statistical variation.

2. An oil spill is an example of:
   (a) a correlated risk.
   (b) a nonrandom risk.
   (c) an unpredictable risk.
   (d) an escalating risk.

3. Correlated risks are risks that affect large numbers of policyholders at once in the same area. True or false?

4. If Tom drives into Bill's car when Bill falls asleep at the wheel and veers into Tom's lane, Bill's actions are an example of:
   (a) negligence.
   (b) an assumption of risk.
   (c) double indemnity
   (d) contributory negligence

5. If a visitor to your home decides to climb on your roof and jump off, this is known as:
   (a) an assumption of risk.
   (b) an attractive nuisance.
   (c) contributory negligence.
   (d) involuntary negligence.

6. Which of the following types of homeowner's policies provides coverage for renters?
   (a) HO-2
   (b) HO-3
   (c) HO-4
   (d) HO-6

7. Which of the following should you do in order to increase your personal liability coverage?

    (a) decrease your deductible

    (b) purchase an omnibus policy

    (c) institute a self-insurance program

    (d) purchase an umbrella policy

8. If you are married and do not smoke cigarettes, you probably have a lower auto insurance premium than if you were single and a smoker. True or false?

9. If your auto insurance provides coverage for a tree falling on your car as it sits in your driveway, you have:

    (a) bodily injury liability.

    (b) property damage liability coverage.

    (c) collision coverage.

    (d) comprehensive physical damage coverage.

10. An insurance agent who works directly for a specific insurer is known as a captive agent. True or false?

Applying This Chapter

1. A classmate suggests that you can save money on renter's insurance by forming a risk pool. All 100 students in the class agree to contribute money to the pool and agree that anyone who experiences loss or damage to personal property in his or her place of residence can make a claim on the pool's funds over the course of the year. How would you decide how much money to charge each person in the class? Is it fair to charge everyone the same amount?

2. Suppose that last year you formed the risk pool described in Question 1. If, at the end of the year, it turns out that the total losses to the group were larger than the amount of money in the pool, what could you do? What are some potential problems associated with this arrangement?

3. Denise is a college student who rents an apartment with three other students. She has just completed a course in personal finance and thinks that she and her roommates should purchase renter's insurance. Help her to convince her roommates by identifying some risks that might subject her and her friends to financial losses.

4. Identify whether each of the following will likely increase or decrease your homeowner's or renter's insurance premium:

    (a) You buy a more expensive home.

    (b) You acquire a valuable comic book collection.

    (c) You move to a high-crime area.

    (d) Your home is made from fire-resistant materials.

    (e) You have a bad credit history.

5. You rear-end another driver at a stoplight because you are talking on a mobile phone and don't see the light change. Your hefty SUV has about $600 in damage to the front bumper, but the sports car you hit is so seriously damaged that the cost of the repairs ($18,000) exceeds the value of the car ($17,000). Also, the other driver suffers a neck injury, which may have long-term consequences. You have a PAP with limits of 50/100/15 and a collision deductible of $250. What coverages apply, and how?

6. How does no-fault insurance work, and why should it be expected to reduce the costs of automobile insurance?

Not-So-Happy Holidays

During the holidays, David and Mary Costanza's Christmas tree caught fire, and they sustained significant damage to their home and personal property. They had to clean and repaint their living room and replace the living room carpet and furniture for $7,000. While the work was being done, the family stayed in a motel for three days, at a total cost of $300. The Costanzas had an actual cash value homeowner's insurance policy with a deductible of $250. The insurance company's adjuster came to the Costanzas' home and looked at the damage. He estimated the actual cash value of the furniture, hand-me-downs from Mary's parents, at $750 and of the carpet, which had needed to be replaced for some time, at $350.

1. How much do you estimate the insurer will pay the Costanzas?
2. If the Costanzas had purchased replacement cost insurance, how much would they have received from their insurer after the loss?

Picture This

Carrie Chandler is a professional photographer and earns $50,000 before taxes. Carrie has been fairly diligent about establishing a financial plan and working toward achieving her financial goals. Two years ago, she bought a condominium, and it has appreciated sufficiently that she has $40,000 in home equity. She has also accumulated $25,000 in savings and paid off her student loan. Recently, Carrie paid off the balance on the automobile loan for her 2002 vehicle. After looking at Carrie's financial situation, her insurance agent suggests that she consider increasing her automobile insurance coverage. Her current coverage is $25,000 Part A bodily injury liability per person, $50,000 per accident, and $15,000 property damage liability. She also has Part B medical expense coverage of $10,000 per person and uninsured motorist protection of $25,000 per person, and $50,000 per accident. She has been carrying property damage insurance on the car.

1. Given the value of Carrie's household assets, what auto insurance liability limits would you recommend? Explain.
2. Assuming that Carrie's car is in fairly good condition and is worth $10,000, should she carry property damage insurance and, if so, what type(s) and in what amount(s)?

Reduce Your Premiums

Go to www.quicken.com/insurance and get some tips on how to save on your insurance premiums. Take the quizzes to see how you're doing.

9

HEALTH AND DISABILITY INSURANCE
Protecting Your Health

Starting Point

Go to www.wiley.com/college/bajtelsmit to assess your knowledge of health and disability insurance.
Determine where you need to concentrate your effort.

What You'll Learn in This Chapter

▲ Types and features of health insurance plans
▲ Disability income needs
▲ Disability income insurance policies

After Studying This Chapter, You'll Be Able To

▲ Evaluate the types of health insurance plans and understand their features
▲ Calculate your disability income needs and select appropriate insurance
▲ Incorporate employer-sponsored retirement plans in your financial plan

INTRODUCTION

Because salary and employee benefits can differ radically between employers, don't take a job without carefully considering the value of the benefits being offered. Remember, employer-provided benefits may make it easier to achieve your other financial goals and to avoid financial crises caused by health and disability risks. In this chapter, we discuss how to evaluate your needs and choices in health insurance and disability insurance. (Life insurance is covered in Chapter 10.) Don't underestimate your risk of needing disability insurance at some point.

9.1 Employee Compensation and Health Insurance

When weighing job offers, the most obvious component of a package is, of course, the salary or hourly wage. But many jobs offer much more in the form of employee benefits, sometimes called fringe benefits. These may include tangible benefits, such as various types of insurance or retirement contributions, as well as intangible elements, such as flexible hours or a pleasant working environment. Take into account all the components of an employment opportunity and estimate the value of the total package before making your decision. In this section, we identify the different types of benefits you might expect and explain the advantages of group provision of certain types of benefits.

9.1.1 Why Benefits Are Preferable to Cash Compensation

Employee benefit packages commonly include vacation and sick days, various types of insurance (health, dental, vision, disability, and life), and retirement plans. Whether your employer will offer any or all of these options depends on the employer's size, the type of employment, and competitive factors. Benefits are sometimes completely paid for by the employer, in which case they're said to be noncontributory. If, instead, you're required to pay some or all of the cost yourself, the benefit plan is called a **contributory plan.** Some employers offer a **cafeteria plan,** in which they provide a sum of money to be used for benefits but allow you to choose the benefits you need from a menu.

Although some employers offer benefits to employees for purely altruistic reasons, in general, competition is the driving force. If a firm is able to provide something that employees value, it will be able to attract the most highly qualified workers and will benefit from reduced turnover and increased employee loyalty, productivity, and job satisfaction. If there are additional advantages of receiving compensation in the form of group benefits, such as tax savings, reduced costs, and better coverage, employees will value the benefits even more.

Let's illustrate the advantages of benefits over cash with the following example. Suppose you're considering two employment opportunities. Company A is offering a salary of $26,000 and fully paid health insurance. Company B is offering a salary of $30,000 and no health insurance. If you take the Company B job, you'll have to purchase individual health insurance on your own. Since both companies are competing in the same market, we'll also assume that the cost to Company A of providing you with health insurance is $4,000 per year, so that the two companies have identical total compensation costs.

Which one would you choose? The reasons you might prefer the job with the benefits rather than the extra salary are related to the advantages of group insurance, availability of private market insurance alternatives, and taxes, as discussed in Section 9.1.2.

9.1.2 Advantages of Group Insurance

Group insurance is insurance purchased on a group basis by an employer for the benefit of employees. The primary advantages of group insurance are related to **group underwriting** and cost. Insurance companies normally consider your individual risk characteristics before selling you an insurance policy, using a process called underwriting. If you have higher risk of auto accidents, you pay a higher rate for your insurance, for example. (See Chapter 8 for more information on auto insurance.)

This is not the case, however, with group insurance. When an insurer insures a group, as in the case of health, disability, or life insurance offered through an employee benefit plan, the individuals in the group are not individually considered for insurability. Since the contract is with the employer rather than the individuals, there is a single application for the entire group, and the insurer's decision is based on the risk of the group as a whole, rather than on characteristics of individual group members.

Members of the group are also protected from the risk of policy cancellation due to changes in their individual risk characteristics during the period of employment. So, for example, if you were diagnosed with a chronic illness, such as cancer or multiple sclerosis, you would continue to have insurance coverage, and the insurer couldn't raise your premium (unless it raised the premiums for the entire group).

Group insurance may offer some cost advantages as well. In general, the administration of a group insurance plan is cheaper for an insurer than individual insurance, and these cost savings can be passed on to the employer and employee. Let's go back to the example given in Section 9.1.1, where Company A is paying the entire health insurance premium and Company B isn't. Could you buy the insurance yourself for the $4,000 salary difference if you took the Company B job? If you're young and healthy, it's possible you could buy comparable health insurance in the private market for less, but if you're older or in poor health, you might find private market alternatives to be much more expensive than $4,000. Similarly, if your employer offers a contributory plan, you'll pay a portion of the per-person group premium, but you'll be paying the cost of the *average* risk in your group. Again, this may be more or less than what you'd pay in the private market, depending on your age and health.

If you participate in a group plan through your employer, you'll enjoy some tax savings as a result. Current tax law allows you to receive qualified employee benefits tax-free, subject to some limits. This applies to the whole cost of the insurance, even when your employer requires you to pay some or all of the premium. So, if your insurance premium is $5,000 and your marginal tax rate is 30 percent, the effective cost of that insurance is only $5,000 \times (1 - 0.3) = \$3,500$.

Whether you participate in an employer plan or purchase individual insurance, however, health insurance is important, because illnesses and injuries can place a tremendous financial burden on your family. Health insurance provides protection against unexpected costs due to illness, accident, or disability. This works in the same way as property and liability insurance, discussed in Chapter 8. Because a particular individual's health-related expenses are not correlated with those of other individuals (except in rare cases of health epidemics such as meningitis, SARS, and AIDS), insurers can pool these risks and spread the cost over many policyholders. Insurers use statistical data to estimate future costs and charge premiums sufficient to cover their expected losses and expenses.

9.1.3 Expected Health Costs

You should begin this component of your financial plan with a realistic estimate of your expected health costs, taking into consideration your family situation and national trends in the costs of medical care. National statistics suggest that more than 40 million people in the United States have no health insurance at all. Although it's true that your risk of experiencing a large health loss is relatively small, particularly if you're currently young and healthy, you don't want to be among those without health insurance. Even regular, predictable medical expenditures, such as annual diagnostic tests, prescription drugs, and office visits for minor illnesses, can rapidly deplete household resources.

As with auto and homeowner's insurance, discussed in Chapter 8, the high administrative costs of insuring small, predictable health costs make it preferable to budget for them rather than insure them. However, budgeting for more serious health problems is another matter. Specialists commonly charge $250 or more for office visits. Regular ambulance services may cost $1,000 or more, and a helicopter ambulance can run as much as $10,000 for one trip.

If you require hospitalization, you can expect to pay several thousand dollars per day—more if you require intensive care. If you have or plan to have children, you can expect to incur costs every year for illnesses, injuries, and wellness care. Having a new baby can be surprisingly expensive. Not including costs for the obstetrician, anesthesia, and hospitalization for the birth, the first-year costs for recommended office visits and immunizations average $1,200 per child.

For some people, expected health-care costs are higher than average because of a family history of cancer, diabetes, or heart disease. In assessing your potential health-care needs, consider your family history, even if you haven't been diagnosed with a particular illness.

9.1.4 National Trends in Health Costs

Even if you're relatively healthy, you can expect your medical care and health insurance costs to rise. For a variety of reasons, including increased quality of care and escalating prescription drug prices, medical costs and health insurance premiums have increased at an alarming rate over the last two decades, and this trend is expected to continue.

As you can see in Figure 9-1, wage increases have not kept up with increases in health insurance benefit costs. Over the last two decades, health-care costs have increased at a much faster rate than wages and the prices of other goods and services. For example, despite a low overall inflation rate of 2.2 percent and average wage increases of only 3.1 percent between the spring of 2002 and the spring of 2003, monthly premiums for employer-sponsored health insurance during that time rose 13.9 percent, according to a Kaiser Family Foundation study.

Figure 9-1

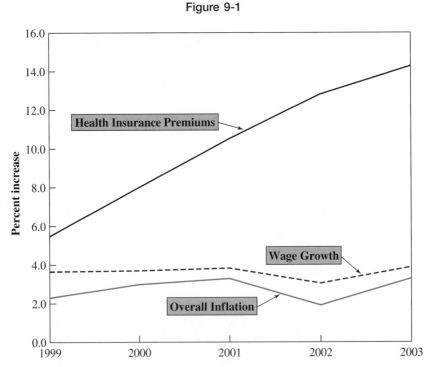

Increasing cost of employer-sponsored family health insurance coverage relative to wage growth and inflation.

Figure 9-2

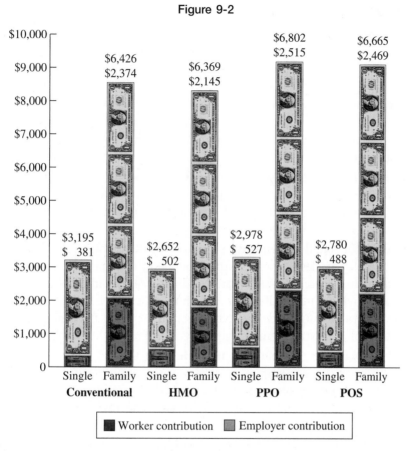

Average annual employer and employee share of health insurance costs, single and family coverage, 2003.

Although health insurance premiums have been rising steadily, the share paid by employers has so far remained relatively stable. Figure 9-2 shows the average dollar amounts paid by employers and employees, respectively, for different types of health plans in 2003. As you can see, employers paid most of the cost of single coverage for conventional health plans ($3,195 of the average $3,576 premium, or 89%) but a smaller percentage of the cost of family coverage ($6,426 of the $8,800 average premium, or 73%).

The average proportion paid by employers is likely to decline, particularly as smaller employers are finding it increasingly difficult to absorb the rapidly increasing costs. In addition, you can expect that employers will add cost-saving measures to their plan design, such as larger deductibles and more limitations on prescription drugs. All of this means that you can expect to pay a larger amount out-of-pocket than you have in the past.

9.1.5 Strategies for Controlling Health-Care Costs

The price you'll pay for medical services in the future is pretty much out of your control. However, there are some ways that you can reduce your expected future out-of-pocket costs for insurance premiums and other health-care expenses:

▲ **Invest in your own health**. Eat healthy, stay active, and don't smoke. If you're healthy, chances are you'll have reduced health expenditures over your lifetime and lower premiums for health, life, and disability insurance.

▲ **Choose an employer who offers generous health insurance benefits**. The best situation is one in which the employer pays the full cost, even for family coverage. But even if your employer's plan is contributory, group insurance is preferable.

▲ **Budget for small expenditures**. Health insurance plans with high deductibles are less expensive than low-deductible plans, and the difference in cost is greater than the difference in deductibles. So if you're paying part or all of the premium, you'll be better off opting for the lower-cost, higher-deductible option and paying the deductible instead of the extra premium.

▲ **Take advantage of beneficial tax rules**. Let the IRS pay part of your health costs. If your employer offers you the opportunity to set up a **flexible spending account (FSA)**, take advantage of it. These arrangements enable you to set aside some of your income pretax for the payment of qualified medical and child-care expenses. The funds can be used to cover health insurance deductibles and copayments as well as a wide range of medical, dental, and vision expenses that might not be covered under your health-care plan. (Health care costs paid for through an FSA cannot also be deducted on your tax return, but it is definitely worth considering. Although you're using your own money to pay these expenses, you're paying less than if you'd had to first pay taxes on that income. Under a new tax rule, you may be able to set up a **health savings account (HSA)** (formerly called a health reimbursement account or medical savings account), which operates similarly to an FSA in that contributions to the account are made from pretax dollars. The differences are that you can earn interest on the amounts in the account, the annual contribution limit is only $1,000 (whereas FSA limits are set by the employer and commonly allow $3,000 to $5,000 per year for medical), and you can roll over unused amounts from year to year.

▲ **Take advantage of opt-out rules**. Some employers allow you to "opt out" of their health plan and either give you the cash instead or allow you to apply it to other benefits. This is a good idea if you have better or cheaper coverage through your spouse's employer.

FOR EXAMPLE

Flexible Spending Accounts

Suppose you have a $600 deductible on your insurance and a marginal tax rate of 40 percent. You would normally have to earn $1,000 to accrue $600 in after-tax income to pay the deductible. By setting up the FSA and paying the deductible out of it, you can pay the deductible with pre-tax dollars and save $400 in taxes. That amounts to $400 more in your pocket. The downside to this beneficial tax rule is that the IRS doesn't allow you to recover or roll over excess dollars in the account at the end of the year. Therefore, the amount you put into the flexible spending account each year should be based on out-of-pocket expenses that you are fairly certain to incur, such as the cost of new eyeglasses or contacts, orthodonture, plan deductibles, over-the-counter medications, and any other regular expenses not covered by insurance.

In the future, your family's medical costs are going to take a bigger bite out of your budget than they do now, even if you're covered by a group plan at your place of employment. Your financial plan needs to take this into consideration. You can, however, keep your future costs down by maintaining a healthy life style and being a good consumer of both health care and health insurance. You also should understand your health coverage options and make choices that best meet your needs.

SELF-CHECK

1. Define group insurance, contributory plan, FSA, and HSA.
2. Is group insurance less expensive than individual insurance?
3. List the major national trends in health care.
4. Give five strategies for saving money on health insurance.

9.2 Types of Health Insurance

Many different types of group and individual health insurance plans are available in the marketplace today. You may have several to choose from at your place of employment. If your employer doesn't provide a health insurance benefit, you'll find hundreds of insurers that sell individual policies in the private market.

To select the right type of insurance for you and your family, you first need to understand the similarities and differences among the different health insurance arrangements. All types of health insurance have certain features in common. They all provide a mechanism for paying the medical care provider (doctor, hospital, or laboratory), whether through reimbursement to you for costs incurred or, more commonly, direct payment to the provider.

Health insurance plans differ in the limitations they place on membership, the services they cover, and the physicians they include. In this section, we examine the features of several types of private and government-sponsored plans. Private health plans are usually categorized as either:

▲ **Fee-for-service plan.** Sometimes called an indemnity plan, a fee-for-service plan reimburses for the actual medical costs incurred (sometimes subject to a limit). So, for example, if you have an x-ray or blood test, the bill is submitted to the insurer, and it pays the provider or reimburses you if you have paid the cost out of pocket.

▲ **Managed-care plan.** This type of plan controls your access to or use of medical services in an attempt to reduce plan costs. Two common examples of managed-care plans are a **health maintenance organization (HMO)**, which limits your selection of providers to those under contract with the plan, and a **preferred provider organization (PPO)**, which gives you financial incentives to use specific providers.

In 1990, most employment-based plans were fee-for-service plans, but today, the vast majority of employees are covered under managed-care plans, as shown in Figure 9-3. Such a large change in only a decade is the result of employers seeking lower-cost alternatives for providing health insurance benefits.

9.2.1 Fee-for-Service Plans

Traditional fee-for-service medical expense coverage is usually divided into two categories: basic health-care and major medical insurance. Another classification is comprehensive medical coverage, which is a special type of major medical. Both basic health-care and major medical insurance can be purchased on either a group basis or an individual basis, although about 90 percent of all medical coverage, including fee-for-service and other plan types, is group insurance.

▲ **Basic Health Care Insurance.** Basic health care insurance benefits include hospital, surgical, and physician expenses. These types of policies usually provide first-dollar coverage—that is, there's no deductible for the policyholder to pay. They may limit the types of expenses they cover, however, and have relatively low maximum dollar limits of protection. For example, a basic health care plan will commonly pay for x-rays and

Figure 9-3

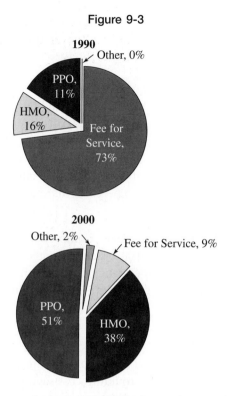

Percentage of full-time employees participating in employment-based health plans by plan type, 1990 and 2000.

lab tests if they're done in connection with hospitalization, but not if they're done in connection with an outpatient procedure.

▲ **Major Medical Insurance.** Major medical insurance adds to the protection offered by basic health insurance by providing coverage for additional expenses and a wider range of medical services. Plans typically have the following features:

- High maximum limits (such as $1 million). The **maximum limit** is the total amount of your covered expenses that an insurer will pay over your lifetime.

- Annual deductibles. The deductible amount might be as low as $250 per person or as high as $2,000 or more. Plans with deductibles set at very high levels are sometimes called catastrophic health insurance plans.

- Coinsurance provisions. Under a **coinsurance** arrangement, the insured person pays a percentage of his or her medical costs, often 10 to 30 percent, up to an annual out-of pocket limit, or **stop-loss limit.**

After your total covered out-of-pocket costs reach the stop-loss limit, the insurer will cover 100 percent of covered charges. Your required contribution is sometimes called a **copay.**

The objective of deductibles and coinsurance is to deter the overuse of medical services by putting you at some financial risk. While you, of course, would never intentionally break your arm, you might consider going to the doctor for a minor cold if you didn't have to pay any of the cost yourself. These provisions also keep down the overall costs of insurance by reducing the number of small claims, which generally involve disproportionately high administrative costs for processing and record keeping—costs that have to be passed on to the policyholders.

▲ **Comprehensive Medical Insurance.** Comprehensive medical insurance is similar to group major medical except that it usually carries a smaller deductible and covers a broader range of inpatient and outpatient services. The objective is to reduce the financial burden of medical costs for the insured.

9.2.2 Managed-Care Plans

The important thing to remember about managed-care plans is that the overall objective is to keep costs down by providing cost-saving incentives to providers and patients. Many types of managed-care plans are available today. Although the lines separating the different types are blurring, they are still primarily distinguishable by the type of arrangement made with the providers of medical services (doctors and hospitals). The major categories are:

▲ **Health Maintenance Organizations.** Health maintenance organizations (HMOs) were the original type of managed-care plan. HMOs attempt to control rising health-care costs by providing relatively comprehensive health insurance, encouraging preventive medicine (checkups, diagnostic tests, and immunizations), and giving health-care providers financial incentives to control costs. For example, a doctor who contracts with a plan might be given a fixed fee per participant per year regardless of the number of office visits, tests, and procedures. The HMO physician also commonly serves as a "gatekeeper" to other medical services; in other words, you must get a referral from your regular HMO physician to see a specialist or to be hospitalized. In a group practice plan, the doctors are actually employees of the HMO, combining medical care and insurance in one organization. The most common HMO arrangement today is an individual practice association made up of independent physicians who have their own practices, which include both fee-for-service patients and HMO participants. The advantage of this type of plan, compared with a group practice HMO, is that you may be able to continue with the same doctor if you switch from a fee-for-service plan to an HMO. The primary disadvantage of the HMO model of health care is that the patient often has a limited choice of physicians and limited access to specialist care. However, your out-of-pocket costs in an HMO (not including your share of the premium) will generally be lower than in a fee-for-service plan. HMOs normally do not require the payment of a deductible and usually charge only modest copays for office visits ($5 to $15 per visit), although the amounts can vary substantially by plan. HMO medical coverage tends to be very comprehensive, most notably in the area of preventive care, which can result in a huge cost saving for families with children. Whereas fee-for-service arrangements typically only cover medically necessary treatment for illness or injury and often exclude or limit certain types of costs (such as mental health services), the philosophy of HMOs is that early intervention can reduce the likelihood of more serious health-care problems later.

▲ **Preferred Provider Organizations.** A preferred provider organization (PPO) is a group of medical care providers who contract with the insurer to provide services at a reduced rate. If you have a PPO plan, you can get the benefit of this discount arrangement by using physicians and hospitals that are "preferred providers." Typically, you will still have coverage when you use a health-care provider that doesn't belong to the plan, but you'll pay a larger share of the cost. For example, once you've paid your deductible, the insurer might pay 90 percent of your expenses when you use a participating provider but only 70 percent if you use a nonparticipating provider. Because the providers are usually paid according to the services they provide, this type of plan looks something like a traditional fee-for-service insurance plan. It is also similar to the HMO model, however, in that limitations on choice result in lower costs.

▲ **Other Managed-Care Alternatives.** A fairly new entrant into the health plan market, a point of service (POS) plan is similar to a preferred provider organization in that it allows participants to seek treatment from both participating and nonparticipating providers but requires greater cost-sharing in the latter case. The advantage of a POS plan is that the participating physicians are affiliated with an HMO, so the coverage is more comprehensive than in PPOs or fee-for-service plans, and copays are smaller. Another alternative is the exclusive provider organization (EPO). An EPO is like a PPO in that it negotiates discounts with certain providers. The difference is that if you don't use an affiliated provider, the plan doesn't pay any of your costs. This type of arrangement is sometimes used for prescription drug plans.

9.2.3 Consumer Choice Plans

A consumer choice plan attempts to control health costs by giving consumers incentives to control their own costs. In the other health insurance arrangements we've discussed, if you go to the doctor and she tells you that you need a particular procedure or prescribes a certain medicine, you have little incentive to say "Are there any cheaper alternatives?" In fact, if you have full coverage, you may actually have the incentive to buy the most expensive health care, to ask for more tests, and to generally overutilize medical providers.

Consumer choice plans, sometimes called consumer-directed health care, attempt to address this concern by making you more sensitive to the cost of medical care and thus wiser in deciding what care to receive, when, and from whom. The For Example, "Winning by Losing: Insurance Incentives for Weight Loss," shows how consumer choice plans are particularly well-suited to providing consumers with incentives to invest in their own health.

Here's an example of a consumer choice plan. Suppose your employer offers a major medical plan with a high deductible ($2,000) in combination with a flexible spending account (FSA) or a health savings account (HSA). The employer could give you an additional amount of salary on a pretax basis ($1,000), which you could deposit in the HSA and use to pay part of the deductible or expenses not covered by the plan. Subject to certain IRS limitations, the HSA funds not used in a given year can be rolled over to the next year, so you essentially get to keep whatever you don't spend on health care. Because you're now paying out of pocket for many medical costs, you have an incentive to choose lower-cost options for medical care. Theoretically, this should result in reduced total medical costs per person.

9.2.4 Government-Sponsored Plans

Government sources of health insurance include state **workers' compensation** insurance, which pays lost wages and medical costs associated with job-related illness or injury; the **Medicare** program, which pays some health-care costs for Social Security participants age 65 and over; and state-run **Medicaid** programs, which provide health-care coverage for the poor.

▲ **Workers' Compensation.** Suppose you're lifting some heavy boxes at work and you strain your back. Who will pay the medical costs? Today, all states have laws that make your employer strictly liable for employment-related injuries or illnesses. Strict liability (see Section 8.2.1) means your employer will be financially responsible for your injury regardless of fault—so you don't have to sue to recover your costs and it won't matter if it was your fault you were injured. In fact, state workers' compensation laws actually limit your right to sue your employer for additional damages, such as pain and suffering. Although state laws differ, all provide for

FOR EXAMPLE

Winning by Losing: Insurance Incentives for Weight Loss

Obesity is epidemic in the United States, according to statistics from the U.S. Centers for Disease Control and Prevention. Some 30 percent of American adults are obese, defined as being at least 20 percent over their recommended weight, and extra weight is associated with many chronic health problems, such as heart disease and diabetes. One study reported that $93 billion per year in health-care spending can be attributed to the obese and overweight; and experts predict that poor diet and physical inactivity may soon surpass tobacco as the leading cause of death in the United States. Tommy Thompson, U.S. Secretary of Health and Human Services, has urged business and insurance companies to help fight the epidemic. Companies can make it easier for workers to exercise every day, and insurers can give discounts to people who lose weight and exercise. Employers are motivated by the prospect of reducing health related costs. An estimated 40 percent of employers offer health management benefits. Common programs include educational materials, on-site fitness centers, health screenings, nutrition counseling, and reimbursement for gym memberships. Insurers are also participating. Destiny Health of Oak Brook, Illinois has consumer driven health plans that incorporate incentives for healthy lifestyles. Participants who lose weight can earn health club discounts, frequent flier miles, discounted movie tickets, and vacation packages. (Sources: Associated Press, "Corporations Launch War on Fat," MSNBC Health, October 31, 2003 (www.msnbc.msn.com/id/3076957); "HHS Secretary Calls on Corporate, Government Forces to Help Fight Obesity," Health and Medicine Week, June 14, 2004, p. 496; Sarah Lueck, "Personal Health (Special Report); Costs; Winning by Losing," Wall Street Journal, October 20, 2003; John A. MacDonald, "Extra Pounds Cost Big Dollars for U.S. Government, Businesses," Knight Ridder/Tribune Business News, August 17, 2003; United Press International, "HHS Campaign to Combat U.S. Obesity," March 11, 2004.)

payment of medical expenses, rehabilitation costs, lost wages, and specific lump-sum benefits for death and dismemberment. Medical costs associated with on-the-job injuries are the responsibility of your employer and won't be covered by your health insurance. If you're injured on the job, you should contact your benefits office immediately to see what to do. Federal and state law requires that this contact information be prominently displayed in the workplace. Because workers' compensation plans often include contractual arrangements with certain providers, you may be required to see a particular physician to get your costs fully paid.

▲ **The Social Security Medicare Program.** Social Security is much more than just a public retirement plan. It also provides disability insurance, income for surviving spouses and children of plan participants, and health insurance. More than 34 million elderly and 6 million disabled individuals are currently enrolled in Medicare, a health insurance program for qualified Social Security participants age 65 and over and anyone who is receiving Social Security disability benefits. While you're employed, a portion of your Social Security payroll tax (2.9% split between you and your employer) goes to Medicare. There is no limit on the amount of income subject to this tax.

Medicare includes three important parts: Part A, Part B, and Part D. Part A is mandatory hospital insurance, including room and board (subject to an annual deductible of $992 and $248 per day coinsurance for days 61–90 and $496 for days 91–50 in 2007), prescription drugs furnished by the hospital, and post hospitalization extended-care services up to 100 days ($124 per day coinsurance for days 21–100). Part B is supplemental medical insurance for which you pay a monthly premium ($93.50 in 2007, regardless of age, health status, or gender) to insure the costs of physicians and surgeons, home health services, and other medical costs, such as x-rays, lab tests, medical equipment, and ambulance service. There's also a deductible ($131 in 2007) and a 20 percent coinsurance payment for most services. As part of the Balanced Budget Act of 1997, Medicare participants are now allowed to opt for Part C, a managed-care plan that combines Parts A and B coverages. Options for these "Medicare+Choice Plans" include HMOs and PPOs. About 14 percent of Medicare participants are in one of these.

Beginning in 2006, you can also buy a Medicare Part D prescription drug plan. If you don't sign up when you're first eligible, there is a penalty to join later. These plans are offered by various government-approved insurers and have different deductibles, premiums, and drug limitations. In Colorado, for example, 55 insurers offered plans in 2006, with deductibles ranging from $0 to $265 and premiums ranging from $16 per month to $83 per month.

▲ **Medicare Supplement Insurance.** Although the Medicare program provides a valuable source of health insurance to many who would otherwise be uninsurable in the private market, participants are exposed to many gaps in coverage. The coinsurance provisions and deductibles can add up to substantial sums each year, and the plan doesn't cover routine checkups, immunizations, vision care, and hearing care.

To fill in the gaps in Medicare coverage, many private insurers offer one or more Medicare Supplement plans, commonly called **Medigap** policies. In 2006, there were 12 standard plans, labeled A through L.

The standardization of Medigap policies makes it easier to compare policies. Still, companies charge differing premiums and provide different services. The Medicare Supplement Buyers Guide, available free from sellers of these products, provides detailed information on the various plan types. The average cost of a group Medigap policy is more than $200 per month, a significant out-of-pocket expense for the typical retiree whose only source of retirement income was Social Security. When you retire, it's important that you purchase Medigap within six months of enrolling in Medicare Part B, especially if your health is poor. After the six-month period has passed, your eligibility for Medigap insurance isn't guaranteed. Medicare Choice Plans don't have the same gaps in coverage as traditional Medicare, so you don't need Medigap if you belong to one of these plans. In fact, it's illegal for an insurer to sell you a Medigap policy under those circumstances. If you're lucky, you may be eligible for group Medigap coverage through a former employer. Although 37 percent of retirees have health insurance through a former employer, government estimates suggest that only 12 percent of all private companies offer health benefits to retirees, and these are primarily large firms. This percentage has been declining steadily, and employers have tightened up requirements and reduced their subsidy of costs.

Medicare is currently in financial difficulty. The aging of the U.S. population and rising health-care costs are putting more pressure on Medicare. The new prescription drug benefits may cost much more than forecasts suggested. Without major changes, the system can't survive. What does this mean for you? As in other areas of your finances, you are responsible for ensuring your future welfare. Instead of assuming that the government will take care of your medical costs in retirement, consider additional savings targeted to these future costs.

▲ **Medicaid.** Whereas Medicare is a federal program, Medicaid is a state-run and federally financed program that provides relatively comprehensive health coverage for more than 28 million individuals with low income and assets. Approximately 3 million people who are over age 65 and poor qualify for both programs and may use Medicaid payments to meet Medicare deductibles and co-pays. The use of Medicaid for long-term care costs will be discussed in Chapter 16. States differ in eligibility requirements and coverage provided. Because the programs place low limits on physician charges to control costs, it's sometimes difficult to find participating providers.

More information on Medicare options can be found in the Medicare & You 2007, published by the Centers for Medicare and Medicaid Services and available at www.medicare.gov.

9.2.5 Dealing with Special Circumstances

The best-laid plans sometimes go wrong. You had a terrific job with an employer that offered a comprehensive benefit package, but you just got laid off. Thousands of workers have faced this reality in the last several years as employers responded to the demands of a recessionary economy. Or maybe you're recently divorced and are no longer covered under your spouse's employer sponsored plan. Perhaps the most important special circumstance is when you have a serious preexisting condition, such as kidney failure, diabetes, or multiple sclerosis. Here, we examine each of these special circumstances:

▲ **Continuation Coverage under COBRA.** The Consolidated Omnibus Reconciliation Act of 1986 (COBRA) is a federal law that applies to all employers with 20 employees or more, with the exception of the federal government and religious institutions. Under this law, if you lose or quit your job, you're eligible to purchase coverage through your previous employer's plan for a period of 18 months (extendable under some circumstances to 36 months). To elect this coverage, you must notify your employer no later than 60 days after your last day of work. However, you'll have to pay the full premium plus an administrative charge of up to 2 percent. In total, your insurance costs can easily amount to from $4,000 to $8,000 per year for family coverage.

▲ **Divorce.** A disproportionate percentage of divorced women, whether employed or not, have inadequate health insurance or are uninsured. This is largely because women are more likely to work for employers that offer limited employee benefits. If you were participating in a health plan through your former spouse's employer before the divorce, you can elect to pay for COBRA continuation coverage under his or her plan for up to 36 months after the divorce (unless your former spouse worked for the federal government, a religious institution, or a firm with fewer than 20 employees). In many cases, this coverage is prohibitively expensive, so you may be better off buying individual insurance. Health insurance continuation should be a factor in divorce settlements, at a minimum requiring inclusion of the children under the employed parent's plan and fair division of their uninsured medical costs, deductibles, and copays. Too often, the health insurance effects of divorce don't become apparent until the ink is dry on the divorce decree.

▲ **Loss of Dependent Status.** Many students are covered under their parents' health insurance plans. What happens if you lose your dependent status? The good news is that, as a relatively healthy young person, you'll probably be eligible for individual health insurance at favorable rates. If you have a serious health condition that makes it impossible to find coverage in the individual market, you have the right under federal law to elect COBRA continuation coverage under a parent's policy for up to 36 months if that parent works for a firm subject to that law. As in the case of continuation after divorce, however, this coverage may be quite expensive. As another option, most educational institutions provide group coverage opportunities for full-time students.

▲ **Preexisting Conditions.** A preexisting condition is an illness or injury, such as diabetes or heart disease, that significantly increases your expected claims costs under an insurance policy and that began before you were covered under that policy. Historically, insurers didn't cover preexisting conditions for new policyholders for a specific period of time (typically three to six months). However, under the Health Insurance Portability and Accountability Act of 1996 (HIPAA), you can't be subject to a preexisting condition waiting period when you move from one plan to another. You should still look carefully at plan exclusions and limitations, though, because an insurance plan can exclude coverage entirely for certain conditions, as long as the exclusion applies to all participants in the plan. The reason for these limitations and exclusions is obvious— to keep costs down for the members of the pool.

9.2.6 Additional Types of Insurance

Medical costs associated with dental and eyecare are normally excluded from health insurance policies. Your employer may offer programs that help you to cover these costs:

▲ **Dental Expense Insurance.** Dental expense insurance, which is primarily available as a group benefit, is very similar to health insurance in that you pay a premium in return for being reimbursed for qualified medical expenses. You'll normally have to pay deductibles and coinsurance as well, and you may be subject to limits on some procedures (such as root canals and crowns) and exclusions of others (such as orthodontic work). Most dental plans provide first dollar coverage for annual cleanings, x-rays, and check-ups, but they usually require the insured to pay a fairly large proportion of the covered charges, often 50 percent. In addition, they typically place a maximum on the total payable by the insurer under the plan in a given year, sometimes as low as $1,000. Thus, if you're considering paying for a contributory plan, weigh whether your out-of-pocket dental expenses for the year will exceed the policy limit less the premium cost. And don't forget human nature—many people miss their regular dental check-ups even when they've paid for dental insurance simply because they hate going to the dentist.

▲ **Vision Care Insurance.** Vision care insurance provides reimbursement or discounts on eye examinations, glasses, and contact lenses. Normally, your regular health insurance will cover care related to diseases of the eye, such as glaucoma or macular degeneration. This implies that vision care insurance policies essentially cover an annual expense that you can easily estimate and budget for. Although nearly every person over the age of 40 requires eye correction of some sort, vision care insurance is often expensive relative to the benefit received. As with dental expense insurance, you should look carefully at what the plan offers before agreeing to pay for it. Particularly in the case of "vision discount plans," which charge a fee in return for special discounts at participating merchant locations, many consumers have found that the discounts are also available to people who don't participate in the plan, so they've paid the premium for nothing.

▲ **Child Care.** Some employers sponsor dependent care programs that allow individuals to defer up to $5,000 per year, tax-free for a licensed day care facility.

SELF-CHECK

1. Explain what COBRA and Medigap are for.
2. List four government sponsored health care programs.
3. Most employer sponsored healthcare is of which type?

9.3 Planning for Disability Income Needs

Most people underestimate their risk of becoming disabled. You may be surprised to know that you have a 33 percent chance of being disabled for at least three months during your working life. In any particular year, your risk of disability is much higher than your risk of death. Without sufficient financial resources, the loss of income during a period of disability can be financially devastating. You may be unable to work, but you'll still have the expenses of daily living. Understanding your disability income needs and sources of disability income insurance are thus essential to your financial plan.

9.3.1 What Is Disability?

In general, a disability is an illness or injury that prevents you from earning your regular income or reduces how much you can earn. Insurance policies may apply more restrictive definitions; for example, they may define a disability as the inability to perform the regular requirements of your job or the inability to work at any job for which you are reasonably suited by education and experience.

> ### FOR EXAMPLE
>
> #### Cindy and Dave Thompson
>
> Our hypothetical couple, Cindy and Dave Thompson, estimate their total monthly expenses at $4,768. In the event that Dave became disabled, however, the family could eliminate discretionary spending on clothing, gifts, entertainment, and charity. They also could temporarily suspend contributions to college and retirement savings. Making these adjustments to their budget leaves approximately $3,200 per month to cover groceries, housing and auto expenses, utilities, and insurance. In the event of a long-term disability, Cindy and Dave could also consider more drastic cost-saving measures such as downsizing their house and cars.

If you were disabled tomorrow and were unable to earn your regular income, how much money would you need to meet your basic needs? You should be able to answer this question easily by reviewing the personal cash flow statement (see Chapter 2), omitting expenditures for anything that isn't necessary, and subtracting any income you receive from investments.

9.3.2 Sources of Disability Income

In the For Example, the Thompsons estimate needing income of at least $3,200 per month if Dave were disabled. Because Cindy left the workforce to care for their new baby, they might be able to at least partially meet their income needs if she returned to work. Other sources of income include government programs, Dave's accumulated paid leave at his place of employment, and **disability income insurance.** Disability income insurance, which replaces lost income during a period of disability, is available from many sources, including:

▲ **Government-Sponsored Disability Income Protection.** Most states require that some type of workers' compensation insurance be carried on all employees, as discussed earlier in this chapter. So if your injury or illness is job-related, you may be eligible for income replacement from that source. However, benefits and waiting periods can vary substantially from state to state, and you can't be sure that the benefits will be sufficient to cover your expenses. If your injuries are serious enough, you may be eligible for Social Security disability insurance. Under that program, you must be unable to work at any job (the most restrictive definition of disability), and you must have been out of work at least five months and expect to remain disabled at least one year. The benefits under Social Security depend on your participation in the Social Security system and your average income over your working career.

▲ **Employer-Sponsored Disability Income Protection.** Employers may provide disability income protection in several ways, including personal days, paid vacation time, sick leave, and group short- and long-term disability income insurance. If you become ill or are injured and expect to be away from your job for more than a few days, you should consult with your employer's benefits office, because there are often specific requirements regarding qualification and waiting periods for each program. Your employer may require that you exhaust all or a portion of your sick days, personal days, and vacation time before accessing short-term disability insurance, for example. Some employers provide short-term disability insurance for workers with a qualifying disability. This type of insurance pays a portion (commonly 60 or 70%) of your predisability earnings after you've exhausted your sick days and you've been unable to work for a specified waiting period (commonly 15 to 30 days). Although plans differ, these policies commonly replace income for from 6 to 12 months. Long-term disability income insurance is often an optional contributory benefit under employee benefit plans, but it can also be purchased by individuals directly from an insurer. Even under a group policy, the premiums are usually age-related, so that older employees will pay more per month to participate in the plan. Like short-term disability insurance, long-term disability plans specify the definition of disability that qualifies you for income replacement, the waiting period before you're eligible to receive benefits (often three to six months of continued disability), the percentage of predisability income replacement (usually 60%), and the length of time benefits will be paid. Many such policies pay benefits to age 65 if the policyholder is permanently disabled. As discussed earlier, it's advantageous to purchase group disability insurance, if available, because individual insurance costs will increase and availability will decrease as your age or health condition becomes less favorable. When you purchase disability insurance through your employer, you're usually given the option of paying for it with either after-tax dollars or pretax dollars. Although it's generally preferable to use pretax dollars for benefits, you should buy disability insurance on an after-tax basis. If you pay for the insurance with after-tax income and later are disabled, the income benefit you receive while disabled will be tax-free. In contrast, if you use pretax dollars for the insurance premium, you'll have to pay tax on the income received. Most disability policies pay benefits equal to 60 percent of your salary; additional taxation could reduce your income to a degree that it wouldn't cover your needs. For example, if Dave Thompson's pretax monthly income is $5,500, then 60 percent income replacement would give the family $3,300 per month, just enough to cover expected expenses. If the insurance benefit were taxed, however, the Thompsons wouldn't have enough income protection.

▲ **Individual Disability Insurance.** If no employer-sponsored plan is available to you, or if you need additional protection, you can purchase coverage in the individual market. Difficulties with fraud and abuse in recent years, however, have resulted in a smaller number of insurers and higher premiums. Although many variations on individual disability insurance policies exist, the best types replace lost income if you're unable to perform the duties of your particular job—often called "own occupation" insurance. For example, a surgeon who has a hand injury could receive income replacement even if he or she could still work in another medical specialty. These policies are usually sold based on a dollar amount of income replacement with limits on what percentage of predisability income will be replaced. For example, you might buy a policy that will pay you $1,000 per month as long as that doesn't exceed 30 percent of your predisability income. Obviously, the more disability income coverage, the higher your premium. Other factors that increase the cost are your profession, your age, and your existing health status. Key features to look for in disability income insurance policies include:

- **Waiting period.** How long do you have to be disabled before you can begin receiving benefits? This period can be anywhere from 30 days to one year.
- **Benefit duration.** How long can you continue to receive benefits, assuming you continue to meet the definition of disability? A policy may pay benefits for a short time, such as two years, or until age 65, or for life. Generally, all else equal, you want a plan that will cover you for as long as possible. The longer the coverage, however, the more expensive.
- **Income replacement.** How much will the benefit be? Your objective is to meet your expenses, but consider that if your disability continues for a long time, these costs may rise with inflation. A cost-of-living increase feature is therefore desirable.
- **Renewability.** If your health deteriorates, can the insurer drop your disability insurance policy? You should look for policies with a guaranteed renewability feature. Some policies also waive your premium if you are disabled.

SELF-CHECK

1. What are the key features of disability insurance policies?
2. Define disability income insurance.
3. Give the sources of disability income insurance.

SUMMARY

Employee benefits can be tangible, such as insurance or retirement contributions, or intangible, such as flextime. Consider the total value of the package being offered by a potential employer. Estimate your health care costs, and factor this in to your employment decisions. Health insurance can be bought individually but is also commonly available on a group basis through employers and through government programs such as Medicare and Medicaid. Government programs can help with health insurance costs, but be aware of national health care trends. The two main types of plans are fee-for-service and managed care. If you are disabled, disability income insurance can replace a percentage of your lost income. In addition to worker's compensation programs mandated by the government, your employer may offer short-term and long-term disability insurance or you can buy individual disability insurance.

KEY TERMS

Basic health care insurance	Health insurance that covers hospital, surgical, and physician expenses.
Cafeteria plan	An employee benefit plan in which the employer provides a sum of money and allows employees to choose the benefits they want from a menu.
Coinsurance	An arrangement providing for the sharing of medical costs by the insured and the insurer.
Consumer choice plan	A health plan that includes financial incentives for preventive care and cost reduction.
Contributory plan	An employee benefit plan for which the employee pays some or all of the costs.
Copay	Dollar amount of medical costs paid by the insured under a coinsurance provision, after meeting the annual deductible.
Disability income insurance	Insurance that replaces the policyholder's lost income during a period of disability.
Exclusive provider organization (EPO)	Health-care plan that only covers medical costs from participating providers.
Fee-for-service plan	A health insurance plan that reimburses the insured for medical expenses incurred or pays the provider directly.

Flexible spending account (FSA)	An account maintained by an employer in which the pretax earnings of an employee are set aside for qualified medical and child-care expenses.
Group insurance	Insurance purchased by an employer for the benefit of employees.
Group underwriting	Underwriting in which the premium is based on the risk of the group as a whole rather than on characteristics of individual group members.
Health maintenance organization (HMO)	A managed-care plan that attempts to control health care costs by encouraging preventive care and limiting participants to providers with whom the plan has contracted.
Health savings account (HSA)	An investment account in which an employer deposits pretax dollars allocated for payment of an employee's health-related expenses.
Major medical insurance	Insurance that covers the costs of most medical services prescribed by a doctor, subject to deductibles and coinsurance.
Managed-care plan	A health insurance plan that attempts to reduce costs through contractual arrangements with providers and financial incentives for low-cost alternatives.
Maximum limit	Lifetime maximum paid by the insurer to an insured person.
Medicare	Federal health insurance program for people age 65 and over.
Medicaid	State-run program providing health-care coverage for the poor.
Medigap policies	Insurance policies designed to pay deductibles and other costs that are not covered by Medicare.
Point of service (POS) plan	Health-care plan in which participating providers are affiliated with an HMO, but participants can still use nonparticipating providers if they are willing to pay a bigger share of the cost.

Preferred provider organization (PPO)	A managed-care plan that provides participants with financial incentives to use certain providers.
Stop-loss limit	The maximum out-of-pocket cost to be paid by an insured in a given year, after which the insurer pays 100 percent of covered charges.
Workers' compensation insurance	State-run program requiring employers to pay lost wages and medical costs associated with job related illness or injury.

ASSESS YOUR UNDERSTANDING

Go to www.wiley.com/college/bajtelsmit to assess your knowledge of health and disability insurance.

Measure your learning by comparing pre-test and post-test results.

Summary Questions

1. Which of the following is *not* a recommended strategy for controlling your health care costs?
   (a) Take advantage of beneficial tax rules.
   (b) Budget for small expenditures.
   (c) Invest in your own health.
   (d) Choose a low-cost provider.

2. Contributory plans are set up by employers to minimize their health insurance costs. True or false?

3. A major difference between a flexible spending account (FSA) and a health savings account (HSA) is that:
   (a) a HSA has a higher annual contribution limit than most FSAs.
   (b) a FSA can rollover unused amounts from year to year; a HSA cannot.
   (c) a HSA can earn interest on amounts in the account; a FSA does not.
   (d) a FSA contribution is made from pretax dollars; a HSA contribution is made from after-tax dollars.

4. Which of the following is *not* one of the typical features of major medical insurance?
   (a) Annual deductible.
   (b) High maximum limits.
   (c) Choice of doctors restricted.
   (d) Coinsurance provisions.

5. HMOs and PPOs are both examples of fee-for-service health insurance plans. True or false?

6. The most common type of employer-based health insurance plan today is the fee-for-service plan. True or false?

7. Insurance policies designed to pay costs not covered by Medicare are called:
   (a) Part C policies.
   (b) Medicare Plus plans.
   (c) Medigap policies.
   (d) Complete coverage policies.

8. The majority of long-term disability insurance plans offered by employers pay benefits for the rest of the policyholder's life. True or false?

9. Which of the following is required in order to qualify for Social Security disability insurance?

    (a) You must be unable to work at your normal job.

    (b) You must have been out of work for at least 5 months.

    (c) You must be expected to remain out of work for at least two years.

    (d) You must be expected to remain out of work permanently.

10. Which is *not* one of the key features to look for in disability insurance policies?

    (a) Renewability.

    (b) Convertibility.

    (c) Waiting period.

    (d) Benefit duration.

Applying This Chapter

1. Margo is a 30-year-old divorced mother of two. Because her employer offers no employee benefits, she's looking for a new job. What are the most important employee financial benefits that she should look for in a compensation package?

2. If Margo normally has $5,000 in child-care expenses each year, how much would she save if she could pay for it out of a flexible spending account, assuming her marginal tax rate is 25 percent?

3. Your health insurance requires the payment of an annual deductible of $500 per person or $1,000 per family. After meeting the deductible, you must pay 20 percent of covered charges until you reach the stop-loss limit of $5,000. If your child requires emergency surgery and the total covered charges are $20,000, all incurred in the same plan year, how much will you end up paying out of pocket?

4. What type of health insurance is each of the following people most likely to have?

    (a) Retired person age 70

    (b) Child living in a low-income household

    (c) Lawyer

    (d) Self-employed independent contractor

5. You've been laid off by your employer and had been participating in its contributory health-care plan. Your share of the health premiums, $200 per month, was 50 percent of the actual cost to the employer. Under what circumstances should you consider getting COBRA continuation

coverage through your employer's plan? How soon do you need to decide?

6. Allison currently earns $3,000 per month and takes home $2,300. Her monthly expenses total $2,000. Her employer provides 5 sick days and a short-term disability policy that kicks in after 30 days of disability. The policy will pay 60 percent of her gross income for up to 12 months. The disability income payments wouldn't be taxable since she used after-tax dollars to pay the premiums. If Allison wants to have sufficient liquid assets to cover the short-term needs that aren't met by her employer's plan, how much should she set aside for this purpose?

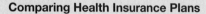

Comparing Health Insurance Plans

Your employer offers two health plan choices and requires that employees pay part of the premium cost. The fee-for-service option will cost you $100 per month for single coverage, does not cover preventive care, and imposes a $300-per-person annual deductible and 20 percent coinsurance to a stop-loss limit of $2,000. The fee-for-service plan also covers prescription drugs after a copay of $30 per prescription. The managed care option (an HMO) will cost you $200 per month, covers all medical services (including preventive care and prescription drugs) but requires a $10 copay for each office visit or prescription. For each of the following scenarios, which cover one year, calculate how much your out-of-pocket expense would be under each plan:

a. You have an annual physical ($200), visit the doctor twice for illness ($50 per visit), and incur prescription drug costs of $500 (10 prescriptions at $50 each).

b. You have an annual physical, have surgery for a skiing injury ($3,000 covered charges), and incur prescription drug costs of $200 (4 prescriptions at $50 each).

What Social Security Disability Benefit Would You Qualify for?

Go to the planner section of the Social Security Web site, www.ssa.gov/planners/, and select the Disability Planner. How much would you qualify for, given your current history of participation in Social Security? Does Social Security provide adequate disability income protection?

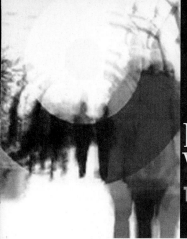

10

FINANCIAL PLANNING WITH LIFE INSURANCE
Thinking Long Term

Starting Point

Go to www.wiley.com/college/bajtelsmit to assess your knowledge of financial planning with life insurance.
Determine where you need to concentrate your effort.

What You'll Learn in This Chapter

▲ Life insurance needs over the life span
▲ Key provisions in an insurance contract
▲ Insurers and policy types

After Studying This Chapter, You'll Be Able To

▲ Assess your life insurance needs
▲ Evaluate insurers and policy types to determine which best meet your needs
▲ Compare the terms and conditions in life insurance policies
▲ Choose the right policy for your needs

INTRODUCTION

We begin the chapter with an assessment of your life insurance needs: What are your risk exposures, and what resources do you have to meet the needs created by those exposures? How might your needs change over the life cycle? After you identify your needs, you need to evaluate alternative methods of meeting them. This chapter describes the types of life insurance available, as well as combinations of insurance and investment plans.

10.1 What Is Life Insurance?

Benjamin Franklin famously wrote, "In this world nothing can be said to be certain, except death and taxes." Even though few would disagree with this sentiment, many people fail to adequately prepare for their deaths. We'll first look at some general characteristics of life insurance and mortality risk. Then we'll consider whether you require life insurance in your financial plan and, if so, how much you need.

10.1.1 How Life Insurance Works

Life insurance basically works in the same way as property and liability insurance (explained in Chapter 8). In fact, it's even simpler than those types of insurance because only one event—a death—can trigger a claim on a life insurance policy, whereas many different events can lead to a property or liability insurance claim. Because people die with a certain degree of predictability and each person's death is, in general, independent of the deaths of others, mortality is a type of pure risk for which the pooling mechanism is particularly well suited.

Like other insurance products, life insurance is based on the concept of risk pooling. You pay a premium that is small relative to the size of your potential loss, and if the bad outcome occurs (you die), your beneficiaries are paid a sum of money, which they can use to offset any losses incurred as a result of your death.

Unlike property insurance, where the insurance benefit is designed to pay you back for a specific dollar loss, life insurance is designed to replace the income you would have earned if you hadn't died prematurely. This is similar in concept to disability insurance (considered in Chapter 9); however, in the case of disability insurance, the policy usually pays out the lost income in installments, whereas it's more common to get a life insurance benefit in a single lump sum.

Because the risk of dying is related to your health and family history, the information that an insurer requires to underwrite your policy (i.e., to decide whether to insure you and how much to charge) is similar to what you have to provide when you apply for individual health and disability insurance. For example, you are commonly asked about your individual and family health history and, for larger amounts of insurance, you usually have to undergo a medical exam and blood test. Obviously, if you have a terminal illness, such as AIDS, an insurer isn't going to be willing to sell you a life insurance policy.

10.1.2 How Life Insurance Differs from Other Insurance

Although life insurance is similar in principle to other kinds of insurance, it's different in an essential respect. Unlike the insurable risks discussed in Chapters 8 and 9, your death will occur with 100 percent certainty. The only question is when. Although advances in medical science have nearly doubled the average human life span, the human body has a natural limit.

The very certainty of the insured event makes life insurance inherently different from property, liability, and health insurance. Also, life insurance policies tend to be longer term in nature than other policies. This makes them different in several ways, as described in this section.

Determinants of Premiums

As with other types of insurance, the premium you're charged for life insurance is directly related to the insurer's estimate of your risk—in this case, your risk of dying during the policy period. As you get older, the cost of insuring your death risk increases. In addition to the expected loss, life insurance premiums include additional amounts to cover the insurer's expenses (such as commissions to agents and claims handling) and its profit to shareholders. They also add a little extra, commonly called the *risk charge*, to account for the chance that their estimate of your mortality risk is inaccurate. These extra charges differ widely among insurers.

FOR EXAMPLE

The Price You Pay for Smoking and Drunk Driving

Everyone knows that, on average, smokers have shorter life expectancies than nonsmokers. Therefore, it's no surprise to find that smokers pay higher life insurance premiums than nonsmokers. The consequences of alcohol abuse can be just as serious and may also disqualify an applicant from paying standard rates. The Society of Actuaries estimates that excessive alcohol consumption can take an average of 10 to 15 years off your life, increasing your risk of heart disease, cancer, accidents, and suicide. The red flags for insurers are a history of drunk driving and blood tests indicating elevated liver enzymes.

As you might expect, larger insurers can often provide better rates than small insurers because they can spread these expense, profit, and risk charges across a larger group of policyholders. Some insurers may also spend more money and time deciding whether to insure you (e.g., requiring more extensive medical tests) in an attempt to limit their pool of policyholders to those with lower-than-average risk of dying during the policy period.

The Investment Component

Insurers invest the premium dollars they receive to earn a return that can help reduce premiums to their policyholders. An important difference between life insurers and property insurers is that the average term of a life insurance policy is much longer; about half of all policies sold today are long-term policies. That means life insurers are receiving extra premium dollars today that will have to be available to pay death claims many years in the future. Because of the long-term nature of their liability, these insurers can invest in long-term securities without worrying about having access to sufficient funds to pay claims. The life insurer's investment experience is therefore very important to its long-term financial performance: Insurers with better investment experience can charge lower premiums and capture larger market shares.

The Benefits of Life Insurance

Life insurance is uniquely suited to meeting certain personal financial goals and to providing a sizable amount of protection at a relatively low cost because the proceeds are free from the claims of creditors and tax authorities. It also offers the following benefits:

▲ **Large amount of coverage:** Life insurance allows you to buy a fairly large amount of protection for a relatively small annual cost. Your greatest need for protection is likely to be at the time in your life when you're still in the wealth accumulation phase. For a young family, household resources are unlikely to be sufficient to meet the financial costs of an untimely death. But for a few dollars a month, the family can buy insurance to cover these costs.

▲ **Protection from creditors:** If you die, the proceeds of your life insurance policy are not subject to the claims of your creditors, whereas your other financial assets are. Thus, with life insurance, you can be sure that the funds will be there to meet the needs of your survivors.

▲ **Tax savings:** The proceeds of a life insurance policy are not taxed. If your policy includes an investment component, the increase in the value of that investment is also free of income tax. And as discussed in Chapter 15, with some minimal planning, you can ensure that your estate will pay no gift and estate taxation on the benefits.

SELF-CHECK

1. Name six ways that life insurance is different from other types of insurance.
2. On what do life insurance companies base their premiums?

10.2 Determining Your Life Insurance Needs

Whether you live a long life or die prematurely, there will be costs associated with your death. At a minimum, the funeral costs will have to be paid. More importantly, your survivors will suffer if they relied on you for financial support. Life insurance pays your beneficiaries a sum of money after you die to help meet the costs of your death. Before you buy life insurance, though, you must first carefully evaluate their needs.

It's not easy to look seriously at your own mortality, or probability of dying, and consider the negative outcomes that might result from your death. Here, we'll get the most unpleasant part out of the way first by thinking about your mortality risk.

10.2.1 What Are the Odds?

What are the odds of dying in the next year, or 10 years, or 20 years? In other words, what is your mortality risk?

In the life insurance business, a person's risk of dying is estimated through the use of standardized mortality tables. These tables, based on many years of statistical data on millions of lives, provide yearly probabilities of dying and surviving based on current age. Women tend to live longer than men, on average, so there are separate tables for each gender. It's also common for life insurers to use different tables for smokers and nonsmokers. The standard tables are updated every 20 or 25 years to account for changes in mortality risks resulting from factors such as better health care and nutrition.

According to the current mortality tables, only 1 of every 1,000 20-year-old males will die before he reaches his 21st birthday, representing a 1/1,000 chance of dying in that year. This may sound like pretty good odds—the chances of dying in any given year are in fact fairly low through your 40s or 50s—but the tables give annual probabilities. The mortality tables show the cumulative probability of surviving to a particular age. For a 20-year-old male, it's about 99 percent. With each successive year, the risk of dying increases, and the cumulative probability of surviving to that age gets smaller. About 94 percent of men born the same year as you (i.e., your birth cohort) will still be alive at age 50, but by the time you reach 70, more than one-fourth of your birth cohort will have died, and only 45 percent will survive to age 80. For women, the odds of surviving are better at all ages.

As you survive to each successive year, your life expectancy, measured as expected age at death, actually increases. The average life expectancy of a child born in 2001 is 77.2 years (74.4 for men and 79.8 for women). This is a gain of 6.4 years from the previous generation—a child born from 1959 to 1961 had a life expectancy of 70.8 (66.6 for men and 73.2 for women). The life expectancy of a child born from 1929 to 1931 was only 59.2 (57.5 for men and 60.9 for women). The 18-year increase in life expectancy over the last two generations is primarily attributable to the availability of antibiotics and vaccines for many previously fatal illnesses.

So what does this mortality information tell you? First, it demonstrates that mortality is a very real risk. In any year of your life, you could die. Second, you have a pretty good chance of living to be very old. It's dangerous to assume that you'll only live the average life expectancy for your age cohort. The new mortality tables give life expectancies through age 120, whereas the previous ones stopped at 99. If you live to be 100, you'll probably live to be 102. The lesson overall is that you need to invest for longevity but plan for mortality.

10.2.2 Why Buy Life Insurance?

Let's say you accept that you're going to die someday. If it happened tomorrow, is there anyone who would experience financial distress as a result? What about your spouse, children, or parents? Would your dog end up with no one to take care of him?

The process of determining the potential financial impact of your death on others is called **needs analysis.** Usually, your needs are motivated by the following:

▲ **Replacing your income and services:** If you're providing necessary income or services to your household, your death will result in a loss to your survivors. This may seem obvious for the major breadwinner of the household, but consider too that a stay-at-home parent's housekeeping, child-care, and transportation services can be very costly to replace.

▲ **Preserving household wealth:** If you die prematurely, your dependents may need to sell the house or spend household resources to meet their living expenses. Life insurance can provide the funds to keep the household running.

▲ **Providing for future family needs:** Even if your survivors would be able to make ends meet financially without you, life insurance can provide greater financial security and can fund the extras—for example, allowing your spouse to work part time until the children are grown or paying for your children to attend a more expensive college.

▲ **Covering business losses:** If you're a partner or other key person in a business venture, your death might cause significant hardship to your surviving partners, who will be faced with the cost of replacing you. Of course, money can't replace things such as creativity and vision. As a result, even with insurance, the loss of a talented CEO can result in significant stock price declines for a company. (If no one likes the CEO, the reverse may be true.) Life insurance that names the company as the beneficiary can, however, offset some of the losses and provide the cash necessary to help the business continue operating. Sometimes, family-owned businesses buy life insurance to cover estate taxes payable at the death of the last surviving parent.

10.2.3 Factors That Affect Your Life Insurance Needs

Not everyone needs life insurance. And those who do require it don't all need to carry the same amount. For example, if you have no one relying on your income or services (no "significant other," no children, no pets, no business obligations), then the only financial cost of your death will be your funeral costs. If you have sufficient assets, then you probably don't need life insurance. You may still want to buy it to provide a financial benefit to someone, but you don't need to buy it.

Over your lifetime, your needs for life insurance may change. The following are some of the factors that influence your life insurance needs over the life cycle:

▲ **The number and age of your dependents:** The more dependents you have and the younger they are, the more life insurance you need.

▲ **Your age and life-cycle stage:** You need more life insurance during the child-rearing years and less when your children are independent.

▲ **Your spouse's earning capacity:** If your spouse can't work or earns a lot less than you, you may need more life insurance.

▲ **Financial wealth and obligations:** The lower your wealth and the higher your financial obligations, the more life insurance you need.

▲ **Your health:** If you have signification health problems, you may need more life insurance because your risk of dying prematurely is higher than average.

▲ **Your dependents' health:** If your spouse or children have health problems, your death might make it difficult for them to maintain health insurance and to meet medical costs, so you may need more life insurance.

10.2.4 Approaches to Life Insurance Needs Analysis

Your existing wealth can obviously be a source of support for your survivors. But because you've already earmarked this wealth for specific purposes (e.g., a college fund for your children or retirement income), you generally buy life insurance to provide whatever else might be needed. Here, we discuss two approaches commonly used to estimate life insurance needs: the income-multiple method and the financial needs method.

The Income-Multiple Method

The simplest approach to estimating life insurance needs, and one that is often used as a shortcut to life insurance needs analysis, is the **income-multiple method.** With this method, you simply multiply your income by a factor of 5 to 10. If you have income of $40,000, for example, you need between $200,000 and $400,000 in life insurance, according to this approach. The idea is that the life insurance should be sufficient to replace your income for a period of time.

One problem is the assumption that one size fits all. As with other financial rules of thumb (e.g., the 70 percent replacement ratio for retirement expenses mentioned in Chapter 14), there's no scientific evidence that this is the "right" amount of insurance. Some people need far more, and others don't need any. Another problem is that there's usually no good explanation for why you should be on the high end or the low end of the multiple.

Furthermore, the multiplier method doesn't take into consideration the resources you already have. Finally, using a straight multiple might not be the best approach to replacing your annual income. Because the income is effectively an inflation-adjusted annuity, it would be more appropriate to estimate what that cash flow stream is worth in today's dollars.

Despite its disadvantages, the income-multiple approach does have the advantage of simplicity, and because most people don't even have the minimum amount of insurance recommended by this approach, it serves the purpose of identifying a shortfall.

The Financial Needs Method

Compared to the income-multiple method, a more accurate method of determining your life insurance needs is to use the **financial needs method** to carefully estimate the funds your family will need after your death.

In general, if you use the financial needs method, you separately estimate your capital needs (i.e., sums earmarked for paying off debts or funding future needs, such as education) and income replacement needs. You then calculate the lump sum amount required to fund the income needs and add it to the capital needs to arrive at a total. From this total, you subtract any financial resources you have to meet the capital needs.

There are various approaches to estimating each type of cost. Your financial needs generally fall into the following categories:

▲ Costs of death
▲ Lump sum needs for dependents' education costs, spouse's retirement plan, and debt repayment
▲ Household maintenance expenses

> ## FOR EXAMPLE
>
> ### The Thompsons' Life Insurance Needs
>
> The Thompsons are evaluating the life insurance component of their financial plan shortly after the birth of their new baby, Julia. Dave has $50,000 in life insurance, and Cindy has none. Cindy has quit her job and plans to stay home until Julia goes to kindergarten. Because Dave is now the sole provider, he needs to carry more life insurance than his wife. However, Cindy's death would result in household expenses for such things as child care and household maintenance. Figure 10-1 shows a needs analysis for Dave and Cindy Thompson. This worksheet, which is also in the Personal Financial Planner in the Appendix, is organized by the different categories of expenses a household might incur in the event of premature death. Some of the costs on this worksheet, particularly the costs at death, are one-time expenses; others are lump-sum capital needs, such as the cost of paying off household debts and setting up an emergency fund. In contrast, some of the costs involve ongoing, long-term cash flow needs, such as continuing household expenses.

When a family member dies, the survivors generally incur a number of one-time costs, including medical costs, funeral costs, and legal costs for settling the estate (discussed in Chapter 15). Out-of-pocket medical expenses depend to a large extent on the cause of death and whether the deceased person had comprehensive health coverage. Funeral expenses vary, but the average is around $10,000. The Thompsons estimate that their uninsured medical costs would be $1,000 and that it would cost $5,000 to settle the estate. They also include $500 to cover the cost of family counseling for the survivors.

Many families include in their life insurance needs analysis sufficient funds to establish an emergency fund, settle large household debts, and fund the future education needs of their children (and sometimes grandchildren) or a retirement fund for a surviving spouse. Although the family may have a plan for financing those needs, the loss of a primary earner often makes continued debt repayment or investment contributions more difficult. For example, Dave Thompson includes enough in his needs analysis to repay the mortgage on the family's house and outstanding car loan. Also, he'll purchase enough life insurance to pay for his children's college fund and Cindy's retirement account. Note, however, that none of these is included in the estimate of Cindy's life insurance needs because Dave's continued income would be sufficient to make the payments.

The most important category addressed in the needs analysis is the cost of maintaining the household. This step of the calculation estimates the net effect on household cash flows by summing the lost income and the cost of services

Figure 10-1

	Dave	Cindy
A. Costs at Death		
1. Uninsured medical expenses (deductible and copay)	$1,000	$1,000
2. Funeral expense (average $10,000, but less for cremation)	10,000	10,000
3. Settlement of estate (estimate 4% of assets)	5,000	5,000
4. State inheritance taxes (if any)		
5. Counseling costs for adjustment to loss	500	500
Total costs at death 1 + 2 + 3 + 4 + 5	$16,500	$16,500
B. Lump Sums		
6. Outstanding debts		
a. Mortage	100,000	
b. Car loan(s)	10,000	
c. Credit cards and other loans		
d. Total outstanding debt to repay 6a + 6b + 6c	110,000	0
7. Education costs for children or spouse (see Chapter 15)	120,000	60,000
8. Spouse retirement fund	100,000	
9. Household emergency fund Monthly household expenses × 3	10,000	10,000
Total lump sum needs 6d + 7 + 8 + 9	$340,000	$70,000
C. Cost of Household Maintenance		
10. Decreased annual after-tax income	52,800	
11. Annual cost of lost support services (child/elder care, housekeeping)		13,000
12. Reduction in family expenses due to death (estimate 20–25%)	13,200	10,000
13. Annual Social Security survivor benefits	26,000	
14. Net income shortfall 10 + 11 − 12 − 13	13,600	3,000
Total household maintenance fund needs		
Line 14 × Number of years to replace 10 YEARS	136,000	30,000
15. Total fund needed (sum shaded cells)	$492,500	$116,500
Available Resources		
16. Total savings and investments	5,000	5,000
17. Group life insurance	50,000	
18. Social Security lump sum benefit		
19. Total resources to meet needs 16 + 17 + 18	$55,000	$5,000
Total life insurance needs line 15 − line 19	$437,500	$111,500

Dave and Cindy Thompson's life insurance needs analysis.

provided by the person who dies and then adjusting for the reduction in household expenses (one fewer person in the household) and expected Social Security survivor benefits. The remainder is the expected annual income shortfall. If Dave were to die, for example, the Thompson family would lose his income, but Social Security survivor benefits would replace almost half of that, and the household's expenses would also be lower by an estimated $13,200 (25 percent of total expenses) per year. The reduction in expenses that would occur with Cindy's death would be less because she doesn't have work-related expenses.

Although Social Security is a retirement program, it also provides survivor benefits. As with the retirement benefits discussed in Chapter 14, your survivors' eligibility for full benefits depends on whether you're considered fully insured under the programs. (You need 40 quarters of covered employment prior to your death or one and a half years of covered employment in the past three years.) Benefits are currently payable for each child under 18 and for a nonworking surviving spouse who stays home with children, up to a family maximum. Because the Thompsons' oldest child, Kyle, is a teenager, the benefits will drop significantly in a few years. But by then, Cindy will likely be able to return to work. Benefits payable to the surviving spouse are phased out, beginning at a fairly low earnings level if the spouse is employed (which is why the Thompsons estimate that no benefits from Social Security would be payable if Cindy were to die).

Using the benefit calculator on the Social Security website, Dave Thompson estimates that the family will be eligible to receive the maximum family benefit, which translates to approximately $26,000 per year in 2004. Based on these estimates, Cindy would experience an annual household income shortfall of $13,600 if Dave were to die. Unlike the lump-sum needs, the income shortfall would presumably continue for years. Household expenses are likely to rise with inflation, but the survivor may invest the proceeds of the insurance policy to earn at least the rate of inflation. The two effects cancel each other out, allowing us to vastly simplify this calculation and simply multiply the total annual income shortfall by the number of years the cash flow will be needed. This multiplier should take into account the number of years the family will have dependent children and also the time until the surviving spouse could earn sufficient replacement income. Cindy estimates that within 10 years, she would be able to earn enough to offset this income shortfall, so her projection needs for this category are 10 × $13,600 = $136,000.

After summing all the categories of financial need, the Thompsons are surprised to see just how underinsured they are; they never dreamed that their combined life insurance needs would add up to more than $600,000. The Thompsons' household financial resources at the moment are very limited, but they decide that they need to look into increasing Dave's life insurance coverage to about $400,000 and buying $100,000 of coverage for Cindy. Of course, it will be necessary to reevaluate their life insurance needs as their circumstances change.

Your life insurance needs change as you move through the stages of the life cycle. As a young single with no dependents, you only need to fund your funeral costs and repay your debt. When you marry, your life insurance needs are greater, especially if you're the primary breadwinner; if you have children, your needs increase even more. Initially, you aren't likely to have much wealth, so you need to rely on insurance in case of death. In middle age, your needs are likely to decline because your financial wealth is probably growing and your children are becoming independent. For most retirees, life insurance is no longer a necessity, but it can be an effective estate planning tool.

SELF-CHECK

1. How is mortality estimated in the life insurance business?
2. List factors that affect your insurance needs over your life cycle.
3. Define **needs analysis**.

10.3 Choosing Life Insurance Companies and Policies

After you determine your need for life insurance, the next steps are to consider which financial institution to do business with and which type of policy best meets your needs. Because some insurers specialize in certain types of policies, you should probably decide on the type of policy first. However, people who don't know much about life insurance usually decide on the insurer first and then rely on their agent to help them decide between policy types.

Although insurers always try to meet customers' needs by creating "new and improved" life insurance policies, there are just two basic types—term (or temporary) and permanent (or long-term) life insurance. There are many variations on these two types, which can make the selection and comparison process somewhat confusing. But if you understand the fundamental difference between the two basic types, you'll be headed in the right direction. In this section, we examine important features of each type.

10.3.1 Term Life Insurance

Term life insurance provides protection for a specific period of time, such as one year or five years, and has no investment component. You pay an annual premium, sometimes in monthly installments; if you die during the contract period, your beneficiary receives the **face value** of the policy. If you don't die, the contract concludes at the end of the period.

Figure 10-2

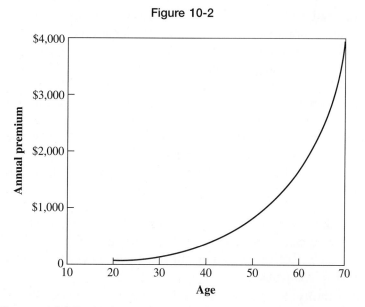

The cost of $10,000 face value yearly renewable term life insurance.

The primary determinant of the price of term insurance is your probability of dying. This probability increases with age and health problems. Thus, the annual premium is fairly low when you're young and healthy and increases with age, as shown in Figure 10-2. For example, a 1-year policy for a 25-year-old woman usually costs less than $100 per year for $100,000 in face value, whereas she might pay $500 per year at age 50 for the same protection.

Term life insurance allows you to buy a fairly large amount of protection for a relatively modest premium, which is a real advantage when your financial needs are large relative to your household resources. When you get older, you can decrease your coverage as your household wealth grows and your dependents' needs are reduced. There are two primary problems with term insurance:

▲ The premiums rise sharply as you get older; beyond a certain age limit, often 65, insurers are reluctant to sell term insurance to you at all.

▲ In the absence of specific provisions in your insurance contract, your term life insurance lapses at the end of the term of coverage, and you may have to go through the application process again, including any required medical examination. If your health makes you no longer eligible, you might lose coverage just when your family needs it most.

To address these problems, insurers make various features available in term insurance policies. Although they may cause your premiums to be higher, you should seriously consider features such as guaranteed renewability and convertibility when you purchase term insurance:

▲ **Guaranteed renewability: Guaranteed renewability** is the right to renew an insurance contract without additional proof of insurability, such as a medical exam. In renewable policies of this type, the face value usually remains the same over time, but the premium increases periodically. At each renewal date, the premium for the policy is adjusted upward to reflect the additional mortality risk for your age cohort. The policy may be renewable annually, adjusted each year according to a predetermined schedule, or it may be renewable at longer intervals, such as every 5 or 10 years. When the premium stays the same for more than 1 year, the rate at the beginning of the term is higher than the rate on an annually renewable policy because the insurer is spreading your mortality risk over a longer period. Note that renewability has limits. Although there are now some exceptions, in general, you can renew term insurance only until you're 65 or 70. Even when it's possible to renew beyond these ages, the premium rates are prohibitively expensive.

▲ **Convertibility:** Sometimes, a term policy may be **convertible,** giving you the right to convert to permanent life insurance without additional proof of insurability. However, permanent life insurance is much more expensive than term. The benefit of the convertibility feature is that it allows you to effectively lock in a premium rate, based on a younger age, while obtaining more protection than you could afford to buy in the form of permanent insurance. If you decide to exercise this type of option, you usually have to come up with the back premiums for the permanent coverage. Although this might not seem to be worthwhile, it's actually less expensive than the alternative—being subject to an annual premium rate for permanent insurance, based on your age.

▲ **Decreasing protection:** With **decreasing term life insurance,** the amount of your premium remains the same from year to year, but that premium purchases smaller amounts of coverage each year. You effectively pay an age-related price per $1,000 of coverage, as you would under a standard term policy, but you reduce the face value of the policy to keep the premium the same. This type of arrangement may make sense if you expect your life insurance needs to decline over time as your household wealth is increasing and your children are growing up and leaving home. It's doubtful, however, that the declines in coverage will exactly match your changing insurance needs.

10.3.2 Permanent Life Insurance

Permanent life insurance provides an investment component along with its protection component. It's called *permanent* because, unlike term insurance, it doesn't need to be renewed—it's intended to be in place for your entire lifetime. The idea is to allow policyholders to stay insured for their lifetimes while paying a guaranteed, level premium.

In the beginning, the premium is higher than that for term insurance of comparable coverage, and the insurer invests the difference. As the policyholder grows older and mortality risk increases, the premium stays the same because the accumulated savings in the policy offset the additional risk. Because of the accumulation of savings, permanent life insurance is also commonly referred to as *cash value life insurance*. The buildup of extra funds that will eventually be used to offset the increased costs of providing protection at older ages is known as the **cash value.**

The primary advantages of permanent insurance are that the accumulated investment returns are not taxable and provide a mechanism for forced saving. However, it's important to carefully consider alternative investment options before deciding to buy permanent life insurance because the rates of return on many policies are not competitive with other alternatives, and the expenses charged to your account may exceed those of comparable-risk mutual funds.

The primary categories of permanent life insurance—whole life insurance universal life insurance, current-assumption whole life, and variable life insurance—are similar to one another in that the policies are long term and don't require renewal. The differences in these categories relate to how premiums are determined and whether you can select how your cash value is to be invested.

Whole Life Insurance

Whole life insurance provides death protection for a person's entire life. If the premiums are also payable over the insured's whole life, the policy is an **ordinary life insurance** policy; if the premiums are paid only for a specified time, the policy is a **limited-payment life insurance** policy.

Although it's common for people to purchase limited-payment life insurance that will be paid up at retirement, typically age 65 or 70, these policies have many payment options. You can even purchase **single-premium whole life insurance** with a one-time premium payment. With such a policy, your beneficiaries will be paid the face amount of the policy, regardless of when you die. You can generally borrow against the cash value at favorable interest rates, subject to a reduction in the death benefit to repay any unpaid loan balance at your death. With a limited-payment life policy, although you no longer pay a premium after a certain point, your cash value continues to earn investment returns, effectively increasing the amount that will be payable to your beneficiaries upon your death. Bundling death protection with an investment product makes sense only if it offers you a cost-effective way of achieving both objectives.

Traditional whole life insurance is often criticized for the relatively noncompetitive rates of return that have been credited to policyholders, particularly during periods when the stock and bond markets have done well. Another problem with traditional whole life insurance contracts is that they are relatively

---

FOR EXAMPLE

How Whole Life Insurance Works

Suppose you purchase a $100,000 whole life policy with a level premium of $1,000 per year, payable for your whole life. If you could have bought term insurance for only $100, then we may assume that the insurer can provide death protection for that amount of money. In other words, $100 will be sufficient to pay your share of the death claims for its pool of insured persons. This implies that the remaining $900 can be invested to help cover your death protection costs in the future, when it will be more expensive (because you'll be older).

In the early years of your policy, the insurer is providing death protection that is nearly equal to the face value of the policy. You haven't paid very much into the policy, so if you die, the insurer will be footing almost the entire bill. Over time, however, a larger share of the death protection comes from the policy's cash value reserves, which implies that the insurer provides less protection. Although you usually aren't credited with any cash value for the first few years, as the insurer recoups its issuance costs (e.g., commissions to agents, processing of your application), you eventually accumulate a cash reserve in the policy. This will be used to cover your mortality costs in later years, when they're greater than the $1,000 premium amount.

---

inflexible. A policyholder who runs into financial difficulties and misses a payment or two can have his or her policy canceled, even when there's substantial built-up cash value.

Universal Life Insurance

Universal life insurance is a type of permanent insurance that attempts to address the shortcomings of whole life insurance. Universal policies promise death protection and a savings component, as whole life policies do, but if the insurance company earns greater-than-expected returns on its investment portfolio, the policyholder shares in some of that benefit, usually through a reduction in the next year's premium.

Universal life also includes a flexible premium option: A policyholder with sufficient cash reserves can choose not to pay the premiums, using accumulated cash value to meet mortality costs for the period, or to take some of the funds out of the policy entirely. On the one hand, this flexibility is a benefit; for example, a policyholder doesn't have to let the policy lapse if he or she experiences some financial difficulties. On the other hand, it tends to undermine the savings element of the policy; if you don't put the money in and keep it there, you can't accumulate savings.

Current-Assumption Whole Life

Another variation on the whole life concept is **current-assumption whole life insurance,** which has some similarities to universal life. This type of policy incorporates a variable premium design in which each premium is recalculated based on the mortality, expense, and investment experience of the insurer, subject to a guaranteed maximum. In theory, this could result in lower premiums over time if the insurer does a good job of underwriting and investing, but it could also result in sharply increased premiums if an economic downturn reduces investment returns.

Variable Life Insurance

The most popular types of permanent life insurance in recent years have been **variable life insurance** and **variable universal life insurance.** Both of these allow policyholders to direct the investment components, usually into managed accounts with different risk characteristics, such as a growth stock account, income stock account, high-grade bond account, or government bond account. The insurer provides professional management of the accounts, and the policyholder selects from among several options, much like the choices in employer-sponsored retirement funds.

The pricing of variable life insurance takes into account investment returns, so if you assume a little more risk, you may benefit from lower premiums and quicker buildup of cash value. Policyholders are generally allowed to transfer money between investment options, subject to some timing restrictions. Variable universal life also includes the flexible premium features of universal life.

Although most variable policies have a stated minimum death benefit, the expectation is that the cash value accumulation from the performance of the selected investments will end up being higher than the stated death benefit. For example, the premium for a $100,000 policy might be determined assuming a 3 percent return on investment, but if you actually earn 8 percent, the cash value will increase beyond what is required to fund your policy. If you were to die, your beneficiaries would receive the face value plus the extra accumulation. You generally get no guarantees regarding the interest rate or cash value for these policies, however. The Securities and Exchange Commission says these products are investment securities and must follow all the registration and disclosure rules applicable to securities.

The real downside of variable life insurance is risk. Although all investments expose you to risk, it may not be appropriate to mix the protection-motivated purchase of life insurance with the wealth-building motivation of investing. During the 1990s, when the stock market was climbing spectacularly, insurers found it difficult to sell minimal-return whole life insurance, but sales of variable products skyrocketed. However, many investors found out the hard way that their cash values could actually go to zero.

SELF-CHECK

1. What are the two basic types of life insurance policies?
2. What are the two problems with term life insurance?
3. List the four types of permanent life insurance.

10.4 Buying Life Insurance

In deciding whether to buy term insurance (i.e., death protection only) or permanent insurance (i.e., death protection plus a savings vehicle), it's a good idea to compare the permanent insurance alternative with a strategy of buying term life insurance and investing the difference.

Premiums for permanent insurance are many times those for term insurance, which can make permanent insurance a prohibitively expensive choice for low- or average-income families. In contrast, term insurance is quite inexpensive if you're young and healthy. Thus, instead of paying high premiums for permanent insurance, you might consider buying decreasing term insurance and investing the premium difference between this product and a permanent life insurance policy in a mutual fund. As the face value of the term insurance declines, the value of your investment portfolio increases, so you can maintain relatively constant total protection plus wealth accumulation. Whether this is a good strategy depends on the following:

▲ **Will you stick with your investment plan?** The strategy of buying term and investing the difference can work only if you really do invest the difference. If you find other things to spend the money on, or if you dip into the investment portfolio on occasion, you'll end up with insufficient protection for your survivors.

▲ **Can you earn more on your investments than the insurer can?** Although life insurers are generally experts at investing, it's not very difficult to find mutual fund alternatives with comparable investment performance.

▲ **Is it cheaper to buy term insurance and invest the difference?** Whether you buy insurance with an investment component or you buy mutual funds on your own, you are exposed to some combination of commissions and management fees. You need to compare these costs.

10.4.1 Choosing an Insurer

Buying life insurance requires homework. Life insurers are not all the same. Insurers differ in terms of the products they offer, their financial arrangements with their agents, how they underwrite and price their policies, and their financial solvency.

Financial deregulation has made it possible for financial institutions to offer products that were previously available only through specialized firms. Thus, you may even find that your bank sells some types of life insurance. In choosing an insurer, you need to think about the following:

▲ **Financial strength:** Keep in mind that, unlike property and liability insurance contracts, which rarely extend beyond one year, life insurance is often a long-term arrangement and involves potentially large sums of money. You don't want to take the chance that a company might not be around to pay your beneficiaries after you die or that it doesn't have sufficient funds to pay them the promised benefit. Luckily, state regulators are also concerned about the safety and soundness of financial institutions, so many information resources are available, including rating agencies such as Best's, Standard & Poor's, Moody's, and Weiss Ratings. A company being rated AAA (the highest rating) now doesn't mean it will always be highly rated, but you can still use these agencies' ratings as a starting point. You may want to consider life insurers rated AA or A in addition to those rated AAA. Some helpful links are: www.insure.com, www.ambest.com, and www.moodys.com.

▲ **Stock vs. mutual:** Another distinction among life insurers is their form of organization. A life insurer can be either a stock company or mutual company. A stock company is owned by the stockholders, who expect to make a profit on their equity investments. In contrast, a mutual insurance company is owned by its policyholders. Policies issued by a mutual company are called *participating policies* because they pay a dividend at the end of the year to compensate the policyholder-owners for their equity interest in the firm. Quoted premiums for **participating policies** are usually higher than those for nonparticipating policies issued by stock companies, but the difference is made up through the dividend. Because dividends aren't guaranteed, the actual net premium you end up paying each year varies, based on the financial performance of the mutual company. Sometimes, stock companies offer participating policies as well.

10.4.2 Choosing an Agent

Depending on the insurance companies you choose to consider, you may need to select an agent. As discussed in Chapter 8, insurance products are sold through many distribution channels. You may be able to buy a policy directly from a company; through an independent agent, who can sell insurance for many different insurers; or through a captive agent, who sells insurance for only a single company.

Although it's often a little less expensive to buy from companies that sell directly—on the Internet or through direct mail, for example—you can't expect to get much personalized service unless you work with an agent. In general, the more complex the product, the better it is to deal with a well-informed agent who can explain the intricacies of various policies. An independent agent, of course, has a wider selection of products than a captive agent. You should look for agents who will provide the service you need, such as coming to your home to get your signature on documents. You should also consider the following:

▲ **Education:** An agent who has appropriate education, professional credentials, and certifications is likely to understand the products he or she is selling. Continuing education is also important, because it shows that the agent makes an effort to keep current in his or her area of specialty.

▲ **Experience:** In general, the more years an agent has been in the business, the more likely he or she will be able to understand and evaluate your needs.

▲ **Reputation:** You should ask your friends and colleagues for recommendations. Have they been satisfied with the professionalism and service provided by a particular life insurance agent? Are there certain local agents they'd recommend you avoid? You can also ask for recommendations from other professionals you trust, such as your lawyer, your financial planner, or your banker.

▲ **Responsiveness:** A good agent should provide you with the information necessary to make appropriate decisions. This should include a realistic analysis of your insurance needs, informative answers to your questions, and clear explanations of product details. You're embarking on what may be a long-term relationship, so you need to feel comfortable sharing your personal and financial information with an agent.

▲ **Ethical behavior:** Because insurance agents primarily work on commission, they may have incentives that aren't compatible with your best interests. Although most agents attempt to be professional and ethical in their sales practices, some do not. In addition to high-pressure sales tactics, practices that may be deemed unethical (and in some states, illegal) include the following:

  • Using unrealistically high rates of interest in illustrating the expected premiums and cash value of a policy.

  • Encouraging you to replace an existing cash value policy with a new one.

  • Promising that cash value buildup will cause your premiums to "vanish" within a few years.

- Suggesting that you should borrow from a whole life policy to buy a variable-annuity product.

SELF-CHECK

1. List the factors to consider in choosing an insurer.
2. List the factors to consider in choosing an agent.

10.5 Important Provisions in a Life Insurance Contract

By state law, a life insurance policy may be required to include certain provisions, such as the grace period (the ability to borrow against any accumulated cash value), and a time limitation on the insurer's ability to get out of the contract. Many other provisions are optional. A policy may thus include one or more of the provisions discussed in this section.

10.5.1 Grace Period

If you don't pay a premium on time, your policy lapses. For example, if you have an annually renewable policy, the premium for the next year's coverage is due on the anniversary of the date your policy originally went into effect. Insurers must provide a grace period for payment, usually one month for fixed-premium policies and two months for flexible-premium policies.

Generally, insurers don't charge interest on overdue payments. If you haven't paid by the last day of the grace period, some insurers still allow you to reinstate your policy, but they aren't required to. If your policy lapses, you have to provide additional proof of insurability, which could be a problem if your health has changed since your first application; you may also have to pay higher rates.

10.5.2 Policy Loans

If you have a cash value policy, you're allowed to borrow from your accumulated funds without terminating the policy. Outstanding loans accrue interest, usually at an attractively low rate, and there's no set schedule for repayment. In the event of death, the death benefit is reduced by any outstanding amounts due. Therefore, you should take out a policy loan only if you've carefully considered your other borrowing options and your family's need for protection.

10.5.3 Incontestable Clause

Under general contract law, a contract is voidable by one of the parties if that party entered into it as a result of misrepresentations made by the other party. Suppose you have a serious medical condition but, when asked about your medical history, you fail to disclose this information on your life insurance application.

If the policy is issued and you subsequently die, the insurer has the right to refuse to pay the benefit to your survivors on the grounds that the policy was void due to your misrepresentation. Because this has the effect of leaving your beneficiaries without protection, states have generally limited insurers' right to contest the claim, or refuse payment, on these grounds to a specific period of time from the policy's issue date, often one or two years. The rationale for this **incontestable clause** is that, without such a limitation, insurers might be tempted to do very limited underwriting investigations, collect premiums for years, and then refuse to pay when the policyholder dies. Making a policy incontestable after a certain amount of time has passed gives insurers the incentive to do more careful up-front underwriting.

10.5.4 Policyholder Dividends

Policies issued by mutual companies are participating policies, which means the policyholders are entitled to dividend distributions, much like stockholder dividends. The Internal Revenue Service treats these dividends as a return of premium, so they aren't taxable. Participating policies must include a clause that describes how and when dividends will be paid—usually on the policy anniversary and conditional on the policyholder's timely payment of premiums.

Policyholder dividends are not guaranteed up front but depend on the insurer's financial performance. Although it's common to apply a dividend to reduce future premiums, policyholders may be given several options for receipt of dividends. Sometimes, a policyholder can opt to take the dividend as cash, put it in an interest-bearing account, or use it to purchase small amounts of additional paid-up insurance or one-year term insurance.

10.5.5 Entire Contract Clause

Most policies include an entire contract clause that explicitly states that the written contract is the entire agreement between the insurer and the insured. This rule applies whether or not the policy explicitly states it, and it is designed to prevent the insurer from imposing its own interpretation or changing the agreement without your knowledge after the contract has been issued.

10.5.6 Nonforfeiture

When you buy permanent insurance with level premiums, the premiums in the early years are greater than the mortality expense for the insurer, and the extra amount is used to build up a cash reserve to cover the greater mortality expenses in the later years. Nonforfeiture laws require that, if your contract lapses before maturity but after some minimum amount of time, such as three years, the insurer must refund a fair amount of the cash reserve. You have the option of receiving it either

▲ In cash.
▲ As a paid-up policy, in whatever amount the cash value is sufficient to purchase.
▲ As a term life policy with the same face value as the lapsed policy but for a period the cash value is sufficient to purchase, given your current age.
▲ As an annuity for retirement income.

Many people find the latter alternative useful in financial planning because they can purchase appropriate protection during their child-rearing years and later convert the accumulated cash value to a cash flow stream to be received in retirement.

10.5.7 Reinstatement

Sometimes, you may be entitled under the terms of your policy to reinstate a policy that has lapsed. For example, suppose you purchased a whole life policy in 1995, and by January 2005, it had a cash value of $20,000. You're laid off from work and can't afford to make the required premium payment for 2005. Although you might decide to surrender the policy for its cash value, under some circumstances, it might be preferable to reinstate the policy when your financial situation allows it. If your policy permits reinstatement, you normally have to provide proof of insurability (commonly, a blood test and physical examination) and pay any missed premiums, with interest.

10.5.8 Beneficiaries

You must designate a primary beneficiary for a life insurance policy—the person, persons, estate, or business entity to receive the proceeds of the policy upon your death. You should normally also name a contingent beneficiary in case the primary beneficiary doesn't outlive you. In naming your beneficiaries, you should be as specific as possible, to avoid problems in identifying the recipients later.

It's important to review your policies regularly to ensure that you always have at least one living beneficiary and that you've included everyone. For example, if your policy names "my sons, James and Robert," but you now have a third child, Jessica, she will be entitled to nothing upon your death.

10.5.9 Suicide Clause

If the insured person commits suicide, his or her beneficiaries may be entitled to payment under the policy. This depends on the terms of the suicide clause, which allows the insurer to deny coverage if the insured commits suicide and the policy has been in force less than a specified period of time, usually two years.

In a particularly sad case several years ago, a businessman, who was in debt and could see no other solution to his problems, purchased a large amount of insurance on his life, naming his wife as beneficiary. The policy included a one-year suicide clause, so he waited until the one-year anniversary and shot himself in his office. Unfortunately, he was mistaken about the effective date of the policy (which was one day after he made his application) and committed suicide one day too early.

10.5.10 Waiver of Premium

Many insurers offer a relatively expensive option called **waiver of premium.** A policyholder who has purchased this option is allowed under some limited circumstances, usually permanent disability, to keep the policy in force without further payment of premium.

10.5.11 Accelerated (or Living) Benefits

Many life insurance policies now offer an **accelerated benefits** option under which terminally ill policyholders can receive a portion of their life insurance proceeds before their death. More than half the states have adopted model regulation governing this type of benefit. The regulation lists the conditions that trigger the benefit, including AIDS, acute heart disease, permanent brain damage due to stroke, and kidney failure. This option may be an automatic feature of a policy, or it may require an additional premium.

Although you might envision using your life insurance for the trip to Europe you never got to take while you were healthy, usually the insurance proceeds are used to help pay for medical treatments and hospice care. Another way to access the value of your life insurance in advance of your death, if allowed in your state, is to sell the policy to someone else.

10.5.12 Accidental Death Benefit

Your life insurance policy may include a rider or an amendment that doubles the face value payable under the policy if your death is caused by an accident instead of natural causes. An **accidental death benefit** is therefore sometimes referred to as a *double indemnity clause*. Because the percentage of deaths that occur due to accidents is fairly small, this is an inexpensive benefit to provide. But individuals tend to overestimate the probability of accidental death and thus tend to overestimate the value of this benefit.

10.5.13 Guaranteed Purchase Option

After you buy a life insurance policy, you might probably want to increase your coverage as your circumstances change. You can simply buy additional policies to meet your growing needs, but if you become uninsurable later, you won't be able to get a new policy. Diagnosis with a serious illness or development of a disability might make it impossible to find insurance or might make the insurance prohibitively expensive.

A guaranteed purchase option gives you the right to purchase additional amounts of insurance in the future without proof of insurability and without "restarting the clock" on the suicide and incontestable clauses. Many group life insurance plans offered by employers also include this feature, allowing you to increase your insurance by from $10,000 to $25,000 per year, as long as you have continuous coverage.

10.5.14 Settlement Options

Settlement options are choices regarding how the beneficiaries will receive the proceeds of the policy. You can make this choice, or you can leave it to the beneficiaries to decide after your death.

SELF-CHECK

1. List the key provisions in a life insurance contract.
2. Define **inconstestable clause, accelerated benefits,** and **wavier of premium.**
3. Who decides how the proceeds of life insurance are paid out?

SUMMARY

Mortality is the one risk that everyone is sure to face. Your mortality risk changes as you age. If you need life insurance, you can consider both term and permanent options. You should do some homework on the best insurer and the best type of policy for your individual situation. You should also reevaluate your needs as your life circumstances change.

KEY TERMS

Accelerated benefits	An option under which a terminally ill policyholder can receive a portion of his or her life insurance proceeds before death.

Accidental death benefit	A life insurance contract provision through which the benefit is doubled for accidental death.
Cash value	The value of the investment component of a permanent life insurance policy.
Convertible	A type of term life insurance policy that allows the insured person to convert a term insurance policy to a permanent life insurance policy without additional proof of insurability.
Current-assumption whole life insurance	A type of permanent life insurance with premiums that depend on the insurer's actual mortality, expense, and investment experience.
Decreasing term life insurance	A type of term life insurance that features a level premium and decreasing protection.
Face value	The dollar value of protection payable to beneficiaries under the terms of a life insurance policy.
Financial needs method	A method for estimating life insurance needs based on expected capital and income replacement needs.
Guaranteed renewability	A feature of term life insurance that gives the insured person the right to renew the policy without additional proof of insurability.
Income-multiple method	A method for estimating life insurance needs as a multiple of income.
Incontestable clause	An insurance contract clause which states that the insurer cannot contest a claim for misrepresentation after a policy has been in force for a specified period of time.
Limited-payment life insurance	Whole life insurance that is paid up after a specified period.
Needs analysis	The process of determining the potential financial impact of a person's death on others.
Ordinary life insurance	Whole life insurance with premiums payable to the time of death.
Participating policies	Life insurance policies issued by mutual insurers that pay dividends to policyholders.
Permanent life insurance	A type of life insurance that provides both death protection and a savings vehicle.
Single-premium whole life insurance	Whole life insurance that is paid up with a one-time payment.

Term life insurance	A type of life insurance that provides death protection for a specified term, often one or five years, and no cash value.
Universal life insurance	A type of permanent life insurance that allows policyholders to benefit from the investment experience of the insurer and provides a flexible premium option.
Variable life insurance	Permanent life insurance that has a fixed premium and allows policyholders to choose from different investment alternatives.
Variable universal life insurance	Permanent life insurance that involves a flexible premium feature and allows policyholders to choose from different investment alternatives.
Waiver of premium	An insurance option that allows the insured to waive premium payments under certain conditions, such as permanent disability.
Whole life insurance	Permanent life insurance that provides death protection for the policyholder's whole life and includes a savings component.

ASSESS YOUR UNDERSTANDING

Go to www.wiley.com/college/bajtelsmit to assess your knowledge of financial planning with life insurance.
Measure your learning by comparing pre-test and post-test results.

Summary Questions

1. Life insurance is based on the concept of:
   (a) diversification.
   (b) actuarial science.
   (c) risk pooling.
   (d) mortality intermediation

2. Which of the following is *not* a benefit of life insurance?
   (a) Tax savings.
   (b) Protection from inflation.
   (c) Large amount of coverage.
   (d) Protection from creditors.

3. A standardized mortality table shows:
   (a) life expectancy of those who live to each age.
   (b) yearly probabilities of dying.
   (c) deaths per 1,000.
   (d) all of the above.

4. A disadvantage of the income-multiple method to determining how much life insurance is needed is its complexity. True or false?

5. The major advantage of term life insurance over whole life insurance is that term life:
   (a) is available without proof of insurability, whereas whole life is not.
   (b) always has a constant premium, whereas whole life does not.
   (c) tends to have lower premiums than whole life.
   (d) has a choice of investments, whereas whole life does not.

6. A term life insurance policy that can be extended for another term without the insured taking a medical exam has:
   (a) convertibility.
   (b) decreasing protection.
   (c) permanent life protection.
   (d) guaranteed renewability.

7. Both universal life and variable life insurance allow policyholders to direct the investment component of their policies. True or false?

8. Which of the following is *not* one of the characteristics you should consider when choosing a life insurance agent?

    (a) Reputation.

    (b) Education.

    (c) Fees.

    (d) Responsiveness.

9. Nonforfeiture laws require that insurers must refund a fair amount of the cash value of permanent life insurance policies if held a minimum number of years. True or false?

10. Without which of the following might insurers be tempted to do very limited investigations before issuing a policy?

    (a) A convertibility clause.

    (b) Guaranteed renewability.

    (c) An incontestable clause.

    (d) A nonforfeiture clause.

Applying This Chapter

1. Elaine has just graduated from college, is single, and has no dependents except for her chocolate lab, Rufus. She has accepted a job with a starting salary of $40,000, and she has $10,000 in student loan debt. Her employer doesn't provide any group life insurance. Does Elaine need any life insurance? Why or why not? If so, how much would you recommend?

2. Carrie and Brad have no children nor any pets. Both are attorneys who make more than $100,000 per year. Because they're relatively frugal, they have only a small mortgage on their jointly owned condo, and they have no outstanding debt. With their high net cash flow and some wise investment decisions, they've accumulated a sizable net worth, and both have good retirement plans with their employers. Does either of them need life insurance? Why or why not? If so, how much would you recommend?

3. Marian, age 45, estimates that she needs to buy $300,000 in life insurance to protect her dependent children from suffering adverse financial consequences in case of her death. As a single parent, she's on a pretty tight budget. Would term or permanent insurance be more appropriate to meet her needs right now? Explain.

4. Richard, age 35, is married and childless. His wife is also fully employed. He would like to have $100,000 in life insurance coverage and is interested in a policy that will also give him some investment earnings. Should he consider term insurance?

5. What are the pros and cons of working with a life insurance agent?

6. What are the pros and cons of buying your insurance online directly from the company?

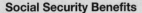

YOU TRY IT

Social Security Benefits

Go to the Social Security Web site, at www.ssa.gov, and click on "Calculate Your Benefits." If you're married or have children, enter your own financial information to see what benefit you or your children could be entitled to collect. If you're not married and don't have children, enter hypothetical information based on what you think your financial circumstances will be 10 years from now.

Life Insurance Needs Analysis

Kate is a single parent who earns $40,000 per year. Her household expenses are $28,000 per year. If she were to die, she estimates that the costs of her death would be $10,000. She has not participated in Social Security long enough to be fully insured. She would also want her life insurance to provide an education fund for her 10-year-old twins and a lump sum for their continued care, which she estimates at $15,000 annually until they are 18.

1. Would an income-multiple approach result in Kate's purchase of sufficient life insurance? Why or why not?

2. Using a financial needs approach, how much life insurance would you recommend that Kate buy?

3. If Kate were fully insured under Social Security and her children would be eligible for total annual benefits of $10,000, how much difference would this make in her life insurance needs?

11

INVESTMENT BASICS
Investing Wisely

Starting Point

Go to www.wiley.com/college/bajtelsmit to assess your knowledge of investing.
Determine where you need to concentrate your effort.

What You'll Learn in This Chapter

▲ Appropriate investment goals
▲ The risk/return trade-off
▲ Passive and active investing strategies

After Studying This Chapter, You'll Be Able To

▲ Develop realistic investment goals consistent with your financial plan, risk tolerance, and life stage
▲ Compare and contrast your investment alternatives
▲ Assess the asset allocation and diversification of your portfolio
▲ Decide whether you will be an active or passive investor and what your primary investment strategy will be

INTRODUCTION

Today, thousands of possible investments compete for your cash, and it's easy to make bad choices. To avoid costly mistakes, you should make sure your personal financial plan includes a plan for developing investment knowledge and for taking an active role in household investment decisions. To accumulate the funds to achieve your goals, you need to save and invest on a regular basis. This requires that you stick to a budget, and it also requires that you make informed investment decisions. Over time, compound interest can help your savings grow. In addition, the more you can earn on your investments, the more quickly your savings will grow. If you leave all your money in low-interest bank savings accounts, it will take much longer to build wealth than if you put money in higher-interest investments.

In this chapter, we look at the basics of investing. We first examine the process of setting investment goals and then consider some fundamental investment concepts. This chapter also provides a broad overview of the investment alternatives available.

11.1 Developing Realistic Investment Goals

In investing, as in other areas of your financial plan, you need to set specific goals that are realistic and within your control. Because you invest in order to accumulate funds to meet other household objectives, your investment process should begin with a reevaluation of your overall plan. Have you established the necessary foundation elements of your plan, prioritized your financial goals, and developed a budget that will allow you to set aside sufficient funds for investing? If so, you can move ahead in the investment planning process.

11.1.1 Establishing a Firm Foundation

Although it might sound like fun to jump right in and start investing, there are a few things you should take care of first. Before you begin to develop an investment plan, you should make sure you have a secure foundation to build on. To see if you're ready for this step, you need to ask yourself the following questions:

- ▲ Have I established my financial goals?
- ▲ Am I living within my budget and meeting my basic needs?
- ▲ Have I reduced my outstanding high-interest credit?
- ▲ Do I have an emergency fund in cash or liquid savings accounts?
- ▲ Do I have adequate insurance coverage?
- ▲ Have I bought a home or established a plan for doing so?

If you can answer "yes" to all these questions, you're ready to begin your investment planning. That doesn't mean you should immediately call a broker and buy 100 shares of Google stock. Before you take any specific action, you need to establish your investment objectives and educate yourself about the investment marketplace and your investment alternatives.

The investment planning process involves these seven steps:

1. Identify your goals.
2. Estimate how much you need to accumulate to achieve your goals.
3. Estimate how much you can apply to your investment program both in current lump-sum and regular future payments.
4. Evaluate your risk tolerance.
5. Learn about your investment alternatives.
6. Select investments that are appropriate for you, given your risk tolerance, time horizon, and investment objectives.
7. Monitor your investment plan.

11.1.2 Investing to Meet Your Prioritized Goals

In developing your investment plan, you should ask yourself "Why am I investing?" The answer is probably that you're trying to achieve one or more of the following financial goals:

▲ Increase current income.
▲ Take a vacation.
▲ Make a major purchase, such as a car or home.
▲ Start a business.
▲ Save for education costs (for yourself or your children).
▲ Meet retirement income needs.

If you've prioritized your financial goals, you know which ones you need to focus on first. How much do you need to accumulate to meet these goals? How much time do you have? How much money can you allocate to this part of your financial plan? Because different types of investments yield different average returns over time, the amount you need to invest to achieve your goals depends on your choice of investments. You also need to consider the risk levels of different investments relative to your preferences and time horizon. If you're saving for a long-term goal, you might be able to weather some ups and downs in your investments, but if you need the money next year for a particular purpose, you can't afford to take much risk.

In setting your investment goals, you should try to make sure that they're realistic, specific, and measurable. Therefore, you should go back to your prioritized financial goals and, for each goal, identify the following:

▲ The purpose of the investment plan.

▲ The amount needed in the future to meet your financial goal.

▲ The amount you can currently allocate to your investment plan.

▲ How much time until you need the money.

▲ How much risk, and what types of risk, you can afford to take.

How much money do you need to save to meet each of your goals? The answer to this question depends on the time value of money. If your accumulating funds earn more interest, then you'll need to save less each month. Conversely, if your investments earn a small rate of return, you'll need to put away more each month to get to your goal. The following table can help you estimate your monthly investment needs. For example, if you want to save $10,000 in five years and your savings account will earn 4%, look down the 4% column to the amount in the row corresponding to five years. The amount given, $15.08, is how much you would have to save to accumulate $1,000 in five years, so you multiply this by 10. This means you will need to save 10 × $15.08 = $150.80 per month to have $10,000 saved by the end of five years.

11.1.3 Getting the Money to Invest

The actual process of investing is not especially difficult. The most common stumbling block is not having the necessary funds to invest. An essential element of your financial plan must therefore be to prioritize your spending so that investing for the future receives sufficient attention. You may have to sacrifice current spending to

Monthly Savings Amount Per $1,000 Investment Goal

(assuming monthly compounding and end of month contributions to savings)

Years to Save	Months to Save	Annual Investment Return				
		2%	4%	6%	8%	10%
1	12	$82.57	$81.82	$81.07	$80.32	$79.58
2	24	$40.87	$40.09	$39.32	$38.56	$37.81
3	36	$26.98	$26.19	$25.42	$24.67	$23.93
4	48	$20.03	$19.25	$18.49	$17.75	$17.03
5	60	$15.86	$15.08	$14.33	$13.61	$12.91
10	120	$7.53	$6.79	$6.10	$5.47	$4.88
15	180	$4.77	$4.06	$3.44	$2.89	$2.41
20	240	$3.39	$2.73	$2.16	$1.70	$1.32
25	300	$2.57	$1.95	$1.44	$1.05	$0.75
30	360	$2.03	$1.44	$1.00	$0.67	$0.44

have money available to devote to your investment plan. Depending on where you are in your career and life cycle, you may need to start out small and build your investment program as your income increases. You may not think investing small amounts is worthwhile. But keep in mind that when saving for long-term goals, the earlier you start, the less you need to save to achieve a specific goal. Taking the first step is the toughest part; when you get started, it's easier to continue.

Here are a few ideas to help make it less painful to find the money in your budget for investing.

▲ **Pay yourself first:** Financial advisors regularly offer this rule of thumb. If your budget includes an amount that you've allocated to saving or investing, you should take it right off the top at the beginning of the month. You can often accomplish this by having the amount automatically withdrawn from your checking account and deposited in your investment account. Most people find that, if they wait until the end of the month to invest what's left over, the funds are no longer there—they are whittled away by small and often unnecessary expenditures.

▲ **Save your raise:** Maybe you truly don't have any excess funds in your budget; all your current income may be going to pay for necessities. But what if you make a deal with yourself that you'll allocate all—or at least a significant portion—of your next raise to your savings and investment plan? This works best if you have a high proportion of fixed expenses in your budget, such as car and loan payments. In that case, when your income goes up, your expenses do not go up proportionally. So if you don't let yourself become accustomed to the extra income but instead immediately set it aside for your investment plan, it won't feel like you're cutting back on immediate consumption.

▲ **Set aside bonuses, tax refunds, and other lump sums:** When the money you're applying to investments has never been part of your regular income, it's not painful to set it aside. You can immediately apply bonuses and other lump-sum windfalls such as birthday gifts, tax refunds, and inheritances to your investment plan. If these lump sums are fairly significant amounts, the dollars can accumulate quickly.

▲ **Continue a payment plan:** When you've finished paying off an installment loan, such as a car loan or student loan, you should consider shifting those dollars immediately to your investment plan. Because you haven't been spending that portion of your income on consumption, you can put it toward this new use without feeling the loss. Your $300 monthly car payment could put you closer to achieving your investment goals by $3,600 per year.

▲ **Participate in employer-sponsored retirement plans:** Your employer may offer you the opportunity to participate in a company-sponsored retirement savings plan. Whether or not your employer also makes contributions to the plan, you should try to contribute regularly. These dollars are generally invested on a pretax basis, which means you avoid paying current federal, state, and local income taxes on this money. Also, the taxes on earnings in your retirement fund are deferred until you take the money out—and that may be many years in the future. Without the eroding effect of taxes, your investments can grow more quickly.

▲ **Stop up a cash leak:** When you developed your cash budget, you may have identified some regular household expenditures that could be avoided or reduced. If so, you can try to allocate to your new investment plan the amount you would have spent on those items. If you normally drive 15,000 miles per year and you can cut down your driving by 10 percent, for example, you'll save between $150 and $300 per year, depending on the fuel efficiency of your car and the current price of gasoline. If you replaced your car with a more fuel-efficient one, you could save more than $1,000 in gas costs per year (although you'd also have to consider the effect this might have on your car payments and auto insurance premiums).

FOR EXAMPLE

Saving Money by Making Little Changes

Suppose you decide to "brown bag" your lunch three times a week instead of eating out every day, saving about $15 per week, or $60 per month. If you take that $60 and invest it instead (at the beginning of the month), you'll accumulate $720 plus interest by the end of the year. Other examples of little budget reductions include taking books out of the library instead of buying them and renting DVDs instead of going to the movies. If you have a gas-guzzling car, you might take public transportation or try biking.

▲ **Go on a financial diet once or twice a year:** Many people find it easiest to tighten their belts in short stretches. You can try being a cheapskate for one or two months a year, trimming your budget down to just the necessities and banking the rest.

▲ **Take a second job:** Although you probably wouldn't want to work two jobs indefinitely, you can consider taking a second job for one or two months and applying all the additional income to accumulating some investment capital.

11.2 Understanding Your Investment Alternatives

When it's time to decide how to invest, you have many alternatives. Before deciding, you need to understand the two major ways to invest. This section presents an overview of the advantages and disadvantages of each and identifies the major categories of investment alternatives.

There are generally two ways to invest: You can be either a lender or an owner. When you lend, you're a **debt investor,** and when you own, you're an **equity investor.** In either case, the return on your investment comes from some combination of

▲ Regular cash flow, such as the payment of interest or dividends.

▲ **Capital gain,** or the growth in the value of your investment over time.

The amounts earned and the risks you're exposed to with these two methods of investing differ in important ways.

11.2.1 The Advantages and Disadvantages of Lending

When you lend—whether to an individual, the government, a financial institution, or other business—your cash flows include regular interest payments and the eventual repayment of your loan. If you sell your debt investment before the loan is due in full, you may realize a capital gain also.

Such investments are called debt investments because they represent a debt obligation to the borrower. They also may be referred to as **fixed-income investments** because the interest cash flows to the lender commonly are a series of equal payments over time. This relative certainty about future cash flows is one of the advantages of debt investing. Of course, the investor runs the risk that the borrower might get into financial difficulty and fail to pay the interest promised or to repay the original amount borrowed.

In the event of financial difficulties, however, the firm's obligation to debt investors is given first priority—the owners do not receive anything unless the debt investors have first been paid what they're owed. There are many types of lending opportunities, and they differ in terms of risk and return.

One of the basic principles of finance is that the lower the risk, the lower the return. Your bank savings account, for example, is a very low-risk, federally insured loan made to your financial institution. In return for your deposit, the bank promises to pay you regular interest on your savings and to return your funds to you upon request; however, because the risk is so low, the interest rate the bank pays is very low as well. In contrast, if you lend money to the government or to a business and commit your funds for a long period of time for the loan (often 20 years or more), you're exposed to greater risk and are therefore paid a higher annual rate on the debt investment. Although debt investments offer the security of receiving regular cash flows, their rates of return in general tend to be lower than those of some of the other investment alternatives.

If you lend to a business, and the business later becomes very profitable, you do not have a right to any of the profits, as you would if you were an owner. As a lender, you don't share in the company's good fortune except insofar as it reduces the risk that you won't be paid what you're owed.

11.2.2 The Advantages and Disadvantages of Owning

If you're an entrepreneur at heart, you can invest by owning a business. This, of course, requires certain skills and a substantial investment of time and money. Alternatively, if you want to share in the profits of a business without having to run the business yourself, you can become a partial owner of a company and allow others to manage it.

This type of investment is often referred to as an equity investment and, as an **equity investor,** you expect to receive a return on your investment in the form of growth in the value of your investment over time and/or regular distribution of business profits. Your cash flows as an owner are much less certain than your cash flows as a lender.

If a company you own does very well, your income stream may increase over time, but you also run the risk that the company's profits will be less than expected or that the company will experience a loss or go out of business. Whereas the company is obligated to make payments to its debt investors, it has no similar obligation to its owners; in a bad year, there may be nothing left to distribute to equity investors.

It's generally less risky to be a lender than it is to be an owner. If the firm gets into financial difficulties, the lenders are paid first. But there's a cost associated with lower risk: The average return on stocks has averaged between 10 and 12 percent over time, whereas the average return on long-term bonds has averaged only 6 to 8 percent.

11.2.3 The Major Asset Classes

Although there are many investment choices, if you're a novice investor, you probably want to stick to the basics—stocks, bonds, mutual funds, and perhaps investment real estate. These categories, commonly referred to as **asset classes,** are broad groups of investments that have certain characteristics in common.

As you gain experience, you may decide to branch out to more complex investments, but you need to start out simple and add to your knowledge base as you go. Your want to build a diversified portfolio, or collection, of investments that fulfills your objectives. You may see many types of investments referred to as **securities,** defined as investments in which the investor contributes a sum of money to a common enterprise, with the intention of earning a profit through the efforts of others.

The law requires that companies selling securities meet certain reporting and disclosure requirements. Stocks, bonds, and mutual fund shares are common examples of financial securities, but many other business ventures might qualify as well. The example "Can a Security Wiggle?" describes an unusual case. The major asset classes are described next.

Common Stock

A share of **stock** in a company represents a share of ownership in a business. If you own a share in a company that has a total of 1 million shareholders, your

---

FOR EXAMPLE

Can a Security Wiggle?

Florida residents John Rowles, Jim Cole, and Wayne Minton decided to supplement their regular income by investing in a worm ranch. They paid $50,000 for a franchise from B&B Worm Farms of Oklahoma and invested another $100,000 in startup costs. B&B promised to buy all the worms they produced for $7 a pound for sale to chicken farms, dairies, and facilities that need worms to process compost. The three friends estimated that they'd recoup their initial investment in less than a year. The worms seemed like a no-risk investment.

Jim's garage was soon too small for their operation, so they expanded to a greenhouse. Unfortunately, with more than 11 million worms ready for market, the entrepreneurs found that B&B was being investigated for securities law violations—which meant that B&B could no longer buy their worms. The state sued B&B.

Jim, John, and Wayne eventually found buyers for the worms, so they didn't lose all their money. They also learned some hard lessons. First, there's no such thing as a "no-risk" investment. Second, it isn't a good idea to have everything tied up in a single investment. Finally, you should always do your homework before investing; a call to the Department of Securities at the outset would have prevented Jim, John, and Wayne from making this mistake.[1-3]

single share means you have a 1/1,000,000 ownership share of the firm. Your share typically entitles you to vote on major issues, such as election of the board of directors of the company. If the board decides to distribute some of the company's profits to its shareholders in the form of dividends, you're entitled to a proportional share of the dividend distributions.

Although neither form of return is guaranteed, stock investors generally expect to make a return on their investment in the form of **dividends,** which are the periodic distributions of profits to equity investors, and capital gains, the increase in the value of their shares over time. Both of these forms of cash flow are fairly risky. Dividends can be paid only if the company has funds available after paying all its other obligations. Shares of stock have no maturity date, so the firm never has to pay you back the amount you've put into the firm, but you can sell your shares to other investors or pass them on to future generations, assuming that the firm is still in existence at that time. Stock investing is covered in more detail in Chapter 12.

Bonds

The most common long-term debt investment is a bond. A **bond** generally has a fixed maturity date (often 20 years or more in the future), at which time the borrower promises to repay the loan in full. Also, the bondholder is entitled to receive a fixed periodic payment of interest, with payments normally made semiannually, or every six months. Unlike mortgage loans, this type of loan is not amortized, so the regular payments include interest only, and the full amount of principal is due at the end of the term. For example, a corporate bond with a $1,000 face value might promise an $80 interest payment per year, or 8 percent of the face value. The investor would receive half of this interest, or $40, every six months and be repaid the $1,000 in full on the maturity date.

Bonds are commonly issued by federal, state, and local governments and by corporations to finance operations and expansion. Like stock investors, bond investors expect to make returns on their investments from both current income (i.e., periodic interest payments) and capital gains (i.e., changes in value of the bond over time). Although the interest payments are usually fixed for the life of the bond, the bond value is not. Chapter 12 describes the factors that affect bond values.

Preferred Stock

In addition to common stock, companies also sometimes issue **preferred stock.** This type of stock has characteristics that make it look like a hybrid of a stock and a bond. Like a share of common stock, a share of preferred stock has no maturity date and represents an ownership interest in a firm. Like a bond, a share of preferred stock produces a constant cash flow for the investor because the dividend is a fixed dollar amount per share per year.

Although the constant cash flow makes preferred stock look something like bonds, it's a riskier investment than bonds because it does, in fact, represent an equity interest. In the event of financial difficulties, the company must make its debt payments before paying any dividends to the preferred shareholders; preferred shareholders do, however, have priority over common shareholders. Preferred stock is discussed further in Chapter 12.

Mutual Funds

Investors can invest in stocks, bonds, and other assets by purchasing shares of a **mutual fund** that invests in these assets. A mutual fund takes investors' funds and hires professionals to select and manage a portfolio of investments on behalf of the fund owners.

As a mutual fund investor, you're a proportionate owner of the fund assets, and you're therefore entitled to share in the income and growth of the investment pool. Mutual fund shares are similar to stock investments, but the return and risk of a mutual fund depends on the return and risk of the assets that each mutual fund invests in. Mutual funds are discussed in Chapter 13.

Real Estate

Home ownership has advantages as an investment, as discussed in Chapter 7, and you may also want to consider other investment in real estate. Real estate offers investors the opportunity to receive cash flows from net rental income and capital gains from the growth in the property's value. The large minimum amount of funds required to get started in real estate investing may preclude you from considering this alternative until you've built up some wealth. Also, you need to consider the added risk you face from having your wealth tied up in an asset that isn't very liquid.

Derivatives

The investment marketplace has expanded to include a large number of complex and risky securities. Many fall into a general category of investments called **derivative securities** because they derive their value from the price movements of some other underlying assets. These assets are highly speculative because they are usually purchased in the hope of making a short-term profit, based on changes in supply and demand. **Speculative investments** don't usually pay dividends or interest, so you're entirely dependent on the change in value to make a return. Although it's possible to make a large return on some types of speculative investments, you run the risk of quickly losing everything you've invested. And this is most likely to happen to inexperienced, uninformed investors.

Commodities are contracts to buy or sell raw materials (e.g., oil, precious metals) and agricultural products (e.g., corn, wheat, sugar) at some point in the future at a price set at the time the contract is made. A similar type of investment is a **futures contract,** which is a contract to buy or sell a financial security, such as a government bond or stock index, in the future. Because the price and date are set in advance, the buyers and sellers of both commodities and futures contracts are making bets on which way prices will go in the future.

Option contracts are like commodities and futures contracts except that with an option contract, the buyer is not obligated to go through with the contract to buy or sell in the future—he or she simply has the option to do so. A buyer of a call option has the right, but not the obligation, to purchase the underlying asset at a set price on or before the call's maturity date. A buyer of a put option has the right, but not the obligation, to sell the underlying asset at a set price on or before the put's maturity date. Although these investments may seem a bit less risky than commodities and futures, the buyer of an option has to pay a price up front for that right, so even if prices move in a favorable direction, the cost of the option itself may offset any profit.

Indexed Securities

An indexed security is an investment whose cash flows mimic the returns and risk of a broad class of securities. For example, if you're interested in investing in stocks, you can buy index shares that track the performance of the 500 large company stocks in the S&P 500 Index or the 30 industrial stocks in the Dow Jones Industrial Average. There are also indexes based on specific industry sectors, such as energy, technology, and financial services, and there are indexes based on different classifications of bonds.

Index investors receive a return on their investment from some combination of price appreciation and dividends.

SELF-CHECK

1. Which type of security looks like a hybrid of a stock and a bond?
2. List the five major asset classes.
3. Define **capital gain**, **dividends**, **commodities**, and **derivatives**.

11.3 Factors That Reduce Investment Risk

One of the most important investing concepts is the relationship between risk and return. Almost all investments expose you to some risk. In general, however, riskier investments provide higher average rates of return over time. Because there are two sources of return—current cash flow and capital gains—there are two kinds of risk that may hurt your ability to meet your financial goals:

▲ The risk that you won't receive expected cash flows from the investment.

▲ The risk that the value of your investment will decline over time.

Depending on the type of investment you make, you may have more or less exposure to these two types of risk. Not everyone is comfortable with investment risk, and it's important that your investments be consistent with your risk preferences. Your investment risk exposure should not be greater than your desire and ability to bear risk.

11.3.1 The Risk/Return Trade-off

How do you know whether an investment is too risky for you? First, you need to understand your own risk tolerance, and then you need to be able to assess the expected returns and risks for each of your investment alternatives so that you can evaluate whether their expected performance is consistent with your risk tolerance.

You may already have a good feel for how much risk you're willing to take in your investments. A **risk-averse person** is someone who prefers an amount of money that is certain over a gamble that would, on average, produce the same amount of money.

Suppose you're offered the following gamble: We'll flip a coin, and if it's heads, you win $100; if it's tails, you get zero. How much would you be willing to pay to play that game? Paying $50 would represent a "fair" gamble—that is, if you could play the game many times, on average, you'd break even. Even so, a risk-averse person wouldn't be willing to pay $50 to play because he or she would rather have the $50 for certain than take the risk. The risk-averse person might, however, be willing to pay $40 or $30 to play. The less you're willing to pay, the more risk averse you are. In other words, a risk-averse person is only willing to take a gamble if he or she gets something extra for taking the risk. In an investment context, the "something extra" is a higher rate of return on investment.

Women tend to be more conservative investors than men. However, a recent study examining transactions in a large mutual fund found that the female investors ended up with better overall performance than the men. Although the women did, in fact, make somewhat more conservative investment choices than the men, the men made more trades, apparently "playing" with their money more. The men's higher transaction costs left them with lower overall returns.

11.3.2 Measuring Risk and Return for Individual Securities

The amount of risk that you're willing to take should depend on whether you expect to be adequately rewarded for taking that risk. Even if an investment were truly risk free, you'd still expect to be compensated for investing your money instead of being able to spend it for current consumption. This minimum return is referred to as the *real risk-free rate*. The additional return you earn from any investment is your compensation for bearing risk.

Investors expect to make money from current income generated by their investments (e.g., interest, dividends, rents) and the gains in the value of their investments over time. These are often referred to collectively as the *return on investment* and may be expressed as a **rate of return** (or yield) in percentage or as a dollar return over a given period of time.

The annual rate of return is calculated as follows:

$$\text{Annual rate of return} = \text{Current yield} + \text{Capital gain yield}$$

$$\text{Current income} / \text{Beginning price} + \text{End price} - \text{Beginning price} / \text{Beginning price}$$

$$\text{Current income} + \text{End price} - \text{Beginning price} / \text{Beginning price}$$

To see how this works, assume that you buy a share of stock for $20. Over the next year, the stock pays you a cash dividend of $1 (which is 5 percent of your original purchase price), and the stock also increases in value to $22 (a gain of $2, or 10 percent of the original purchase price). The combined value of the dividend income and the gain in value gives you a $3 return for the year, so you have earned a rate of return, or yield, of $3 / $20 = 15 percent on the stock investment.

11.3.3 Risk Premiums

As we've seen, investors require a premium to be willing to bear risk. An easy way to think about the relationship between risk and return is that investors will require a certain amount of return, or a risk premium, for each type of risk to which they're exposed. For debt securities, these may include inflation risk, interest-rate risk, reinvestment risk, default risk, liquidity risk, and market risk. Equity investments expose you primarily to inflation risk, reinvestment risk, and market risk. An investment with more of these components of risk will generally provide a greater level of return than one that has very few. The types of risk are:

▲ **Inflation Risk.** Even if an investment were virtually risk-free, you'd require compensation for delaying consumption. With most investments, you'll also be exposed to inflation risk—the loss in spending power over the investment period. Thus, the minimum rate of return you'd expect from any investment would include compensation for delaying consumption and for bearing inflation risk. This minimum rate of return is usually called the nominal risk-free rate—a rate that is higher during periods of rising inflation than during periods of low inflation. The shortest-term debt security issued by the federal government, a 13-week Treasury bill, is an investment that is expected to earn the nominal risk-free rate since it doesn't expose you to any of the other types of risk discussed below. Inflation risk normally increases with the term to maturity, so a one-year Treasury bill will have a slightly larger inflation-risk premium than a 13-week Treasury bill.

▲ **Interest-Rate Risk.** Although interest rates can have an effect on all investments, some types of securities—bonds and preferred stock—are more influenced by interest-rate changes. When interest rates go up, the present value of cash flows to be received in the future goes down. This causes prices to fall. When rates go down, prices go up. The longer the term to maturity, the more the price of the security is affected. This is commonly called interest-rate risk, although it's sometimes called maturity risk or price risk, because of the strong interrelationship among interest rates, maturities, and prices. Investors expect to be compensated for this risk with an interest-rate risk premium. Short-term securities have a lower interest-rate risk premium—they provide a lower return on investment, all else equal—than longer-term securities. A corollary to interest-rate risk is **reinvestment risk**—the risk that you'll have to reinvest returns at a time when rates of return have fallen. Whereas interest-rate risk is greatest for long term debt securities, reinvestment risk is highest for short-term debt investments.

▲ **Default Risk.** The risk that you won't receive expected cash flows from an investment is called default risk. Although any company can run into financial difficulties, some corporations and government entities are considered more likely to default than others. The issuers of risky bonds must offer investors a higher rate of return to compensate them for default risk. For equity investors—who can't technically be defaulted on, since they haven't been promised any particular return—there's still the risk of business failure. In a bankruptcy proceeding, the value of an equity investment is likely to be zero.

▲ **Liquidity Risk.** Liquidity risk is the risk that you won't be able to convert your investment to cash on short notice without losing value. This risk is lowest for securities that have active markets—such as publicly traded stocks and bonds. In contrast, real estate is fairly difficult to sell on short notice. Investors expect to receive a premium when they invest in less liquid assets, but it may be insufficient to offset the cost of not being able to sell something when you need to.

▲ **Market Risk.** In addition to individual risk, all investments expose you to market risk, the risk associated with general market movements and economic conditions. In a recession, when businesses are cutting back on spending and unemployment rates are high, investment values tend to decline, resulting in a "bear market." When times are good, as in the late 1990s, the result is a "bull market," characterized by increasing asset values fueled by high business profits, low interest rates, and economic growth. Although both debt and equity markets are influenced by market conditions, they don't necessarily move together. You could, for example, simultaneously have a bull stock market and a bear bond market. Market risk is related not only to economic conditions in the United States but also to global risks. After the events of September 11, 2001, and their well-publicized effect on financial markets around the world, it's easy to see why global and political factors are important to investors.

11.3.4 Reducing Risk in a Portfolio

If you could see the future and know with certainty which of your investments would do best, you could put all your money there and never lose a dime. But in reality, no one can accurately predict the ups and downs of specific companies or even of broad asset classes. By spreading your money over a selection of investments and asset classes—that is, by diversifying your investments—you reduce the risk that one bad choice will cause you to lose everything.

FOR EXAMPLE

The Benefit of Perfect Foresight

If you had invested $1 in short-term federal government debt securities (i.e., Treasury bills [T-bills]) in 1933 and then reinvested the principal and interest each year, your portfolio would have grown to about $15 by 2004. If the same dollar had instead been invested in the S&P 500 Index, which is composed of large company stocks, and you'd reinvested all your dividend income each year, you'd have had about $3,000 by 2004, more than 200 times as much as if you'd invested in T-bills.

Suppose that in this same investing scenario, you'd had a crystal ball that could perfectly predict the future. Each year, you'd look ahead to see which investment would earn a higher return in the coming year—the S&P 500 Index or T-bills. When you foresaw stocks outperforming T-bills, you'd move all your money to stocks for the year, and when you foresaw T-bills doing better, you'd move all your money there. With perfect foresight, your single dollar in 1933 would have grown to around $65,000 by 2004, resulting in a portfolio more than 20 times greater than stocks alone and more than 4,000 times your accumulation in T-bills alone.

Although no one has the ability to perfectly predict the market, there are two lessons here. First, despite its ups and downs, the stock market has produced far greater returns over time than low-risk investments such as T-bills. Second, even if you can't predict with perfect accuracy, a little knowledge goes a long way. Even if you just avoided the 5 worst loss years in the stock market, you'd have had about $12,500 at the end, more than four times what you'd have had if you'd left the money in the stock market for the entire 70 years.

The principle of **diversification** can be summed up this way: Don't put all your eggs in one basket. In practice, deciding exactly which "baskets" to use and how many "eggs" to put in each is difficult. Suppose you have $10,000 to invest in a portfolio of stocks. At the beginning of the year, you put half the money in Stock A and half in Stock B. Both are expected to earn a return of 10 percent per year, on average. But these are risky investments, so the actual return in each year is not always 10 percent. Rather, the returns fluctuate around an average of 10 percent and may even, in some years, be negative. Over a two-year period, the actual annual returns for your investment portfolio, including dividends and capital gains, are as follows:

Actual Returns

	Year 1	Year 2
Stock A	18%	2%
Stock B	4%	16%
Average	11%	9%

As you can see, if you'd put all your money in Stock B, you would have realized a return of only 4 percent on your investment in Year 1. Because Stock A earned 18 percent in Year 1, however, you were able to earn an overall return of 11 percent on your two-stock portfolio. In Year 2, Stock A earned only 2 percent, but Stock B earned 16 percent, so again, your average return was near the expected return of 10 percent. Splitting your money between these two stocks reduced the risk that your investment portfolio return would deviate too far from your expected return. You paid a cost for reducing the risk, however: Although your returns were higher than if you had happened to have only the poorly performing stock in a given year, they were lower than if you had happened to have only the higher-performing stock.

As you increase the number of investments in your portfolio, the variability of the returns on your portfolio declines because the ups and downs of individual investments cancel each other out. That's because many of the things that affect a given firm's profitability are company specific. One company may have a labor dispute when another introduces a new product. One company might be named in a product liability lawsuit while another is expanding its operations into South America. Your objective in diversification is to have enough investments so that all these company-specific risks average out, resulting in reduced variability of return for your total portfolio.

Figure 11-1 illustrates the risk-reducing effect of adding more stocks (or other investments) to your portfolio: The more you have, the lower your risk. Although the graph shows that random asset selection gets rid of most company-specific

Figure 11-1

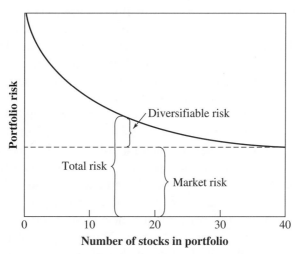

Number of stocks in portfolio

The risk-reducing impact of diversification.

risk after you have about 40 stocks in your portfolio, there isn't a "magic number" of investments that results in perfect diversification.

Diversification depends on many factors, including your choice of invest-ments, the relationships between the investments you hold, market conditions, and your own risk tolerance. Even if your portfolio is well diversified, it still isn't risk free. After all the company-specific, or diversifiable, risks are canceled out, what is left is market risk. Market risk, unlike company-specific risk, cannot be avoided through diversification.

What if you're pretty sure that an investment is going to do so well that you want to put all your money in it? Suppose you work at a terrific company that gives you stock bonuses or contributes stock to your retirement plan. The value of that stock has been rising at a rate faster than the market as a whole. Is it still necessary to diversify? In 2001, thousands of employees of Enron Corpora-tion found out the hard way that being undiversified—holding nothing but Enron stock in their portfolios—involves a lot of downside risk. When the com-pany went bankrupt after allegations of accounting irregularities, these people not only lost their jobs but also lost most of their nest eggs.

Although financial advisors have for years warned about the hazards of being undiversified—having all your financial and human capital tied to the perfor-mance of one firm—people like to invest in what they understand or think they understand. The company you work for may seem like a good investment, but you should resist the urge to go overboard. As a general guideline, you should invest no more than 10 percent of your total portfolio in any single investment.

Asset allocation is the method by which you achieve diversification. **Asset allocation** is the process of deciding which proportion of your portfolio to invest in each of several broad investment classes—stock, bonds, real estate, cash—as opposed to individual security selection within an asset class.

Most investment professionals say that asset allocation is the most important component of building an investment portfolio. Some academic studies have shown that as much as 90 percent of the overall performance of a long-term portfolio is attributable to the asset allocation mix, as opposed to individual investment selection of assets within each asset class.

Your allocation of funds between broad asset classes should change over your life cycle to be consistent with your investment objectives, family situation, time horizon, and risk tolerance. There's no hard-and-fast rule, but most people should allocate a higher proportion of their portfolios to stocks when they're younger. With a longer time to invest, young people can afford to take more risk, so they should have more wealth in assets that have the potential for greater returns. As you approach retirement and your investment horizon shortens, it's advisable to gradually shift toward lower-risk asset classes. Your goal then is to maintain your wealth, so you don't want to take too much risk. When you retire, you spend rather than save, but you need to earn enough to offset the eroding effect of inflation. Thus, even in retirement, you want to allocate some money to stocks. If you retire at 65 and expect to live to be 90, you still have a long investment horizon.

Although there's no magic formula for asset allocation over the life cycle, investment advisors commonly provide their clients with rules of thumb for asset allocation decisions. These rules aren't universally accepted and haven't been scientifically validated. But they have the positive effects of discouraging overly conservative investment behavior at young ages and encouraging risk reduction at older ages. For example, an advisor might suggest the following rule: The percentage of money you should invest in stocks is 110 minus your age and the rest of your portfolio should be equally allocated to bonds and cash. If you followed that rule, at age 25, you would invest 85 percent in stocks, and at age 65, you would invest only 45 percent in stocks. The remainder of your portfolio would be a combination of bonds and cash. Figure 11-2 shows how this allocation might evolve over a typical person's life cycle. Note, however, that a different financial advisor might advise you to allocate based on a different formula—perhaps 100 minus your age.

SELF-CHECK

1. Define **rate of return** and **asset allocation**.
2. What is the problem with having all your eggs in one basket?
3. What is the financial goal in retirement?

Figure 11-2

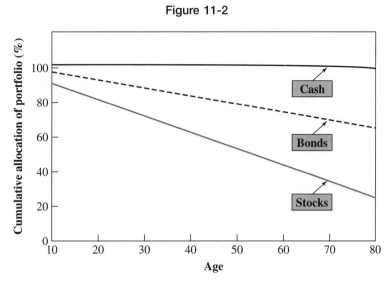

Possible asset allocation over the life cycle.

11.4 Establishing Your Investment Strategy

After you have developed realistic financial goals, learned about your investment alternatives, and determined your risk level, the next step in the investment planning process is to establish an investment strategy that's appropriate for your risk tolerance, expertise, time, and life cycle stage. This section explains why it's advisable to be a passive investor and describes passive investment strategies.

11.4.1 Active vs. Passive Investing

Do you want to be an active or a passive investor over the long term? An **active investor** attempts to identify investments and asset classes that are undervalued in the short run and to make returns by buying those that are underpriced and selling those that are overpriced. In the extreme, an active investor might be what is called a "day trader"—one who makes many trades in a single day, attempting to capitalize on new information or temporary imbalances in supply and demand. In contrast, a **passive investor** attempts to carefully select a combination of investments that will, over the long term, result in achieving his or her investment return goals.

The objective of an active investor is to "beat the market," or to make greater returns than would normally be expected for the level of risk in the portfolio. Passive investors are happy to do as well as the market, on average, earning a return that is appropriate for the portfolio risk. In general, individual investors are well advised to choose from the passive investment strategies described here. Let's look at two eternally debated questions.

Can Active Investors "Beat the Market"?

As you learn more, you may be tempted to capitalize on your newfound knowledge by doing some active investing. Before you do, however, you should consider the evidence: Many studies show that portfolios actively managed by professional money managers achieve lower annual returns, on average, than the market as a whole. This means that investors have paid for the services of professionals when they might have been better off simply buying shares of an indexed security.

But aren't some professional investors more successful than others? The evidence shows otherwise: The managers who achieve the highest returns in a given year are rarely at the top the following year. Because you're not as experienced or knowledgeable as these professionals, you probably won't be able to do any better. If this is true, why do so many investors think they can beat the odds? There are many psychological forces at work, which result in often-irrational financial decisions.

Are Markets Efficient?

A commonly offered explanation for why investors are unlikely to make short-run returns from active investing is that markets for financial securities are relatively efficient. In all of financial economics, no topic has been the subject of more study than market efficiency; the originator of the theory, Eugene Fama, received a Nobel prize for his work on this subject.

Market efficiency means that, at any given time, all publicly available information has already driven security prices to the correct level, given that information. If, as the theory implies, financial assets are always correctly priced, you can't make any extra profit by buying underpriced securities and selling over-priced securities—the essence of an active investment strategy. So investors receive the return justified by the risk of the investment but aren't able to get any extra return by incurring additional trading costs or by investing time in research or education. Stock analysts and investment managers, who make a living doing exactly that, are not too keen on this theory.

On a very basic level, market efficiency can be thought of as being related to how quickly prices react to news. Because information is so easily available today and there are so many investors in the marketplace, all trying to identify undervalued securities, the window of opportunity for capitalizing on any new information has to be fairly small. If, for example, you hear that a company is introducing an innovative new product and you believe it will cause the stock price to rise, you may want to buy some shares at the current price and sell them after the price rises with the good news. But everyone else has heard the good news, too, so investors will immediately start buying up as many shares as possible, and the price will rise. By the time you buy the shares, the stock price may already be high. Market efficiency means that it's difficult, although not impossible, to profit from new information. You have to be at the front of the line.

Today, the efficiency of the market makes it riskier than ever to be an active investor. Prices of actively traded stocks and bonds react to information so quickly that they sometimes even move in advance of the actual public announcement, on the strength of expectations. Generally, if information is reported in the financial press, it's too late to act on it for quick profits.

11.4.2 Passive Investing Strategies

Although being a passive investor implies that you're not making regular changes in your portfolio, most passive investors continue to build their portfolios over time. Therefore, they must make regular investment contributions and selections. The most common strategies for doing so include buy-and-hold, dollar cost averaging, and direct investment and reinvestment plans.

Buy-and-Hold

In general, passive investment strategies by their very nature fall into the category of **buy-and-hold.** This strategy means selecting an asset allocation appropriate for your life stage and risk tolerance and then choosing a diversified set of securities within each asset class. You hold your securities for the long term, making changes only as necessary to maintain your asset allocation and to reflect changes in information about investments.

The advantages of a buy-and-hold strategy are that you can capture the long-term gains for each asset class while avoiding most of the transaction costs associated with buying and selling. You pay less in commissions, and you defer the taxes on your gains until you sell.

Dollar Cost Averaging

Many investment advisors recommend a strategy for passive investors called **dollar cost averaging.** This strategy involves buying in equal dollar amounts at regular intervals rather than making a large purchase at one time. Because most individual investors attempt to make regular contributions to investments from current income, this strategy is a natural fit for their financial plans.

The logic behind dollar cost averaging is that you can't predict whether market prices today are high or low compared with what they'll be later. By spreading your purchases over time, however, you average out the ups and downs of purchase prices. When prices are rising, your payment purchases fewer shares at the higher prices. When prices are falling, you can buy more shares at lower prices, which means that the average purchase price per share in your portfolio is lower than the long-term average price for the investment.

Dollar cost averaging doesn't always result in higher portfolio values. If the stock price had continually risen over the year, you would have missed out on the gain in value on the shares you could have purchased earlier at the lower price, and you'd end up with fewer shares. Also, the profits you make on smaller transactions may be offset by your transaction costs.

Direct Investment and Dividend Reinvestment Plans

In general, it's beneficial to stick to a plan for making regular investments. While you can do this many ways, it's best to avoid brokerage commissions on small trades. Most large corporations have a **direct investment program** whereby you can purchase stock directly from the company without being charged a commission. For a list of companies with these plans, call the Direct Stock Purchase Plan Clearinghouse at (800) 774-4117 or check its website, www.enrolldirect.com. Mutual funds also encourage regular contributions and can arrange for automatic monthly transfers from your checking or savings account for mutual fund shares.

If you hold stock in a company or mutual fund that pays regular dividends, you are likely to have the opportunity to reinvest your cash dividends in the stock through a **dividend reinvestment plan (DRIP).** Such plans automatically use any cash distributions to buy additional shares. Suppose, for example, that you're entitled to a $20 dividend distribution on the 100 shares you own of a company's stock, which is currently valued at $10 per share. Under a dividend reinvestment plan, you'd receive two additional shares instead of the dividend. To find out which companies offer DRIPs, consult Standard & Poor's Directory of Dividend Reinvestment Plans.

Indexing

Recall from earlier in this chapter that an index is an investment whose risk and return track those of a broad asset class, such as large-company stocks. You can buy shares of an index security directly, or you can buy a mutual fund that tries to mimic that market. For example, a mutual fund that is indexed to the Dow Jones Industrial Average is invested in all 30 stocks that make up that index. Indexing is a good way for passive buy-and-hold investors to achieve their objectives with fairly low expenses. We discuss this investment strategy in more detail in Chapter 13.

Timing

Just because you're a passive investor doesn't mean you should have your blinders on and ignore what's going on around you. Some investors attempt to avoid general downturns and take advantage of general increases in particular markets by strategically reallocating their portfolios, a strategy called **timing.**

Suppose you thought the stock market was about to take a nosedive. You could pull all your money out of stocks and put it into cash to avoid such losses. This is an example of market timing, in which you try to anticipate major moves in certain asset markets. Alternatively, you might try to implement a business cycle timing strategy, in which you put more money into your investment portfolio when the economy is expanding and you pull out when the economy is contracting.

The problem with timing strategies is that even the experts aren't very good at correctly predicting what the market is going to do. In practice, investors probably get it right less than half the time. In the late 1990s, for example, when the market moved continuously upward, many business cycle timers pulled money out of the stock market too soon and missed out on the strong returns at the end of the decade. Other individual investors waited too long to start investing in the stock market in the late 1990s, buying at the high point, and shortly after watched their portfolio values decline sharply. In response to the stock market crash of October 1987, investors sold more than $15 billion in stock mutual funds in 1988, missing out on a 17 percent gain on the S&P 500 Index for the year.

Even missing a few of the best days of a bull market can significantly reduce your portfolio's performance. From 1980 to 2002, if you'd missed the top 10 days, you'd have ended up with 40 percent less than you would have by using a simple buy-and-hold strategy. Although some timers have had good success over the long term, you're probably better off selecting a diversified portfolio and letting it ride.

SELF-CHECK

1. List five passive investing strategies available to you.
2. Define **timing**, **DRIP**, and **market efficiency**.
3. What type of investor looks for undervalued assets?

SUMMARY

When you have analyzed your financial plan, your risk tolerance, and your life stage, you can put together investment goals that result in a balanced, diversified portfolio. Your investments depend on your strategy and the market risk in general. You should make sure to invest across different asset classes. If you are an active investor, the odds are against you, but as a passive investor, your strategy should pay off.

KEY TERMS

Active investor	An investor who actively buys and sells securities, attempting to make short-run gains.
Asset allocation	The process of deciding what proportion of a portfolio to invest in each asset class.
Asset classes	Broad groups of investments that have certain characteristics in common.

Bond	An investment representing a loan to a governmental or business entity, which usually pays a fixed interest rate for a fixed period of time.
Buy-and-hold	A passive investment strategy in which the investor identifies his or her target asset allocation and then selects appropriate securities to hold for the long run.
Capital gain	Growth in the value of an investment over time.
Commodities	Contracts to buy or sell raw materials or agricultural products in the future.
Debt investor	An investor who lends money to an individual, a government entity, a financial institution, or another business.
Default risk	The risk of not receiving promised cash flows from an investment.
Derivative securities	Investments that derive their value from some underlying security's changes in price over time.
Direct investment program	A program offered by a publicly traded company to allow investors to automatically purchase shares of the company's stock on a regular basis without incurring brokerage fees.
Dividend reinvestment plan (DRIP)	Program that allows investors to receive dividends in the form of additional shares of stock instead of cash.
Diversification	An investment strategy that involves spreading money across a range of investments in order to reduce the overall risk of the portfolio.
Dividends	Periodic distributions of profits to equity investors.
Dollar cost averaging	An investment strategy in which you invest equal dollar amounts at regular intervals, regardless of fluctuations in price.
Equity investor	An investor who has an ownership interest in a business.
Fixed-income investment	A debt investment that provides a fixed interest payment to the investor over the term of the investment.
Futures contract	A contract to buy or sell financial securities in the future.
Inflation risk	The risk that inflation will erode the purchasing power of investment returns.

Interest-rate risk	The risk of price changes due to changes in interest rates.
Liquidity risk	The risk of not being able to convert an asset to cash without losing value.
Market efficiency	A theory which suggests that prices immediately adjust to reflect all publicly available information.
Market risk	The risk of portfolio fluctuations caused by common market factors.
Mutual fund	A collection of investments, managed by a professional investment firm, in which investors can buy shares.
Option contract	A contract that gives the holder the right, but not the obligation, to purchase or sell a specified investment at a set price on or before a specified date.
Passive investor	An investor who invests to make long-run returns and doesn't actively engage in buying or selling.
Preferred stock	A type of stock that pays a fixed dividend.
Rate of return	The total income earned on an investment over a period of time, including interest or dividends and capital gains, divided by the original amount invested. Also known as yield.
Reinvestment risk	The risk that short-term investments will have to be reinvested at lower rates when they come due.
Risk-averse person	A person who has a tendency to dislike risk and to be unwilling to invest in risky securities unless they earn higher investment returns than lower-risk securities.
Securities	Investments in which the investor contributes a sum of money to a common enterprise, with the intention of making a profit through the efforts of others.
Speculative investments	High-risk investments made in the hope of making a short-term profit.
Stock	An investment security that represents a proportionate ownership interest in a corporation.
Timing	An investment strategy in which you attempt to shift your asset allocation to capture upturns and avoid downturns in specific markets.

ASSESS YOUR UNDERSTANDING

Go to www.wiley.com/college/bajtelsmit to assess your knowledge of investing. *Measure your learning by comparing pre-test and post-test results.*

Summary Questions

1. The first step in the investment planning process is to:
   (a) estimate how much you need to accumulate.
   (b) evaluate your risk tolerance.
   (c) identify your goals.
   (d) learn about investment alternatives.

2. Saving your next raise is a recommended way to find the funds to invest. True or false?

3. If you start doing your own laundry instead of taking it to the cleaners, this is an example of:
   (a) paying yourself first.
   (b) going on a financial diet.
   (c) stopping up a cash leak.
   (d) continuing a payment plan.

4. Which of the following is an example of a fixed-income investment?
   (a) common stock
   (b) bonds
   (c) futures
   (d) options

5. A disadvantage of debt investments is:
   (a) that they tend to be riskier than many other types of investments.
   (b) that they tend to have lower liquidity than many other types of investments.
   (c) that they tend to have lower rates of return than many other types of investments.
   (d) all of the above.

6. A major difference between stock and bond investments is that:
   (a) it is possible to earn current income on bonds but not on stocks.
   (b) stocks have a fixed maturity, but bonds do not.
   (c) bonds can be issued by governments, but stock cannot.
   (d) all of the above.

7. Diversification reduces not only the risk of an entire portfolio but also the risk of individual securities in the portfolio. True or false?

8. Which of the following statements regarding asset allocation is false?

   (a) If you have invested in several broad investment classes, you are practicing asset allocation.

   (b) Studies have shown that as much as 90 percent of overall long-term performance of a portfolio is attributable to the asset allocation mix.

   (c) An investor's asset allocation mix should not change over time.

   (d) All of the above are true.

9. Active investors:

   (a) are willing to accept much higher risk than passive investors.

   (b) believe the market is inherently efficient, whereas passive investors do not.

   (c) are more interested in short-term gains than passive investors.

   (d) are more likely to invest in stock than passive investors.

10. Actively managed portfolios, such as those run by professional money managers, tend to outperform the market as a whole. True or false?

Applying This Chapter

1. For each of the following, indicate which type of risk it relates to.

   (a) Interest rates are expected to rise over the next several years.

   (b) The prices of goods and services are rising rapidly.

   (c) A company's management is indicted for fraud, and the company declares bankruptcy.

   (d) The United States declares war on Iraq.

2. You invest $1,000 in Xenon Corporation stock (10 shares at $100 per share) and $1,000 in Xenon Corporation bonds (1 bond at $1,000), which pay 8 percent interest. That's right. Xenon has a phenomenal year and distributes $5 per share to its shareholders. The stock value also increases to $115 per share. The bond value stays at $1,000. What is your return on investment for each of these investments in that year?

3. Continuing with Question 2, the following year, Xenon experiences a loss. It pays no dividends, and its stock price falls from $115 to $105. The bond value stays the same. What is your return on investment for each of these investments in that year?

4. Kenny has $5,000 to invest, and this amount represents his entire net worth. He decides to split his money evenly among five stocks in different industries. Is Kenny diversified? Why or why not?

5. You're 30 years old. Using the allocation rule described in Section 11.3.3, how much should you be allocating to stocks, bonds, and cash, respectively?

6. Explain why market efficiency makes it difficult to be successful at active investing.

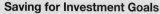

YOU TRY IT

Saving for Investment Goals

Maria would like to accumulate $300,000 by the time she retires twenty years from now. If she earns 6% on her investments, how much should she contribute each month in order to meet her goal?

Growing Your Investment

Maria contributes $150 per month to her investment account at the end of each month, and she earns 4 percent per year after taxes. How much will she have after six years?

Allocating Your Assets

Your mother received a $50,000 judgment (after taxes) as the outcome of a lawsuit, and she has asked you to recommend an asset allocation strategy for investing it. She is 45 years old, divorced, and in danger of being laid off from her job in the next two years. She has an emergency fund equal to three times her monthly expenses, she doesn't own a home, her credit card debt currently totals $5,000, and she owes $3,500 on a car loan.

1. Should your mother invest the entire $50,000?

2. Should she pay for the services of an investment advisor?

3. What proportion of the funds, if any, should she invest in stocks? Explain your reasoning.

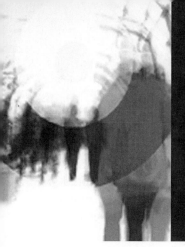

12

INVESTING IN STOCKS AND BONDS
Equity and Debt Investing

Starting Point

Go to www.wiley.com/college/bajtelsmit to assess your knowledge of investing in stocks and bonds.
Determine where you need to concentrate your effort.

What You'll Learn in This Chapter

▲ Types of stock issues
▲ Bonds and their classification
▲ How stocks and bonds work
▲ Preferred stock

After Studying This Chapter, You'll Be Able To

▲ Categorize stocks according to their characteristics
▲ Buy and sell stocks and bonds, with the help of a broker
▲ Categorize bonds according to their characteristics
▲ Analyze investment alternatives and evaluate portfolio performance
▲ Analyze bond investment alternatives and evaluate performance

INTRODUCTION

Stocks tend to provide higher returns than other asset classes, but this isn't true of every stock, nor is it true at all times. Most investors should also have some of their portfolio invested in fixed-income securities, such as bonds and shares of preferred stock, which are generally less risky than common stock. You should regularly track the performance of your portfolio to see if it's successfully moving you toward your financial goals. As discussed in this chapter, you need to know methods of performance evaluation.

12.1 Common Stock

When you buy stock, you're actually becoming a part owner of a business. You wouldn't buy into a local business without checking whether the business is in good financial shape. You want to know, among other things, whether it's making a profit. Does the company have good prospects for the future so that you'll make a reasonable rate of return on your investment? Your decision to buy stock isn't really so different, and it deserves just as careful deliberation.

12.1.1 What Is Common Stock and Why Is It Issued?

Common stock represents a share of ownership in a **corporation,** a type of business organization that exists as a legal entity separate from its owners, the shareholders. The corporate form of organization enables the company to have many owners with limited rights and obligations.

In contrast, the owners of companies organized as sole proprietorships and partnerships have more extensive rights (e.g., the ability to directly participate in the management of the business), but they also have greater responsibility (e.g., personal liability for the debts of the business). Corporations can be classified as private or public. Private corporations have few shareholders, and their stock isn't usually bought or sold.

In this chapter, we're primarily concerned with public corporations, whose stock is traded (i.e., bought and sold by individual investors) in the securities market. When you purchase shares of common stock in a public corporation, you're buying an ownership interest. Each shareholder owns a proportionate share of the firm equal to the number of shares owned, divided by the total number of shares.

A common shareholder's claim on the firm is said to be a **residual claim,** which means the person shares in the assets and income of the corporation, but only after other, higher-priority claims (e.g., interest payments on bonds) are satisfied. If the firm goes bankrupt, each shareholder is entitled to a proportionate share of whatever is left over after all the firm's creditors are paid back.

Even multi-billion-dollar companies such as Wal-Mart and Microsoft began as small private companies with only a few owners. Those owners eventually found it necessary to sell shares of stock to the public to get the funds needed to grow their companies. As a company continues to grow, it may again need funds, which can come from current earnings, borrowed funds (i.e., bonds, as discussed in Sections 12.5 and 12.6), or the sale of additional shares of stock. Most large publicly traded companies have millions of shares of stock outstanding.

12.1.2 Stockholder Rights and Obligations

Investors who buy stock in a firm hope to share in the future income and growth opportunities of that firm. Their investment has very few strings attached. They have limited rights to influence the management of the firm and also have limited liability for the firm's losses. Stockholders' rights and obligations are described in this section.

Voting Rights

Each common stockholder has the right to vote for members of the board of directors at an annual election. The board is responsible for selecting the top-level management, or officers, of the firm and for making major policy decisions for the company. The day-to-day operations of a corporation are handled by the officers, led by the chief executive officer (CEO) and sometimes the chief financial officer (CFO). In general, corporations follow a 1 vote-per-share system, so if you own 100 shares of a particular firm's stock, you cast 100 votes. Of course, your 100 votes don't make a big difference in an election if there are 5 million shares outstanding. Also, large blocks of shares are often held by a few shareholders. Bill Gates, for example, owns about 9.5 percent of Microsoft stock (937 million out of a total 9.8 billion shares outstanding in December 2006, so his vote makes a big difference. If you don't go to the annual meeting, you're allowed to pass your voting right to someone else through a written agreement called a **proxy.**

Limited Liability

Limited liability means that the most you can lose when you own a share of stock is the value of the share itself. Without the limited liability right, no one would be willing to buy shares of stock because doing so would put their personal assets at risk of being taken to pay for corporate debts in the event of company failure.

Claim on Income

In return for providing equity capital, a common shareholder expects to share in the company's profits, either through dividends or price appreciation. If the firm's revenues are greater than its expenses, the board of directors can decide to distribute a cash dividend to the shareholders, or it can decide instead to reinvest the funds for future growth. Shareholders benefit either way. If you receive dividend income, you have the immediate benefit of cash flow to spend or invest. If the firm reinvests the money instead of distributing it to you, the value of your shares should go up to reflect the firm's new investment in earning power and the potential for future dividends. If you sell at that point, you realize a capital gain—the difference between the price at which you sell and the price you paid.

Sometimes, a firm issues a **stock dividend** in place of a cash dividend. In this situation, rather than receiving cash, you get additional shares of the firm's stock in proportion to the number of shares you already hold. While a stock dividend doesn't really benefit you currently as much as a cash dividend or capital gain, it may provide benefits later. Because all stockholders receive these additional shares, everyone's percentage of ownership remains the same. In fact, the value of each share usually declines after an announcement of a dividend to reflect the new value of each share. What if you and three friends pool your funds to buy an apple pie for $12, each paying $3 for your share? If you cut it in 12 slices, you each get 3 slices, but the total value of your share is still $3. Getting a stock dividend is similar to cutting up your pie into smaller slices. You have more slices, but each one is worth less. So if you originally owned 100 shares at $10 per share and the firm gave you 3 shares as a dividend, you'd end up owning 103 shares at $9.70 per share—still a $1,000 ownership interest.

One of the risks of stock ownership is that firms are not required to pay dividends. Even if a firm has issued dividends before, it may choose to reduce or eliminate them. Conversely, firms that have never issued dividends may begin doing so. This creates uncertainty for stockholders because they never know in advance how much income they'll earn. But for bearing this risk, stockholders have unlimited opportunity for gain. If the firm does unusually well, the stockholders share in the bounty; however, if it does poorly, the stockholders might lose all their investment.

Preemptive Rights

When companies sell additional shares of stock, it's also like cutting the pie into more slices, so current stockholders risk seeing the value of their shares decline. Sometimes, though, shareholders are entitled to maintain their proportionate interest in a company as the number of shares outstanding increases with new issues. This is called a **preemptive right.**

Stock Splits

Corporations sometimes decide to declare a stock split, which is similar to a stock dividend in that each shareholder gets a number of new shares in proportion to the number of shares already held. However, in the case of a stock split, the price of the shares is adjusted so that the total value of your investment remains the same as it was before the split.

The most common type of stock split is a two-for-one split, but three-for-one or three-for-two splits are also relatively common. To use our pie analogy, a two-for-one stock split is like splitting each of the 12 pie slices in two, for a total of 24 pieces. If you owned three slices before the split, you now have six, but you still have one-fourth of the pie. Similarly, if you own a share of stock worth $100 per share and the corporation announces a two-for-one split, after the split you'll own two shares valued at $50 per share.

Investors tend to view a stock split as favorable information about the corporation's prospects for future growth, so the stock price often increases a little when a company announces a split. Your $50 shares might soon be worth $51 if the company does well, so the split would result in an increase in wealth for you. Why is a split good news? Management likes to keep the share price below some maximum value that is perceived as affordable. Announcement of a split is seen as a signal that management expects the stock price to rise above this maximum value. To the extent that this is news to investors, they respond by buying the stock and driving up the price. Many investors attempt to buy shares just as the announcement is made and then sell after the stock price increases in response to the announcement of the split—a type of active investing strategy. However, with market efficiency, the price change occurs incredibly fast.

12.1.3 The Stock Market

Stocks are bought and sold in the stock market. This market has two parts:

▲ The **primary market,** where stocks are sold to the public by the issuing corporation for the first time.

▲ The **secondary market,** where stocks that have already been issued are traded between investors.

Primary Market vs. Secondary Market

Even though most individual investors' transactions occur in the secondary market, it's useful to understand the role of both of these parts of the market. When a company issues stock for the first time, we say it's "going public," and the stock issue is called an **initial public offering (IPO).** For example, the company that started the Google search engine went public during 2004. Cofounders Larry Page and Sergey Brin in addition to CEO Eric Schmidt retained ownership of a significant block of voting shares.

The IPO process is usually handled by one or more investment banking firms (the Google IPO had more than 25), such as Merrill Lynch or Goldman Sachs, which underwrite the issue. Underwriting involves helping the firm determine a price for the new issue, facilitating the paperwork, and managing the selling process. Sometimes, it's difficult to determine exactly how much a new company is worth, particularly if it's expected to grow quickly after the infusion of cash from the sale of stock.

FOR EXAMPLE

Google IPO Scam

If something looks too good to be true, it probably is. In late 2003, Shamoon Rafiq, age 30, sold nearly $3 million in bogus "pre-IPO" Google stock. He falsely represented that he was able to obtain pre-IPO shares by saying he was a college buddy of the Google founders and a partner in an investment firm handling the IPO. In fact, the IPO date had not even been set, and Rafiq had no connection with Google. In 2004, he plead guilty to wire fraud and was given 51 to 63 months in jail.

The underwriter may guarantee a minimum price to the issuing firm, or it may buy the entire issue itself and then resell it to the public. In an innovative departure from the usual process, Google decided to set its IPO stock price through an auction in which interested investors placed bids, naming the number of shares they were willing to buy and the price they were willing to pay.

New stock issues are advertised in the financial press in a format called a **tombstone ad.** If you see a tombstone in *The Wall Street Journal*, you can ask the company for a **prospectus,** a document that includes all the important information about the company and its stock.

Although you may someday have an opportunity to purchase shares directly from a company through an IPO, it's more likely that your transactions will be with other investors in the secondary market.

Securities Exchanges

Trading among investors can be accomplished through an organized **securities exchange,** which is a physical location where trades are implemented, or through an electronic marketplace referred to as the **over-the-counter (OTC) market.** The oldest, largest, and best-known securities exchange is the New York Stock Exchange (NYSE), where approximately 2,800 stocks valued at nearly $18 trillion are traded. The NYSE recently merged with the Archipelago Exchange and the Pacific Exchange and is planning to merge with Euronext, a large European exchange. Other exchanges include the American Stock Exchange (AMEX; the second largest exchange), and the Philadelphia Stock Exchange. A stock can be traded on more than one exchange. Each exchange has its own rules for how a stock can qualify to be a **listed security,** or offered on the exchange.

To make trades at securities exchanges such as the NYSE, you must have a seat on the exchange. There are a limited number of seats on any given exchange, and most are owned or rented by brokerage firms. For this reason, individual investors must use the services of a brokerage firm to execute trades. These are the steps in a typical stock transaction:

1. The buyer places an offer to purchase the stock with a broker whose employing firm is a member of the exchange; similarly, the seller indicates to his or her broker a desire to sell a number of shares.

2. To implement the buyer's request, the brokerage firm contacts its representative at the securities exchange to relay the price offer, or **bid price**, and the seller's broker relays the sale offer, or **ask price**, through their respective representatives at the exchange.

3. Both brokerage representatives then go to the **specialist** for that stock at a physical location on the floor of the exchange called the *specialist's post*. The specialist is the person at the exchange who is responsible for matching up the buy and sell orders for a particular stock.

4. Based on the bid and ask information received from many buyers and sellers, the specialist is able to match up buyers and sellers fairly. If there are too many buyers relative to sellers, or vice versa, the specialist actually sells or buys the shares as necessary to meet the market's demand. For this reason, specialists are sometimes referred to as *market makers*.

5. When a match is made, the brokerage firms relay the information back to the buyer and seller of the shares. Transfer of money and shares is then accomplished through accounts at the respective brokerage firms.

The OTC market is not a formal exchange and doesn't have a physical location. Instead, it's a network of securities dealers that communicate electronically to quote the prices (bid and ask) at which they're willing to buy and sell securities. About 35,000 companies have stocks that are traded over the counter. About 3,300 of the most frequently traded OTC stocks participate in an electronic reporting system called the **NASDAQ**, which stands for National Association of Securities Dealers Automated Quotation System. If you want to buy a NASDAQ stock, your broker can post your bid on the system, and a NASDAQ dealer will match you up with a seller. Generally, the small size and lower liquidity of stocks traded exclusively over the counter make them riskier investments than stocks listed on organized exchanges.

SELF-CHECK

1. Define **NASDAQ**, bid price, proxy, and specialist.
2. List the five steps in a typical stock transaction.
3. Name the rights of a stockholder.
4. What are the differences between primary and secondary stock?

12.2 Classification of Common Stock

Common stock is usually classified according to broad, and sometimes overlapping, categories. Although these classifications have no official status, understanding them helps you comprehend what you read in the financial press. An important caution is that the companies within each of these classifications differ widely, so you need to analyze the individual companies independently rather than rely solely on their classifications.

12.2.1 Income vs. Growth Stocks

Investors usually expect to receive some combination of current cash flow and price appreciation in return for providing capital to a firm. Stocks are often classified based on whether the company tends to reward its investors primarily with current income or with capital gains.

An **income stock** is one that pays investors a regular dividend rather than concentrating on reinvestment of profits. Because these stocks pay most of their profits in dividends instead of reinvesting for future growth, there is usually less capital appreciation. The relative certainty of a dividend cash flow stream makes these stocks attractive to more conservative stock investors and to those who desire a regular income stream, such as retirees.

A **growth stock** is one that compensates investors primarily through increases in the value of the shares over time. Stocks issued by younger companies that are experiencing high growth in earnings and assets are likely to be classified as growth stocks. During this high-growth phase, firms tend to reinvest profits to meet capital needs rather than distribute profits as dividends. Many of these types of stocks are traded in the OTC market.

Obviously, the attraction of growth stocks to investors is the opportunity to share in the future profits of these companies as investments in growth eventually pay off. Growth companies expose investors to uncertainty because there are no guarantees that today's reinvestment will translate into tomorrow's growth in value. Young investors are more likely to focus on growth investments, while investors who want investment income and stability are less inclined to do so. Some growth stocks are highly risky—their prices fluctuate widely, and they have very uncertain future prospects. During the 1990s, many internet companies issued stock despite the fact that they had failed to show any profit. In spite of the uncertainty, investors flocked to buy these stocks, and a few of the companies succeeded. However, for every success story, such as eBay.com and Amazon.com, there are a dozen failures—companies whose anticipated future profits never materialized or were overestimated.

12.2.2 Blue Chip Stocks

A **blue chip stock** is one issued by a large, stable, mature company. These firms' earnings and growth tend to track the growth in the overall market. As consistent performers, they're considered less risky than growth stocks; however, they don't offer opportunities for unexpectedly high earnings. They are the slow-and-steady performers, often leaders in their industry, and they commonly pay dividends besides offering the opportunity for some growth in value over time. Examples of blue chip stocks include Anheuser-Busch, Procter & Gamble, and Coca-Cola.

12.2.3 Cyclical vs. Defensive Stocks

A **cyclical stock** exhibits above-average sensitivity to the business cycle—that is, it tends to perform well during strong economic climates and poorly in downturns. Cyclical companies include firms that produce consumer durable goods and luxury items—for example, cars, appliances, furniture, and sporting equipment—because purchases of such goods can nearly always be put off when money is tight. Companies connected to the home-building industry (e.g., Home Depot) and companies that provide services or goods to other businesses (e.g., transportation and technology firms) are also cyclical because during recessions, construction and investment projects tend to be put on hold.

The opposite of a cyclical stock is a **defensive stock**—one that is less sensitive to market ups and downs and therefore can help stabilize a portfolio during market downturns. Stocks that are related to food and beverages (e.g., Anheuser-Busch, Coca-Cola), pharmaceuticals (e.g., Pfizer), and utilities (e.g., Duke Energy) are examples of defensive stocks because these companies' products are in demand regardless of economic conditions.

12.2.4 Industry and Sector Stocks

Stocks are often categorized by the industry or sector of the issuing companies. Some classifications and representative companies include the following:

▲ Airlines (e.g., United Airlines).
▲ Banking (e.g., Bank of America).
▲ Financial services (e.g., Merrill Lynch).
▲ Food and beverage (e.g., Coca-Cola).
▲ Technology (e.g., Intel).

12.2.5 Market Capitalization

Market capitalization is the total value of a company's shares at its current market price. It is calculated as follows:

Market capitalization = Current market price × Number of shares outstanding

On the basis of capitalization, companies are classified as large cap, mid cap, or small cap. Some investors also refer to subsets of the largest and smallest groups. Here, we consider the general parameters for these classifications, but these definitions aren't engraved in stone—investors tend to include companies in these groups based on not only market capitalization but also revenues, growth potential, and past history.

Large-Cap Companies

Large-cap companies have market capitalization of $5 billion or more (although some investors and reporting services classify companies as large cap with as little as $3 billion). These are the largest firms in the country. They typically have been in existence for many years, and their stock tends to experience less price fluctuation than the stock of mid-cap and small-cap companies. Consequently, their stock is perceived as being less risky and is often preferred by more conservative stock investors. Examples include McDonald's, with market capitalization of $33 billion, and Disney, with market capitalization of $48 billion.

Mid-Cap Companies

Mid-cap companies have $1 billion to $3 billion in market capitalization—they're large but not giants. Mid-caps tend to be niche players that are not well known outside their industries. They have some advantages of both large and small companies because they are still small enough to grow yet have already reached a level of stability that small-cap companies don't yet possess.

Small-Cap Companies

A **small-cap company** generally has market capitalization of less than $1 billion and annual revenues of under $250 million. That might not seem very small, but these firms are small relative to many others and generally are young, growing companies. Small-cap companies rarely pay dividends (because they reinvest their profits to promote growth) but have historically seen larger investment returns than other asset classifications. However, small-cap stock prices tend to be more sensitive to market movements, which means their investors experience larger losses in economic downturns. This effect is even more pronounced for micro-cap companies—those with less than $100 million in capitalization.

SELF-CHECK

1. Which type of stock compensates investors through increases in the value of their shares?
2. List the classifications of common stock.
3. Define **income stock, blue chip stock, and market capitalization.**

12.3 Buying and Selling Stocks

Buying stock isn't like making a consumer purchase—you can't just go out and buy stocks directly from other investors. Transactions in the secondary market require the services of a licensed broker as an intermediary. In this section, we walk through the process you'd follow if you wanted to buy some shares of a particular company. For this example, let's assume that you'd like to buy 100 shares of Dell Inc. To implement this transaction, you need to know the current price and place a specific order with a broker.

12.3.1 Looking Up a Stock Price

To determine how much you must pay for a stock, you must first look up the current price. There are numerous sources of information on stock prices. Besides several websites that give price quotes, *The Wall Street Journal* and other financial newspapers report stock prices. Figure 12-1 shows how information is reported in the stock section of *The Wall Street Journal*.

The highlighted section of the exhibit shows the information reported for Dell Inc. (a NASDAQ-listed stock) on July 16, 2004. Every publicly traded stock has a ticker symbol, which is a universally accepted shorthand reference for the company. The ticker symbol—DELL in our example—is shown in bold-face type. The annual dividend is reported in the column immediately after the company name; in this case, we see that DELL shareholders didn't receive a dividend. If you look at the next-to-last column, you see that the **close price** reported for the stock was $34.87. This is the price the stock sold for in the last transaction on July 15, 2004, the previous trading day. The other reported information is defined in the figure. For more current price information, go to finance.yahoo.com and enter the ticker symbol in the space marked "Get Quotes." These and other financial websites will typically provide prices that are about 15 minutes delayed.

12.3.2 Placing an Order

Suppose you think the reported $34.87 price for Dell stock makes it a good investment. You decide to place an order for 100 shares. Orders are normally made in a **round lot,** or a unit of 100 shares. If you want to buy fewer than 100 shares (an odd lot), you may have to pay an extra fee. Regardless of the type of brokerage firm you use, there are three types of orders you can make: market order, limit order, or stop order.

Market Orders

When you make a **market order,** you ask the broker to execute your trade at whatever the market price is at the time your trade is actually finalized. You say, "Buy 100 shares of Dell at market." The broker will have quoted you the most

Figure 12-1

YTD %CHG	52 week HI	52 week LOW	STOCK (SYM)	Yield DIV	Yield %	Yield PE	VOL 100s	CLOSE	NET CHG
−15.7	11.50	5.98	Datastream **DSTM**		...	26	z44284	6.62	0.01
193.3	26.24	6.46	DawsnGeo **DWSN**		...	73	1562	22	0.03
11.4	27.01	17.58	DebShop **DEBS**	.50a	2.1	24	z5592	23.97	−0.28
31.4	31.07	6.50	DeckrsOutdr **DECK**		...	30	4717	26.93	−1.07
−5.1	13.80	2.45	deCodeGntcs **DCGN**		...	dd	1709	7.77	0.14
−9.4	11.36	8.25	Dcomalnt **DECA**	.28g	...	...	22	9.33	0.14
2.6	37.18	30.70	Dell **DELL**		...	33	139777	34.87	0.03
147.1	15.93	4.31	DeltaPet **DPTR**		...	cc	3185	15	−0.20
28.5	16.72	5.36	Dendreon **DNDN**		...	dd	3718	10.36	−0.32
2.5	19.77	12.12	Dendritelnt **DRTE**		...	30	2762	16.09	0.03
14.5	52.84	41	DENTSPLY **XRAY**	.21	.4	19	2520	51.72	−0.22
−34.4	8.97	4.67	DepoMed **DEPO**		...	dd	z53127	4.65	−0.08
−12.0	30.60	19.30	Deswell **DSWL**	1.18e	5.2	14	z8197	22.89	−0.34
−26.0	6.28	1.75	DialgSemi ADS **DLGS**		...	...	7	3.22	0.02
−20.9	12	3.90	DiamondClstr **DTPI**		...	dd	z63918	8.07	−0.12
−10.2	49.45	25.71	DigeneCp **DIGE**		...	cc	1600	36.01	0.63
12.1	12.33	5.36	DIGI Intl **DGII**		...	35	1691	10.76	0.78

Columns	Explanation
YTD % CHG	The percentage change in price since the beginning of the calendar year, adjusted for stock splits and dividends that exceed 10% of the stock price. Dell's price has increased 4%.
52 WEEK HI LO	The high and low stock prices over the course of the last year. Dell's price has ranged from $29.23 to $37.18 over the last 52 weeks.
DIV	The annual dollar dividend per share. Dell doesn't pay a dividend so there is no entry in this column.
%	Dividend percent yield, which equals the dividend divided by the close price. Since Dell pays no dividend, this isn't applicable.
PE	The price-to-earnings ratio is 33, which is the current price per share divided by earnings per share. Note that although EPS isn't reported, you can calculate it by dividing the price by the PE.
VOL 100s	The number of shares traded, reported in round lots of 100. For Dell Inc., the reported volume of 157382 means that 15.7 million shares traded that day.
NET CHG	Dell's price changed by 0.03% since the previous day.

Source: WALL STREET JOURNAL. Copyright 2004 by DOW JONES & CO INC. Permission granted via Copyright Clearance Center.

How to read stock market quotes in *The Wall Street Journal*.

recent price, but the price may change before you get your shares, even if the broker acts quickly. This may result in a more favorable price, or it may mean you end up paying more for your shares than you had intended. For example, if the price has fallen to $34.00 by the time your trade is executed, you pay that price per share (plus the commission to the broker).

Limit Orders

What if the stock price is creeping upward and you're worried that it might increase beyond what you can afford or beyond what you think the stock is worth? For example, suppose you don't want to pay more than $36 per share for the Dell stock. In that case, you can give a **limit order** to the broker, in which you say, "Buy 100 shares of Dell stock for me as long as the price is no more than $36."

You can also give a limit order to sell, in which you specify the minimum price that you're willing to accept from a potential buyer. If the current price is too high (or too low, in the case of a sell order) to execute the order, the limit order remains in effect until you cancel it, so you might get the shares you want a few days or weeks later.

If you don't want to leave your order open, you can place a time limit on it, the most common limit being a day order, in which your order expires at the close of trading for the day. An order can also be a fill-or-kill order, which means that it's canceled if not immediately filled.

Stop Orders

A **stop order** is commonly used to minimize losses or protect gains on a particular stock. For example, suppose you buy the Dell stock at $35 and it subsequently goes up to $38 per share. You can sell it and take the profit of $3 per share, or you can hold on to it in the hope that the price will increase even more. If you hold on to it, you don't want to take the chance of losing all the profit you've gained on paper if it were to subsequently decline in value. To protect against that possibility, you can place a stop order with your broker that says, "Sell all my Dell shares if the price drops to $36.50." If the price begins to fall, this order will be executed, and you'll have locked in $1.50 profit per share.

Now suppose instead that your Dell stock has dropped from its original $35 purchase price to $33 per share. You may not want to sell it now and take the $2 loss—perhaps you think there's a chance it will recover in value. But you also may not want to lose much more money. In this case, you can place a stop order instructing the broker to sell your shares if the price falls below, say, $30 per share. This type of stop order is often called a stop-loss order, for obvious reasons. If the order results in a sale at $30 per share, you'll have lost $5 on your original $35 investment, or about 14 percent, but you'll have cut off the risk of further losses if the stock price continues its drop. With 20-20 hindsight, many investors regret their failure to use stop-loss orders during market declines.

12.3.3 Selling Long vs. Selling Short

As a long-term investor, you'll primarily be a buyer of stocks rather than a seller. When you're a buyer and hold stock in your portfolio, you're said to be *long in stock*. You make money when the stock price goes up and lose money when the stock price goes down. Your objective is to buy low and sell high, in that order.

Investors sometimes talk about **selling short.** This happens when they issue a sell order to their broker but don't actually have the stock to sell; instead, they borrow it from their broker's account. They're betting that the price of the stock will go down so that they can replace the stock later at a lower price and make a profit on the difference. A short seller's objective is therefore to sell high and buy low, in that order.

Although short sellers can sometimes be quite successful, earning a return without putting up much cash, they're counting on being right about the direction the price will move. What happens if the stock price goes up instead of down? They end up paying the market price as well as repaying the broker for any missed dividends.

12.3.4 Full-Service vs. Discount Brokerage Firms

A **stockbroker** is a licensed professional who facilitates securities transactions for clients. Generally, a stockbroker works for a particular brokerage firm, such as Merrill Lynch or Raymond James Financial, and the firm is a member of one or more organized exchanges.

Brokers and the brokerage firms they work for are categorized based on the level of service they provide to their clients. All brokers, of course, trade on their clients' behalf, but there is a distinction:

▲ Full-service brokers provide such services as account management, investment research, recommendations on specific securities and asset allocation, and loans.

▲ Discount brokers, which include a wide range of financial services firms and online brokerage sites, are generally much less expensive than full-service brokers but are likely to offer fewer services. Some discount brokers primarily take orders over the phone, and some operate online.

Competition in the brokerage marketplace is blurring the lines between broker types; full-service brokers are providing low-cost trading services to their clients, and discount brokers are offering investment research services. The end result is good news for small investors, who now have more access to information and incur lower costs for trading than they did a decade ago. You can find reliable information on brokers at the National Association of Securities Dealers' Web site, www.nasd.com.

12.3.5 Brokerage Accounts

When you do business with a brokerage firm, you are required to open a brokerage account and keep a minimum amount there, in either cash or securities. Your funds may be insured against brokerage firm failure by the Security Investor Protection Corporation (SIPC). Although your account records include the specific shares you own, the actual documents that evidence your ownership interest—your stock certificates—are held in the name of the brokerage firm and maintained at its office.

Most brokers offer three types of accounts: cash accounts, margin accounts, and discretionary accounts. If you have a cash account, you're required to make payment in full within three days of a buy order. Because three days isn't enough time to mail a check, you need to have an electronic transfer system between your bank and your brokerage account. If you have sufficient funds in your brokerage account, your broker can execute buy orders using those funds.

But what if you don't have sufficient funds? If you have a margin account, you can buy more stock than you have the funds for, borrowing the rest from the brokerage firm. This is called **buying on margin.** Although margin trading allows you to buy more stock than you could if you used only your own money, it's also riskier because you have to earn enough on the stock to pay back the loan with interest. The advantage is that, if the stock goes up in value, you don't have to share the gain with the brokerage firm—you only owe the amount of the loan plus interest.

The Federal Reserve requires that the margin—that is, the equity in the account divided by the stock value—be at least 50 percent. To guard against the possibility that the value of the stock is less than the loan amount, brokers also set a maintenance margin (e.g., 30 percent). Thus, if stock prices fall sufficiently, you may get a **margin call** from your broker, requesting that you deposit additional funds into your account so that you can meet the maintenance margin limit.

FOR EXAMPLE

Buying on Margin

Say you buy $5,000 in shares, using $2,500 of your own money and $2,500 borrowed from your brokerage firm. In this case, you have a 50 percent margin. If the share prices fall, so that the shares in your account are worth only $3,500, your margin is now (3,500 − 2,500) / 3,500 = 28.6 percent, which is less than the 30 percent minimum. You need to pay back at least $50 to meet the required minimum.

The last type of brokerage account is a discretionary account, in which you delegate the decision-making authority for buying and selling to the broker. Because the broker makes more money by making more trades, you run the risk that the broker might make lots of trades just to get the commissions. There are ethical restrictions on **churning,** or excessive trading, in discretionary accounts, but how much is too much is subject to disagreement.

Brokers charge a commission fee—either a dollar amount per transaction or a decreasing percentage, based on the size of the trade. As mentioned earlier, shares usually trade in round lots of 100 shares, so an order for an odd lot, which has fewer than 100 shares, may require the payment of an additional fee. Brokers' fees cover their costs of handling transactions and general overhead expenses, and they can differ substantially from firm to firm. Full-service brokerage firms charge higher commissions than discount brokers, and fees also vary among firms. You might pay as little as $5 per trade with an online broker or many times more for a full-service broker. Your choice of broker should be based on your individual needs. Some specifics that you may want to investigate include the following:

▲ Is the account insured by the SIPC?

▲ Does the brokerage firm have a useful website, and, if trades are to be executed on the site, can it provide evidence of past reliability during high-traffic trading periods?

▲ What is the commission structure?

▲ Will the broker pay you interest on any uninvested cash in your account? If so, at what rate?

▲ What services does the broker provide besides executing trades?

Many individual investors are choosing the convenience and reduced transaction costs of online investing. Online brokers offer investor education, banking and financial services, quick transactions, access to extensive investment databases, and portfolio management tools. Before you start investing this way,

SELF-CHECK

1. Define **margin call, churning, selling short, round lot,** and **close price.**

2. What are three types of orders you can make?

3. What are some criteria for choosing a broker?

however, a few cautions are in order. You should only use a reputable online broker, and you shouldn't let the ease of trading lure you into being a **day trader**—someone who buys and sells during the day to make a quick profit—because that type of active trading is highly risky and thus unlikely to be consistent with your financial planning objectives.

12.4 Stock Selection and Performance Evaluation

Your selection of individual stocks for your investment portfolio should be based on your evaluation of expected returns as well as on an assessment of how much risk the investment will add to your portfolio. In this section, we introduce several return and risk measures and explain how to evaluate an investment's performance by comparing it with benchmark indexes.

12.4.1 Measuring Expected Stock Returns

Besides looking at historical rates of return, investors commonly use the earnings per share and the price-to-earnings ratios to help them estimate future rates of return.

Chapter 11 defines the annual rate of return on an investment as the current yield plus the capital gains yield. For stock investors, the current yield is usually called the dividend yield because the current income to a stock investor is the annual dividend payment. The two components of a stock's rate of return, **dividend yield** and **capital gains yield**, are therefore defined as follows:

Dividend yield = Annual dividend / Market price of stock

Capital gains yield = Annual change in price / Market price of stock

---

FOR EXAMPLE

Comparing Yields

You're considering purchasing a stock with a market price of $50 per share. If the stock pays an annual dividend of $1 per share, you'll earn a dividend yield of $1 / $50 = 0.02, or 2 percent. Your total annual return on the stock will be the 2 percent dividend yield plus the expected capital gains yield. If, historically, the stock has increased an average of 10 percent annually, you might expect the price to rise to $55 by the end of the year. If it did, you'd earn a total rate of return of 12 percent on your stock investment for the year—2 percent in dividend yield and 10 percent in capital gains yield. Normally, the price you use for the denominator of this equation is the price you paid (or expect to pay) for the shares.

Investors usually estimate future dividends based on dividends paid in the previous year, but it can be much more difficult to estimate expected capital gains. For this reason, investors sometimes use various ratios that have been found to be good indicators of future performance.

Perhaps the most-watched ratio is the company's **earnings per share (EPS),** which is measured as follows:

$$\text{EPS} = \text{After-tax net income / Number of shares outstanding}$$

Because stock investors own a proportionate share of the company, they have an interest in a proportionate share of the firm's annual after-tax net income, or earnings. The company can use those dollars to pay dividends, or it can reinvest them to grow the firm. Either way, stockholders stand to benefit if earnings go up.

When a company reports better-than-expected earnings, its stock price tends to go up because investors see that as a good sign for the future. When earnings fall or are lower than expected, the stock price tends to fall also. The EPS ratio provides a rough measure of profitability and can be compared over time for a particular firm. However, it's not very useful as a decision-making tool because there isn't a universally accepted "good" or "bad" value (as long as EPS is positive).

Generally, differences in company size, industry, and share price all make it difficult to directly compare companies based on EPS. You can sometimes use EPS to compare companies if you consider it relative to some other variable. For example, you can use the **price-to-earnings (P/E) ratio,** which measures the relationship of share price to earnings per share. The P/E ratio is calculated as follows:

$$\text{P/E ratio} = \text{Stock price / EPS}$$

The P/E ratio is used as a measure of future earnings potential. Thus, a high P/E ratio is generally considered a positive indicator of the firm's potential for future growth. The implication is that investors perceive the firm as being worth the extra price. However, a high P/E ratio can also be an indication that a stock is currently overpriced.

Although P/E ratios differ over time and across industries, the average for large company stocks is usually between 15 and 25, whereas P/E ratios for high-growth stocks can be much higher.

12.4.2 Measuring Stock Risk

All stock is risky. When you buy stock, there's no guarantee that you'll receive any cash flow, and you're not entitled to the return of your capital. In addition, the actual return varies. Although, on average, you can expect to receive a higher average rate of return for bearing more risk, in the short run, you are likely to experience ups and downs in your portfolio value. Investors require higher rates

Figure 12-2

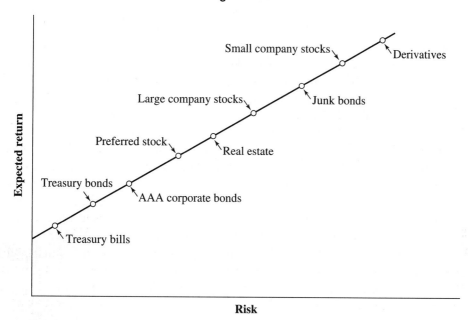

The risk/return relationship.

of return for riskier investments. Figure 12-2 illustrates this relationship graphically for several investment classes. The relationship between risk and return is not a perfect continuum as in the graph, but over the long term, this relationship holds true.

Treasury bills (T-bills) expose you to very little risk; if you hold them to maturity (which is no more than one year), you receive the **yield** you expected when you bought the securities—about 5 percent at the beginning of 2007. The primary risk you face is that your purchasing power may be affected if inflation changes drastically in the short time you hold the T-bills.

Bonds, considered in Sections 12.5 and 12.6, generally fall on the lower portion of the graph because the risk of investing in bonds (with the exception of junk bonds, which are issued by less creditworthy companies) is relatively low. Stocks pose more risk, and derivatives still more. Remember that the measure of investment risk is the variability of the returns you can expect from the investment: The more variable the returns, the higher the risk.

How can you incorporate investment risk in your investment decision process? Investors use different measures for risk. When stocks are put together in a portfolio, some of the individual company risks are canceled out (see Section 11.3.3). Thus, if you're a diversified investor, you're not primarily interested in how variable a particular stock is by itself; rather, you want to know how it will affect the variability, or risk, of your overall portfolio. This requires that you have a way of measuring the market risk of individual securities—the components of risk that can't be diversified away. One measure commonly used to estimate the risk of stock investments held in a diversified portfolio is the **beta.** A stock's beta measures its degree of market risk, or how much it tends to move with the overall market. A beta equal to 1 means that the stock has about the same degree of risk as the overall market (and should therefore give you about the same percentage of return if held in a diversified portfolio). A beta less than 1 means the stock is less risky than average and may give you proportionally lower return, and a beta greater than 1 means the stock is riskier than average and may give you proportionally more return. Although stocks rarely have negative betas (which would imply that they would have negative returns when the market had positive returns), there are occasional examples where this happens.

Most financial services firms, brokers, and investment advisors can provide you with an estimate of the beta for a particular stock. Most technology and Internet companies have high betas; the type of business they're in has increased market risk because sales tend to slump in recessions and surge forward during recovery periods. Investors expect to receive a much higher return to compensate them for this higher risk.

Let's take a look at how you could apply what you know about risk to selecting stocks. Suppose you're a bit conservative and don't want your portfolio to be highly sensitive to general market movements. You can use screening tools on various websites to identify low-beta stocks (i.e., stocks with betas of less than 1) in each of several industries; you can create your portfolio from these stocks. The beta for the portfolio is the average of the betas for the stocks you select, weighted according to the proportions of the stocks held in the portfolio. Note that you can use this concept to offset the risk of a single investment also. For example, if you've bought a relatively risky stock such as Dell, you can balance that with a stock with low market risk, such as Anheuser-Busch.

12.4.3 Evaluating Portfolio Performance Against Stock Indexes

A **stock market index** tracks the performance of a particular group of stocks. This helps gauge general market conditions and is also used to assess the performance of specific stocks and portfolios. Some portfolio managers identify a certain index as their benchmark, making their goal to perform at least as well as the stocks in the index while maintaining a similar risk level.

In evaluating performance, it doesn't make sense to look just at your own past returns as a benchmark. A diversified stock portfolio should be compared to a diversified index that includes stocks with similar risk and return characteristics. Even if your portfolio returns were lower than you'd hoped based on your past returns, you can still pat yourself on the back if you've beaten the market index. This section looks at the most common stock market indexes.

The Dow Jones Industrial Average (DJIA)

When you hear in the news that "the market" has gone up or down, the newscaster is usually referring to the Dow Jones Industrial Average (DJIA), commonly referred to as the Dow. The Dow, which includes 30 blue chip stocks considered representative of the overall U.S. stock market, is the most widely watched and reported index in use today. It might seem that too much emphasis is placed on this index of only 30 stocks. But the fact is that these 30 companies are so large and have so many investors that they represent a significant percentage of the value of the broader market. Even though the S&P 500 and the NASDAQ include many more stocks than the Dow, the returns of these three indexes tend to move together.

Originally, the value of the Dow was determined by adding up the share prices of the stocks in the index (which is called price weighting because stocks with higher prices have more effect on the value of the index). Now, however, the value is calculated by summing the share prices of the Dow stocks and then dividing by a factor that takes into account stock splits, spin-offs, and dividends. This adjustment is necessary so that the Dow can be compared over time. Because of the adjustment, the Dow is not actually an "average," despite its name.

S&P 500 Index

Standard & Poor's, an investment advisory service, offers several indexes. The most popular is the S&P 500 Index, which tracks the performance of 500 large companies, most of them traded on the NYSE. Because this index represents a broader cross-section of U.S. industry than the DJIA, the S&P 500 is probably a better indicator of market performance. The S&P 500 is the benchmark most commonly used by mutual funds and money managers to assess performance.

In contrast to the price weighting of the DJIA, the S&P 500 index is value weighted. This means that companies with higher market capitalization have a greater impact on the index than those with lower capitalization. The rationale for this method of calculation is that it better reflects the influence of large companies on the market as a whole.

Other Stock Market Indexes

Both the Dow and the S&P 500 measure the performance of large-cap stocks. If your portfolio includes smaller companies or is weighted more heavily toward a certain sector (e.g., technology, financial services), you might want to compare its performance against that of some other subsection of the market.

Both Standard & Poor's and Dow Jones offer indexes that track other groups of stocks, including those in particular industry sectors, such as financial services and technology, and those of companies in different size groups, such as small-cap and mid-cap companies. In addition, the NYSE Composite Index and the AMEX index track price movements for the groups of stocks that trade on their respective exchanges. The NASDAQ Composite Index tracks the over-the-counter market, which includes more small-company stocks.

Another broad market indicator, the Wilshire 5000 Index, includes around 6,500 of the most actively traded stocks.

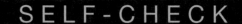

SELF-CHECK

1. Define **EPS**, **P/E ratio**, **stock market index**, and **beta**.
2. If a stock has the same market risk as the entire market, what is its beta?

12.5 Investing in Bonds

A **bond** is a type of financial security that represents your long-term loan of money to a company or government entity and gives you the right to receive interest payments and to have your loan repaid in the future.

Why are bonds issued? In general, an organization seeks outside investors when it doesn't have enough current cash flow to support its needs. A business may need cash because it's growing rapidly or its revenue is insufficient to cover its costs. Similarly, a government entity—whether federal, state, city, or municipal—may need money to pay for a large construction project or to cover other costs. Although government entities can't issue stock, businesses can choose to issue additional shares of stock instead of bonds. However, debt generally costs less than stock to the issuer, it has more favorable tax treatment, and it does not result in loss of control to the current owners. For these reasons, businesses and government like to use long-term bond issues to fund projects that they expect to have a long-term payoff. If these entities need funds for only a short time, they're likely to issue short-term debt or take out a short-term bank loan instead.

12.5.1 Advantages of Owning Bonds

Bonds generally provide a lower rate of return to investors than stocks. But fixed-income securities make up a substantial proportion of individual investors' portfolios, for the following reasons:

▲ **Diversification:** In a stock market downturn, bond income can help offset stock losses.
▲ **Predictable source of income:** Some investors need or want a steady stream of income. When you retire, for example, you could purchase long-term bonds and live off their interest. The interest payments are usually a fixed amount for the life of the bond, so you know with certainty how much income you'll be receiving.

▲ **Profit on price changes:** Bond prices go up and down over time in response to changes in market interest rates: When interest rates go up, bond prices go down and vice versa. If you're a buy-and-hold investor, this doesn't matter to you because you'll be holding the bond to maturity. If you must sell a bond before its maturity date, however, you may find that the market price is more (or less) than what you paid for it, resulting in a capital gain (or a capital loss). Active bond investors attempt to buy bonds in anticipation of interest rate declines, to profit from future price increases. Or when they think rates will be rising, they might sell bonds short in anticipation of price declines. For these strategies to work, an investor's return must be enough to offset trading costs; and the investor must correctly anticipate interest rate changes in advance of the rest of the market, which isn't easy.

▲ **Lower risk:** If you've assessed your risk tolerance and find that you prefer to bear less risk, even though it may mean receiving a lower return, you may prefer bond investing to stock investing. When you buy a bond from a creditworthy company, you know that you'll most likely receive your promised interest payments and that your principal will be repaid at maturity. For many investors, this level of certainty is more important than the uncertain possibility of greater returns from a risky stock.

▲ **Matching time horizon:** Because bonds have a fixed maturity date, some investors like them because they can match the time horizon of their investment with their future needs. Similarly, the fixed period of payments may be consistent with an investor's needs. For example, a retired couple might buy 20-year bonds so that they will have 20 years of interest income during their retirement period.

12.5.2 Bond Terminology

To become familiar with bond terminology, look at the advertisement for a new bond issue that's shown in Figure 12-3. Here, Cavalier Corporation is telling potential investors that it's interested in raising $10 million by selling bonds to the public. The firm may need this money to finance an anticipated expansion or to purchase needed assets. In return, investors will be paid 7.2 percent interest per year through 2024.

The following are some terms used in relationship with bonds:

▲ **Prospectus:** As with new stock issues, a bond issuer must provide pertinent information about the company and the security in a document called a prospectus. If you were interested in a particular company's bonds, you'd probably want to know, for example, what the company's primary business is, how the funds raised by the bond issue will be used, the financial strength of the issuer, and how the company plans to

Figure 12-3

This announcement under no circumstances should be construed as an offer to sell or as a solicitation of an offer to buy any of these securities. The offering is made only by the Prospectus.

CAVALIER CORPORATION
$10,000,000
7.2% Senior Debentures due 2024

Copies of the Prospectus may be obtained in any state or jurisdiction in which this announcement is circulated from only such of the undersigned or other dealers or brokers as may lawfully offer these securities in such state or jurisdiction.

Merrill Lynch & Co.
A.G. Edwards
Wachovia Securities
Wells Fargo Securities
Stifel, Nicholaus & Company
TD Waterhouse
H&R Block Financial Advisors, Inc.
Deutsche Bank Securities

Advertisement for a new bond issue by Cavalier Corporation.

make good on its promises to pay interest and to repay the principal at maturity. To learn more about the Cavalier bond issue, you'd contact the management firm identified in the advertisement.

▲ **Indenture:** The contract between a bondholder and the issuer of the bond is a legal document called an **indenture.** The indenture specifies all the important terms of the bond agreement, including the rights and obligations of the bondholders and the issuer. A trustee, usually a bank trust department, is assigned to keep an eye on the company, making sure that the bondholders' rights are protected. If, for example, the trustee finds that the company has violated a promise specified in the indenture, it can bring a legal action on behalf of all the bondholders to force the company to remedy the situation.

▲ **Face value:** The **face value,** or par value, of a bond is the amount that will be repaid to the bondholder when the bond matures, or comes due. Corporate bonds are usually issued with a face value of $1,000, but the face value can be larger. If we assume that the Cavalier Corporation bonds have a face value of $1,000 and the company initially sells each bond for a price equal to the face value, it needs to sell 10,000 bonds to raise the $10 million it requires. Unlike car loans and mortgages, bonds are not amortized. This means the issuer does not pay back any of the principal of the loan until the end, often 20 years or more from the date of issue. Over that period, the bonds are likely to be traded in the secondary securities market, just as common stocks are. No matter what happens to the price of the bonds in the secondary market, however, the face value remains at $1,000; whoever owns the bond on the maturity date receives that amount.

▲ **Maturity date:** The maturity date is when the bond comes due—when the issuer must repay the loan in full. Most corporate bonds are issued for 20- to 30-year terms. The maturity date for the Cavalier Corporation bonds is 2024. Because the bonds were being issued in 2004, they have a 20-year maturity. Government bonds also can have long terms but are issued for shorter periods, too, in which case they are usually called *notes* instead of bonds.

▲ **Coupon rate and payment:** The coupon rate on a bond is the fixed interest rate that the issuer pays the holder of its bonds each year; it is quoted as a percentage of the face value. For example, the Cavalier Corporation is offering to pay 7.2 percent on its bonds. The coupon rate is determined when the bond is issued, based on prevailing market rates for similar bonds. Thus, when market interest rates are relatively low, bonds are issued with lower rates than when market rates are high. At any given time, a company may have several outstanding issues of bonds that pay different fixed rates of interest because they were issued at different points in time. Knowing the face value and the coupon rate, you can calculate the **coupon payment**—the dollar payment of interest per year—as follows:

$$\text{Coupon payment} = \text{Coupon rate} \times \text{Face value}$$

Thus, Cavalier Corporation will pay 7.2 percent of $1,000, or $72, interest per year on each bond until the bonds mature.

▲ **Call provisions:** Sometimes, a bond issuer might want to repay the loan early. For example, suppose the issuer is currently paying a high fixed interest rate on a bond issue (because the bond was issued in a high-interest-rate environment), but the current rate on similar bonds is much lower (because market rates have since declined). Clearly, the company could save costs on interest payments by refinancing. Because callable bonds are better for the company, most corporate bonds have call provisions, although some may include restrictions on the company's right to call.

▲ **Sinking funds:** When the Cavalier bonds come due in 2024, the company will be obliged to repay the $10 million it borrowed from the bondholders. Although the company may be able to issue new bonds at that time to pay off the old ones, it's hard to tell right now if it will be in good enough financial shape to be able to do so. Because it's unlikely that a firm will have enough to pay the bondholders back out of its annual cash flow in the year of maturity, many bond indentures include provisions that require the company to establish a **sinking fund**, a pool of funds set aside to pay future bond obligations. The existence of a sinking fund reduces the risk of future defaults for investors.

▲ **Convertibility:** Some bond issues include a special provision that allows the bondholders to convert the bonds to shares of common stock in the future. The contract specifies how many shares a bondholder can get for each bond. Because convertibility is an attractive feature, a convertible bond usually pays a coupon rate that's 1 to 2 percentage points lower than a comparable nonconvertible bond. This reduced income potential may be offset by capital gains so that when the stock price rises, the value of the convertible bond also rises.

12.5.3 The Bond Market

The bond market is very similar to the stock market. New bond issues must be registered with the Securities and Exchange Commission, an independent agency of the federal government charged with enforcement of the securities laws and oversight of the securities market, OTC trading, brokers, and dealers. The issuers originally sell their bonds in the primary market, and then investors trade their bonds in the secondary market, both at organized exchanges and, more commonly, over the counter through bond dealers.

The biggest difference between the stock and bond markets has to do with volume—the number of trades per day. Other than Treasury securities, which have a fairly active market, bonds tend to be buy-and-hold investments, so trading can be quite "thin." This means that bond investors are exposed to greater liquidity risk than stock investors because they may not be able to find a buyer or seller to trade with at a particular time.

12.5.4 Types of Bonds

Bonds are issued by corporations and various government entities. Because these issuers have different prospects for the future and different sources of cash flow, their bond issues are distinctly different in terms of their risk characteristics. This section looks at the various types of bonds, including corporate bonds, Treasury bonds, and municipal bonds.

Corporate Bonds

Corporate bonds are long-term, interest-bearing debt securities issued by a corporation to help finance its long-term assets or operations. They are usually issued in denominations of $1,000 and promise semiannual interest payments, based on a fixed rate. Terms to maturity can vary from 5 to 30 years or more, with the most common maturities being 20 and 25 years.

U.S. Treasury Bonds

The U.S. government regularly issues debt with various terms to maturity. We've previously considered T-bills, which have maturities of 1 year or less. Although T-bills may be an appropriate choice for funds you've allocated to short-term objectives, such as an emergency fund or a money market account, the rate of return is too low to be an option for your intermediate- and long-term investment plans. In this section, therefore, we consider only Treasury notes and bonds.

If the term is 10 years or less, the security is called a Treasury note; if the term is more than 10 years, it's a Treasury bond. Other than maturity, the only real difference between the two types of securities is that some older Treasury bonds are callable (at par value) during the last 5 years before maturity. More recent issues don't have a call provision.

The primary reason for the issuance of Treasury securities is that the federal government rarely, if ever, stays within its budget. Some investors may also find Treasury securities attractive because the interest paid on them, while federally taxable, is exempt from state and local income taxes. Because of the minimal risk and the tax benefits, the yield on this type of debt investment is lower than that on corporate bonds with similar maturities.

Agency Issues

An agency issue is a bond issued by a federal agency, such as the Government National Mortgage Association (Ginnie Mae), the Federal National Mortgage Association (Fannie Mae), the Federal Home Loan Mortgage Corporation (Freddie Mac), or the Student Loan Marketing Association (Sallie Mae). These bond issues are generally backed by pools of mortgages or, in the case of Sallie Mae, pools of student loans. Agency bonds are issued in large denominations (a minimum of $25,000) and bought primarily by large institutional investors, such as pension funds and insurance companies.

Municipal Bonds

A **municipal bond** is a long-term debt security issued by a state or local government entity. The money raised from a municipal bond offering might be earmarked to pay for airport construction, public schools, parks, infrastructure improvements (e.g., roads, bridges), or ongoing government expenditures. One of the most important features of municipal bonds is that interest payments are exempt from federal income tax. If the investor lives in the state of issuance, interest payments are usually exempt from state and local taxation also. However, capital gains earned on the sale of a municipal bond are still taxed.

FOR EXAMPLE

Bonds Delayed at Airport

Sometimes, the projects financed by revenue bonds are subject to construction delays or fail to generate as much revenue as expected. The construction of the Denver International Airport was partially financed by a municipal bond issue. As the airport neared completion, problems associated with its state-of-the-art baggage-handling system caused bond-rating agencies to sharply downgrade the bonds to reflect a higher risk of default. Because the bonds had been paying an interest rate appropriate for a lower rate of risk, the increased risk caused the bond prices to crash in the secondary market. Investors who bought them cheaply at that time have realized a very good rate of return on their initial investment.

A "muni"—as a municipal bond is often called—can be either a general obligation bond or a revenue bond. If it's a general obligation bond, the interest and principal payments come from the normal operating cash flows of the issuing entity, and the security for the bond is just the "full faith and credit" of that entity. Normally, general obligation bonds can be issued only by states, cities, and other entities that have the power to assess taxes. In contrast, a revenue bond is repaid from the income generated by the project it is issued to finance.

Municipal bonds can sometimes be fairly risky investments. State and local governments with serious budget problems may find it difficult to make good on their obligations. (See the example "Bonds Delayed at Airport.") Default rates have generally been higher on revenue bonds than on general obligation bonds. To reduce this risk, investors can purchase insured municipal bonds, but these bonds pay a lower interest rate.

Like corporate bonds, municipal bonds may also have call provisions, but most are protected from early calls for the first 5 to 10 years. Such call provisions still increase the reinvestment risk associated with these bonds.

12.5.5 Classification of Bond by Characteristics

Besides the classifications based on type of issuer, bonds are sometimes classified into categories based on differences that affect their return and risk, such as whether they are secured and coupon arrangements.

Secured Vs. Unsecured Bonds

Most corporate and government bonds are **debentures**, which is a legal term for unsecured bonds. When a bond issue is unsecured, the promise of payment of interest and principal in the future is backed only by the creditworthiness of the company or government body, which will presumably rely on regular cash flows to make the payments.

In contrast, some bonds are secured. With a **secured bond**, the issuer has pledged specific assets or future cash flows as collateral. In the event of nonpayment, the bondholders, through their trustees, have the right to take the pledged assets in payment of the debt. Although the existence of collateral for the loan can reduce the risk of default to bondholders, the amount of risk reduction (and consequent reduction in yield) depends on the value of the security and its resulting cash flows. Examples of secured bonds include mortgage bonds, which are backed by real estate (much the same as a home mortgage), and equipment bonds, which are backed by valuable equipment or vehicles.

Coupon Arrangements

Bonds can be classified according to how interest is calculated and paid. Although the most common arrangement is for bond coupon payments to be fixed until maturity and paid in semiannual installments, variations exist. For example, with floating-rate bonds, interest payments are tied to current market interest rates and adjusted periodically, similarly to an adjustable-rate mortgage. A variation on the floating-rate bond is the indexed bond. Here, the interest rate is tied not to another interest rate but to a general price index or the price of a commodity or another market index. Treasury Inflation Protected Securities (TIPs) protect investors from inflation by adjusting the face value of the bond.

A **zero-coupon bond** makes no coupon payments but is instead discounted at the time of sale. Thus, the price you pay for a zero-coupon bond with a face value of $1,000 is always less than the $1,000 to be received at the maturity date. Your entire yield comes from the capital gain, the face value less the price you pay for the bond. Zero-coupon bonds are issued by both corporations and governments, with the U.S. Treasury being the primary issuer. If you aren't interested in current income but have a specific investment goal in mind, such as paying for your child's education 18 years from now, it might appear that a zero-coupon bond would be an attractive investment.

The major problem with zero-coupon bonds is that the IRS considers the annual appreciation in the value of the bond to be "undistributed interest" and requires that you recognize it as taxable income. These bonds are best held in tax-deferred accounts or by minor children who are subject to low tax rates. Another disadvantage of zero-coupon bonds is that, because their only cash flow is the $1,000 to be received many years in the future, they expose investors to greater interest-rate risk than coupon bonds. Although an increase in interest rates causes all bond prices to decline, the prices of zero-coupon bonds tend to experience larger declines as a percentage of value. Zero-coupon bonds also expose you to inflation risk if actual inflation turns out to be greater than what was expected at the time of issue. Nevertheless, zero-coupon bonds are very

Figure 12-4

General Rating	Moody's	Standard & Poor's	Explanation
Very high quality	Aaa Aa	AAA AA	High-grade bonds. Extremely strong or very strong capacity to pay interest and principal. Companies that have been profitable over the years and are unlikely to default.
High quality	A Baa	A BBB	Medium-grade bonds. Strong or adequate capacity to pay but can be susceptible to adverse economic conditions or changing circumstances.
Speculative	Ba B	BB	Low-grade bonds. Capacity to pay interest and repay principal is speculative. It may still have some good elements, but there is great uncertainty about the company's exposure to adverse conditions.
Very poor quality	Caa C	CCC D	These bonds pose the highest risk, and some may already be in default. C-rated bonds are income bonds that are no longer paying interest, and D-rated bonds are in default on interest and/or principal. There is little chance of recovery.

Bond ratings.

popular with buy-and-hold investors who plan to hold the bonds to maturity and aren't concerned with interim swings in value.

Risk

Bonds are often classified according to risk. Several rating agencies, including Moody's, Standard & Poor's, Duff & Phelps, and Fitch Investors Service, regularly evaluate large corporate and municipal bond issues and provide ratings based on default risk. The two most popular rating systems—Moody's and Standard & Poor's—are described in Figure 12-4.

Bonds rated Baa and above under the Moody's system and BBB and above in Standard & Poor's are called **investment-grade bonds,** whereas those with lower ratings are called speculative-grade bonds, or **junk bonds.** Because higher risk usually translates into higher returns, junk bonds are also called high-yield bonds. Certain financial institutions, such as pension funds and insurance companies, are heavily invested in bonds, but they're often required to hold only investment-grade bonds. For this reason, if a bond issue is downgraded to spec-ulative grade, the value is likely to fall substantially as these investors sell them. Junk bonds are riskier than bonds issued by low-risk companies, not only because of the difference in default risk but also because of liquidity. Junk bonds are much less actively traded and tend to be more sensitive to economic condi-tions than investment-grade bonds.

SELF-CHECK

1. List the advantages of buying bonds.
2. Define **face value, zero-coupon bond, municipal bond, junk bond, and debentures.**
3. Cite three bond classifications.

12.6 Buying and Selling Bonds

It's useful to evaluate bonds in terms of their expected yield, or return on invest-ment. The return on a bond investment has two components:

▲ **Coupon yield:** The coupon yield, or current yield, is the return on investment that comes from receiving regular payments of interest.

▲ **Capital gains yield:** The capital gain (or loss) is the difference between the price you pay for the bond and the amount you get for it at maturity (or upon sale to another investor).

Section 12.4 explains that a stock investor's yield also comes from current yield (or dividend yield) and capital gains yield. Unlike the uncertainty cash flows from stock investments, when you buy a bond and hold it to maturity, both of these components of yield are known with certainty at the outset, subject only to the risk of default by the issuer.

Long-term investors often evaluate their bond investments using **yield to maturity (YTM),** which is the annualized yield you get if you hold a bond to maturity, receive all promised cash flows from the date of purchase, and reinvest annual payments at the same rate. In the simplest case, where you pay exactly the face value for a bond, the YTM is the same as the coupon rate. Because there is no difference between the $1,000 you pay at the beginning and the $1,000 you receive at the end, your only income is the annual interest received. There-fore, your total yield is the current yield. However, if you don't pay face value for the bond, the YTM includes any change in price (which can be a loss or gain) between the time you buy the bond and the maturity date. Thus, your YTM is the coupon yield plus the annualized capital gains yield. You can approximate the YTM by using the following equation:

$$\text{Approximate YTM} = \frac{\text{Annual coupon payment} + \text{Face value} - \text{Price} / \text{Years to maturity}}{\text{Face value} + \text{Price} / 2}$$

12.6.1 Bond Risk in a Diversified Portfolio

Although both bonds and stocks are affected by market interest rates, their price changes are not perfectly correlated. Thus, holding both bonds and stocks in a diversified investment portfolio can reduce the risk of the portfolio.

An investor who maintained a 50/50 allocation between bonds and stocks would have had lower returns during the stock market run-up in the 1990s than an all-equity investor but would have softened the blow of the market downturn because the interest rate declines during the 2001 to 2003 period caused bond prices to rise. The net result on the portfolio would have been slightly lower average return and significantly lower risk.

12.6.2 Bond Investment Strategies

Your investment plan should include determining your investment strategies in addition to regularly reevaluating your portfolio and your progress toward your goals. You can be an active or a passive investor (see Section 11.4), but the risks of active investing, along with the time and energy required, may not make it practical.

Most of the investment strategies discussed in Section 11.4 can be applied to bond investing also—for example, diversification, buy-and-hold, dollar cost averaging, and timing. In addition, laddering and maturity matching are strategies that are unique to fixed-income securities:

▲ **Laddering:** Laddering is a type of buy-and-hold bond investing strategy in which you purchase a collection of bonds with different maturities spread out over your investment horizon. If, for example, you have a 10-year investment horizon, you could buy bonds that mature in 1, 2, 3, 4, 5, 6, 7, 8, 9, and 10 years. As each bond matures, you use the money to buy a bond that matures in 10 years (so that you always have one bond from each maturity in the portfolio). The advantage of this strategy is that it balances the risk and return elements in the portfolio because the bonds with shorter terms to maturity are not as sensitive to interest rate changes, while the bonds with longer terms to maturity give slightly higher yields.

▲ **Maturity matching:** Maturity matching is similar to laddering, but it requires that you purchase assets with cash flows that coincide with the period in which you need the funds. Thus, if your time horizon is 10 years from now, you purchase only bonds with 10 years to maturity. Zero-coupon bonds are often used for this purpose because they don't pay any interest in the interim and you receive the full principal at maturity. Alternatively, you might buy bonds that will make interest payments for the period when you'll need the funds—let's say 20-year coupon bonds that will make interest payments over the expected 20-year period of your retirement.

12.6.3 A Bond Transaction

Let's walk through the process of actually buying a bond. Individual investors buy bonds in the same ways they buy stock—usually through a broker. If you use a full-service brokerage firm, the broker provides you with advice and information about prices and yields. In return for this, though, you pay a higher commission. If you already know what you want, you can save money by using a discount broker or buying online.

In this section, we assume that you've decided to invest in Ford Motor Credit bonds. First, we look at how you can look up the price of these bonds, and then we walk through the transaction.

Reading Bond Quotations

The Wall Street Journal regularly reports prices and yields for Treasury issues and some municipal and corporate bonds. Figure 12-5 shows how the information on corporate bonds was reported in the July 16, 2004, issue of the *Journal* (with information from the close of the previous day). It includes the coupon rate, maturity date, prices, and yields for transactions of $1 million or more for the 40 most actively traded corporate bonds (in order from highest to lowest volume of trading).

Let's look more closely at the Ford Motor Credit bond. Note that the bond reported for Ford pays a 7.45 percent coupon rate per year, or $74.50, which is 7.45 percent of the face value of $1,000. Although it doesn't say so, these bonds pay their coupons semiannually, so you'd receive $37.25 every six months if you owned one of them. The bond will mature July 16, 2031, which tells you the coupon payments are made on January 16 and July 16 of each year and the last coupon will be paid on July 16, 2031, 27 years from the date of the newspaper report, when the investors will also receive their $1,000 par value.

The "Last Price" column reports the price as a percentage of the face value. The Ford bond is priced at 95.455 percent of the face value, so it is selling for $954.55 per bond. The "Last Yield" column is the YTM if you bought the bond for the current price, but not including the interest that accrues between coupon

Figure 12-5

Corporate Bonds

Thrusday, July 15, 2004
Forty most active fixed-coupon corporate bonds

COMPANY (TICKER)	COUPON	MATURITY	LAST PRICE	LAST YIELD	*EST SPREAD	UST†	EST $ VOL (000'S)
Electronic Data Systems (EDS)	6.000	Aug 01, 2013	96.095	7.090	261	10	234,039
Merrill Lynch (MER)	5.450	Jul 15, 2014	99.818	5.474	99	10	212,310
Glaxo Smith Kline Capital Inc (GSK)	4.375	Apr 15, 2014	94.777	5.060	57	10	132,428
Ford Motor Credit (F)	7.375	Oct 28, 2009	107.396	5.727	204	5	132,149
Sprint Capital (FON)	6.900	May 01, 2019	102.363	6.645	216	10	114,510
Ford Motor Credit (F)	7.450	Jul 16, 2031	95.455	7.858	264	30	113,856
AT&T Corp (T)	6.000	Mar 15, 2009	96.750	6.824	314	5	101,999
General Motors Acceptance (GM)	8.000	Nov 01, 2031	102.995	7.733	252	30	93,336
General Motors (GM)	8.375	Jul 15, 2033	105.504	7.889	268	30	86,314
Citizens Communications (CZN)	9.250	May 15, 2011	109.125	7.511	303	10	85,160
Altria Group (MO)	7.000	Nov 04, 2013	103.264	6.524	204	10	81,121
Morgan Stanley (MWD)	4.750	Apr 01, 2014	93.697	5.600	112	10	78,494
Ford Motor Credit (F)	7.000	Oct 01, 2013	102.015	6.701	222	10	77,398
Credit Suisse First Boston (USA (CRDSUI)	5.125	Jan 15, 2014	98.082	5.386	90	10	74,104
Merrill Lynch (MER)	3.700	Apr 21, 2008	99.094	3.961	27	5	72,780
Harrah's Operating (HET)	8.000	Feb 01, 2011	112.191	5.735	125	10	71,456
HSBC Bank USA (HSBC)	4.625	Apr 01, 2014	94.707	5.330	85	10	69,535
National Rural Utilites Cooperative Finance (NRUC)	7.250	Mar 01, 2012	114.422	4.952	46	10	66,555
General Motors Acceptance (GM)	4.150	Feb 07, 2005	100.985	2.327	n.a.	n.a.	64,543
Schering-Plough (SGP)	6.500	Dec 01, 2033	102.680	6.536	132	30	63,987
Ford Motor Credit (F)	5.800	Jan 12, 2009	101.809	5.340	166	5	62,863
General Motors Acceptance (GM)	6.750	Jan 15, 2006	104.941	3.315	71	2	62,189
Wyeth (WYE)	5.500	Feb 01, 2014	96.971	5.920	144	10	60,892
Sprint Capital (FON)	8.375	Mar 15, 2012	116.157	5.735	125	10	56,676
Tyco International Group SA (TYC)	6.375	Oct 15, 2011	107.437	5.130	65	10	55,849
UFJ Finance Aruba AEC (UFJ)	6.750	Jul 15, 2013	107.300	5.700	121	10	55,629
International Business Machines (IBM)	6.220	Aug 01, 2027	102.183	6.043	82	30	55,003
General Electric Capital (GE)	2.850	Jan 30, 2006	100.225	2.698	9	2	54,472
Verizon Global Funding (VZ)	4.375	Jun 01, 2013	92.943	5.386	90	10	53,886
General Motors Acceptance (GM)	6.875	Sep 15, 2011	102.649	6.405	192	10	52,583
International Business Machines (IBM)	4.750	Nov 29, 2012	98.706	4.940	46	10	52,048
Ford Motor Credit (F)	5.625	Oct 01, 2008	101.877	5.120	143	5	51,908
Kellogg (K)	6.600	Apr 01, 2011	110.383	4.769	27	10	51,667
Vodafone Group PLC (VOD)	7.625	Feb 15, 2005	103.210	2.031	n.a.	n.a.	51,628
Time Warner (TWX)	7.700	May 01, 2032	110.625	6.839	162	30	49,421
J.P. Morgan Chase (JPM)	5.900	Nov 15, 2011	104.796	5.105	62	10	49,266
Merrill Lynch (MER)	4.125	Jan 15, 2009	99.536	4.240	56	5	48,758
Target (TGT)	7.500	Feb 15, 2005	103.111	1.975	n.a.	n.a.	48,721
SBC Communications (SBC)	5.875	Aug 15, 2012	103.695	5.305	82	10	47,238
Time Warner (TWX)	6.875	May 01, 2012	109.100	5.424	94	10	46,120
Tyco International Group SA (TYC)	6.375	Feb 15, 2006	105.116	3.011	41	2	44,310

Volume represents total volume for each issue: price/yield data are for trades of $1 million and greater. *Estimated spreads, in basis points (100 basis points one percentage point), over the 2, 3, 5, 10 or 30-year hot run Treasury note/bond. 2-year: 2.750 06/06; 3-year: 3.125 05/07; 5-year: 3.625 07/09; 10-year: 4.79 05/14; 30-year: 5.375 02/31. †Comparable U.S. Treasury issue.

Source: Wall Street Journal. Copyright 2004 by Dow Jones & Co Inc. Permission granted via Copyright Clearance Center.

The Wall Street Journal, corporate bonds, July 16, 2004.

payment dates. The Ford bond's annual yield is 7.858 percent, reported in the "Last Yield" column.

The difference between the yield on the Ford bond and a Treasury security of comparable term to maturity (the number of years given in the UST column)—called the estimated spread—is in the column labeled "Est Spread." The unit in which the estimated spread is given is the basis point, which is 1/100 percent, so the estimated spread of 264 means the Ford bond will give you an estimated 2.64 percentage points more yield than the 30-year Treasury security. The last column, labeled "Est $ Vol (000's)," gives the total value of bonds that traded on that day, which was $113,856,000. You can find bond quotations for most traded bonds at www.investingbond.com.

A Brokered Deal

The process of buying a bond is similar to that for buying a stock. As noted, you can find out the price at which a particular bond traded on the previous day. A broker will quote you a higher price that includes trading costs. The broker's price is also adjusted to reflect any portion of the next coupon payment that should accrue to the person selling the bond. For example, if you buy a bond three months from the date of the semiannual coupon, you have to give the seller half of the interest for that period, and the price you're quoted reflects this. The broker implements the trade at an organized exchange if the bond you want is traded in that way. Most bonds, however, are traded by bond dealers, so the broker actually contacts a dealer and buys your bond through that firm. You pay a commission to your broker, and the dealer makes a profit called a markup. For a $1,000 bond, you can expect your transaction costs to be anywhere from $25 to $60, the equivalent of almost a full year's interest payment.

SELF-CHECK

1. List some bond investing strategies that are available.
2. Define **YTM** and **laddering**.
3. Where can you find out the price of a bond?

12.7 Preferred Stock

Besides common stocks and bonds, you may want to invest in preferred stock, which offers the advantage of paying regular, fixed dividends that take precedence over dividends to common shareholders. Here, we review the most important features of preferred stock.

Figure 12-6

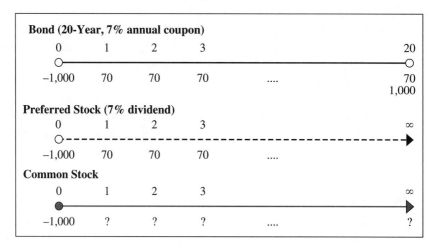

Comparison of annual cash flows for bonds, preferred stock, and common stock.

Preferred stock shares have similarities to both common stock and bonds. Like both bonds and common stock, preferred stock is issued by companies as a means of raising capital. Like bonds, most preferred stock pays a fixed cash flow to investors. Like common stock, though, preferred stock has no set maturity date, and the company never has to repay the original investment amount.

Figure 12-6 shows the differences in cash flow streams that might be realized by a bond investor, a preferred stock investor, and a common stock investor, assuming an initial investment of $1,000 in each case. At this point, the actual dollar amounts of the cash flows are not important. Instead, let's focus on the timing and certainty of the cash flows.

Note that the bond's cash flow stream has a specific end date, whereas the cash flows of the two types of stock extend to infinity (or at least, as long as the company is in existence). Note also that the owners of the bond and the preferred stock know what the amount of their cash flow will be with certainty (assuming that the issuer doesn't miss any payments or default), whereas the owners of common stock don't know what the dividends will be in the future. As with bonds, the current price of a share of preferred stock may be higher or lower than its par value and depends on the dividend rate relative to market rates at the time. When rates on similar risk investments are higher than the dividend rate, the price is lower than the par and vice versa.

The primary attraction of preferred stock is its steady dividend stream, which provides a yield that is usually greater than the pretax yield on long-term bonds of similar risk. These dividends are taxable income to the investor and are not deductible by the issuer. A special tax rule allows corporations that hold the stock of other corporations to exclude 70 percent of the dividends from taxable income. Although this is good for corporate investors, it's a disadvantage to individual investors because these tax-advantaged investors are willing to pay more for the stock and therefore drive up the price.

The most important risks preferred stock investors face are interest rate risk, call risk, and default risk. Much like bond values, preferred stock values are extremely dependent on market rates of interest. You might expect that falling rates would benefit the investor through increased prices and above-market yield. However, in the case of callable preferred shares, the issuing corporation is likely to exercise its call rights and retire the stock. Thus, the investor gets the worst of both worlds—the price declines when rates rise, and stock is called when rates fall. Default risk depends on the issuing firm's business risk. Riskier companies, on average, pay higher dividend rates than less risky companies.

If the company has a cash shortfall, preferred stock investors, particularly holders of cumulative preferred stock, are in a better position than common stock investors. Although bondholders still get paid first, preferred shareholders must be paid their dividends before the company can declare a dividend for the common shareholders, making this investment generally less risky than common stock and more risky than bonds. As with bonds, ratings agencies such as Moody's and Standard and Poor's regularly provide ratings of credit risk for issues of preferred stock.

SELF-CHECK

1. Who rates preferred stock?
2. Cite the main advantage of preferred stock as an investment.

SUMMARY

Common stock gives stockholders the right to share in the future performance of a corporation. You should, however, diversify your portfolio with bonds or preferred stock. You can evaluate stocks based on several risk and return factors. Bonds provide a steady stream of income and are generally less risky than stock. You should stay on top of your portfolio to get the best return for your level of risk tolerance.

KEY TERMS

Ask price	The stock price requested by a potential seller.
Beta	A measure of the market, or nondiversifiable, risk of a stock.
Bid price	The stock price offered by a potential buyer.
Blue chip stock	A stock that is issued by a large, stable, mature company.
Bond	Type of financial security that represents your long-term loan of money to a company or government entity.
Buying on margin	Using borrowed funds from a broker to make a trade.
Capital gains yield	The component of a stock investor's total return that is equal to the ratio of the annual change in price to the market price of a stock.
Churning	Excessive trading in a discretionary account.
Close price	The last price at which a stock sold at the close of the previous business day.
Corporation	A form of business organization that exists as a legal entity separate from its owners, who have limited liability for corporate losses.
Coupon payment	The annual dollar interest payment on a bond, equal to the coupon rate multiplied by the face value, usually paid to investors in two equal installments.
Cyclical stock	A stock exhibiting above-average sensitivity to the business cycle.
Day trader	An active investor who buys and sells many times during the day in an attempt to make quick profits.
Debentures	Unsecured bonds.
Defensive stock	Stock that is relatively insensitive to the business cycle.
Dividend yield	The component of a stock investor's total return that is equal to the ratio of annual dividends to the market price of a stock.
Earnings per share (EPS)	A measure of company profitability equal to annual earnings divided by the number of shares outstanding.
Face value	The dollar amount the bondholder will receive at the bond's maturity date.
Growth stock	Stock that compensates investors primarily through increases in value of the shares over time.

Income stock	Stock that compensates investors primarily through the regular payment of dividends.
Indenture	A legal document that details the rights and obligations of the bondholders and bond issuer.
Initial public offering (IPO)	A company's first stock offering to the public.
Investment-grade bonds	Medium- and high-grade bonds with low risk of default on interest or principal.
Junk bonds	Bonds with a high risk of default.
Limit order	A request to buy stock at any price up to a specified maximum or to sell stock at any price above a specified minimum.
Limited liability	A statutory right of corporate shareholders that limits their potential losses to the value of the shares they hold.
Listed security	A security that is approved to be bought or sold on a particular exchange.
Margin call	A request from a brokerage firm that the holder of a margin account add money to the account to maintain the required minimum.
Market capitalization	The total outstanding value of a company's stock at current market prices. It is calculated as the current stock price multiplied by the number of shares outstanding.
Market order	An offer to buy stock at the market price.
Municipal bond	A long-term debt security issued by a state or local government entity.
NASDAQ	An electronic reporting system for frequently traded over-the-counter stocks. Stands for National Association of Securities Dealers Automated Quotation System.
Over-the-counter (OTC) market	An electronic network for trading securities through securities dealers.
Preemptive right	The right of a stockholder to maintain his or her proportionate ownership when the company issues additional shares of stock.
Price-to-earnings (P/E) ratio	Measure of a company's future earnings potential calculated as market price divided by earnings per share.
Primary market	The market in which securities are sold by corporations to the public for the first time.

Prospectus	A document that gives potential investors financial information about a stock issue and the issuing company.
Proxy	A written agreement in which a shareholder gives another person the right to vote in his or her place.
Residual claim	A common shareholder's right to the firm's assets and income after all the other claimholders are paid.
Round lot	A group of 100 shares of stock; stock is normally traded in round lots.
Secondary market	The market in which previously issued securities are traded between investors.
Secured bond	A bond for which interest and principal payments are backed by assets or future cash flows pledged as collateral.
Securities exchange	A physical location at which securities are traded; the largest securities exchange is the New York Stock Exchange.
Selling short	A strategy in which an investor borrows stock from a broker, sells the stock, and later buys stock on the market to replace the borrowed stock.
Sinking fund	A fund accumulated to pay an amount due at a specific time in the future, such as when a bond issue comes due.
Specialist	A person responsible for matching a particular stock's buy and sell orders at a specific securities exchange.
Stock dividend	A dividend given to shareholders in the form of shares of stock instead of cash.
Stock market index	An indicator that shows the average price movements of a particular group of stocks representing the market or some market segment.
Stockbroker	A licensed professional who buys and sells securities on behalf of clients.
Stop order	An order to buy or sell stock holdings when the market price reaches a certain level.
Tombstone ad	A formal advertisement of a stock issue in the financial press.
Yield	The annual return on investment, including current yield and capital gains yield.
Yield to Maturity (YTM)	Annualized return on a bond, if it is held to maturity and all interest payments are reinvested at the same rate.
Zero-coupon bond	A bond that doesn't make interest payments but instead is discounted at the time of sale.

ASSESS YOUR UNDERSTANDING

Go to www.wiley.com/college/bajtelsmit to assess your knowledge of investing in stocks and bonds.
Measure your learning by comparing pre-test and post-test results.

Summary Questions

1. The major reason companies issue stock is to spread the risk among a large number of investors. True or false?

2. A written agreement that gives your common stock voting rights to someone else is known as a:
   (a) preemptive right.
   (b) proxy.
   (c) forfeit agreement.
   (d) voting assignment.

3. A stock issued by a large, stable, mature company is known as:
   (a) an income stock.
   (b) a growth stock.
   (c) a large-cap stock.
   (d) a blue chip stock.

4. Which of the following would be considered a defensive stock?
   (a) Home Depot.
   (b) Coca-Cola.
   (c) Ford Motor Company.
   (d) Delta Airlines.

5. If your stock has made a profit and you want to protect your gains, you would most likely do a:
   (a) market order.
   (b) limit order.
   (c) stop order.
   (d) fill-or-kill order.

6. What does a short seller try to do?
   (a) Buy low now and sell high later.
   (b) Sell high now and buy low later.
   (c) Buy on margin and repay with borrowed funds.
   (d) Sell on margin and repay with borrowed funds.

7. A stock paying an annual dividend of $1.10 and selling at a price of $27.50 would have a dividend yield of 2.5 percent. True or false?

8. The ratio most often seen as a measure of future earnings potential is the:
   (a) EPS.
   (b) P/E ratio.
   (c) dividend yield.
   (d) capital gains yield.

9. When you buy bonds issued by a company, you become an owner of the company. True or false?

10. Bonds that are rated BBB or better by Standard & Poor's are referred to as:
    (a) top-notch bonds.
    (b) risk-free bonds.
    (c) investment-grade bonds.
    (d) recession-proof bonds.

11. If you determine that the maximum maturity for your bond portfolio will be 4 years and you allocate 25 percent of your portfolio to one-year bonds, 25 percent of your portfolio to two-year bonds, 25 percent of your portfolio to three-year bonds and 25 percent of your portfolio to four-year bonds, you are practicing:
    (a) bond spreading.
    (b) maturity matching.
    (c) laddering.
    (d) timing.

12. The primary reason to invest in preferred stock is the potential for large capital gains. True or false?

Applying This Chapter

1. Explain the difference between the bid price and the ask price for a stock.
2. For each of the following stocks, identify the appropriate classifications:
   (a) Microsoft Corporation, $283.1 billion market capitalization
   (b) JetBlue Airways, $2.95 billion market capitalization
   (c) Longs Drug Stores, $801 million market capitalization
   (d) Trump Hotel & Casino Resort, $59 million market capitalization

3. Use the excerpt from *The Wall Street Journal* given in Figure 12-1 to find the following information about Deb Shops, Inc., a clothing retailer:

    (a) ticker symbol

    (b) annual dividend

    (c) close price

    (d) 52-week high

4. You can attempt to make investment gains by either buying stocks you think will increase in value or selling short stocks you think will decrease in value. In either case, you take the risk that the price will go in an unfavorable direction. Explain why selling short is an inherently risky investment strategy.

5. You have a margin account with a minimum maintenance margin of 30 percent. You buy 100 shares of stock at $20 per share, using only $1,200 of your own money. If the stock price fell to $15, would you get a margin call?

6. Seesaw Incorporated has a P/E ratio of 45 and beta of 2.2, while SlowMo Corporation has a P/E ratio of 12 and beta of 0.75. Which stock is riskier? What can you tell from the P/E ratios?

7. The coupon rate on a corporate bond issue is 8.5 percent. If you own one bond with a face value of $1,000, how much interest will you receive every six months from this investment?

8. Indicate appropriate classifications for each of the following bonds:

    (a) a bond issued by the state of Texas to finance construction of an interstate highway, with payments to be made from tolls

    (b) a bond issued by a fairly young, high-growth technology company that pays interest at 5 percentage points over the 10-year Treasury bond yield

YOU TRY IT

Play the Market Risk Free

Give yourself some play money and try your hand at stock investing at http://finance.yahoo.com. Decide on how you will diversify your stock portfolio across different classifications as discussed in this chapter (e.g., by industry, capitalization, risk). Start your account by selecting at least 10 stocks. Then track your portfolio over several weeks. Compare your performance to that of a benchmark index over the same time period.

Blue Chip Dividends for You

You own 400 shares of a blue chip company's stock, which currently is worth $65 per share. The company pays a quarterly dividend of $0.90, for a total of $3.60 per year.

1. How much will your dividend check be this quarter?

2. What tax rate will be applicable to this dividend if the stock is held in a taxable account and you're in the 15 percent federal income tax bracket?

3. What is the dividend yield on this stock (pretax)?

Bond Yields

You buy a semiannual fixed-rate coupon bond that has a face value of $1,000 and 10 years to maturity. The current market price is $910, and the coupon rate is 8 percent. Use the formula given in Section 12.6 to calculate the approximate YTM. What would be the approximate YTM if the current price is $1,080?

13

INVESTING IN MUTUAL FUNDS
Pooling Your Money

Starting Point

Go to www.wiley.com/college/bajtelsmit to assess your knowledge of investing in mutual funds.
Determine where you need to concentrate your effort.

What You'll Learn in This Chapter

▲ Benefits and costs of investing in mutual funds
▲ Types of mutual funds
▲ The process of selecting funds for your portfolio

After Studying This Chapter, You'll Be Able To

▲ Classify mutual funds by their investment objectives and portfolio composition
▲ Establish strategies for selecting among mutual funds and evaluating fund performance
▲ Compare and contrast funds based on portfolio composition and investment objective

INTRODUCTION

Buying individual stocks and bonds is not a realistic alternative for everybody. If you don't have much money to invest right now, buying individual stocks and bonds probably won't enable you to achieve enough diversification in your portfolio, at least in the beginning, and the trading costs are likely to be too high relative to your returns. Also, many people are too busy to take the time to make informed stock and bond investment decisions. This is why more than half of all U.S. households own mutual funds. In this chapter, you'll learn how mutual funds can enable you to participate in the stock and bond markets while achieving better overall diversification with lower transaction costs. We explore the types of funds that are available and how to evaluate and select funds for your portfolio.

13.1 What Is a Mutual Fund?

A **mutual fund** is technically an open-end investment company, but the term is often applied more broadly to any arrangement in which investors' funds are pooled and used to purchase securities. Although the mechanism can differ across funds, the cash flows generated by the securities in the pool are later distributed to the investors. Investors who purchase shares in mutual funds are like other corporate shareholders: They have no say in the day-to-day decisions about buying and selling securities for the pool, but they have an equity interest in the pool of assets and a residual claim on the profits of the pool.

What does a mutual fund investor actually own? One measure of the value of an investor's claim on mutual fund assets is called the **net asset value.** This is calculated as assets minus liabilities, per share:

$$\text{Net asset value} = \frac{(\text{Market value of assets} - \text{Market value of liabilities})}{\text{Number of shares}}$$

For example, suppose you own one share of a mutual fund that has 5 million shares outstanding. The fund portfolio is currently worth $100 million, and its liabilities include $2 million owed to investment advisors and $1 million in rent, wages, and other expenses. The per share net asset value is calculated as:

$$\text{Net asset value} = (\$100,000,000 - \$3,000,000)/\ 5,000,000$$

$$= \$97,000,000/\ 5,000,000$$

$$= \$19.40$$

If the securities that are held in a mutual fund increase in value, the net asset value of the shares of the mutual fund should also increase in value, even though these increases are technically unrealized capital gains. A mutual fund shareholder can capture that gain in value by selling his or her shares of the fund for a price that reflects the higher net asset value. The objective of fund managers is thus to invest in assets that will continue to grow in value over time.

As you learn more about this type of investment, it is important to keep in mind that mutual fund values tend to track the performance of the assets they invest in. So if the stock market is down, stock mutual fund values decline too because the assets they have invested in have lower market values.

13.1.1 The Increasing Popularity of Mutual Funds

Mutual fund investing by individuals has increased dramatically. Fewer than 6 percent of households owned mutual fund shares in 1980, compared with nearly 50 percent in 2003—more than 50 million households. Although some of this growth is due to an increase in defined contribution employment retirement plans, which invest primarily in mutual funds on behalf of employees, the bull market of the 1990s had an effect too. The lure of double-digit increases in portfolio value was hard to resist, and the number of individual investors more than doubled during that decade.

Over the past three decades, probably in response to investor demand, the number and variety of mutual funds has risen significantly. Figure 13-1 shows recent growth in the number of mutual funds, the value of the funds, and the number of accounts. Whereas there were only 1,000 U.S. mutual funds in existence 20 years ago, today investors have more than 8,000 to choose from.

As mentioned previously, a mutual fund is technically a type of **investment company**—usually a corporation but sometimes a partnership or trust. Investment companies are financial intermediaries that provide the service of pooling small dollar amounts from many investors and investing those funds in a wide variety of assets. Each investor buys shares in the company, and the company uses the dollars to make investments on behalf of the investment pool.

Until the enactment of comprehensive securities laws in the 1930s, investors had little confidence in this type of investment. Today, however, these investment shares are legally considered securities and are thus entitled to all the protections afforded to other financial assets. That means the investment company must provide all potential investors with disclosure information, similar to the information provided for a stock or bond investment, and it must make regular reports to the Securities and Exchange Commission, which regulates them. Because fund investors depend on the managers to make decisions that are in their best interests, actions that are in conflict with this fiduciary duty create negative publicity for the entire industry.

Although different types of investment companies are often lumped together in a discussion of mutual funds, several distinct types provide pooling opportunities for individual investors. This section discusses these types of companies.

Figure 13-1

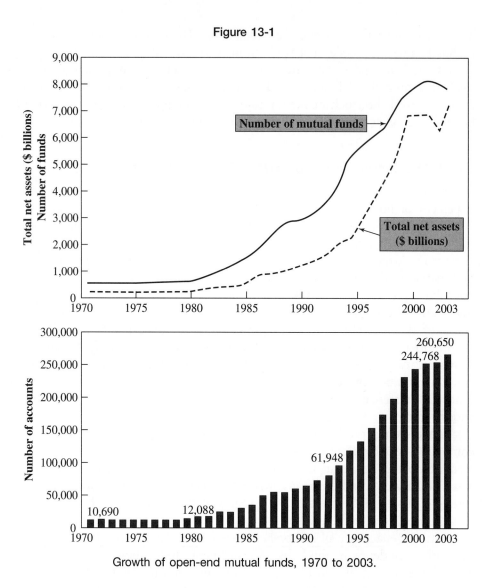

Growth of open-end mutual funds, 1970 to 2003.

Open-End Funds

When people talk about mutual fund investing, they're generally referring to buying and selling shares of open-end investment companies, or **open-end funds.** By far the most common type of investment company, an open-end fund is different from the other types discussed in this section in two respects:

▲ It is required to buy back shares at any time an investor wants to sell.
▲ It continuously offers new shares for sale to the public.

The price for purchases and sales is usually the net asset value plus trading costs, which are explained later in this chapter. The issuing company provides the only market for the shares because they aren't traded in the secondary market between investors. The investment company is free to issue new shares at any time to raise additional funds for investment and to meet investor demand for the shares. Open-end funds can be very large, with many billions of dollars under management.

Closed-End Funds

A **closed-end fund** is an investment company that issues a fixed number of shares that trade on a stock exchange or in the over-the-counter market. The process of issuing shares is very similar to that for stocks. The initial public offering of shares is sold directly to investors, after which the shares trade between investors in the secondary market. Closed-end funds hire professional managers to invest the funds in a diversified set of assets intended to meet stated objectives. Closed-end funds trade primarily on the major stock exchanges, such as the New York Stock Exchange, the American Stock Exchange, and NASDAQ. Many financial Web sites provide price and dividend information for available closed end funds and allow you to screen for desired characteristics. Although closed-end funds are only a small proportion of the total number of mutual funds in existence (around 600 in the United States, compared with 8,000 open-end funds), they are growing in popularity. The number of closed-end funds increased more than 20 percent from 2000 to 2003.

Exchange-Traded Funds

An **exchange-traded fund (ETF)** combines some of the characteristics of open-end and closed-end funds. It is technically an open-end fund because the company is free to issue new shares or redeem old shares to increase or decrease the number of shares outstanding. But like a closed-end fund, an ETF is traded on an organized exchange, and share prices are determined by market forces. Investors buy ETF shares through a broker just as they would purchase common stock shares of any publicly traded firm.

Although the number of ETFs is still small relative to other types of investment companies, their size and popularity are growing rapidly. This is largely because many are designed to be index funds, investing in a set of securities that mimic the performance of a particular market index, such as the S&P 500 Index, with low expenses (because they aren't actively managed). Also, most have fairly low minimum investment amounts. For these reasons, the financial press has been strongly advocating this type of fund for individual investors seeking diversification and low costs. Investors who buy shares in ETFs based on the S&P 500 (called "Spiders") see an increase in the value of their shares when the S&P 500 increases in value. Similarly, investors in "Diamonds," which are ETFs based on the Dow Jones Industrial Average (DJIA), benefit when the Dow goes up. Fortunately, these gains don't have to be recognized for tax purposes until the shares are sold at some point in the future.

Unit Investment Trusts

A **unit investment trust (UIT)** is an investment company that buys and holds a fixed portfolio of securities for a time determined by the life of the investments in the trust (usually, fixed-maturity debt securities). Because there isn't any change in the portfolio, this type of fund is essentially unmanaged. The manager of the pool, called the *trustee*, initially purchases the pool of investments and deposits them in a trust. Owners are issued redeemable trust certificates, which entitle them to proportionate shares of any income and principal payments received by the trust and a distribution of their proportionate share of the proceeds at the termination of the trust. The investors generally pay a premium over what it costs the trustee to purchase the underlying assets, providing the equivalent of a commission to the trustee for the service of pooling the funds and distributing the income and principal.

Because UIT funds are unmanaged, the fee should be lower than that for a comparable managed fund, but it can be as high as 3 to 5 percent. Why would an investor by willing to incur such a high cost? The answer lies in the type of securities that make up UITs. About 90 percent of these assets are fixed-income securities, primarily municipal bonds. Each trust specializes in a certain type of security, so one might hold only municipal bonds and another only high-yield corporate bonds. The high cost of individual bonds (usually $1,000 minimum) makes it otherwise difficult for individual investors to include these investment classes in their portfolios. The availability of UIT shares means that small investors can still participate in a relatively diversified pool of specialized debt securities. Although there isn't an active secondary market for the trust certificates, the trustee usually buys them back on request.

A UIT continues in existence only as long as assets remain in the trust. Thus, a trust invested in short-term securities might exist for only a few months, whereas a trust holding municipal bonds might have a life of 20 years or more, depending on the maturities of the bonds held.

Real Estate Investment Trusts

A **real estate investment trust (REIT)** is a special type of closed-end investment company that invests in real estate and mortgages. By law, a REIT must have a buy-and-hold investment strategy, a professional manager (the trustee), and at least 100 shareholders. The trustee initially issues shares of stock and then uses the funds to invest in a portfolio of assets according to the terms of the trust, much as in a UIT. The difference is that the REIT doesn't have a limited lifespan because most real estate investments don't have fixed maturities.

REITs offer individual investors the opportunity to diversify their investment portfolios into real estate. Many investors wouldn't otherwise have access to this investment class because of the high initial investment required and the liquidity risk involved. In many respects, REITs look like stock investments and closed-end funds, trading on national exchanges and distributing profits to the investors through dividends. They aren't as liquid as stocks, however, and they must distribute most of their income each year to investors, resulting in higher tax obligations for investors. Even though recent tax law changes reduced the tax rate on most corporate dividends, REIT dividend distributions are still generally taxable as ordinary income. REITs are usually distinguished by the types of real estate investments they make. Equity REITs, which make up about 90 percent of the market, specialize in making direct investments in rental and commercial properties, such as office buildings and shopping centers. Mortgage REITs focus on mortgage investments such as residential and construction loans.

During the stock market downturn from 2000 to 2002, if you had been invested primarily in stock mutual funds, as so many investors were, you would have lost at least one-third of your wealth. If instead you had some, or all, of your portfolio in REITs, you would have fared substantially better. In fact, REITs were the only bright spot on the equity investment landscape. Although the S&P 500 fell 40.1 percent from December 1999 to December 2002, equity REIT values increased 48.3 percent during that same period. The fact that REIT returns are not highly correlated with overall stock market returns makes them valuable for diversifying your portfolio.

13.1.2 The Advantages of Mutual Fund Investing

For individual investors, mutual funds have some advantages that make them preferable to investments in stocks, bonds, and other financial assets. Although these points apply to most types of investment companies, we focus specifically on open-end funds in several of the examples because they represent such a large share of the total number of funds. The advantages of mutual funds include the following:

▲ **Diversification:** Suppose you have $200 per month to invest. If you buy stocks or bonds directly, it is difficult to buy more than one company's securities at a time, and you might even have to save up for several months before you can make certain investments, such as buying bonds (which often cost around $1,000 each). Also, if one of the companies you've invested in goes downhill, a big chunk of your investment portfolio goes downhill, too. Consider instead what happens if you split the $200 and invest half in a diversified stock mutual fund and half in a diversified bond mutual fund. You'll not only be able to allocate your money between two asset classes, but you'll also become an owner (although admittedly a small one) of a diverse pool of investments in each asset class. If a single company's stock or bond price declines in value, it should have only a minimal impact on your portfolio. About two-thirds of all mutual fund assets are stocks, the remainder is invested in a wide variety of assets, including government, municipal, and corporate bonds. To determine the asset allocation of a particular fund, you have to look at its annual report, which lists all the fund's holdings as of the end of the reporting period. Mutual funds normally specialize in one or a few asset classes.

▲ **Transaction costs:** If you trade individual stocks, you must pay brokerage fees. Although these costs can be relatively low, you still must recoup them before you start to earn a profit on your investments. Because mutual funds make large-volume trades, their costs per trade are likely to be substantially lower than yours as an individual. Of course, you may also pay fees to invest in some mutual funds. Another cost savings to consider is the time you would spend making decisions for an investment portfolio made up of individual stocks and bonds. Investment companies provide reports to help you track your investments, including your capital gains distributions, dividends, purchases, and sales.

▲ **Professional money management:** One reason investors like mutual funds is that the individual investment selection decision is taken out of their hands. The investment company hires professionals whose job is to manage the funds, generally making use of the most current data and analysis tools available. Many of the largest companies (not including those that simply buy and hold) have full-time staffs of security analysts.

FOR EXAMPLE

Diversification Within Quaker Mutual Fund

Figure 13-2 shows the distribution of fund assets for the Quaker Mid-cap Value A fund in June 2004. This fund has 94.8 percent of its assets in stocks and the remainder primarily in cash. Although it's classified as a mid-cap fund, the allocation by market cap indicates that the fund still holds some large- and small-cap stocks. With more than $6 billion invested in more than 12 industry segments, this fund has far more business sector diversification than most small investors could hope to achieve by buying stocks individually. Its largest allocations are in industrial materials (25.97 percent), business services (16.14 percent), and financial services (13.63 percent). Many mutual funds are invested in thousands of different securities, and their quarterly investor reports, which list the exact holdings, are dozens of pages long.

Figure 13-2

Fund Name: Quaker Mid-cap Value A		
Market Capitalization: $6.69 Billion		

Allocation of Portfolio by Sector		*Allocation of Portfolio by Market Cap*	
Information sector		Giant	1.23%
Software	0.05%	Large	18.33
Hardware	7.23	Medium	70.38
Media	0.08	Small	10.06
Telecommunications	2.28	Micro	0.00
Total	9.64%	Total	100.00%
Service sector		*Allocation of Portfolio by Asset Class*	
Health care	2.68%	Cash	4.1%
Consumer services	7.70	Stocks	94.8
Business services	16.14	Bonds	0.0
Financial services	13.63	Other	1.1
Total	40.15%	Total	100.0%
Manufacturing sector		*Allocation of Portfolio by Country*	
Consumer goods	8.26%	United States	91.3%
Industrial materials	25.97	Foreign	8.7
Energy	8.34	Total	100.0%
Utilities	7.64		
Total	50.21%		

Asset allocation in a mutual fund portfolio, June 2004.

Of course, even the experts aren't always right, so professional management is no guarantee of performance, but you can probably assume that a professional money manager knows more than you do and that his or her overall objective is the same as yours—to increase the value of the investment.

▲ **Liquidity:** Liquidity is the ability to convert an asset to cash without loss of value. Mutual funds are somewhat liquid. It's fairly easy to sell mutual fund shares if you own a closed-end fund, but the price depends on market supply and demand. If you own shares in an open-end fund, you can nearly always sell them back to the investment company, but the price you get depends on the value of the total portfolio when you sell. In either case, you may have to pay a transaction fee. Although the shares of a mutual fund may not be quite as liquid as some of the stocks and bonds the fund invests in, they can be far more liquid than other investments you might make. Municipal bonds and real estate, for example, have fairly low liquidity, so holding shares in a mutual fund that invests in these assets provides you with much more liquidity than you'd have if you invested in the assets directly.

▲ **Dividend reinvestment:** Most mutual funds allow you to automatically reinvest dividends and capital gains distributions, similar to the dividend reinvestment plans for stocks discussed in Chapter 11. Instead of receiving immediate cash flow, you use your dividends and distributions to buy additional shares in the mutual fund. Because the majority of mutual fund investors are still in the wealth accumulation phase and thus don't need the current cash flow, this is a very desirable feature.

▲ **Beneficiary designation:** When you open a mutual fund account, you can usually designate where you want the funds to go when you die. This is an advantage because it allows your heirs to avoid the costs and hassles of probate, as discussed in Chapter 15.

▲ **Withdrawal options:** Although you initially invest in a mutual fund to save for a goal, the time will come when you want to start converting the shares to cash. Mutual funds provide several options for this process. You can receive a set amount per month, redeem a certain number of shares per month, take only the current income (i.e., distributions of dividends and capital gains), or make a lump sum withdrawal of all or part of the account. For funds designated as tax-qualified retirement accounts, specific limitations apply to when you can begin withdrawing the money.

13.1.3 The Costs of Mutual Fund Investing

The benefits offered by mutual funds—such as liquidity, professional management, and diversification—don't come free. Fund investors can thus expect to pay a variety of fees and expenses. A fund is required to disclose its fees and expenses in a standardized fee table at the front of its prospectus. The fee table must break out the fees and expenses shareholders can expect to pay so that they can easily compare the costs of different funds. These costs fall into two categories:

▲ **Shareholder fees:** Fees paid directly by shareholders may include the following:
  - A one-time sales charge, commonly known as a "load," to compensate a financial professional for arranging the transaction.
  - A redemption fee to cover the costs, other than sales costs, of the investor's sale of shares back to the company.
  - An exchange fee when an investor transfers money from one fund to another within the same fund family.
  - An annual account maintenance fee charged to cover the costs of providing services to investors who maintain small accounts.

▲ **Fund expenses:** As well as the charges paid directly by investors, funds incur expenses that are deducted directly from the funds' assets before earnings are distributed. These expenses impose indirect costs on investors because they reduce returns. They may include the following:

- An annual management fee charged by the fund's investment advisor for managing the portfolio.

- Annual distribution fees, commonly known as 12b-1 fees, to compensate sales professionals for marketing and advertising fund shares. These fees are increasingly being used to compensate professional advisers for services provided to fund shareholders at the time of purchase but are limited to a maximum of 1 percent of fund assets per year.

- Other operational expenses, such as the costs of maintaining computerized customer account services, maintaining a Web site, record keeping, printing, and mailing.

Comparing Costs of Mutual Funds

As mentioned previously, the prospectus for each fund must include a standardized fee table so that investors can compare the costs of different funds. Also, many other resources can help you to make direct comparisons of expenses. Many Web sites provide information on fees and expenses. In comparing different funds, it's useful to understand the differences between load and no-load funds and how to interpret the expense ratio.

As noted previously, mutual fund purchasers may pay a commission or sales charge, called the load. Mutual funds are thus classified as either load, if they charge a fee, or **no-load funds,** if they don't. Most open-end mutual funds assess a **front-end load** at the time of purchase. The load can be as high as 8.5 percent of the purchase price of the shares; however, the average is around 5 percent, and some loads are as low as 2 percent. Some load funds charge a **back-end load,** officially known as a *contingent deferred sales charge*, if you sell your shares back to the fund too soon after your purchase. These fees often become smaller over time and are intended to encourage investors to hold on to their shares. For example, you might have a charge of 6 percent if you sell the first year, 5 percent the second year, and so on.

A fund that carries a front-end load has the effect of reducing your investment. For example, if you have $1,000 to invest and the fund has a 5 percent load, or $50, you pay $1,000 but get only $950 worth of shares. As with other types of transaction costs, you need to earn a rate of return on your investment that's sufficient to offset the costs and also compensate you for the risk you bear. In other words, if you receive a dividend distribution this year in the amount of $50, you won't really have earned a positive return on your investment—you'll only be back to the $1,000 you started with. Because front-end loads are charged only at the time of purchase, a buy-and-hold investor is not very affected by them.

Over a 10- or 20-year holding period, a one-time $50 sales charge is relatively insignificant. But if you're an active investor, it isn't a good idea to buy load funds.

A no-load fund charges no commission at the time of purchase or at the time of sale. Although this saves you money, you need to look carefully at what you're giving up by purchasing a no-load fund and at the fund's other expenses and charges to see if it is really a better deal than a low-load fund (a load of up to 3 percent is considered low). Instead of charging investors at the time of purchase or sale, no-load funds tend to have higher management expenses. Whereas load funds generally provide investors with advice from brokers and financial planners (who receive a portion of the load charge), a no-load fund has to either skimp on this service or charge in a different way, often through 12b-1 fees. To be designated as no-load, however, a fund can't impose a 12b-1 charge of more than 0.25 percent.

As mentioned earlier, management expenses include trading costs, operating expenses, the costs of professional investment management, security analysis, and legal and accounting services. Even though all funds charge their investors for providing these services, some are much more efficient in managing costs than others and pass the savings on to investors. For this reason, it's important to take expenses into account when evaluating potential mutual fund purchases. A fund's **expense ratio** is measured by the expenses per dollar of assets under management, as follows:

$$\text{Expense ratio} = \text{Total expenses} / \text{Total assets in fund}$$

All else being equal, the lower this ratio, the better. The expense ratio must be disclosed in the fund's prospectus; it's usually between 0.5 and 1.25 percent but can be as high as 2 percent. Because many of the fund's operating costs are related to trading, you can expect the expense ratio for an index fund that does very little trading to be much lower than that of an actively managed fund that frequently buys and sells securities within the portfolio. Some funds with higher expense ratios give investors better returns, so you need to consider this variable in light of all the information you have about a fund. If the expenses are paying for better analysis, security selection, investor advisory services, Web site tools, or other things of value to you, it might be worth paying the cost.

Mutual Fund Classes, by Fee Structure

Just as a corporation can sell different types of stock (e.g., common and preferred), a mutual fund can offer a menu of share classes that differ in load and expenses. For example, Class A shares usually have front-end loads of 4 to 5 percent; Class B shares carry a back-end load and impose a 12b-1 fee; and Class C shares have no back-end load but charge a higher 12b-1 fee. Some funds also have Class D shares, which carry a front-end load and a smaller 12b-1 fee.

If you like a particular mutual fund but aren't sure which class of shares to purchase, the most important consideration is your time horizon. Front-end loads are a one-time charge, whereas management fees and 12b-1 fees are incurred annually. Thus, if you plan to hold a mutual fund for a long time, the front-end load might be the best option, because you'll incur it only once. Back-end loads are also less important if you plan to hold the mutual fund beyond the point at which it disappears. A 5 percent load on Class A shares may seem like a lot, but you'll pay up to 1 percent per year in 12b-1 fees annually if you buy Class C shares instead.

SELF-CHECK

1. Define **net asset value** and **ETF**.
2. Distinguish between open- and closed-end mutual funds.
3. What are the advantages of investing in mutual funds?

13.2 Mutual Fund Investment Classifications

Mutual funds are usually classified based on investment objectives and portfolio composition. As the number of mutual funds in the marketplace increases, each fund has more incentive to try to distinguish itself from its competitors. This has created so much diversity that it isn't always easy to categorize funds. The classifications suggested in this section aren't uniformly applied, but will familiarize you with some of the terms commonly used to describe mutual funds. In general, the most important distinctions among funds are the type of investment (equity vs. debt), the source of expected return (income vs. capital gain), and the tax status.

13.2.1 Classification by Investment Objective

Each mutual fund has a specific investment policy, which is described in the fund's prospectus. For example, money market mutual funds, discussed in Chapter 4, consider the preservation of capital to be an important investment objective. The fund managers must invest in short-term, low-risk debt securities. Investors know this in advance and thus have specific expectations about the performance of the fund, based on its objectives.

The most common general investment policy categories are capital appreciation (growth), income, and preservation of capital, but the objectives of a given fund may include more than one of these.

Growth Funds

The primary objective of a **growth fund** is capital appreciation. Managers attempt to select assets for the portfolio that will experience above-average growth in value over time. Because growing companies tend to be riskier than stable companies, growth mutual funds are most appropriate for investors who are willing to bear a little more risk to achieve a higher long-run return.

Growth funds are often placed in subcategories, depending on the level and type of risk represented by the investment portfolio. For example, an aggressive growth fund invests only in risky companies that pay no dividends, whereas a moderate growth fund, while still focused on capital appreciation, might invest in larger companies that pay stable dividends but have the potential for good appreciation in value. Aggressive growth funds, as you'd expect, are much riskier and expose you to greater potential losses in the event of a market downturn.

Income Funds

The objective of an **income fund** is to invest in stocks and bonds that will provide high current income, either in dividends or interest. These funds tend to be less risky than growth funds because the investor is realizing immediate gains rather than taking the risk of waiting for future gains. As with growth funds, there are various subcategories, most commonly based on the source of the income (e.g., interest vs. dividends) and the risk level (e.g., high-quality debt vs. junk bonds).

Growth and Income Funds

Some funds try to straddle the fence between income and growth, providing reasonable income to investors while still investing in companies that have good potential for growth in value. Primarily invested in growth-oriented blue chip stocks, these funds have generated respectable returns over time and have been more stable than the market as a whole.

Balanced Funds

A balanced fund, sometimes called a *hybrid fund*, provides investors with the opportunity to benefit from investments in both stocks and bonds. Because they are better diversified than funds that are entirely invested in stocks, and because they tend to focus on high-grade securities, balanced funds tend to have stable returns over time. These funds are similar to income funds but focus more on reducing investment risk.

Value Funds

A **value fund** manager attempts to invest in companies that are currently undervalued by the market—companies with good fundamentals whose stock prices are low relative to the companies' perceived potential. Of course, many other investors seek these same undiscovered gems, so the risk of being wrong is fairly high.

Value stock funds tend to be invested in companies with relatively low P/E ratios and good growth potential so are a little less risky than growth funds but offer fairly good returns.

Life-Cycle Funds

A **life-cycle fund** attempts to capture the asset allocation needs of individual investors at particular points in their life cycle. Thus, a fund designed for individuals under age 40 might be invested primarily in growth stocks, whereas a fund designed for a retiree would be more heavily allocated to fixed-income securities. These funds usually allow investors to move their invested dollars to new life-cycle funds as they reach different points in the life cycle at no cost.

Given the financial planning emphasis on changing needs over the life cycle, the idea behind the design of these funds is sound. There's still some disagreement as to what the ideal portfolio composition should be for each life stage, however. And because these funds are relatively new in concept, they don't yet have particularly long track records.

13.2.2 Classification by Portfolio Composition

In addition to being classified by investment objective, funds are commonly defined by their portfolio composition. This can occur through some combination of asset class, industry representation, and index benchmark.

Asset Class Funds

Mutual funds commonly confine their investments to certain asset classes, such as stocks vs. bonds, although as you've seen, some funds hold both stocks and bonds. Within each broad asset class, funds may be further classified according to such features as size of company (e.g., large-cap, mid-cap, small-cap) or type of asset (e.g., long-term Treasury bonds, high-grade corporate bonds, municipal bonds).

When you invest in a mutual fund concentrated in a particular asset class, its performance is likely to mimic the overall performance of that asset class. Your share values respond to economic conditions in much the same way as investments in individual stocks and bonds in that class.

Industry or Sector Funds

A **sector fund** specializes in particular industries or business sectors. Common examples include technology, financial services, telecommunications, health care, and utilities. These funds tend to focus on growth rather than income, enabling investors to allocate more of their money to the sector offering the most attractive returns. Because this strategy results in less diversification, sector funds tend to be riskier than those that cover more industry groups. For example, during the stock market run-up of the late 1990s, technology stocks were the stars—but they also took the biggest hit in the following downturn.

FOR EXAMPLE

What Does It Cost to Feel Good?

Some investors screen their investments based on social responsibility criteria. They like integrating their values, ethics, and societal concerns with their investing. In her senior honors thesis, Jennifer Gagnon compared the risk and return on several Lipper funds classified as socially responsible investors (SRI) to those on similar non-SRI funds for the period 1999 to 2003. SRI funds buy the securities of corporations with good employee relations, strong records of community involvement, excellent environmental impact policies and practices, respect for human rights around the world, and safe products. They avoid companies related to tobacco, alcohol, gambling, firearms, and nuclear power.

Being socially responsible costs money, and customers aren't always willing to pay more for goods produced by socially responsible companies. Thus investors in SRI mutual funds often earn a lower return than those in non-SRI funds.

However, Gagnon found the cost of "feeling good" isn't that large, and how much it costs depends on the type of fund and the holding period. Based on her analysis, an investor would have earned almost 4 percent less per year investing in a mixed capitalization SRI fund (which invests in companies in different capitalization categories), but in small-caps, an investor would have been 0.5 percent better off over the five-year period.[1]

Geographical Location Funds

When the U.S. stock market is down, investors can benefit from global diversification. An **international fund** invests exclusively in securities from other countries. Some include securities from a particular region, such as Latin America or Asia; others, known as country funds, specialize in a particular country. In contrast, a **global fund** attempts to diversify globally, investing in U.S. and foreign securities.

Index Funds

Many funds try to mimic the performance of a particular index, such as the S&P 500 Index, but without buying every stock that is included in the index. With other types of funds, a fund manager's performance is judged at the end of a period, compared to the benchmark index's performance, to see if the manager's efforts produced the desired outcome. Many academic studies have shown that it's difficult for an actively managed fund to beat its benchmark index.

As an alternative, index funds sometimes attempt to buy and hold a selection of stocks that can mimic the market more exactly and at lower cost. If the index fund is targeting the DJIA or the S&P 500, for example, it usually buys all the stocks in that index, in about the same proportions, and is thus able to track the index almost exactly. For indexes that include a much larger number of stocks—such as the New York Stock Exchange Index, which has more than 3,000 different stocks—the index fund might try to buy a smaller selection of representative stocks.

Because index funds buy and hold, trading costs for them are minimal.

Socially Responsible Funds

If the "bottom line" is not your primary focus, you might be interested in a **socially responsible fund**. The manager of this type of fund is charged with selecting stocks issued by companies that meet some predefined standards for moral and ethical behavior. Although the objectives of various funds differ, common issues are a company's policies toward employees and the environment. Socially responsible funds also commonly avoid securities of companies that are involved in "sin industries," such as tobacco, alcohol, and gambling. Investors pay a price for being socially responsible because the performance of these funds, on average, has slightly lagged behind the performance of other funds.

SELF-CHECK

1. Name some mutual fund classifications based on investment objective.
2. List some mutual fund classifications based on portfolio composition.
3. What's the difference between a growth fund and an income fund?

13.3 Selecting and Evaluating Mutual Funds

Assuming that you've decided to buy one or more mutual funds, now it's time to do homework. How do you pick the best funds for you? You need to return to the decision-making process outlined in Chapter 1. You consider your goals, evaluate your alternatives, and select the investment alternatives that best meet your needs. An outline of the steps to take is provided in Figure 13-3.

13.3.1 Matching Fund Classification with Investment Objective

The first step in the mutual fund decision process is to identify your investment objective, which includes a number of factors:

▲ The outcome you'd like to achieve.
▲ The time horizon you have for achieving it.

Figure 13-3

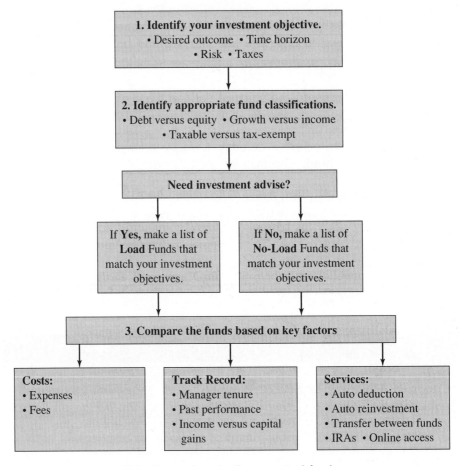

Selecting and evaluating a mutual fund.

▲ The amount of risk you're willing to take.

▲ Minimizing taxes owed.

To see an example of matching fund classification with investment objective, let's look again at Cindy and Dave Thompson. At age 32, the Thompsons want to start contributing to a retirement savings account for Cindy in 2005, and they plan to invest $3,300 the first year. The Thompsons decide to target a large-cap growth fund initially. As Cindy's investment portfolio grows, she'll probably spread her money among several stock funds and, as she nears retirement and her objectives turn toward preservation of capital, she can gradually shift her investments to a less risky asset allocation.

In the For Example in this section, Cindy and Dave Thompson are planning to buy a mutual fund, with the primary objective of building retirement wealth. Because Cindy is only 32 years old, she has a long time horizon—at least 30 years. The Thompsons are prepared to take some risk in exchange for a possibly greater return, and they want to keep their current tax cash outflows to a minimum. After determining their objectives, they identify fund classifications that would be appropriate. They should, at a minimum, determine whether they'll invest in debt vs. equity, income vs. growth, and taxable vs. tax-exempt funds.

With their time horizon and wealth-building objectives, the Thompsons are more interested in growth than income. Receipt of current income would just require that they reinvest the money, and they can afford to take a little more risk with such a long time horizon. Most financial planners recommend that investors with long time horizons allocate more of their portfolio to equity securities because that asset class has historically generated greater returns over time than other classes.

Another aspect of fund classification selection is taxes, but because this is a retirement account, the Thompsons plan to set it up as an individual retirement account (IRA). The choice between traditional and Roth IRAs is discussed in Chapter 14, but in either case, no current taxes will be due on the income and capital gains earned by the fund. If the Thompsons were saving for a goal other than retirement, they'd have to pay taxes on distributions from the fund. In that case, they might want to avoid income funds and those that trade frequently to capture capital gains because these investment activities generate a bigger current tax liability.

With respect to taxes, it's important to remember that tax consequences are often factored into the prices of investments. The current yield on a tax-exempt security (i.e., tax-free interest income divided by the price) is often comparable to the after-tax current yield for a taxable security (i.e., after-tax interest income divided by the price), with similar risk characteristics.

To see how tax consequences are often factored into the prices of investments, suppose you had two similar bonds, paying the same amount of interest each year, one with taxable income and one tax exempt. If the tax-exempt bond was priced the same as the taxable bond, people who invested in the tax-exempt bond would realize a greater after-tax return. Clearly, all investors would want that bond, and they wouldn't want the taxable bond. With higher demand for the tax-exempt bond, the price would rise, and the return would go down because the same amount of interest divided by a higher price gives a smaller yield. The opposite would happen to the taxable bond: Its price would fall until the after-tax returns on the two securities were equal. What does this mean? If your tax situation is different from the average investor's, certain securities may be a better or worse "deal" for you than for others. For example, if you're investing through a tax-deferred or tax-exempt retirement account, you don't want to be investing in tax-exempt bonds. They offer you no tax savings and have higher relative prices that reflect the average investor's tax savings, not yours.

An example from the opposite point of view involves the tax effects of investing in a very actively managed mutual fund, which generates a lot of capital gains income that is taxable. If you're investing through an IRA, you don't have to worry because you don't have to pay the tax. In addition, the fund might be advantageously priced, reflecting the taxes that must be paid by other investors.

The final decision Cindy and Dave need to make before narrowing their mutual fund choices is whether they're willing to pay a load. They know that some funds charge high fees and that these expenses can erode their long-run returns. They definitely want to consider the historical expense ratios on the funds they're evaluating. Because they don't plan to withdraw the money until far in the future, they're willing to bear a small front-end load but would like to minimize the management expenses and 12b-1 fees each year.

13.3.2 Identifying Fund Alternatives

After Cindy and Dave Thompson narrowed their choices to large-cap growth funds, they had to find particular funds that met their objectives. Although in many cases, the name of a fund gives a hint as to its investment objectives—such as "Value Fund" or "Life Cycle A"—this isn't always the case, so you need to do your homework to ensure that you've identified all likely prospects. The Thompsons used a financial Web site's fund screener to identify the best performers in the large-cap growth classification over the past few years. Because they were interested in funds with low expenses, they also screen on this criterion. Let's assume that their screens result in a list of 20 mutual funds.

13.3.3 Comparing Funds Based on Key Factors

After the Thompsons identified their options, they narrowed their selection based on the criteria most important to them. These criteria can include ratings, expenses, net asset value, manager tenure, and services provided.

Morningstar and other mutual fund services firms provide the names and job histories of fund managers, as well as analysis of performance. Why is the fund manager important? Suppose you're considering a fund that has had a fairly good track record but now has a new manager. The past performance was attributable—at least in part—to the skill of the previous fund manager, so the future performance could be totally different. Although a fund is supposed to stick with its investment objectives, some managers are better than others, and how the objectives are interpreted may vary among managers, too.

Another factor to consider is whether the fund is part of a **fund family,** an arrangement in which a single company, such as Fidelity or Vanguard, operates several separately managed mutual funds with different investment objectives.

There are some advantages to choosing a fund that is part of a family. Firms that offer families usually allow you to transfer money between funds within a family at little or no cost, which makes it easy to shift asset allocation. So if Cindy decides in the future that she'd like to invest some of her portfolio in a different type of fund, she can easily switch within the same family.

All life-cycle funds belong to fund families, because the assumption is that you would shift to a different life-cycle fund as your life progresses. Based on their criteria, the Thompsons narrowed their selection to three funds. In making this type of comparison, it helps if you organize the key information for each fund you're considering. Figure 13-4 provides an example of Cindy and Dave's analysis. (A blank worksheet is provided in the Personal Financial Planner in the Appendix.) Cindy ultimately decided to invest in the Future Progress mutual fund, based on its low expenses, the long tenure of its manager, and its short- and long-run performance.

13.3.4 Determining How Many Funds to Invest In

A common misconception of mutual fund investors is that investing in a lot of different mutual funds is better and will reduces their risk. It's true that having more funds from different fund families reduces the risks related to investment company failure or wrongdoing. But having more funds won't unless you invest in funds that include different asset classes and different securities within those asset classes. Many funds are highly invested in the same stocks—large-cap funds are heavily invested in companies that make up the DJIA and the S&P 500, for example.

If Cindy and Dave had decided to split their money among several large-cap funds that track the same index, and the stock market experienced a decline, all their mutual funds would likely lose value, too, and they'd have incurred higher expenses than if they had only bought shares in one fund. But suppose you want to diversify your mutual fund holdings. Diversification is a good investment strategy. Instead of investing in several similar funds, you should buy shares in funds that focus on different areas. For example, you might invest in a large-cap fund, a small-cap fund, an international fund, an investment-grade bond fund, and a REIT.

13.3.5 The Mutual Fund Transaction

After you've decided what mutual fund or funds you want to buy, you must actually make the purchase. Here's what you do:

1. **Determine the current price:** You can find the current price of mutual funds in the financial newspapers and on many financial Web sites. For open-end funds you can look up the net asset value as of the previous day, the daily change in value, and the year-to-date return. Closed-end fund information includes the exchange on which the fund trades, the net asset value, the market price (usually with a 15 to 20 minute delay),

Figure 13-4

1. Investment objective: _____ Retirement fund _____
2. Appropriate type of fund: ___ Equity, growth, taxable, no load ___

| | Mutual Fund Alternatives | | |
	A	B	C
Company name	Excel Growth	ABC Fund	Future Progress
Fund objective	Growth	Growth	Growth
Price per share	$45	$32	$29
Net asset value	$40	$35	$28
Minimum initial purchase	$1,000	$2,000	$1,500
Minimum additional purchase	$500	$100	$200
Past performance			
1-year	15%	13%	17%
3-year	8%	7%	4%
5-year	6%	6%	8%
Expenses	2%	1.5%	1%
Front-end loan			
Back-end loan	√	√	
12b-1 fee	0.5%	1.0%	0.5%
Fund manager tenure	3 years	2 years	10 years
Services			
Auto deduction	√	√	√
Auto reinvestment	√	√	√
Transfer between funds	√	√	√
IRAs	√	√	√
Online access	√	√	√
Ratings (Morningstar)	5-star	5-star	5-star

Choosing a mutual fund for the Thompsons.

the percentage difference between the market price and the net asset value, and the 52-week return, based on market price plus dividends.

2. **Make the purchase:** There are several ways to purchase shares of a mutual fund, and many people are surprised to find that they don't have to use a broker. Because brokers receive commissions for sales, many investment companies keep their costs down by marketing their funds directly. They advertise through the mail, by phone, in print media, and on the internet. You call them to set up an account and purchase shares. About half of all funds are sold through brokers, and in many cases, shares of funds are available through "financial supermarkets." In these arrangements, a supermarket firm such as Fidelity Networks or Charles Schwab & Co. gives investors access to a large number of funds from different fund families under its umbrella. The great advantage of this arrangement is that you can purchase from several fund families, switch money among them easily, and still receive a consolidated financial report from the supermarket company.

13.3.6 Tracking Your Portfolio

After you make a mutual fund purchase, your job isn't done. You need to keep track of your portfolio and continue to contribute to your investment fund.

Cindy and Dave Thompson will probably want to set up a mutual fund account with an automatic deposit arrangement. They should also regularly review the performance of their fund relative to its investment objective and the index that it tracks. A worksheet for tracking your mutual funds is provided in the Personal Financial Planner.

SELF-CHECK

1. Define **fund family**.
2. What are the steps in purchasing the best mutual fund for you?

SUMMARY

If you don't have time or want to research stock and bond investments, mutual funds are a good alternative. Mutual funds are a way to invest in a diversified mix of stocks and bonds with relatively lower transaction costs. Funds are usually classified by investment objective and portfolio composition. You need to study your alternatives to find the funds that best match your investment goals and to filter out what won't work for you from the thousands of alternatives. You also need to monitor your funds periodically to check whether they're helping you meeting your goals.

KEY TERMS

Back-end load	A charge that mutual fund investors pay at the time they sell shares.
Balanced fund	A mutual fund invested in both stocks and bonds.
Closed-end fund	An investment company that has a fixed number of shares, which are traded in the secondary market.
Exchange-traded fund (ETF)	An investment company that has professionally, but not actively, managed assets, often intended to track a market index, and shares that trade in the secondary market.
Expense ratio	The ratio of annual mutual fund expense charges to fund assets.
Front-end load	A commission or sales charge paid by mutual fund investors at the time they purchase shares.
Fund family	An arrangement in which a single company operates several separately managed mutual funds with different investment objectives.
Global fund	A mutual fund that invests in U.S. and foreign securities.
Growth fund	A mutual fund that focuses on capital appreciation.
Income fund	A mutual fund that focuses on providing stable dividend and interest income.
International fund	A mutual fund that invests primarily in securities from countries other than the United States.
Investment company	A financial intermediary that invests its funds in securities or other assets.
Life-cycle fund	A mutual fund that designs its asset allocation to meet the needs of individuals in a particular life stage.

Mutual fund	An open-end investment company that uses its investors' funds to purchase stocks, bonds, or other financial assets.
Net asset value	The market value of a mutual fund's assets less the market value of its liabilities, per share.
No-load fund	A mutual fund that doesn't charge a front-end or back-end load.
Open-end fund	An investment company that sells its shares directly to investors and buys them back on request.
Real estate investment trust (REIT)	A closed-end fund that invests primarily in real estate or mortgages.
Sector fund	A mutual fund that invests primarily in securities from a particular industry or sector.
Socially responsible fund	A mutual fund that limits its holdings to securities issued by companies that meet certain ethical and moral standards.
Unit investment trust (UIT)	An investment company that buys and holds a fixed portfolio of securities for a period of time determined by the life of the investments in the trust.
Value fund	A mutual fund that invests in companies that the market perceives to be undervalued.

ASSESS YOUR UNDERSTANDING

Go to www.wiley.com/college/bajtelsmit to assess your knowledge of investing in mutual funds.
Measure your learning by comparing pre-test and post-test results.

Summary Questions

1. The net asset value of a mutual fund is calculated as the market value of assets less the market value of liabilities divided by the market value of the assets. True or false?

2. ABC Fund has 9 million shares outstanding. The fund's portfolio is now valued at $300 million, and the fund owes $18 million to the fund advisors and $5 million for rent and wages. What is the net asset value of the fund?
   (a) $30.78
   (b) $31.33
   (c) $33.00
   (d) $34.78

3. Mutual funds:
   (a) are primarily geared for larger investors.
   (b) can only be formed as corporations.
   (c) have a fiduciary responsibility to fund investors.
   (d) are subject to less stringent securities regulation than other types of securities.

4. The issuing company provides the only market for the shares in:
   (a) an open-end fund.
   (b) a closed-end fund.
   (c) an exchange-traded fund.
   (d) an over-the-counter fund.

5. Which of the following statements regarding UITs is false?
   (a) UIT owners are issued redeemable trust certificates.
   (b) The major type of asset in UITs is U.S. Treasury bonds.
   (c) UITs are essentially unmanaged investments.
   (d) The term of a UIT depends on the maturities of the securities held.

6. Which type of mutual fund tends to be invested in companies with relatively low P/E ratios and good growth potential?
   (a) growth fund
   (b) growth and income fund

(c) balanced fund

(d) value fund

7. A mutual fund whose entire portfolio is invested in stocks of financial service companies would be considered:

(a) an undiversified fund.

(b) a sector fund.

(c) an income fund.

(d) a life-cycle fund.

8. Index funds:

(a) always buy all the securities in the index they are following.

(b) generally outperform the index they are imitating.

(c) are expected to be very low-risk investments.

(d) generally have minimal trading costs.

9. When a single company operates several separately managed mutual funds with difference investment objectives, this is a fund family. True or false?

10. Investing in several large cap stock funds from different fund families reduces market risk. True or false?

Applying This Chapter

1. You have the following information from the January 1, 2005, balance sheet for the Balanced Growth and Income mutual fund sponsored by Frontier Investment Company:

(a) $150 million in assets.

(b) $10 million in liabilities.

(c) 12.3 million shares.

Task a: Calculate the net asset value.

Task b: If the value of the assets in Frontier's portfolio increased in value during 2005, what would happen to the net asset value?

2. Suppose you're considering a fund that offers the following classes of shares:

(a) Class A: front-end load, 5 percent.

(b) Class B: back-end load, 5 percent (reduced 1 percent per year); 12b-1 fee, 0.5 percent.

Under what circumstances would the Class B shares be preferable to the Class A shares?

3. Suppose you want to split your money between stocks and bonds. You could choose a fund that has a specific asset mix, or you could buy a

stock fund and a bond fund to achieve the same type of diversification. What would be some of the advantages and disadvantages of each strategy?

4. For a 20-year-old woman saving money for a down payment on a home, suggest some mutual fund classifications consistent with the stated investment objective and time horizon. Explain your reasoning.

5. Help out a 60-year-old retired couple looking for a regular source of income by advising them on mutual fund classifications that would meet their needs.

6. Suggest mutual funds for a 30-year-old couple saving for their 5-year-old child's college education.

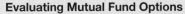

YOU TRY IT

Evaluating Mutual Fund Options

Elena is divorced and has two daughters, ages five and six. Her ex-husband is paying $100 per child per week in child support. Because the kids are in school full time, Elena has returned to work as a high school math teacher; she earns sufficient income to support the family. Elena has decided to put the child support money in a college fund for the girls. For the past year, she's been depositing the money in a savings account that earns only 3 percent annual interest, and she's accumulated $10,600. She realizes that she needs to invest this money to earn a better return.

1. What is Elena's specific investment goal?
2. What types of mutual funds might be appropriate to meet Elena's goal? Explain.

Researching Mutual Funds for Yourself

Select a class of mutual funds that interests you (e.g., large-cap value, mid-cap income). Use the mutual fund screener at finance.yahoo.com to find the top funds in your chosen category. Answer the following questions:

1. What have been the top performers in the past year?
2. On what criteria is this assessment based?
3. Are there any other criteria you should consider?

Bond Mistake?

In June 2003, at the age of 60, Gabe decided to retire. He and his wife Della, also 60, decided that she would continue to work until she could qualify for Social Security benefits. Gabe took the money from his 401(k) retirement plan ($600,000) and bought shares in a long-term, AAA-rated, corporate bond fund, thinking he wanted to be conservative with their nest egg. Recent stock market declines had reinforced his belief that stocks were too risky. In June 2003, 20-year AAA corporate bonds yielded about 5.0 percent. Gabe and Della figured that the income from their bond fund, combined with Della's income, would be plenty to live on. The first year, Gabe's mutual funds generated $30,000 in income before taxes. Although this was about half what he had earned while working, he was pleased to find that they didn't have to dip into the principal to support their lifestyle. But as rates on AAA corporate bonds rose to about 6 percent by June 2004, Gabe was alarmed to see that the value of his bond mutual fund shares declined to $533,000. He and Della were confused; they had thought that bonds were safe investments. They wonder if they should switch to a different type of investment.

1. Is the asset allocation chosen by this couple appropriate for their life situation and risk tolerance? Explain.
2. Explain why the value of Gabe and Della's bond mutual fund has declined. (Hint: consider what happens to the prices of bonds when interest rates rise.)

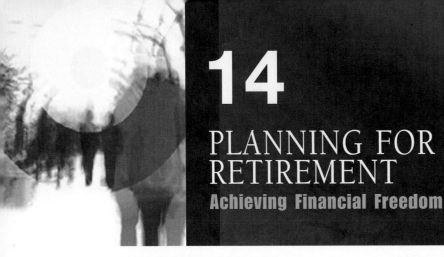

14

PLANNING FOR RETIREMENT
Achieving Financial Freedom

Starting Point

Go to www.wiley.com/college/bajtelsmit to assess your knowledge of planning for retirement.
Determine where you need to concentrate your effort.

What You'll Learn in This Chapter

▲ Retirement income needs
▲ Employer-sponsored retirement plans
▲ Social Security
▲ Traditional and Roth IRAs

After Studying This Chapter, You'll Be Able To

▲ Estimate your retirement income needs
▲ Evaluate your future benefits from employer-sponsored retirement plans and Social Security
▲ Determine your retirement wealth goal and monthly savings target
▲ Assess your alternatives for personal retirement saving
▲ Evaluate your options for retirement income payouts

INTRODUCTION

To successfully plan for distant goals, you need to apply many concepts emphasized throughout this text. Establishing realistic goals, estimating their costs, and evaluating the most appropriate ways to achieve them are essential. Here, we apply the steps in the planning process (from Chapter 1) to funding your retirement. The earlier you begin planning, the more successful you'll be at meeting your long-term objectives, and the easier it will be to weather the unknowns.

You begin the planning process by reviewing your goals. Your objectives for retirement may start out fairly vague—"live comfortably in retirement" or "retire at age 55," for example—but you need to be much more specific. This chapter also explains how to estimate more accurately your retirement income so that you know how much to save on a regular basis.

14.1 Estimating Retirement Income Needs

Retirement may seem to be pretty far off. But most of us find that the time goes by all too fast. And unlike many of your personal financial goals, this one is going to eventually cost you much money, probably more than a million dollars. Consequently, it's especially important to begin planning for retirement as early as possible. If you do so, you'll be able to save a smaller proportion of your current income, and you'll be more likely to meet your retirement objectives.

You need to identify your needs, which requires that you estimate how much retirement income your investments will need to generate. You first need to settle on your goals, such as when you'll retire and how much income you'll need at that time. From this, you'll subtract any income you expect to receive from other sources to arrive at the income shortfall your investments will have to generate. These steps are discussed in the following sections.

14.1.1 Determining Your Retirement Goals

One person's ideal retirement isn't the same as another's, which implies that the cost of paying for retirement isn't the same for everyone. And, of course, because you have to save for this future expense now, you have to make a trade-off between current and future consumption. If you're willing to accept a lower standard of living in retirement, you can spend more today. But if you want to retire young, travel, golf, and spoil your family, you'll probably need to sacrifice some current spending to achieve your retirement goals.

When do you plan to retire? Obviously, the younger you retire, the longer your retirement period and the shorter the time you have to accumulate the wealth necessary to support yourself during your retirement. When surveyed,

Figure 14-1

Directions: For each of the following retirement goals, indicate its importance to you by checking the appropriate box.

Retirement Goal	Very Important	Somewhat Important	Not at All Important
Economic security			
Maintain standard of living	☐	☐	☐
Improve standard of living	☐	☐	☐
Financial independence	☐	☐	☐
Afford to keep home	☐	☐	☐
Family			
Bequests to heirs	☐	☐	☐
College costs	☐	☐	☐
Support children or parents	☐	☐	☐
Continue family business	☐	☐	☐
Medical			
Cover health-care costs	☐	☐	☐
Extras			
Better/more vacations	☐	☐	☐
Increased hobby costs	☐	☐	☐
Contributions to charity	☐	☐	☐
Other			
_____			
_____			

Developing and prioritizing retirement goals.

most people say they want to retire "early," which usually means in their mid- to late 50s. This is extremely optimistic, and many people have to revise their expectations as they approach their target retirement age.

Although the average age of retirement has declined slightly over time, particularly for men, the most common retirement age is still 65. As the age for normal Social Security retirement is gradually being increased to 67, as explained later in the chapter, it's likely that more people will delay retirement to that age. Nevertheless, it's not a bad idea to have an optimistic target date if it means you'll be more aggressive about saving toward that goal today.

To help you formulate some specific objectives, take a look at the list in Figure 14-1. For each item, you need to indicate its importance to you. If you have any additional goals, you should add them to the list. It's important to remember that your goals and priorities will likely change between now and your retirement date, so you'll need to revisit this step. For your convenience, the Retirement Planning Worksheet is also included in the Personal Financial Planner.

Unless you're independently wealthy or expect to receive a large inheritance prior to retirement, you're not likely to reach the goals you've identified in Figure 14-1 unless you take steps today to accumulate sufficient wealth in time for retirement. Unfortunately, most households have unrealistic expectations about the retirement they can afford, given their current savings patterns.

According to one study, the baby boom generation is saving at only one-third the rate necessary to meet its retirement goals. Unless these people increase their savings rate substantially, they'll find themselves delaying their retirement dates, relying on their children, or having a much lower standard of living in retirement than they have today. The example "Why Don't People Plan Better for Retirement?" summarizes some of the psychological biases you may have to overcome to do a good job of retirement planning.

After you establish some goals for the kind of retirement you'd like to have, the next step is to estimate how much it will cost. This isn't a particularly easy task because there are so many factors to consider. As a result, many people simply omit this step in their retirement planning. That's a mistake, though, as it is likely to lead to poor planning and insufficient saving. If you don't know how much you'll need, how will you know if you're saving enough to get there? The Retirement Planning Worksheet in the Personal Financial Planner will help you to work through the following steps, which are explained in more detail below.

1. Estimate your future retirement expenses
2. Subtract your expected income from employer-sponsored defined benefit retirement plans and Social Security to arrive at your expected retirement income shortfall.
3. Estimate how much wealth you need to accumulate by the date of retirement and how much you need to save each month to meet that goal. The following sections walk you through the steps in this process.

FOR EXAMPLE

Why Don't People Plan Better for Retirement?

Why do so many people fail to prepare adequately for retirement? As in much of the rest of personal finance, the answer boils down to psychological factors. Although it's unlikely that you'll be able to avoid all the psychological biases identified here, recognizing them is half the battle:

▲ **Myopia:** More than ever, our society embraces a "live for today" ethos. Myopia, or near-sightedness, is the term economists use to describe this phenomenon. Households are constantly bombarded with advertising that reinforces natural tendencies for current spending and immediate gratification, which makes it difficult to allocate funds for far-distant goals such as retirement.

▲ **Inflation illusion:** Most people don't understand inflation. As a result, they underestimate the amount of money they'll need to fund an inflation-adjusted income in retirement.

▲ **Focus on averages:** People tend to focus on averages rather than look at the full range of possible outcomes. This mistake can create a number of difficulties, particularly in estimating life expectancy and investment returns. Based on average life expectancy, you probably understand that you'll live into your mid-80s. But if you use this age to estimate how much you need to save for retirement, you have a 50 percent chance of saving too little. As medical treatments continue to extend life, it will become increasingly common for people to live to 100 years of age, approximately doubling the average retirement period. We're guilty of the same bias in estimating investment returns, often using a long-run average return in forecasting instead of recognizing the variability to which we're exposed.

▲ **It Won't Happen to Me:** A common psychological bias is the tendency to think that bad things happen to everyone else but us. Despite the high rates of divorce, widowhood, and disability, most people don't have a plan for how they'll deal with these issues if they come up. These events produce income shocks that inevitably affect the ability to accumulate funds for retirement.

14.1.2 Determining Your Expenses in Retirement

These two methods are most commonly used for estimating retirement income needs:

▲ **Replacement Ratio Method:** The **replacement ratio method** assumes that your retirement expenses will be some fixed proportion of your pre-retirement expenses, such as 70 or 80 percent. For example, suppose you've estimated that your current household expenses are $40,000 per year. If you assume that your expenses after retirement will be 80 percent of current expenses, the replacement ratio method yields an estimate of $32,000 in today's dollars. Although this method is relatively commonly applied, the problem is, you have no guarantee that your expenses will drop in retirement.

▲ **Adjusted Expense Method:** The **adjusted expense method** for estimating retirement income takes a little more time to use than the replacement ratio method but results in a more accurate forecast. This method is the one applied in step 1 of the Retirement Planning Worksheet. Here, you take your current expenses, by category, and adjust each one, based on your estimates of expenses in retirement. For example, if you expect to have a larger mortgage payment in the future (e.g., with the purchase of a larger home), or if you have arranged to have your mortgage paid in full by the time you retire, you adjust the mortgage expense amount accordingly. If you'll need to pay for your own health insurance after you leave your current employer (which is highly likely, given current trends), you add the additional insurance premium cost. You can use the goals you've developed to help identify the necessary adjustments. (Keep in mind that you do this estimate in today's dollars, so if it would cost you $5,000 a year for golf club membership today, that's the figure you use on the worksheet.)

14.1.3 Adjusting for Inflation

After you've estimated your expenses in current dollars by using either of the methods in Section 14.1.2, you need to adjust this amount for inflation between now and retirement to arrive at your total income needs in your first year of retirement. Although inflation has been lower in recent years, the long-run average is between 3 and 4 percent, so 4 percent provides a more realistic estimate. The method of calculating this number is based on the time value of money discussed in Chapter 1. You can expect your expenses to grow from year to year at 4 percent, so you need to compound that out to the number of years until your retire. You can use the following equation, where N is the number of years until you retire:

$$\text{Expected expenses at retirement} = \text{Current expenses} \times 1.04^N$$

where N is the number of years to retire.

To make this easy, you can estimate the answer from Table 14-1. To do so, you pick the expense amount level closest to your own and then look down the first column to find the value that corresponds to it. Let's assume that you've estimated your retirement expenses at $30,000 in today's dollars and that you expect to retire in 40 years, and that you think inflation will average 4 percent between now and then. Looking down the $30,000 column in the table to the row for 40 years, you can see that, assuming that inflation averages 4 percent between now and then, your expenses in the first year of retirement will be $144,031. Although $144,031 may seem like a lot of money, keep in mind that it will be equivalent in spending power to $30,000 today.

Table 14-1: Estimating First-Year Retirement Income Needs (at 4% Inflation per Year)

Years to Retirement	Total Expenses in Today's Dollars					
	$20,000	$30,000	$40,000	$50,000	$60,000	$70,000
10	$29,605	$44,407	$59,210	$74,012	$88,815	$103,617
15	$36,019	$54,028	$72,038	$90,047	$108,057	$126,066
20	$43,822	$65,734	$87,645	$109,556	$131,467	$153,379
25	$53,317	$79,975	$106,633	$133,292	$159,950	$186,609
30	$64,868	$97,302	$129,736	$162,170	$194,604	$227,038
35	$78,922	$118,383	$157,844	$197,304	$236,765	$276,226
40	$96,020	**$144,031**	$192,041	$240,051	$288,061	$336,071
45	$116,824	$175,235	$233,647	$292,059	$350,471	$408,882

How much difference will it make if inflation over the next 40 years is more or less than what you've estimated? The short answer: a lot. If, for example, inflation averages only 3 percent, the future value of your expenses is only $97,000, about one-third less than your estimate. If inflation averages 5 percent, your expenses will be around $211,000, about 50 percent more. You can see why it's so important to take inflation into account.

SELF-CHECK

1. List the two methods used to calculate retirement income needs.
2. Why is it important to take inflation into account in estimating your future expenses?

14.2 Sources of Retirement Income

When you have an estimate of your retirement income needs, the next step is to consider the ways you can meet those needs. The "three-legged stool of retirement income" is a metaphor originated in the Congressional discussions that led up to the passage of the act that created Social Security many decades ago. The fact that it's often mentioned in government policy discussions today demonstrates its continued relevance.

Each individual's retirement income security can be visualized as a three-legged stool, with the three legs being

▲ Social Security.
▲ Employer-sponsored retirement plans.
▲ Private savings.

For retirement planning, the stool is a particularly apt analogy: Like a three-legged stool, your retirement plan can be expected to topple over if one of the legs is too short. Unfortunately, most retirees today rely too much on Social Security, making the stool a bit lopsided. Many of them (24 percent of retirees in 2002 find it necessary to continue to work in retirement to supplement their income or to have access to affordable health benefits (so we could say that their stool has to have an extra leg to support their retirement).

Not counting employment income, the Social Security Administration estimates that 25 percent of aggregate retirement income comes from earnings on assets, 22 percent from government and private pensions, and 53 percent from Social Security benefits. More than two-thirds of all retirees get at least half their income from Social Security, and 31 percent rely on it to provide more than 90 percent of their total income.

Today's workers, who will be tomorrow's retirees, face many challenges in balancing the three legs of the stool, including higher levels of household debt, uncertainty about the future of Social Security, and increased investment risk in employer retirement plans. For women, this problem is exacerbated by persistent differences in labor market experience that make it more difficult for them to retire.

FOR EXAMPLE

Why Do Women Have Lower Retirement Income Than Men?

A disproportionate percentage of elderly women are poor. While this is nothing new—Congress used this statistic in justifying the creation of Social Security many decades ago—the persistence of this gender-based retirement income gap is of concern to public policy makers. A recent research report sponsored by the AARP found that much of the retirement income gender gap is caused by differences in labor market experiences.[1] Women continue to earn less than men during their working years, and they have shorter working careers; both of these factors lead to reduced Social Security benefits. Also, there is evidence of occupational segregation: Women are more likely to work in firms and industries that don't have employer-sponsored retirement plans. These factors, combined, make it more difficult for women to adequately prepare for retirement than for men.

It is important, in your own planning, that you make decisions today that will maximize your access to multiple sources of income in retirement. As discussed in Chapter 9, you might want to seek employment with a firm that sponsors a generous retirement plan for its employees. This, combined with Social Security benefits, will reduce the amount of income shortfall that you have to finance from your investments or from later retirement.

14.2.1 Estimating Your Benefits from Employer-Sponsored Plans

Chapter 9 discusses the various types of tax-qualified retirement plans. For each type, plan sponsors are required to report certain information to participants at least annually. These reports give the current value of each investment account and an estimate of the benefit that's likely to result from the plan, under current assumptions. Make sure that your employer provides current written information on any plans that are offered in your workplace.

If you're eligible for an employer-sponsored retirement plan, you can use this information to complete step 2 of the Retirement Planning Worksheet, as discussed next.

Retirement Income from Defined Benefit Plans

Your future benefit from a defined benefit plan is usually based on a formula that takes into account the number of years you've worked for the employer and how much you earn. For example, an employer might use the following formula: 2 percent of final salary for each year of service, up to a maximum of 80 percent. If you work for this employer for 35 years, you'll receive a benefit equal to 70 percent of your salary at retirement. If you have a generous defined benefit plan that also adjusts benefits for inflation during retirement, your risk of outliving your assets may not be too great. In the extreme, you may find that the benefits you receive over your lifetime far exceed the amounts contributed.

Even though your employer provides a benefit estimate, you need to adjust the amount given because it will be based on your current salary and years of employment (rather than your projected final salary and years of employment at retirement), and there's no guarantee that you'll stay with the same employer.

One way to estimate your expected income shortfall is to estimate your future salary, apply the appropriate percentage, and then deduct it from your income needs. For example, suppose your current salary is $40,000, and you'll retire in 20 years, at which time you will have 35 years of service. You can use Table 14-1 to see how much your salary will grow if you receive annual 4 percent raises. For example, if you look down the $40,000 column to the row for 20 years, you see that the future value is $87,645. Using this salary amount, you can then estimate your projected pension benefit based on the applicable benefit formula. For example, if the formula is 2 percent for every year of service, 35 years of service will give you a benefit of 70 percent of $87,645, or $61,351 in the first year.

If you expect to receive income from more than one employer-sponsored defined benefit plan, you should estimate each income amount separately. Note, however, that if you have a vested benefit from a previous employer's plan that uses salary in its formula, the benefit amount is calculated based on your final salary with that firm, not on your earnings when you actually retire.

Income from Defined Contribution Plans

If you work for an employer that sponsors a 401(k) or other type of retirement savings program, contributions to your account can be expected to continue, and even to increase, until you retire. When you retire, you'll probably convert this fund to an income stream, either by purchasing an annuity or by spending the investment earnings and principal during retirement. Unlike with a defined benefit plan, the amount of income this fund will generate for you in retirement is fairly uncertain because it depends on how much is contributed each year and the rate of return on invested assets for many years.

Although you receive an annual report that tells you how much you have saved so far, it's harder to translate this to a specific amount of retirement income. Instead, you may want to consider this as part of the total wealth you are accumulating to meet your retirement income shortfall discussed below.

14.2.2 Estimating Your Social Security Benefits

We've already discussed some aspects of Social Security, but in this section, we review a few key features to see how to estimate your future benefits. We also examine the financial problems the program is expected to experience in the near future and whether you should expect those problems to affect your benefits.

How Is Social Security Funded?

Social Security is a defined benefit program administered by the U.S. Social Security Administration. In addition to the health, disability, and survivor benefits identified earlier, the program is intended to provide at least subsistence-level retirement income to program participants, who include nearly all workers in the United States. About 40 million people currently receive retirement benefits from the program.

Social Security is funded by a payroll tax called FICA, authorized by the Federal Insurance Contributions Act. The tax burden is shared by employers and employees (5.3 percent each on the first $87,900 of income per year in 2004, a maximum that increases annually with inflation). An additional shared tax of 1.8 percent (0.9 percent each) goes to the disability program (also subject to the income limitation), and 2.9 percent (1.45 percent each) goes to the Medicare program (but is assessed on total income). Self-employed people pay both portions of all three of these tax components, for a total of 15.3 percent.

Social Security is referred to as a "pay-as-you-go" system because the money received from current workers is used to pay benefits to current beneficiaries. As the number of workers per retiree has decreased over the years (from 42 in 1945 to fewer than 4 today), the payroll tax has gradually increased to keep the system in balance.

Who Is Eligible to Receive Social Security Benefits?

You can be eligible to receive Social Security benefits either based on your own earnings history (in which case you must be fully insured) or based on your spouse's:

▲ **Fully insured status:** To be fully insured, you must have participated in the system, paying FICA payroll taxes on your earnings, for a total of 40 three-month periods (quarters) totaling 10 years and earned at least a specified minimum dollar amount in each of those quarters. Fully insured participants who retire at the normal retirement age are entitled to benefits, as defined by law. The normal retirement age, originally age 65, is now age 67 for anyone born in 1960 or later. Participants can also opt for "early retirement" at age 62, in which case they receive a reduced benefit to account for the reduced years of payroll tax contributions and increased years of expected benefit receipt. Even though the early retirement reduction is fairly substantial—$6\frac{2}{3}$ percent for each year prior to the normal retirement age—many people opt for early receipt of benefits.

▲ **Spousal benefits:** Another way you can qualify for Social Security benefits is to have a spouse who is fully insured. Because Social Security was designed in an era when single-earner households were the norm rather than the exception, Congress included some protections for women. Today, these protections might seem unnecessary, but they have significantly reduced the poverty rate for elderly women. Consider an example: Barbara and Dave are 65 years old. Barbara didn't work outside the home until her last child left for college. At that time, she was 57 years old, so she's only contributed to Social Security for seven years—not enough time to achieve fully insured status. However, Dave is eligible for a monthly benefit of $1,600. Barbara is eligible for a spousal benefit equal to 50 percent of her husband's benefit. Furthermore, even if Barbara did qualify on her own earnings history, the law would allow her to receive a benefit based on either her own earnings or 50 percent of her husband's benefit, whichever was greater. And if Dave dies before her, she'll receive a survivor benefit equal to 100 percent of Dave's benefit. Divorcees who haven't remarried are eligible for Social Security benefits equal to 50 percent of their ex-husbands' benefits as long as the marriage lasted at least 10 years. Conceivably, the same man could have been married four times, each for

10 years, and all four of his ex-wives could receive benefits at retirement equal to 50 percent of his benefit, as long as they hadn't remarried.

How Much Will I Get from Social Security?

Social Security benefits are based on a multistep calculation. The Social Security Administration first calculates your **average indexed monthly earnings (AIME)**, using your top 35 years of earnings (up to the taxable maximum for each year), adjusted for inflation to current-year dollars. If you've worked for less than 35 years, you have some zeros averaged in. The AIME is then used in a formula to calculate your **primary insurance amount (PIA),** the monthly benefit you'd be entitled to if you retired at the normal retirement age. The dollar amounts in the formula are adjusted annually for inflation.

The PIA formula is designed to have a redistributive effect by replacing a larger percentage of pre-retirement income for low-income retirees than for average- and high-income retirees. A low-income person (AIME = $1,000) retiring in 2004 would have been eligible for a monthly benefit of $671.48, an amount that would have replaced about two-thirds of his or her pre-retirement income. At the other end of the spectrum, a person who consistently earned at least as much as the income maximum in 2004 ($87,900 / 12 = $7,325 per month) would have been eligible for the maximum benefit under the program that year, $2,071.24, which would have replaced less than one-third of his or her pre-retirement income: On average, Social Security beneficiaries receive a retirement benefit of $900 ($1,500 for a couple) per month. The benefit amount is annually adjusted for inflation, which ensures that a retiree's purchasing power does not decline over time. To estimate your future Social Security benefits, you can use the retirement calculator on the SSA Web page (www.ssa.gov).

Will Social Security Be Around When I Retire?

Your eligibility for Social Security benefits makes a big difference in the amount of income shortfall you'll need to fund. Chances are good that Social Security will be as generous as it is today, but there's a strong possibility that it won't be. It's important to remember that Social Security is a pay-as-you-go system: Current payroll taxes are used to fund current benefit payments. When payroll taxes collected exceed the total being paid out in benefits to current retirees, as has been the case for the past several years, the Social Security Administration invests the extra money in special-issue Treasury bonds. The accumulated value of these bonds is called the Social Security trust fund. What this means is that the federal government has borrowed the money from Social Security in return for an IOU that eventually has to be repaid.

Tax inflows currently are much larger than benefit payments to retirees, so the Social Security trust fund is growing steadily, accumulating the extra funds that will be necessary to pay benefits to future retirees. Despite this, the Social Security Administration currently predicts that the retirement of the baby boomers will place a large drain on the program. Based on current projections, tax inflows will start to lag benefit outflows in 2018, and the trust fund will be depleted (meaning all the bonds will have been cashed in) by 2044. This doesn't even take into account the fact that the federal government is somehow going to have to come up with the funds to make good on its pile of IOUs to the Social Security trust fund. This potentially negative outcome has occurred, in part, because people are living longer and are therefore collecting benefits over longer periods. Another reason is that the baby boom generation is larger than the generations that preceded and followed it. This means that as baby boomers retire, more and more retirees will be receiving benefits, and there'll be fewer workers paying taxes to cover those benefits. In another 20 years, when the bulk of the baby boomers have retired, there'll be only 2 workers paying into the system for every retiree receiving benefits. It doesn't take a math genius to figure out that this won't work!

Prospects for Social Security Reform

It has become apparent that some type of Social Security reform is necessary, and various proposals have been discussed. When the stock market was booming, many thought a defined contribution approach was the way to go. In this type of plan, a portion of each worker's payroll tax would be deposited in an investment account, and his or her benefits would depend on the growth in value of this account over time—much like a 401(k) plan sponsored by an employer. Although it's possible that such a plan might find support in Congress, there will be several problems with its implementation. First, older participants don't have the time to accumulate enough in an investment account to replace their current benefit promise, so they'll have to continue under the old program rules. In addition, increasing federal budget deficits make it unlikely that the government will be able to help fund the transition period, so the younger participants' payroll taxes will have to be sufficient to cover the projected benefit obligations under the revised benefit and insurance formulas, their own account contributions, and the "grandfathered" retirees under the old system. Finally, recent market volatility raises concerns about the increased risk an individual account approach would place on plan participants.

Instead of introducing a major reform of Social Security, it's much more likely that politicians will choose to take small steps—perhaps raising the normal retirement age a little more, tweaking the PIA formula, or limiting benefits for the wealthy. In striving not to alienate older voters who are counting on the current system to remain unchanged, politicians are likely to dodge the bullet, leaving the problems for future generations. In light of this, you should be conservative about your estimated Social Security benefit so that you don't underestimate your retirement income shortfall.

14.2.3. How Much Nest Egg Will Be Enough?

If you take your estimate of retirement income needs and then subtract the benefits you'll receive from other retirement plans and Social Security, you're left

Table 14-2: Retirement Wealth Needed

Years in Retirement	*Retirement Wealth Factor* *Investment Return During Retirement*				
	5%	*6%*	*7%*	*8%*	*10%*
5	4.6721	4.5423	4.4181	4.2992	4.0759
10	9.1258	8.6720	8.2506	7.8590	7.1550
15	13.3715	12.4265	11.5752	10.8067	9.4811
20	17.4189	15.8399	14.4591	13.2475	11.2384
25	21.2771	18.9432	16.9607	15.2685	12.5659
30	24.9551	21.7646	19.1308	16.9420	13.5688
35	28.4612	24.3297	21.0133	18.3277	14.3264
40	31.8036	26.6617	22.6462	19.4751	14.8987

with an amount that represents your retirement income shortfall. You'll need enough money saved to be able to pay yourself this amount the first year of retirement and each year until you die, increasing at the rate of inflation. Calculating this value can be complicated, but all you really need is an approximation so that you can target how much to save each month. You can use Table 14-2 to arrive at an approximate savings goal and Table 14-3 to determine how much you

Table 14-3: Annual Savings Target

Amount Needed	Rate of Return	*Annual Investment Amount to Achieve Goal* *Years to Retirement*			
		10	*20*	*30*	*40*
$250,000	4%	$20,823	$8,395	$4,458	$2,631
	6%	$18,967	$6,796	$3,162	$1,615
	8%	$17,257	$5,463	$2,207	$965
$500,000	4%	$41,645	$16,791	$8,915	$5,262
	6%	$37,934	$13,592	$6,324	$3,231
	8%	$34,515	$10,926	$4,414	$1,930
$750,000	4%	$62,468	$25,186	$13,373	$7,893
	6%	$56,901	$20,388	$9,487	$4,846
	8%	$51,772	$16,389	$6,621	$2,895
$1,000,000	4%	$83,291	$33,582	$17,830	$10,523
	6%	$75,868	$27,185	$12,649	$6,462
	8%	$69,029	$21,852	$8,827	$3,860

should save per year to reach that goal. These tables take into account that you want to have retirement income that increases each year with inflation and that you will be earning interest each year.

SELF-CHECK

1. In what year will Social Security outflows outpace inflows?
2. List the three legs of the "retirement stool."
3. Which of the three legs is now overrelied upon by American retirees?

14.3 Personal Retirement Savings Options

The third leg of the retirement stool is your personal savings and investments. You need to decide what form your personal retirement savings should take. Possibilities include investments in taxable and tax-deferred accounts, investments in income-producing real estate, and home equity. We focus on retirement savings accounts here.

Congress has established several programs designed to encourage increased personal retirement saving. These programs generally provide tax incentives to low- and middle-income individuals and small business owners who make contributions to certain types of retirement plans. Individual retirement accounts (IRAs) are defined and briefly discussed in Chapter 4. In this section, we review the differences between the types of IRAs, explain the rules for using them, and cover the tax advantages they offer to individual savers in more detail.

14.3.1 Individual Retirement Accounts

Since the early 1980s, individuals have had the opportunity to make tax-deferred contributions to IRAs, which are easy to set up through financial institutions. The Tax Reform Act of 1986, the Tax Relief Act of 1997, and the Economic Growth and Tax Relief Reconciliation Act of 2001 together define the types of IRAs that are available, the tax preferences involved, and the contribution limits.

There are two main types of IRAs: traditional IRAs and Roth IRAs.

Traditional IRAs

Traditional IRAs are subject to very similar rules to those that govern employer-sponsored defined contribution plans. Your contributions are tax deductible in the year in which you make them if you're not an active participant in an employer-sponsored retirement plan. If you participate in an employer-sponsored plan, the deductibility of IRA contributions depends on your adjusted gross income. For each of the tax years discussed here, your IRA contribution is fully deductible if your income is less than the lower number in the salary range given and partially deductible if your income is within the range given. If your income is greater than the highest end of the range, you can't deduct your IRA contribution at all.

So, for example, if you were married and filed a joint return in 2006, you could fully deduct an IRA contribution if your joint adjusted gross income was less than $75,000 (or $150,000 if only one spouse has access to an employer retirement account). Even when the contribution is not deductible, the earnings are tax deferred until withdrawal, at which time they're taxed as ordinary income. If you withdraw funds before you reach age $59\frac{1}{2}$, however, the withdrawal is subject to a 10 percent penalty unless you use the funds to pay for qualified educational expenses, medical expenses, or a first-time home purchase. The maximum allowable annual IRA contribution per person is the person's adjusted gross income or the limit on the IRA schedule, whichever is smaller.

Recent changes include gradual increases in the deductible amount, as well as catch-up provisions for taxpayers age 50 and over. The limit adjusts annually for inflation in increments of $500.

Roth IRAs

A Roth IRA takes a different approach from a traditional IRA, requiring that contributions be made with after-tax dollars but allowing investments to accumulate tax free, with no tax due on withdrawals, as long as the taxpayer has reached age or is using the proceeds for qualified educational, medical, or first-time home purchase expenses.

The contribution limits for the Roth IRA are the same as for the traditional IRA, but the income limits are higher, making this an option for middle-income households. Full contributions can be made by singles with an adjusted gross income of no more than $95,000 and married joint filers with an adjusted gross income of no more than $150,000. Above that income level, the contribution is phased out up to the income limits of $110,000 for singles and $160,000 for joint filers. To encourage retirement saving by low-income households, there is a tax credit for up to 50 percent of contributions to IRAs and employer plans, depending on income, with a maximum credit of $2,000. For example, a qualifying taxpayer could make a $1,000 contribution to an IRA, and he or she would get a $500 reduction in taxes owed for the year. In effect, that individual has to pay only $500 to accumulate $1,000 in his or her account. This credit was set to expire in 2006, but was made permanent by the Pension Protection Act of 2006.

> ## FOR EXAMPLE
>
> ### The Importance of Starting Early
>
> You may estimate the monthly savings required to meet your goal and find that you can't afford to save much right now. You can still reach your retirement savings goal by saving less now and more later. However, the power of compound interest will be greatest for your earliest contributions. To illustrate this effect, use Table 14-3 to consider the impact of getting a late start on your investments. Suppose you wait 10 years before starting to save for retirement. To accumulate the same $500,000 at 6 percent interest, you need to save $6,324 per year for 30 years but only $3,231 per year for 40 years, almost half as much. Clearly, early contributions make a big difference in the end.

The income limits ($25,000/$50,000 AGI for single/joint filers) will increase with inflation in future years.

14.3.2 Investing in Taxable Accounts

IRAs offer some tax advantages, but with them, you give up some financial flexibility because your retirement assets are not very liquid: Although you can cash them out before retirement in an emergency, you pay a premium to do so. Suppose, for example, that you're subject to a 20 percent marginal tax rate and you have a financial emergency that requires withdrawal of $10,000 from a deductible IRA account. In the year of withdrawal, you pay $3,000 to the government—$2,000 to taxes and $1,000 as the 10 percent penalty for withdrawing before the appropriate age. This represents a substantial drain on your retirement funds.

For some individuals, IRAs provide the discipline they need to leave their money alone for a long period of time. For others, it may be advisable to put some of their investment funds in taxable accounts.

14.3.3 Asset Allocation in Retirement Accounts

In addition to choosing the type of account to use for your savings, you need to make decisions about what to invest in. You have many options. You can put your retirement funds into everything from CDs to stock mutual funds. You can have them professionally managed, or you can manage them yourself.

A few fundamentals here about investing (covered in detail elsewhere in the text) have direct application to asset allocation decisions for your retirement accounts:

1. **Take into account your time horizon:** If retirement is a long time from now, you can probably afford to take a little more risk to get a bigger possible return.

2. **Don't forget about taxes:** If you're holding your funds in a taxable account, it might be worthwhile to consider investments that are exempt from certain taxes (such as federal or municipal bonds). It's not a good idea to hold tax-exempt investments in an IRA because the higher price you pay for these bonds will not be offset by any tax savings. You can also use a taxable account for investments that grow in value over time but don't produce current income (such as growth stocks) because you don't have to pay tax on the increase in value until you sell. However, the same isn't true of stock mutual funds (even if they're growth funds) because the investors normally receive distributions of capital gains and income each year that would be taxable. In general, you should avoid holding investments that generate a lot of currently taxable income (e.g., corporate bonds) in a taxable account, but they might be a good choice for an IRA.

3. **Diversify:** This recommendation should go without saying: In addition to being diversified across your entire household portfolio, it's important to be diversified within your retirement portfolio. Many individuals who had allocated their IRAs and employer-sponsored investment accounts primarily to high-risk stocks in the 1990s (and accumulated substantial wealth as a result) were dismayed to see their portfolio values plummet when the market turned. Those in their 40s still have time to recover, but older investors may find themselves retiring a little later than they'd hoped.

SELF-CHECK

1. What are two main types of savings vehicles?
2. What is the penalty for early withdrawal from an IRA?

14.4 Preparing for Retirement Payouts

You may not be ready to think about the decumulation stage of your life—when you'll be spending your wealth instead of saving. Nevertheless, our discussion of retirement planning wouldn't be complete without a few words of advice on this component of your plan. A little advance planning can save you money in the long run.

14.4.1 Distributions from Retirement Accounts

In general, distributions from employer plans are taxable when they're received. On the other hand, you may have other sources of cash flow, such as Roth IRAs, that you can access without owing any taxes. Because it's always better to pay taxes later rather than sooner, your financial plan for receipt of retirement income should include strategies for delaying the receipt of cash flows that trigger taxation.

If you have other sources of income, you can wait to claim defined benefit annuities to which you're entitled for a few years, and you can deposit defined contribution plan assets in an IRA (commonly called a "rollover") to delay paying the taxes due. You eventually have to pay the tax, of course. Tax rules require that you begin taking payouts from both employer plans and IRAs by April 1 of the year after you reach age 70½.

When you retire under an employer plan, you may receive a lump sum, an annuity, or some combination of the two, depending on the plan terms and your own choices. With a lump sum payout, you need to manage the funds yourself, but it also gives you more flexibility. An annuity provides you with monthly or annual payments, which can be helpful in budgeting.

In some cases, you may be able to choose between several types of annuities:

▲ **Annuity for a specific term:** An **annuity for a specific term** provides a stream of equal payments for a certain number of years, often 10, 15, or 20 years. These payments are likely to be larger than life annuity payments, but they expose you to a significant risk of income shortfall if you live longer than the term of the annuity. If you die before the end of the term, your beneficiaries are usually entitled to receive the remaining payments.

▲ **Single life annuity:** A **single life annuity** promises to pay you an amount per year until you die, but there are no payments to beneficiaries after your death.

▲ **Joint and survivor annuity:** A **joint and survivor annuity** pays an amount per year to you and your spouse until the last one dies. Some joint and survivor annuities allow the option of a reduced annuity after the first spouse dies in return for a greater annuity while both spouses are living.

Obviously, the same amount of wealth produces a lower benefit in the case of joint and survivor annuities than when invested in the other types, but such an arrangement protects the last spouse to die. It is unfortunately all too common an occurrence for an elderly woman to become impoverished as a result of her husband's final illness.

14.4.2 Tapping Your Home Equity

If you've paid off your mortgage or you have substantial home equity at retirement, another option for generating tax-free retirement income is to use some of your equity. While in years past this might have required that you sell the home, today it's relatively easy to get a home equity loan or a home equity line of credit. Both of these require that you make payments, but you may be able to spread out the payments for a fairly long time. The interest you pay is tax deductible, and you still benefit from any increase in the value of your property while you continue to own it.

Another alternative you might consider is a reverse annuity mortgage, discussed in Chapter 7. In this type of arrangement, you trade your home equity for an income stream, and you're allowed to remain in the home for the period of the annuity, which may be a period of years or for life, after which the lender assumes ownership of the home. Given average home values, a reverse annuity mortgage may not provide a big enough income stream to risk losing your equity if you die prematurely. If your home is worth $150,000 and you buy a 20-year annuity, for example, you'll get around $12,000 per year.

14.4.3 What Happens if You Don't Have Enough Money to Retire?

You may find that your ideal retirement age arrives but you can't afford to retire. Whether this is due to children's college costs, bad investments, divorce, health issues, or some other cause, the end result is unpleasant. To meet your income needs, you may need to consider some of the following options:

▲ **Reduce expenses:** Downsizing housing, cars, vacations, and other expenses makes it possible to live on a more modest income.

▲ **Continue to work:** If your health permits, delaying retirement allows you to continue your retirement savings program and reduces the number of years of retirement income that your nest egg must support. Working after you've begun to collect Social Security may result in reduced benefits, however.

▲ **Increase savings:** If you still have a few years to go before retirement, you can attempt to increase your savings rate. Taking an extra job and allocating all that income to retirement saving may be an option.

▲ **Rely on family:** In earlier times, families were often called on to support their parents and grandparents. Although this is less common today than it used to be, it still occurs. Family members may simply provide financial support, or older family members may actually move in with younger ones to stretch retirement savings.

▲ **Rely on public assistance:** Many elderly people live below the poverty level and qualify for public assistance, such as food stamps.

Hopefully, none of these outcomes will apply to you. If you start planning for retirement now, establish goals, and work toward meeting those goals, you'll have a better chance of funding a comfortable retirement.

SELF-CHECK

1. List the three types of annuities.
2. What's the disadvantage of the reverse annuity mortgage?

SUMMARY

To make sure you will be financially secure in retirement, you must first establish retirement goals and then estimate your income needs and savings targets to meet those goals. Your options for funding your retirement include future benefits from employer-sponsored retirement plans, Social Security, and personal savings. The federal Social Security program is under financial strain that is expected to intensify, so you should not rely on it completely. Understanding the different tax-deferred alternatives for employer-sponsored and personal retirement saving will help you achieve your retirement goals.

KEY TERMS

Adjusted expense method	A method for estimating after-tax retirement income needs in current dollars by adjusting current expenses for changes expected in retirement.
Annuity for a specific term	An annuity that provides a stream of equal payments for a specific period of time.
Average indexed monthly earnings (AIME)	The average of a person's 35 highest years of monthly earnings, adjusted for inflation, used in computing that individual's Social Security benefit.
Joint and survivor annuity	An annuity that provides a stream of equal payments until the death of the second spouse.
Primary insurance amount (PIA)	The Social Security benefit payable to a program participant who retires at the normal retirement age.
Replacement ratio method	A method for estimating after-tax retirement income needs in current dollars by multiplying current expenses by a factor of 70 to 80 percent.
Single life annuity	An annuity that provides a stream of equal payments until death.

ASSESS YOUR UNDERSTANDING

Go to www.wiley.com/college/bajtelsmit to assess your knowledge of planning for retirement.

Measure your learning by comparing pre-test and post-test results.

Summary Questions

1. Inflation is a major reason many people underestimate the amount of money needed for retirement. True or false?

2. Which of the following methods for estimating retirement income needs assumes that retirement expenses will be some fixed proportion of your pre-retirement needs?

   (a) Replacement ratio method.

   (b) Fixed ratio method.

   (c) Adjusted expense method.

   (d) Percentage adjustment method.

3. A majority of studies have shown that expenses in retirement are approximately 70 percent of pre-retirement expenses. True or false?

4. To reach fully insured status under Social Security, you must have participated in the system for at least:

   (a) 20 quarters.

   (b) 30 quarters.

   (c) 40 quarters.

   (d) 50 quarters.

5. If your retirement benefit is based on years of service and a percentage of your highest salary, you are enrolled in a:

   (a) defined benefit plan.

   (b) defined contribution plan.

   (c) fixed salary plan.

   (d) variable salary plan.

6. Unlike traditional IRAs, Roth IRAs do not have a tax deduction for contributions, even if you are not participating in an employer retirement plan. True or false?

7. Compared to a traditional IRA, a Roth IRA:

   (a) is easier to set up.

   (b) has a lower minimum age for tax-free withdrawals.

   (c) allows investments to accumulate tax free, whereas a traditional IRA does not.

   (d) allows deductible contributions, whereas a traditional IRA does not.

8. An annuity that pays an equal annual amount until death is:

(a) an annuity for a specific term.

(b) a single life annuity.

(c) a fixed annuity.

(d) a variable annuity.

9. If you don't have enough money to retire, you may need to:

(a) increase savings.

(b) rely on family.

(c) rely on public assistance.

(d) all of the above.

10. If you purchase an annuity that will pay you $10,000 per year for 10 years, you have purchased a single life annuity. True or false?

Applying This Chapter

1. You have 20 years until retirement and your current expenses are $20,000 per year. Using Table 14-1, calculate your future expenses in retirement.

2. You estimate that your first year retirement income expenses will be $100,000 and that these expenses will increase at an inflation rate of 4 percent per year for the 20 years you will be retired. Use Table 14-2 to estimate how much wealth will you need to have accumulated by the time you retire if you expect to earn 6% on your retirement investments.

3. Marissa worked as a homemaker until she was 50. Because then, she has worked part-time as a retail clerk, and she is now ready to retire at age 65. Her husband's Social Security AIME is $3,000, and hers is only $500. Will she be able to qualify for benefits based on her husband's earnings history?

4. Your friend Ravi is considering putting money in either a traditional IRA or a Roth IRA. Explain to him the tax consequences of his decision.

5. You participate in a defined contribution plan at work and earn $40,000. Your wife works part-time and earns $3,000 per year. Can you and your spouse each contribute to an IRA in 2006 if you file joint taxes?

6. You are 37 years old and expect to retire at age 67. Your current expenses are $50,000 per year and you do not have an employer sponsored retirement plan. Your estimated retirement benefit in future dollars according to the Social Security website is $60,000. Estimate your retirement income needs (using Table 14-1), your retirement wealth needed (Table 14-2), and how much you should save each year to meet your goal (Table 14-3).

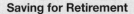

YOU TRY IT

Saving for Retirement

You are 37 years old, and you plan to retire in 30 years. You've estimated that you need to accumulate $1 million by the time you retire in order to fund your retirement income shortfall.

1. If you invest your funds to earn 8 percent per year, how much do you need to save each month?

2. What if you can earn not 8 percent but 10 percent, how much do you need to save each month?

The Effect of Early Investing

Tory decides to get an early start on retirement and, beginning at age 22, she invests $3,000 a year in a Roth IRA for 10 years in a row. At that point, she stops contributing to the account but leaves the money invested until age 65 (a period of 33 years). Tory's brother Harry doesn't start investing until he's 32 but from then on invests $3,000 in a Roth IRA each year for 33 years until retirement at age 65. If both of them earn 10 percent annually on their investments, compounded annually, which one has more in the account at the end? How much more?

15

PRESERVING YOUR ESTATE
Keeping It All in the Family

Starting Point

Go to www.wiley.com/college/bajtelsmit to assess your knowledge of estate planning.
Determine where you need to concentrate your effort.

What You'll Learn in This Chapter

▲ Estate taxes
▲ Wills and estate planning
▲ Types of trusts

After Studying This Chapter, You'll Be Able To

▲ Identify the key elements of your estate plan
▲ Draw up, with an attorney's help, a valid will to benefit your heirs
▲ Estimate the size of your estate and the taxes that would be owed upon your death
▲ Choose trusts, gifts, and charitable contributions to minimize estate taxes

INTRODUCTION

This chapter is all about death and taxes—preparing for the first and avoiding the second. The failure to plan for what will happen upon your death can result in significant hardship, both personal and financial, for your survivors. Whether you consider these issues as they apply to someone else or in the context of your own estate plan, this chapter provides a roadmap for getting started by helping you understand the process and the legal rules. It begins with an overview of the estate-planning process, and then covers the key components of an estate plan. It then explains why everyone needs a will and how to make sure yours is legally valid. The last section of this chapter explains the current system of taxation and what you might expect in the future.

15.1 What Is Estate Planning?

The objective of **estate planning** is to distribute your wealth according to your wishes after your death and to plan for the care of your dependents. In this context, your **estate** is your net worth at death—all your assets less all your debts, as defined in Chapter 2. Although federal estate taxes are gradually being phased out, the long-term status of these taxes is uncertain, and current law still imposes a hefty tax on larger estates. Thus, one of the additional objectives of estate planning is to avoid paying extra estate taxes. This section provides an overview of estate planning and why it should be a component of your financial plan.

15.1.1 The Estate-Planning Process

Estate planning is the process of developing a plan for what will happen to your wealth and your dependents when you die. It involves both financial and legal considerations, and it usually also requires the advice of a professional, such as an estate lawyer or a financial professional. Nevertheless, you can save both time and money if you do some work before you seek professional guidance.

The purpose of this chapter is not to tell you everything there is to know about estate planning but rather to provide you with an understanding of the fundamentals so you can begin making important decisions. As with other elements of financial planning, the estate-planning process requires that you first evaluate your financial situation. By estimating the value of your estate, you can determine whether additional tax planning is necessary to reduce your potential tax liability. If you have children, you must plan for what will happen to them after you die. You have to make a will, and you may also want to consider several other legal documents discussed in this chapter to ensure that your wishes are carried out upon your death.

Who needs an estate plan? Everyone will eventually die, everyone should have an estate plan. Even if you're not wealthy, you should have an estate plan if you want to

▲ Make sure your assets go where you intend for them to go after you die.
▲ Have a say in who becomes the guardian of your child(ren).
▲ Reduce the chance of family discord over the distribution of your assets.
▲ Minimize the costs of settling your estate.

Because people's needs—and their estates—can be quite different, so some estate plans are necessarily more complex than others. If you have no dependents and negative net worth, your plan will be simple. Your biggest problems might be: Who would take care of your pet? Do you want to be cremated? Which kinds of life-extending measures do you want taken if you're physically or mentally disabled in the future? If you are wealthy, have dependent children, or own property in multiple states, your plan will be more complicated. More importantly, the consequences of failing to plan could be much more serious. The legal process of settling your estate—paying your debts and distributing your assets according to your wishes—is called **probate**. This process is supervised by a local court, which appoints someone to administer the distribution of assets. Because only certain assets have to be distributed through the probate process, one of the objectives of your estate plan should be to arrange for as much of your wealth as possible to avoid the probate process. If you die without a valid will or if your family can't locate necessary documents, the probate process can take a long time—months or even years. In some cases, your survivors may experience financial hardship if they don't have access to necessary funds during the probate process.

15.1.2 What Happens if You Fail to Plan?

Most people in the United States don't have adequate estate plans. More than half don't even have valid wills. If you die without an estate plan or a will, the value of your estate may be unnecessarily eroded by the following costs:

▲ Federal estate taxes (top marginal rate 45% percent in 2007, depending on the size of the estate).
▲ State inheritance taxes (0 to 10 percent, depending on the state you live in).
▲ Probate costs (2–5 percent).

Much of this chapter is about tax planning. Estate taxes can take a large bite out of your wealth, so careful tax planning can save your heirs a lot of money. Remember that tax avoidance (which is legal) is not the same as tax evasion (which is illegal). As discussed in Chapter 3, good financial planning requires that you take advantage of rules and regulations that allow you to legally reduce or avoid the taxes you pay. Also, your heirs may experience personal costs such as:

▲ Delays in settlement of the estate.

▲ Distress over having to make difficult health care decisions on your behalf.

▲ Distress over having to make funeral arrangements without knowing your wishes.

▲ Disagreements among family members regarding distribution of your personal effects.

▲ Potential financial hardship for your spouse or children if the state's distribution of your assets leaves them with insufficient financial resources.

▲ Personal upset for your dependent children if they don't like the state-appointed guardian.

15.1.3 Estate Planning over the Life Cycle

Like other parts of your financial plan, your estate plan must change as your life situation changes. Suppose you consult an estate-planning attorney and set up a plan that meets your needs today. Many people make the mistake of assuming that once they've established a plan, they're set for life, but this is not the case.

You need to revisit your estate plan whenever you have a major change in circumstances. At a minimum, such changes include divorce, remarriage, birth or adoption of a child, death of anyone named in your will, change of state of

---

FOR EXAMPLE

Time for New Wills

While getting their financial plan in order, Cindy and Dave Thompson consulted an estate-planning attorney and discovered problems with both of their wills, which were written before their marriage. Under Cindy's old will, her ex-husband is her primary beneficiary. Dave's old will leaves everything to his brother Tom. The provisions in Cindy's will favoring her ex-husband, by law, will have been automatically revoked, or canceled, but not the provisions in Dave's will, favoring his brother. With Cindy and Dave's marriage, the legal status of both old wills is questionable, but clearly both wills are inconsistent with their current intentions. Although Cindy's old will includes a provision for guardianship of her son from her previous marriage, the named guardian is her ex-husband's mother, who is now deceased. Neither will provides for additional children, so even if Cindy and Dave's wills were found to be valid, their new daughter, Julia, would not be entitled to anything should they both die. The Thompsons' attorney advised them to write new wills promptly.

residence, change of job, acquisition of new assets, and change in dependent status of your children. Optimally, you should reconsider your estate plan regularly—perhaps as often as annually, when you reevaluate your financial plan.

Although your plan is likely to be fairly simple when you're young, it should grow in complexity with the complexity of your family circumstances and finances. Through your 40s and 50s, your primary estate-planning concerns are probably the protection of your spouse or children, but as you age, they are likely to shift to providing for your spouse's retirement and passing your wealth to your heirs or your favorite charities.

SELF-CHECK

1. Define **estate** and **estate planning**.
2. What's the purpose of estate planning?
3. List three potential financial costs of not planning.

15.2 Key Components of an Estate Plan

Although estate plans can be very different from one another, most share certain key components. These may include a will, a living will, a letter of last instruction, and any trust instruments deemed necessary. We look at each of these components here.

15.2.1 The Will

The most important component of your estate plan is your will. A **will** is a legal document that specifies how you want your property to be distributed upon your death. A person or an entity designated to receive something from your estate after your death is called your **heir.**

Your will can also specify who will have responsibility for the care of your surviving minor children (under age 18) and other dependents. Different types of wills and the legal requirements for a valid will are discussed in Section 15.3. Whether you have a will or not, state law requires that your assets be distributed after your death.

If you die **intestate**—that is, without a valid will—there are rules in every state as to how your property will be distributed. Although the manner of distribution differs among states, these rules will not necessarily divide up your assets in the way you would have chosen had you drafted a will. Also, you will have no say in who becomes the guardian for your children.

In most states, for example, without a will in place, your spouse will get no more than half your assets, with the other half going to surviving children or your parents. If you have no children, your spouse will likely have to share the wealth with other relatives, which might leave him or her in financial difficulty. If you die without a will and have no living relatives, all your assets will become the property of the state government through a legal rule called **escheat.**

15.2.2 The Living Will or Durable Power of Attorney

In addition to having a will, you may also want to have a **living will.** Whereas wills have been around for thousands of years, living wills are a by-product of modern medical care. In this document, you specify what kind of medical care you want to receive if you become unable to make decisions due to terminal illness or physical or mental disability.

A living will can greatly ease the burden your family bears if you become incapacitated. If you don't express your wishes in advance, your family may be unable or unwilling to make the tough decisions for you, instead bearing significant and continuing financial and emotional burdens.

The most difficult part of drafting a living will is deciding what limitations to place on the level of extreme medical care you desire. For example, you can be fairly vague and specify just that no "heroic measures" be taken to keep you alive by artificial means. In that case, it will be up to your family to decide exactly what constitutes a heroic measure (e.g., respirator, kidney dialysis, feeding tubes), and they may disagree with each other on this point. Or you might limit the living will's applicability to situations in which your brain function is severely reduced to the extent that you have no reasonable chance of living a productive life. Although greater specificity can be helpful to your family who must make the difficult decisions, you need to be general enough to cover all possible circumstances. You wouldn't necessarily want your living will to prevent you from benefiting from advances in medical knowledge or improved chances of survival as time goes on.

The format of living wills can vary greatly, depending on your preferences, and many lawyers draft one along with your regular will at no additional charge. Most states have a particular legal form that they recognize for this purpose, but other forms are acceptable if they include the necessary elements. An example of a living will is provided in Figure 15-1.

A **durable power of attorney** is similar to a living will but should be used in conjunction with one. In it, you designate a person to make decisions on your behalf in case you are temporarily or permanently unable to do so. You can give very explicit instructions to the designee about what you want, or you can give the designee broad powers to make decisions as he or she sees fit. Also, a durable power of attorney can be designed to cover health care decisions only (in which case it may be called a health care power of attorney), or it can be broader, enabling the holder to make both financial and legal decisions.

Figure 15-1

Living Will

To my family, my physicians, my attorney, my minister, and any person or institution responsible for my health and welfare, I make this declaration while I am of sound mind and after full reflection.

This statement is intended to apprise you of my wishes in the event that I can no longer make medical decisions on my own behalf.

If I should ever become in a terminal state and there is no reasonable expectation of my recovery, I direct that I be allowed to die a natural death and that my life not be prolonged by extraordinary measures. I do, however, ask that medication be mercifully administered to me to alleviate suffering even though this may shorten my remaining life.

I direct that, if a terminal diagnosis, the physicians supervising my care discontinue feeding and hydration, should the continuation of feeding and hydration be judged to result in unduly prolonging my life.

I hereby authorize my family to effectuate my transfer from any hospital or other health care facility in which I may be receiving care should that facility decline or refuse to carry out the instructions in this document.

I hereby release any and all hospitals, physicians, and others for myself and for my estate from any liability for complying with this instrument.

Signed _____ Date _____

Address _____

Social Security Number _____

Witness _____ Date _____

Copies of this request have been given to my physician and attorney.

Sample living will.

15.2.3 The Letter of Last Instruction

Although not a legal document, the **letter of last instruction** helps your survivors through the process of your death. You could use this document to communicate your personal wishes regarding funeral arrangements, to identify people who should be notified of your death, and to list important information, such as bank accounts and personal identification numbers, contact information for insurance companies and brokerage firms, and safe deposit box locations and numbers.

Although specific bequests must be in your will to be legally binding, you can also use a letter of last instruction to give advice about how to distribute some of your minor personal property (e.g., your favorite CDs, your old football jersey, family items that have sentimental but not financial value). The letter of last instruction should be copied and distributed to several people (including your attorney) to ensure that it is found in the event of your death.

FOR EXAMPLE

Life or Something Like It: The Case of Terry Schiavo

Imagine that you suffer a heart attack, and the loss of oxygen to your brain leaves you in what your doctors term a "persistent and irreversible vegetative state." Your husband and your parents disagree on whether your feeding tubes should be removed. This is what happened to Terry Schiavo of Tampa, Florida. In 2003, after 13 years on life support, her husband Michael convinced a court to allow him to remove the tubes that were keeping Terry alive. Then the state legislature passed a controversial bill ("Terry's Law") that gave Governor Jeb Bush the right to order reinstatement of the feeding tube. A circuit court judge later struck down the bill as an unconstitutional invasion of privacy. Although Michael Schiavo and two other relatives testified that Terry wouldn't have wanted this type of medical intervention, she didn't have a living will. If you don't want this to happen to you, write down specific instructions concerning the circumstances and conditions under which you want heroic measures taken to keep you alive.

15.2.4 Trusts

For many estate plans, it's desirable to set up legal arrangements called trusts. A **trust** is a legal entity that holds and manages assets on behalf of someone else. Trusts are commonly used in estate planning for a variety of purposes, as is discussed in Section 15.4.

SELF-CHECK

1. What document designates somebody to make financial decisions on your behalf.
2. What should be included in a living will?
3. Define **intestate**, **heir**, and **letter of last instruction**.

15.3 Types and Formats of Wills

The failure to have a valid will can easily result in your assets being distributed contrary to your wishes. So why do so few people have valid wills? Many assume that their property will pass to their spouses or that they don't have enough assets to worry about having a will. But the failure to have a will is sure to complicate the settlement process and create added hardship for survivors. This section focuses on ensuring that your estate goes where you want it to go. Along with having a valid will, your decisions regarding legal ownership of certain assets are important.

15.3.1 Preparing a Valid Will

A will enables the person writing it, the **testator,** to direct the disposition of his or her assets to specific **beneficiaries,** those who will receive the assets. Wills can be very simple or very complicated but must satisfy certain legal requirements to be valid. If your will is declared to be invalid, your property will be distributed as if you had died intestate, so it is generally worthwhile to hire a lawyer to draft or at least review your will. The cost of having a simple will drawn up may be as little as $200 but can be much higher for more complex estates.

The following are the minimum requirements for a valid will in most states:

▲ You must be of legal age (usually 18).
▲ You must have the mental capacity to make a will:
  • You must understand the nature and extent of your assets.
  • You must understand to whom you intend your assets to be distributed.
  • You must understand how you are distributing your assets.
▲ You must intend for the document to be your will.
▲ The will must be in writing and, with some limited exceptions, typed or printed.
▲ The will must be dated.
▲ The will must be signed in the presence of two witnesses who are not your relatives or named beneficiaries in the will.
▲ The will must name an executor.

Even if all the other requirements are met, a will can be declared invalid if the testator did not have the legal **capacity** to make it. For this reason, many wills begin with the language "I, [testator name], being of sound mind and body . . . ." In this context, "of sound mind" addresses the requirement of legal capacity. The testator is considered to be of sound mind if he or she understands the nature and content of the document, is mentally capable of making decisions regarding the distribution of assets, and is not acting under threat or coercion. Capacity is a requirement for making any legally binding contract, but in the case of a will, it is particularly important because the elderly are often unwitting victims of greedy relatives and scam artists.

A will usually includes the following clauses:

▲ **Introduction:** A will usually begins with a set of introductory declarations in which the testator identifies himself or herself and the state of residency, and states that the will replaces all previous wills that he or she may have written. You may revise your will several times over the years, so it's important to date it and to identify each new one as your last will. To ensure that a previous version of your will is not inadvertently identified, you should notify your attorney and your relatives when you write a new will. It's also a good idea (although not necessary for validity) to destroy any old ones.

▲ **Payment of debts and taxes:** This clause instructs the estate to pay your debts and expenses, including funeral expenses, medical expenses, and any taxes due. Because creditors are generally protected by other laws, the most important component of this clause is the instruction to pay taxes. In the absence of such a clause, most states have laws that allocate the taxes among the beneficiaries, based on their shares of the estate. Thus, if you want to be sure that Aunt Grace gets $10,000 from your estate, you need to include a clause that directs payment of taxes before distribution of specific bequests to ensure that her $10,000 isn't reduced by a share of the estate tax.

▲ **Distribution of assets:** The primary purpose of a will is usually the distribution of assets. You can distribute your assets very simply, or you can provide detailed instructions. A very simple will might give the entire estate to the beneficiaries, such as spouse or children, without any specific bequests. Other wills direct that specific personal effects be given to beneficiaries before the distribution of the rest of the estate. If you have a long list of items to be distributed, you may want to include this list with your letter of last instruction instead of in the will itself. That way, you can make any changes that become necessary without having to draw up a new will. After gifts have been distributed, the remainder, called the *residual estate*, goes to the residual beneficiaries, as named in the will.

▲ **Appointment of executor or executrix:** In your will, you need to name the person who will handle the settlement of your estate, called the **executor** (**executrix** if female) or, sometimes, the personal representative. This person has the legal and ethical obligation of ensuring that your assets are distributed as you have directed and that taxes are paid. If your estate is complex, you should consider naming a lawyer or bank trust department instead of a family member. You should also be realistic about the other time commitments of any person you're considering naming as your executor and whether the person lives close enough to handle the details of financial transactions related to settlement of the estate.

Besides naming your executor, your will can provide for the executor to be compensated for his or her services and expenses incurred in settling the estate. This compensation is commonly a small percentage of the total value of the estate.

▲ **Appointment of guardian:** If you have minor children, your will should identify the person or persons who will take care of them and who will manage their inheritance (the **trustee**) until they reach the age you have designated in your will. If your child's other parent is living, you'll probably designate him or her as the primary guardian and trustee. However, it's important to designate a secondary guardian and trustee in the unfortunate event that both of you die at the same time. The guardian and the trustee do not have to be the same person. What if you have one or more children who are over the age of 18, which is the age of majority in most states? At the age of majority, a child legally becomes an adult and can manage his or her own affairs and may even act as a guardian for younger siblings. Nevertheless, your will can specify that your children will receive their inheritance at a later age if you prefer. Some wealthy parents, fearing that the promise of a future inheritance will adversely affect their children's incentives for achievement, have established wills that provide for guardianship and financial support until a specific age, after which the entire residual is given to charity. Others require satisfaction of specific goals, such as graduation from college, as conditions of inheritance.

▲ **Execution:** A will is not valid until executed, a legal term for the process of signing and witnessing a document to make it legally valid. To be properly executed, a will must be in writing and signed by the testator in the presence of at least two witnesses, who also must sign the will in each other's presence. In general, witnesses should be people who are not named in the will as beneficiaries. To avoid having to locate the witnesses later for verification, most states accept the execution of the will if the witnesses sign a statement, in the presence of a notary public, declaring that they observed the testator sign the will while of sound mind and under no undue influence. (Standard will forms usually have a statement of this sort printed in the place where witnesses are supposed to sign.) Even though it's unlikely the witnesses will have to come forward later, it's still a good idea to include contact information for them, just in case. The purpose of the witnesses' signatures is to verify that the testator had the capacity to make the will—was of sound mind and was not acting under coercion. Most challenges to wills are made by family members who question whether this was, in fact, the case. Some famous examples have resulted in lengthy legal battles, such as that resulting from the decision of Howard Hughes, the eccentric multibillionaire, to leave his large estate to a very young female companion. A holographic will—one that is completely handwritten and signed by the maker—doesn't have to be witnessed if it can be shown that the person actually wrote it and if it meets the other requirements for a valid will. The holographic will is a very limited exception to the general requirements, summarized at the beginning of this section, that wills be typed and witnessed. All this leads to a simple rule of thumb: If you want to make absolutely sure your will is valid, you should have it witnessed by people who can validate that you wrote it with full mental capacity.

Should a lawyer draft your will? Many websites, software packages, and self-help books suggest a do-it-yourself approach to writing a will, but this is an area where you don't want to be "penny wise and dollar foolish." It would be a shame for your will to be invalidated based on a legal technicality. No matter how small your estate is, you should consult a professional, particulary if you have children for whom you need to appoint a legal guardian or establish a trust.

To minimize the cost, you should assemble all the necessary information before meeting with the lawyer. You should think through the important issues, such as whom to appoint as executor and guardian. You might even prepare a rough draft. Most lawyers charge a flat price for preparing a simple will. What if you truly can't afford the expense at the moment? Because it's clearly better to have a will than not to have one, you can at least draw up and properly execute a simple will on your own. But you should get a legal review of your will as soon as you can.

You can change or revoke your will at any time, as long as you still have the mental capacity to execute a new will. You should review your will periodically as your circumstances change to make sure it still accurately reflects your intentions. You may want to add or subtract beneficiaries, make additional charitable bequests, or name a different executor or guardian. You can use a **codicil** to change a named guardian or trustee, for example, or to add a new baby to your list of heirs. Because

FOR EXAMPLE

When Only a Small Change is Needed

Suppose that six years ago, you wrote a will identifying your unmarried sister as the guardian of your three children. Since that time, she has married and has had three children. Although she might be a wonderful mother, having six children to raise might be too great a burden for her. Instead, you could now name your unmarried brother as the guardian (if he agrees, of course). To make small changes such as this to your will, you can write a codicil, a short (usually single-page) document that reaffirms your original will except for a small provision that is being changed.

the codicil is a legal document, it should be drawn up, executed, and witnessed in the same way as a will. For larger changes, rather than adding a codicil to your will, you should make a new will and revoke the old one.

15.3.2 Passing Property Outside a Will

Any wealth transferred by will is part of your estate and must go through probate, which, depending on the complexity of your estate, can be a lengthy process. Any assets of which you are the sole owner must go through probate. It follows, then, that you can keep property out of probate by using a different mode of ownership. You can accomplish this by holding assets jointly with your heirs and by naming beneficiaries for life insurance and retirement accounts.

When you die, your retirement accounts—such as funds held in IRAs and 401(k) plans—will pass to the person you've named as the beneficiary. One of the great tax advantages of employer retirement accounts and IRAs (see Chapter 14) is that they allow investments to grow tax deferred or, in the case of Roth IRAs, tax exempt. If your spouse will not have immediate need for your retirement assets, you might consider naming a younger child as the beneficiary of your retirement account to allow the funds to maintain their tax advantages for a longer time. Other assets can be owned in various ways. When two people own property in a **joint tenancy with right of survivorship,** the ownership of the property automatically passes to the surviving owner upon the death of the other, without going through probate. The property is also free of claims from creditors, other heirs, or executors. Joint ownership of this type is not divided; all the owners share ownership of the entire property. Thus, if you and your brother own your parents' former home as joint tenants, you don't own the other half of the property, and you thus can't leave your interest in the property to your heirs. Total ownership of the property automatically passes to your brother upon your death.

In some states, a special form of ownership, called *tenancy by the entirety,* applies to married couples and is essentially the same as joint tenancy with right of survivorship.

Joint ownership involves both advantages and disadvantages. The primary advantage is that the survivor gets immediate ownership of the property, without going through probate. Consider, for example, what would happen if household checking and savings accounts were not owned jointly: The surviving spouse might not have access to the necessary funds to pay household expenses during the process of probate. Joint ownership is also easy and inexpensive to set up. The disadvantages of joint ownership with right of survivorship as an estate-planning tool are as follows:

▲ You lose some control over the property during your lifetime. While living, joint tenants have to agree on all decisions regarding the property, much as in a partnership. Having a falling out with the other joint tenant could spell disaster.

▲ You lose complete control over what happens to the property after you die. The property will eventually pass according to the will of the last to survive. Suppose you're married and both of you have adult children from previous marriages. If you own a home together as joint tenants and you die first, your wife will then own the home. Upon her death, her estate will pass according to her own will, and your children might receive nothing.

▲ The transfer may result in greater tax liability. Although the transfer to a spouse initially bypasses the estate tax, as discussed later in Section 15.4, it may result in higher taxes when he or she dies because the estate might then be large enough to trigger the tax.

▲ You lose the ability to have the property pass to a trust. If the property is owned in joint tenancy, it is no longer yours to dispose of according to any other terms of your will.

Despite these disadvantages, joint tenancy with right of survivorship is the most common form of joint ownership, particularly for married couples. The flexibility it offers to the surviving spouse in the form of immediate access and control of the assets is thought to outweigh the disadvantages.

An alternative to joint tenancy with right of survivorship is a type of ownership called **tenancy in common.** Here, each tenant retains the right to transfer his or her ownership interest independently. Your portion of the property will be included in your estate and passed by the terms of your will.

Finally, some states have a form of property ownership for married couples called **community property.** In these states, it is assumed that any property acquired during the marriage is owned jointly by both spouses. One spouse's share of the property can be willed to someone other than the surviving spouse, however, as in a tenancy in common.

SELF-CHECK

1. Define **testator, beneficiaries, execution,** and **codicil.**
2. List five requirements for a valid will.
3. Name three types of ownership of property.

15.4 Estate and Gift Taxes

If you have a large estate you'd like to pass on, you can do so either while you are living, through gifts, or after you die, through bequests in your will. In either case, the money may be taxed. Because gifts and bequests are alternative ways to accomplish the same end—passing your wealth to the next generation—estate tax and gift tax laws work together. This section shows how gift and estate taxes are calculated and then discusses ways you can minimize taxes for those to whom you give inheritances or gifts.

15.4.1 Federal Gift Taxes

Under federal law, you may be subject to a tax on gifts if they exceed certain limits. In 2007, you and your spouse can each give up to $12,000 per person per year, tax free, to as many people as you like. This limit is scheduled to increase annually for inflation in increments of $1,000.

If you give more than the allowed annual amount to anyone, you have to file a gift tax return (IRS Form 709), and the excess amount will reduce the amount of your estate that is exempt from the estate tax. Effectively, this means your estate will have a lower estate tax exclusion (i.e., reduced by the amount of taxable gifts at the time of your death). The lifetime limit on tax-free gifts is currently $1 million.

There are two important exceptions to the limits on gifts:

▲ There is no limit on how much you can give your spouse.
▲ There is no limit on gifts for the payment of medical expenses or certain educational costs, provided that you make the payments directly to the service provider or educational institution. This means that your rich great uncle can pay the bill for your college tuition and fee expenses directly to the school without exceeding the gifting limit.

Like federal income taxes, estate and gift taxes have increasing marginal tax rates, going from 37 percent for the lowest bracket up to the maximum tax rates, which are shown in Figure 15-2. The rate schedule is the same for both gifts and estates that exceed the exclusion amounts.

Under the Economic Growth and Tax Relief Reconciliation Act of 2001, the maximum rate will be gradually reduced until the estate tax is eliminated altogether in 2010. At that point, the gift tax maximum rate will be equal to the individual income tax maximum rate (35 percent), with the first $1 million exempt from tax, as before. In 2011, however—unless the estate tax repeal is made permanent by Congress in the meantime—the tax rates and exemption amounts will revert to previous levels, as indicated in Figure 15-2.

15.4.2 Federal Estate Taxes

If you don't give your away wealth while you're living, you can give it away at your death. Under current law, the amount of your estate that exceeds the allowed exclusions may still be highly taxed (45 percent on estates of over $2 million in 2007). As discussed in Section 15.4.1, the estate tax is due to be

Figure 15-2

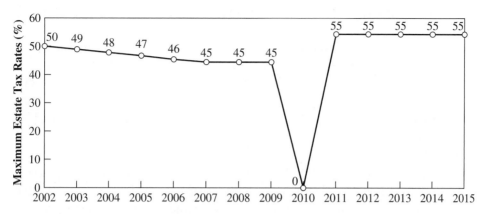

Maximum estate tax rates under the Economic Growth and Tax Relief Reconciliation Act of 2001 and after the Sunset Provisions.

repealed in 2010 but will be reinstated in 2011 (with a maximum tax rate of 55 percent) unless Congress passes further legislation to make it permanent.

An important feature of estate tax law for married couples is that the surviving spouse can inherit the entire estate without paying any tax, regardless of the size of the estate. Thus, the primary purpose of estate tax planning is actually to minimize the taxes payable by your surviving spouse's estate (or your estate, if you leave your wealth to someone other than your spouse). You can use the Calculation of Taxable Estate worksheet in the Personal Financial Planner to estimate the amount of your estate that could be subject to estate tax at your death. The following are the steps in this calculation:

1. **Calculate gross estate:** To calculate your taxable estate, first estimate your net worth, as explained in Chapter 2. Although you know the value today, you need to consider its future value. Even if you have fairly little wealth today, in another 10 years, your savings and investment portfolio will have grown substantially, and it pays to plan ahead. Your gross estate will also include the proceeds of life insurance policies if, during your lifetime, you retained the right to change beneficiaries, turn in the policy for its cash value, or borrow against the cash value. Similarly, your checking and savings accounts, investment accounts, annuities, employment pension and retirement plan assets, IRAs, and other assets will be part of your gross estate, even though they will bypass probate if you have designated a beneficiary. To avoid probate, it's thus important to name a beneficiary and also a contingent beneficiary (in case the beneficiary dies before or when you do). In completing the first step on the worksheet, enter your expected net worth and

then subtract the value of any assets that you have effectively excluded from your estate. You can remove them from your gross estate by placing them in certain types of trusts, as discussed in Section 15.5. No estate tax will be owed on amounts transferred to your spouse, so these estate-planning strategies will be important only if you list someone other than your spouse as the beneficiary on your life insurance policy or retirement account.

2. **Calculate adjusted gross estate:** Reduce your gross estate by funeral costs and settlement expenses to arrive at your adjusted gross estate.

3. **Calculate taxable estate:** Start with your adjusted gross estate, subtract all marital and charitable bequests (which are unlimited), and add any taxable gifts made during your lifetime that exceeded the allowed annual or lifetime exclusions. Finally, you subtract the applicable exemption amount. The amount you end up with—the remainder of your estate—will be taxed if the total exceeds the allowed exemption amount for that year. Although prior law allowed a tax credit for state estate taxes paid, this credit was repealed as of 2005.

FOR EXAMPLE

What Will Your Daughter Inherit?

Suppose you plan to leave your entire estate to your adult daughter. Your life insurance policy will provide her a benefit of $250,000, and your net worth is $1.2 million, $1 million of which is your 401(k) plan. You haven't made any taxable gifts, and you aren't leaving anything to charity. You anticipate that the expenses of settling your estate will be $10,000. If you died in 2007, your adjusted gross estate would be calculated as follows:

Net worth	$1,200,000
Life insurance	+250,000
Gross estate	$1,450,000
Expense of death	−10,000
Adjusted gross estate	$1,440,000

Because the exemption amount for 2007 is greater than $1,440,000, your estate will not owe taxes, and your daughter can receive the entire amount tax free. If you were to die in 2011 or later, however, the exemption amount would revert to $1 million, so $440,000 of your estate would be taxed. You can avoid this by gifting the life insurance to an irrevocable trust, with your daughter as beneficiary, thereby excluding that asset from your estate.

What will happen to estate and gift taxation after 2010? Despite some politicians' assertions that the estate tax is dead, a Democratic Congress makes it less likely that the tax repeal will be made permanent. Federal budget shortfalls have been growing quickly in recent years, and this trend is expected to continue. Also, the retirement of the baby boom generation is expected to cause Social Security outflows to exceed inflows, as discussed in Chapter 14. Due to the uncertainty about the future of the estate tax, you should plan for the worst-case scenario.

As illustrated by the steps in calculating a taxable estate, there are several ways to reduce your potential taxes. In Section 15.5, we examine ways you can legally reduce your taxable estate and thus minimize future taxes. Even if the estate tax stays low, it won't hurt to implement these strategies. It isn't costly and will not hurt your current financial situation.

Almost half of U.S. states impose some type of tax on property received from someone who has died. Federal estate tax law currently gives you a credit against taxes owed for the amount of state estate taxes you pay, but this credit provision has been repealed for future years. States calculate their taxes in different ways. Some apply a flat percentage of the value of the property transferred (usually with exemptions for marital and charitable transfers), and others simply charge an amount equal to the state estate tax credit under federal law. The effect of the latter has been to simply shift money from the federal to the state government—the same taxes would have been owed to the federal government if the state had not imposed its tax. Many states will have to revise their estate tax laws to continue to receive revenue from this source.

SELF-CHECK

1. What is the lifetime limit on tax-free gifts?
2. List three exceptions to the limit on gifts.
3. Describe the three steps used to calculate your taxable estate.

15.5 Reducing Taxes Through Trusts and Gifts

The larger your taxable estate, the greater the likelihood that your heirs or your spouse's heirs may be subject to estate taxation. There are two general ways to reduce the size of your taxable estate:

▲ You can move money or assets to legal vehicles called *trusts*.
▲ You can give away your assets, either as gifts before your death or through charitable bequests in your will.

In this section, we discuss these strategies in more detail.

15.5.1 When Are Trusts Useful?

A trust is a legal entity that holds and manages assets on behalf of someone else. The **grantor,** the person putting the assets in the trust, transfers the assets to the trust, which is managed by a trustee for the benefit of the beneficiary of the trust. Trustee services are commonly provided by banks, financial institutions, and law firms. Trusts are used for several purposes:

▲ To bypass probate, providing your heirs with immediate access to the property upon your death.

▲ To remove property from the taxable estate, thereby minimizing taxes owed.

▲ To ensure that the estate achieves certain purposes after the grantor's death, such as providing income to surviving dependents.

If this all sounds very technical, it's because it is. Trusts are fairly sophisticated legal arrangements, and will require the advice of an experienced estate-planning lawyer. He or she can give you advice on which type of trust will best meet your needs and can draft the appropriate legal documents. The trust that will best meet your needs depends on your objectives.

15.5.2 Revocable vs. Irrevocable Trusts

If your primary purpose in creating a trust is to reduce estate taxes, then you need to set up an **irrevocable trust,** which means that you can't change the terms of the trust once it is established. Irrevocable trusts bypass probate and are not subject to federal or state estate taxes. If, instead, you create a **revocable trust,** you retain the right to change the terms of the trust during your lifetime. The trust will still bypass probate but will be subject to any applicable state and federal estate taxes.

15.5.3 Living vs. Testamentary Trusts

You can set up a trust that takes effect now or one that will not exist until the occurrence of some future event, such as your death. A **living trust,** or *inter vivos* trust, is established while you are alive. In contrast, a **testamentary trust** is established through the terms of a will.

Common Types of Living Trusts

Although living trusts can be revocable or irrevocable, a fairly common practice is to set up a revocable living trust that becomes irrevocable upon your death or incompetence. You place your assets in the trust, but you can still use them, receive income from them, or sell them while you're alive. If you can no longer manage them, either because of death or incompetence, the trustee takes over. This type of arrangement does not reduce estate taxes, but it does bypass probate so that your assets are immediately transferred to your beneficiaries after your death.

Because it allows you to give directions to the trustee regarding distribution of the trust assets, a living trust is similar in effect to a will. In addition to the living trust, you may want a **pourover will,** a legal document simply stating that any of your assets which have not been specifically transferred to a trust by the time of your death are "poured over" into one or more trusts at that time.

If any of the following apply, you should consider establishing a revocable living trust:

▲ You own property in more than one state. By holding the property in a trust, you avoid the costs and aggravation of multiple probate proceedings.

▲ You want the terms of your will to be private. When a will is probated, it is a public record, whereas a trust document is not.

▲ You would like to receive income from your assets but do not want to manage them. A trustee can be given the responsibility of managing all your assets for your benefit during your lifetime.

▲ You are concerned about what would happen to your assets in the event that you become incompetent.

Two specific types of living trusts are life insurance trusts and qualified personal residence trusts:

▲ **Life insurance trusts:** You form an irrevocable life insurance trust to keep life insurance proceeds out of your estate. The insurance policy names the trust as beneficiary, and the trustee is given instructions on how to distribute the proceeds. This is useful for life insurance policies that name a beneficiary who is not the spouse of the deceased. For many heirs, the proceeds of a life insurance policy can be the single largest component of the total estate. Note that the payment of premiums is considered a gift for tax purposes under this arrangement, so the allowable annual tax-free gift limits ($12,000 per person per year in 2007) apply.

▲ **Qualified personal residence trusts:** A qualified personal residence trust removes one or more personal residences from your estate. If you retain the right to live in the residence, it will pass to the person designated in the trust without going through probate. However, your estate will still include the value of the residence for the purpose of paying estate taxes.

Common Types of Testamentary Trusts

Unlike a living trust, a testamentary trust is created by your will and goes into effect after your death. These trusts are commonly used to avoid estate taxes and to provide asset management for children or grandchildren who are too young or too irresponsible to manage the estate proceeds. The most important types of trust in this category are the standard family trust and the qualified terminable interest property (Q-TIP) trust:

▲ **Standard family trust:** The **standard family trust** goes by many names, including credit shelter trust, residuary trust, A-B trust, unified credit trust, and exemption equivalent trust. The purpose of this type of trust is to allow you to transfer your entire estate to your spouse and then to his or her heirs (e.g., your children) upon his or her death, without any estate taxes being paid. In the absence of such a trust, you could transfer everything to your spouse free of tax in your will, but your spouse's heirs might later owe taxes when the estate passes to them.

▲ **Q-TIP trust:** If you're concerned that your spouse will remarry and the assets will never reach your children, you can set up a Q-TIP trust. A **Q-TIP trust** is much like a standard family trust except that the grantor retains control over the ultimate beneficiaries of the estate. Instead of being transferred by your spouse's will, the trust automatically transfers to your children (or other designated beneficiary) upon your spouse's death.

15.5.4 Charitable Trusts

Trusts can be established for charitable institutions. Your will can transfer wealth to charities free of estate tax, so the purpose of this type of trust is not to avoid estate taxes but to allow a charity to benefit from your assets during your lifetime

---

FOR EXAMPLE

The Benefit of Q-TIP Trusts

Suppose that you and your spouse have an estate valued at $4 million. You die first, in 2006, and leave your half of the estate to your wife, tax free (due to the unlimited marital deduction). It's possible that your wife will live long enough to deplete the estate, but suppose instead that she dies a year after you, and the $4 million estate is still intact. The 2007 exemption amount under the Economic Growth and Tax Relief Reconciliation Act is $2 million, so your estate will be subject to estate taxes on the other $2 million (the maximum rate, 45 percent in 2007). If, instead, your will had designated a Q-TIP trust to receive your $2 million estate, to be used by your wife during her lifetime, with the rest going to your children when she died, then no estate tax would be due upon her death because the trust assets would not be included in your wife's estate. This simple strategy would save your heirs several hundred thousand dollars.

while allowing you to retain either the use of or the income from an asset and to take a tax deduction for the donation.

A charitable remainder trust allows you to give away an asset but retain the cash flow generated by that asset during your lifetime. Upon your death, the charity is the beneficiary of the trust assets. In contrast, a charitable lead (or income) trust provides income to the charity during your lifetime or for a period of years, after which the property goes to your beneficiary.

15.5.5 Gifting Alternatives

In making gifts, it's important to consider the tax consequences. If charitable giving is one of your estate-planning objectives, it makes sense to gift in a way that will reduce your taxes too. Charitable gifts are not subject to estate or gift tax and, while you're alive, are deductible from your current income in calculating your federal income tax.

You can also reduce estate taxes by gifting your tax-deferred retirement plan assets to a charity. Because the contributions to these accounts were made with pretax dollars, the assets are subject to income tax when distributed (while you're alive or after you die). However, these taxes can be avoided if you specifically designate in your will that qualified retirement account assets go to a charity. These organizations are tax exempt, so you can effectively give the charity the full amount of your account, whereas anyone else you give it to receives only the net after taxes.

You can also give away some assets while you are alive. Gifts that you make to individuals are subject to the annual and lifetime limits discussed earlier in this chapter. Exceeding these limits may result in greater estate taxes being owed upon your death. However, because you can give the allowed annual amount to any number of people, individuals with sizable estates should seriously consider gifting during their lifetime. Not only will they have the immediate gratification of seeing the results of their gifts, whether to charity or individuals, they will also reduce the likelihood that their estates will be eroded by taxes when they die.

SELF-CHECK

1. List two ways to reduce your taxable estate.
2. Define **grantor, Q-TIP trust,** and **testamentary trust.**
3. Which type of trust can be changed during your lifetime?

SUMMARY

Develop an estate plan that will protect your family from undue financial hardship and excessive payment of taxes upon your death. Regardless of the size of your estate, you need a valid will to ensure that your assets are distributed according to your wishes and that your children are assigned a guardian of your choice. You can use trusts, gifts, and charitable contributions to minimize estate taxes. Estate taxes are now being phased out, their future is uncertain.

KEY TERMS

Beneficiaries	The individuals or entities receiving a distribution under the terms of a will.
Capacity	The mental competence to make a will, including understanding the nature and content of the document and not acting under threat or coercion from anyone.
Codicil	A legal amendment to a will.
Community property	A property law in some states by which any property acquired during a marriage is considered to be jointly owned by both spouses.
Durable power of attorney	A legal document in which a person designates another to make decisions on his or her behalf if the person is incapacitated.
Escheat	The legal process by which the state government acquires the estate of a person who dies without a will and has no living relatives.
Estate	A person's net worth at death.
Estate planning	The development of a plan for what will happen to your wealth and dependents when you die.
Executor/executrix	A person designated to carry out the provisions of a will.
Grantor	A person or an entity who legally passes ownership to another person or entity.
Heir	A person or an entity designated to receive something from your estate after your death.
Intestate	Without a valid will.
Irrevocable trust	A trust that the grantor cannot revoke. An irrevocable trust is not subject to probate or estate taxes.

Joint tenancy with right of survivorship	A form of property ownership in which, after the death of one owner, the property passes to the surviving owner without going through probate.
Letter of last instruction	A nonbinding document that provides helpful information to survivors after the writer's death.
Living trust	A trust established during the grantor's lifetime.
Living will	A legal document that specifies a person's preferences as to medical care in the event that he or she becomes unable to make decisions due to illness or disability.
Pourover will	A will that leaves a person's remaining assets to a trust.
Probate	The legal process of settling an estate.
Qualified terminable interest property (Q-TIP) trust	A trust for married couples in which the grantor retains control over the ultimate beneficiaries of the estate.
Revocable trust	A trust whose terms the grantor can change during his or her lifetime. A revocable trust bypasses probate but is still subject to estate taxes.
Standard family trust	A trust for married couples that is designed to avoid estate taxes on the estate of the surviving spouse.
Tenancy in common	A type of ownership in which each person owns his or her share independently and retains the right to transfer that share by sale or will.
Testamentary trust	A trust established by the terms of a will.
Testator	The writer of a will.
Trust	A legal entity that holds and manages assets on behalf of someone else.
Trustee	A person or an entity who manages assets on behalf of another.
Will	A legal document that transfers property upon the death of the property owner.

ASSESS YOUR UNDERSTANDING

Go to www.wiley.com/college/bajtelsmit to assess your knowledge of estate planning. *Measure your learning by comparing pre-test and post-test results.*

Summary Questions

1. The process of developing a plan for what will happen to your wealth and dependents when you die is known as probate planning. True or false?

2. The legal process of settling an estate is known as:
   (a) liquidation.
   (b) trust management.
   (c) a will.
   (d) probate.

3. If you die without a valid will, this is known as:
   (a) contested.
   (b) intestate.
   (c) escheat.
   (d) interred.

4. A legal document that designates another to make decisions on your behalf in the event of incapacity is:
   (a) a living will.
   (b) a trust.
   (c) a durable power of attorney.
   (d) escheating.

5. A person designated to carry out the provisions of a will is called:
   (a) a guardian.
   (b) an executor.
   (c) a trustee.
   (d) a beneficiary.

6. The major purpose of having witnesses sign a will is to make sure:
   (a) there is no case of forgery.
   (b) the testator (testatrix) is actually who he (she) claims to be.
   (c) the testator (testatrix) had the capacity to make the will.
   (d) the distribution of assets is done fairly.

7. Under 2007 tax law, you and your spouse can give up to $10,000 per person per year tax free, with no limits on the number of people you gift. True or false?

8. Which of the following is the formula for adjusted gross estate?
   (a) Gross estate – Marital and charitable bequests + Taxable gifts.
   (b) Gross estate – Funeral costs and marital and charitable bequests.
   (c) Gross estate – Funeral costs and settlement expenses.
   (d) Gross estate – Marital and charitable bequests.

9. If your primary purpose in setting up a trust is to reduce estate taxes, you should set up:
   (a) a revocable trust.
   (b) an irrevocable trust.
   (c) a living trust.
   (d) a testamentary trust.

10. A trust that is established by a will is called:
    (a) a revocable trust.
    (b) an irrevocable trust.
    (c) an *inter vivos* trust.
    (d) a testamentary trust.

Applying This Chapter

1. For a single college student, age 20, with negative net worth, identify estate-planning goals that would be appropriate. Do the same for a 30-year-old married couple with two children and $150,000 net worth.

2. Eva is about to take a trip away from her family, and she's concerned about the fact that she doesn't have a will. Because she left the task of writing one to the last minute, she doesn't have time to consult an attorney. So she decides to write up a simple will on her own and take care of the details when she returns from her trip. After writing her will and signing it, Eva gets two of her neighbors to witness it. Her will is as follows:

   I, Eva Malone, being of sound mind, declare this to be my last will. I give all that I have to my beloved husband, James Malone. I nominate my daughter, Katie Malone, to be the executrix of my estate, because she is the only one in the family with any sense.

   Eva Malone

   Do you think Eva's will is valid? Why or why not?

3. Your adjusted gross estate is worth $5 million. If you leave everything to your husband, will any estate taxes be payable at your death in 2007?

4. You'd like to leave all your wealth to your grandchildren when you die, but you want to be sure that you and your wife will have enough to live on in the meantime. What type of trust could you use to accomplish this?

5. You have a portfolio of bonds that generate substantial income annually. You've heard that your alma mater is having some current cash flow problems. How can you help out your alma mater but still leave all your assets to your children when you die? Does this strategy offer any current tax advantages to you?

6. Which estate planning tool would you use to ensure that your daughter ends up with the family china (instead of your sister who lives closer and will likely clean out your belongings after you die)?

7. Which estate planning tool would you use to ensure that you aren't kept alive by artificial means when there's no chance of your recovery from a terminal illness?

8. Which estate planning tool would you use to provide for your children's college education after you die?

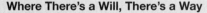
Where There's a Will, There's a Way

Mina is a successful entrepreneur. She started a small bakery when she graduated from college and has turned it into a multi-million-dollar business. Mina is divorced and has had sole custody of her daughter Naitra, age 10, since her ex-husband left them 6 years ago. He provides no financial support for Naitra. Mina has spent a great deal of time running her business—so much that she has sometimes neglected her financial plan. Recently, though, she consulted a financial planner, who was adamant that she immediately take care of a few very important elements of her financial plan. First and foremost, he wants her to make a will right away. Mina and her ex-husband had made wills many years ago, but they predated Naitra's birth. In her old will, Mina left all her wealth to her husband. Mina's current assets are as follows:

Equity in family home	$100,000
Business assets	$250,000
Retirement account	$200,000
Other investments	$50,000
Total net worth	$600,000

In the event of her death, Mina wants her sister Janna to be Naitra's guardian. Janna is aware of Mina's wish and has agreed to act in this capacity. Mina's brother Sanjay was named as the executor in her prior will and will probably be willing to continue in that role.

1. Does Mina need a will? What would happen if she died today, before drafting a new will?

2. What features should Mina incorporate in her will?

3. Does Mina need to include a trust in her will? Why or why not?

4. If Mina names Janna as Naitra's guardian but Janna dies before she does, who will end up being guardian?

5. What duties will Sanjay have to perform as executor of the estate?

ENDNOTES

Chapter 3

1. Internal Revenue Service (IRS), Topic 303, "Checklist of Common Errors When Preparing Your Tax Return," www.irs.gov/taxtopics/tc303.html. Washington, DC: IRS.

Chapter 6

1. U.S. Department of Education.
2. Pahl, Greg, *The Unofficial Guide to Beating Debt.* Hoboken, NJ: Wiley (2001), pp. 166–169.

Chapter 11

1. "Lots of Wiggle Room," *Tampa Tribune*, January 16, 2003.
2. "Worm Ranch in Sticky Situation," *Tampa Tribune*, April 15, 2003.
3. Monies, Paul, "States Sue Worm Buy Back Scam Companies," *The Oklahoman*, April 15, 2003.

Chapter 13

1. Gagnon, Jennifer, *What Is the Cost of Being Socially Responsible?* (senior honors thesis), Colorado State University, April 2004.

Chapter 14

1. Mitchell, Olivia S., Phillip B. Levine, and John W. Phillips, The Impact of Pay Inequality, Occupational Segregation, and Lifetime Work Experience on the Retirement Income of Women and Minorities, AARP Public Policy Institute #9910, September 1999.

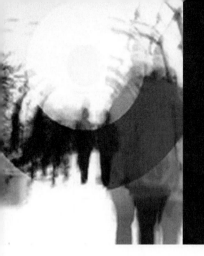

APPENDIX—PERSONAL FINANCE WORKSHEETS

WORKSHEET 1   Organizing Your Financial Records

Financial Record General Category	Specific Items Within Category	Filed	Lockbox	Safe Deposit
Auto	Insurance policy			
	Title information			
	Repairs/expenses			
	Auto loan/lease information			
Bank	Checking statements and records			
	Savings statements and records			
Credit	Records for each loan or credit account			
	Credit reports			
	Applications for credit			
Home	Mortgage documents and records			
	Homeowner's insurance			
	Receipts for repairs/capital improvements			
	Rental contracts			
Children	Report cards			
	School photos			
	School policies/procedures manual			
	Records of child-care expenses			
	Birth/adoption certificates			
Life/estate	Life insurance policies			
	Billing records			
	Copy of wills			
	Copy of estate plan			
Medical	Billing and insurance records			
	Prescription drug records			
	Health insurance policy			
	Health/immunization records			
Employee benefits	Periodic reports from retirement plans			
	Employer information			
	Other insurance and benefits			
Taxes	Tax statements from employer(s)			
	Tax statements from investments and loans			
	Tax returns			
	Receipts for next tax year			
Budget and bills	Current bills payable			
	Bill receipts			
	Budget records			
Investments	Records of purchases and sales			
	Account activity statements			

WORKSHEET 2   Personal Balance Sheet

Directions: 1. List the current values of your assets and your debts.
              2. Compute Net worth = Total assets − Total debts

              = _____

Assets		*Debts*	
Checking accounts	$ _____	Current bills	
Savings accounts	_____	1. _____	$ _____
Money market accounts	_____	2. _____	_____
U.S. savings bonds	_____	3. _____	_____
Cash value of life insurance	_____	**Total current bills**	_____
Other short-term investments	_____		
Total liquid assets	_____	Credit card balances (list)	
Cars	_____	1. _____	
Home furnishings	_____	2. _____	
Jewelry/art/collectibles	_____	3. _____	
Clothing/personal assets	_____		
Total personal property	_____	Alimony/child support owed	_____
Market value of investments (stocks, bonds, mutual funds)	_____	Taxes owed (above withholding)	_____
		Personal loans	_____
Employer retirement plan(s)	_____	Car loans	_____
Individual retirement account(s)	_____	**Total short-term debts**	_____
Other retirement savings	_____	Home mortgage balance	_____
College savings plan	_____	Home equity loans	_____
Other savings plans	_____	Other real estate loans	_____
Total investment assets	_____	Student loans	_____
Market value of home	_____	Other investment loans	_____
Market value of investment real estate	_____	Other liabilities/debts	_____
Total real property	_____	**Total long-term debts**	_____
Total assets	_____	**Total debts**	_____

WORKSHEET 3 Personal Cash Flow Statement

Directions: 1. List all your cash inflows and outflows.
               2. Compute Net cash flow = Total cash inflows − Total cash outflows

               = _____

	Cash Inflows			*Cash Outflows*	
	Monthly	January 1 to December 31		Monthly	January 1 to December 31
Salary/wage income (gross)	_____	_____	Income and payroll taxes	_____	_____
Interest/dividend Income	_____	_____	Groceries	_____	_____
Other income (self-employment)	_____	_____	Housing		
			Mortgage or rent	_____	_____
			Property tax	_____	_____
Rental income (after expenses)	_____	_____	Insurance	_____	_____
Cash from sale of assets	_____	_____	Maintenance/ repairs	_____	_____
Student loans	_____	_____	Utilities		
			Heating	_____	_____
			Electric	_____	_____
Scholarships	_____	_____	Water and sewer		
Other income	_____	_____	Cable/phone/ satellite	_____	_____
Gifts	_____	_____	Car loan payments	_____	_____
Total Cash Inflows	_____	_____	Car maintenance/ gas	_____	_____
			Credit card payments	_____	_____
			Other loan payments	_____	_____
			Other taxes	_____	_____
			Insurance		
			Life	_____	_____
			Health	_____	_____
			Auto	_____	_____
			Disability	_____	_____
			Other insurance	_____	_____
			Clothing	_____	_____
			Gifts	_____	_____
			Other consumer goods	_____	_____
			Child-care expenses	_____	_____

WORKSHEET 3   Personal Cash Flow Statement (*cont.*)

Sports-related expenses	_____	_____
Health club dues	_____	_____
Uninsured medical expenses	_____	_____
Education	_____	_____
Vacations and travel	_____	_____
Entertainment	_____	_____
Alimony/child support	_____	_____
Charitable contributions	_____	_____
Required pension contributions	_____	_____
Magazine subscriptions/books	_____	_____
Other payments/ expenses	_____	_____
Total cash outflows	═══════	═══════

WORKSHEET 4   Spending Log

<u>Directions:</u>   Copy this worksheet and use it to keep careful track of all your expenditures for one or more weeks.

Monday		Tuesday		Wednesday	
Description	$	Description	$	Description	$

Thursday		Friday		Saturday/Sunday	
Description	$	Description	$	Description	$

WORKSHEET 5 Personal Financial Ratios

Directions: Use your personal financial statements to calculate your personal financial ratios. Record them on this worksheet, critically evaluate your current financial situation, identify areas to work on, and reevaluate periodically to track your progress.

Personal Financial Criteria	__/__/__	__/__/__	__/__/__
Net worth			
Net cash flow			
Liquidity ratio $= \dfrac{\text{Liquid assets}}{\text{Monthly expenses}}$			
Debt ratio $= \dfrac{\text{Total debt}}{\text{Total assets}}$			
Debt payment ratio $= \dfrac{\text{Total monthly debt payments}}{\text{After-tax monthly income}}$			
Mortgage debt service ratio $= \dfrac{\text{Monthly mortgage debt service}}{\text{Gross monthly income}}$			
Savings ratio $= \dfrac{\text{Monthly savings}}{\text{After-tax income}}$			
Overall evaluation of current finances:			
Specific areas that I need to work on:			

WORKSHEET 6 Household Credit Summary

Type of Debt	Interest Rate (APR)	Annual Fees	Minimum Payment	Most Recent Finance Charge	Balance Still Owed
Credit cards	_____	_____	_____	_____	_____
	_____	_____	_____	_____	_____
	_____	_____	_____	_____	_____
	_____	_____	_____	_____	_____
Student loans	_____	_____	_____	_____	_____
	_____	_____	_____	_____	_____
	_____	_____	_____	_____	_____
Auto loans	_____	_____	_____	_____	_____
	_____	_____	_____	_____	_____
	_____	_____	_____	_____	_____
Other consumer loans	_____	_____	_____	_____	_____
	_____	_____	_____	_____	_____
	_____	_____	_____	_____	_____
Home equity loans	_____	_____	_____	_____	_____
	_____	_____	_____	_____	_____
	_____	_____	_____	_____	_____
Mortgage loans	_____	_____	_____	_____	_____
	_____	_____	_____	_____	_____
Totals				_____	_____

WORKSHEET 7   Assessing Your Creditworthiness Using the Five C's of Credit

<u>Directions:</u>
1. Complete a consumer credit application.
2. Using this information, rate yourself on each of the five c's of credit, using the following scale:
   4 = excellent; 3 = good; 2 = needs work; 1 = unacceptable.
3. Based on your assessment, identify goals for improving your creditworthiness.

	<u>Score</u>	<u>Notes:</u>
Capacity		
Wage, salary, and other income sufficient to make payments		
Affordable current monthly payment obligations	_____	
Capital		
Positive net worth, appropriate for life-cycle stage	_____	
Collateral		
Valuable assets in addition to income (checking, savings, investment accounts)		
Adequate collateral for loan (if applicable)	_____	
Character		
Previous experience with credit		
Past credit history indicates a good attitude toward repaying debts		
No history of bankruptcy		
Stable employment and residency	_____	
Conditions		
Job and employer security		
General economic conditions favorable	_____	

Plan for improving creditworthiness:

WORKSHEET 8   Automobile Costs Log Sheet

	Date	Lease/ Loan Payment	Fuel	Auto Insurance	Tolls and Parking	Repairs and Maintenance	Registration and License	Monthly Total
January								
February								
March								
April								
May								
June								

WORKSHEET 8   Automobile Costs Log Sheet (*cont.*)

	Date	Lease/ Loan Payment	Fuel	Auto Insurance	Tolls and Parking	Repairs and Maintenance	Registration and License	Monthly Total
July								
August								
September								
October								
November								
December								

WORKSHEET 9   Automobile Options Checklist

Before shopping for a car, evaluate your needs and wants.

	Must Have	Would Like
Automatic transmission	☐	☐
All-wheel drive	☐	☐
Dual front airbags	☐	☐
Side curtain airbags	☐	☐
Air conditioning	☐	☐
Antilock brakes	☐	☐
Power seats	☐	☐
Power windows and doors	☐	☐
Sunroof	☐	☐
Upgraded music system	☐	☐
Computer navigation system	☐	☐
Extra-sized gas tank	☐	☐
Split rear seat	☐	☐
Leather interior	☐	☐
Driver seat lumbar adjustment	☐	☐
Third row seats	☐	☐
Cruise control	☐	☐
Other _____	☐	☐
Other _____	☐	☐

WORKSHEET 10   Lease Versus Buy—Automobile

Cost of Leasing

Capitalized cost reduction and security deposit   _____

Foregone interest on capitalized cost
  reduction and security deposit   _____

Total lease payments (= monthly payment × _____ months)   _____

Expected end-of-lease charges   _____

Less return of security deposit   _____

Total cost of leasing   _____

Cost of Buying

Down payment   _____

Foregone interest on down payment   _____

Total loan payments (= monthly payment × _____ months)   _____

Less expected end-of-loan value   _____

Total cost of buying   _____

WORKSHEET 11   Lease Versus Buy—Housing

Cost of Renting	1 year	5 years
Total rent payments (= monthly × 12/year)		
Renter's insurance (= $_____/year)		
After-tax interest lost on security deposit		
(= ___ months rent @___%/year)		
Total cost of renting		

Cost of Buying	1 year	5 years
Total mortgage payments (= monthly principal and interest × 12/year)		
Property tax		
Homeowner's insurance		
Private mortgage insurance (if < 20% down = 1/2% of mortgage/year)		
Repair and maintenance expenses		
Down payment		
Closing costs		
Lost after-tax interest on down payment and closing costs (@___%/year)		
Subtotal: costs		
Less savings from repaying principal		
Less appreciation of home (@___%/year)		
Less tax savings from interest deduction		
Less tax savings from property tax deduction		
Less tax savings from points deduction		
Subtotal: savings		
Total cost of buying = (costs − savings)		

WORKSHEET 12   Calculating Affordable Home Price

STEP 1.

Monthly amount you can allocate to total housing costs   _____

STEP 2.

a. Expected cost of property taxes   _____

b. Expected cost of homeowner's insurance   _____

c. Expected cost of repairs and maintenance   _____

d. Expected cost of association dues   _____

e. Total nonfinancing housing costs (= a + b + c + d)   _____

Total available for financing costs (principal and interest)
(= Step 1 − 2e)   _____

STEP 3.

a. Mortgage factor$_{,i,n}$ (Exhibit A-6, 6%, 360 months)   _____

b. Total available for financing costs (from Step 2)   _____

c. Maximum affordable mortgage amount (= 3a × 3b)   _____

STEP 4.

a. Down payment available   _____

b. Gifts from parents or others   _____

c. Expected closing costs   _____

d. Maximum house you can afford (= 3c + 4a + 4b − 4c)   _____

WORKSHEET 13   Evaluating Mutual Fund Alternatives

Directions:

Identify an investment objective for which mutual fund investments would be appropriate. Based on your objectives, time horizon, and risk tolerance, identify the fund classification(s) you wish to consider. Evaluate alternative funds by completing this worksheet.

1. Investment Objective   _____

2. Appropriate type of fund   _____

	Mutual Fund Alternatives		
	A	**B**	**C**
Company name	_____	_____	_____
Fund objective	_____	_____	_____
Price per share	_____	_____	_____
Net asset value	_____	_____	_____
Minimum initial purchase	_____	_____	_____
Minimum additional purchase	_____	_____	_____
Past performance			
1-year	_____	_____	_____
3-year	_____	_____	_____
5-year	_____	_____	_____
Expenses			
Front-end load	_____	_____	_____
Back-end load	_____	_____	_____
Expense ratio	_____	_____	_____
Fund manager tenure	_____	_____	_____
Services			
Auto deduction	_____	_____	_____
Auto reinvestment	_____	_____	_____
Transfer between funds	_____	_____	_____
IRAs	_____	_____	_____
Online access	_____	_____	_____
Ratings			
Agency_____	_____	_____	_____
Agency_____	_____	_____	_____

WORKSHEET 14 Mutual Fund Tracker

	Mutual Fund 1	Mutual Fund 2	Mutual Fund 3	Mutual Fund 4	Mutual Fund 5	Mutual Fund 6	Total Portfolio
Fund name							
Fund family							
Investment objectives							
Portfolio composition							
Industry or sector							
Net asset value							
Price per share							
Number purchased							
Front-end load paid							
Total initial investment							

Date				Market or Net Asset Values			

WORKSHEET 15 Retirement Goals

Directions:

For each of the following retirement goals, indicate its importance to you by checking the appropriate box.

Retirement Goal	Very Important	Somewhat Important	Not At All Important
Economic security			
Maintain standard of living	☐	☐	☐
Improve standard of living	☐	☐	☐
Financial independence	☐	☐	☐
Afford to keep home	☐	☐	☐
Family			
Bequests to heirs	☐	☐	☐
College costs	☐	☐	☐
Support children or parents	☐	☐	☐
Continue family business	☐	☐	☐
Medical			
Cover health-care costs	☐	☐	☐
Extras			
Better/more vacations	☐	☐	☐
Increased hobby costs	☐	☐	☐
Contributions to charity	☐	☐	☐
Other			
_____			
_____			

WORKSHEET 16 Retirement Planning

STEP 1. Estimate before-tax income needs.

    a. Enter current household expenses. _____

    b. Adjust for changes in expenses in retirement.

        Possible reductions: Employment expenses _____ _____

                              Retirement savings _____ _____

                              Housing expenses _____ _____

                Total reductions _____

        Possible increases: Health care/insurance _____

                              Leisure activities _____

                              Gifts/donations _____

                Total increases _____

    c. Adjusted expenses in current dollars (1a − 1b + 1c) _____

    d. Adjust for inflation to future dollars
(i = expected inflation; n = years to retirement).
Aftertax income needs = Adjusted expenses in current dollars $\times (1+i)^n$ = _____

    e. Calculate before-tax total income needs.
        $ Before tax = $ After-tax/(1 − average tax rate) = _____

STEP 2. Estimate annual retirement income from defined benefit retirement plan(s).
Use most recent statement from your pension sponsor or estimate based on known benefit formula.

        Plan 1_____

        Plan 2_____

Total income from defined benefit plans = _____

STEP 3. Estimate annual retirement income from Social Security.
Use calculator at www.ssa.gov to estimate in future dollars. = _____

STEP 4. Calculate retirement income shortfall. (1e − 2 − 3) = _____

STEP 5. Estimate total retirement wealth needed.

    a. Retirement wealth factor: _____
(from Figure 14-2, assuming ___ years in retirement and ___ % average investment return)

    b. Retirement income shortfall × Retirement wealth factor = _____

STEP 6. Estimate retirement savings goal

    a. Value of current retirement savings accounts = _____

    b. Future value of current accounts (= 6a $\times FVIF_{i,n}$) = _____

    c. Retirement savings goal (5b−6b) = _____

STEP 7. Estimate monthly savings required to meet savings goal. = _____
(Use time value of money calculation for payment.)

WORKSHEET 17 Life Insurance Needs Analysis

	Yourself	Your Spouse

A. Costs at Death

1. Uninsured medical expenses (deductible and copay) _____ _____
2. Funeral expense (average $10,000, but less for cremation) _____ _____
3. Settlement of estate (estimate 4% of assets) _____ _____
4. State inheritance taxes (if any) _____ _____
5. Counseling costs for adjustment to loss ══════ ══════

Total costs at death $1 + 2 + 3 + 4 + 5$ _____ _____

B. Lump Sums
6. Outstanding debts
   a. Mortgage _____ _____
   b. Car loan(s) _____ _____
   c. Credit cards and other loans _____ _____
   d. Total outstanding debt to repay $6a + 6b + 6c$ _____ _____
7. Education costs for children or spouse (see Chapter 15) _____ _____
8. Spouse retirement fund _____ _____
9. Household emergency fund
   Monthly household expenses $\times$ 3 _____ _____

Total lump sum needs $6d + 7 + 8 + 9$ ══════ ══════

C. Cost of Household Maintenance
10. Deceased annual after-tax income _____ _____
11. Annual cost of lost support services
    (child/eldercare, housekeeping) _____ _____
12. Reduction in family expenses
    due to death (estimated 20–25%) _____ _____
13. Annual Social Security survivor benefits _____ _____
14. Net income shortfall $10 + 11 - 12 - 13$ _____ _____

Total household maintenance fund needs
    14 x Number of years to replace _____ years ══════ ══════

15. **Total fund needed (sum double-underlined values)** ══════ ══════

D. Available Resources to Meet Needs
16. Total savings and investments _____ _____
17. Group life insurance _____ _____
18. Social Security lump sum benefit _____ _____
19. **Total resources to meet needs** $16 + 17 + 18$ ══════ ══════

Total life insurance needs $15 - 19$ _____ _____

WORKSHEET 18 Estate Tax Calculation

1. Calculate gross estate:
   Net worth   _____
   Less assets excluded because of
   type of ownership or beneficiary
   designation:
   Assets transferred through family limited partnerships   _____
   Life insurance held in irrevocable trusts   _____
   Other irrevocable trust assets   _____
   Gross estate   _____

2. Calculate adjusted gross estate:
   Funeral expenses   _____
   Executor's fee   _____
   Legal fees   _____
   Court fees   _____
   Estate administration fees   _____
   Total estate expenses   _____
   Adjusted gross estate = Gross estate − Estate expenses   _____

3. Calculate taxable estate:
   Amount to spouse   _____
   Amount to charity   _____
   Total unlimited deductions   _____
   Taxable estate = Adjusted gross estate − Unlimited deductions   _____

4. Unified exemption ($1.5 million in 2005)   _____
   Amount subject to tax = Taxable estate − Exemption   _____

WORKSHEET 19 Comparison Shopping for Auto Insurance

In comparison shopping for property and liability insurance, it's important to provide the same information to each potential insurer so that your quotes will be comparable.

Automobile
Vehicle characteristics (year, make, model)_____
Insured characteristics (age, sex, driving record, full-time or occasional driver)

_____

Potential discounts (good student, driver education)_____

Company Name			

Agent's name
  Address
  Phone			

Policy term (6 or 12 months)			
Total premium			

Liability coverage
  Per person
  Per accident
  Property			

Deductibles
  Collision
  Comprehensive			

Medical payments Per person			

Uninsured motorist
  Per person
  Per accident			

Other coverage			
Other factors to consider (e.g., multiple policy discounts, insurer reputation)			

GLOSSARY

Accelerated benefits An option under which a terminally ill policyholder can receive a portion of his or her life insurance proceeds before death.

Acceleration clause A loan term that requires immediate repayment of the total amount due on an installment loan that is in default.

Accidental death benefit A life insurance contract provision through which the benefit is doubled for accidental death.

Active investor An investor who actively buys and sells securities, attempting to make short-run gains.

Adjustable-rate mortgage (ARM) Mortgage loan with an interest rate that, by contract, varies over time with market conditions.

Adjusted expense method A method for estimating after-tax retirement income needs in current dollars by adjusting current expenses for changes expected in retirement.

Adjusted gross income (AGI) Earned income and unearned income minus certain allowed adjustments to income.

Agent A person who is acting on behalf of another through a contractual agreement.

Alternative minimum tax (AMT) A federal income tax designed to ensure that people who receive certain tax breaks pay their fair share of taxes.

Annual percentage rate (APR) The standardized annual cost of credit, including all mandatory fees paid by the borrower, expressed as a percentage rate.

Annual percentage yield (APY)   The amount of interest paid each year, given as a percentage of the investment. The APY makes it possible to compare interest rates across accounts that have different compounding periods.

Annuity for a specific term   An annuity that provides a stream of equal payments for a specific period of time.

Ask price   The stock price requested by a potential seller.

Assessment ratio   The proportion of market value used to calculate assessed value of real estate on which the property tax rate will be assessed.

Asset allocation   The process of deciding what proportion of a portfolio to invest in each asset class.

Asset classes   Broad groups of investments that have certain characteristics in common.

Assets   Everything you own, including liquid assets, real and personal property, and investments.

Assumption of risk   A defense to a claim of negligence that is available when the injured party voluntarily took on the risk.

Attitudes   Opinions and psychological differences between people that affect their decisions.

Average daily balance   The average of the balances owed on each day of the billing cycle.

Average indexed monthly earnings (AIME)   The average of a person's 35 highest years of monthly earnings, adjusted for inflation, used in computing that individual's Social Security benefit.

Average tax rate   The proportion of a taxpayer's total taxable income that goes to paying taxes.

Back-end load   A charge that mutual fund investors pay at the time they sell shares.

Balanced fund   A mutual fund invested in both stocks and bonds.

Bank credit card   A credit card issued by a depository institution.

Bankruptcy   The legal right to ask a court of law for relief of certain debts and obligations.

Basic health care insurance   Health insurance that covers hospital, surgical, and physician expenses.

Beneficiaries   The individuals or entities receiving a distribution under the terms of a will.

Beta   A measure of the market, or nondiversifiable, risk of a stock.

Bid price   The stock price offered by a potential buyer.

Billing date   The last day of a billing cycle. Credit card transactions made after the billing date appear on the next month's bill.

Blue chip stock   A stock that is issued by a large, stable, mature company.

Bond   1. An investment representing a loan to a governmental or business entity, which usually pays a fixed interest rate for a fixed period of time. 2. Type of financial security that represents your long-term loan of money to a company or government entity.

Brokerage firm   A nondepository financial institution that helps its customers buy and sell financial securities.

Buy-and-hold   A passive investment strategy in which the investor identifies his or her target asset allocation and then selects appropriate securities to hold for the long run.

Buyer broker   A real estate broker who works exclusively for the buyer and owes no legal duty to the seller.

Buying on margin   Using borrowed funds from a broker to make a trade.

Cafeteria plan   An employee benefit plan in which the employer provides a sum of money and allows employees to choose the benefits they want from a menu.

Capacity   The mental competence to make a will, including understanding the nature and content of the document and not acting under threat or coercion from anyone.

Capital gain   Profit on the sale of an investment. This profit is subject to a lower tax rate if the investment has been held for more than one year.

Capital gains yield   The component of a stock investor's total return that is equal to the ratio of the annual change in price to the market price of a stock.

Cash advance   A cash loan from a credit card account.

Cash management   Management of cash payments and liquid investments.

Cash reserve   Liquid assets held to meet emergency cash needs.

Cash value   The value of the investment component of a permanent life insurance policy.

Certificate of deposit (CD)   An account that pays a fixed rate of interest on funds left on deposit for a stated period of time.

Chapter 7 bankruptcy   Requires the liquidation, or sale, of most of the debtor's assets.

Chapter 13 bankruptcy   A method of protecting a debtor from creditors' claims while that person develops and implements a plan to repay his or her debts.

Churning   Excessive trading in a discretionary account.

Claims adjuster   A person designated by an insurer to assess whether a loss is covered by the insured's policy and to assign a dollar value to the loss.

Close price   The last price at which a stock sold at the close of the previous business day.

Closed-end credit   Loans for a specific purpose paid back in a specified period of time, usually with monthly payments.

Closed-end fund   An investment company that has a fixed number of shares, which are traded in the secondary market.

Closing   A meeting to finalize a home purchase.

Codicil   A legal amendment to a will.

Coinsurance   An arrangement providing for the sharing of medical costs by the insured and the insurer.

Collateral   Valuable assets or real property that can be taken by a lender in the event of loan default.

Collision coverage   Insurance that covers loss or damage to the insured's vehicle caused by an automobile accident.

Commercial bank   A depository institution that offers a wide variety of cash management services to business and individual customers.

Commission   A percentage of the sales price paid to the brokers and agents who assist in the sale of a home.

Commodities   Contracts to buy or sell raw materials or agricultural products in the future.

Community property   A property law in some states by which any property acquired during a marriage is considered to be jointly owned by both spouses.

Compounding   The frequency with which interest is calculated and added to an account.

Comprehensive physical damage coverage   Insurance that covers loss or damage to the insured's vehicle caused by a peril other than an automobile accident.

Compulsory automobile insurance laws   State laws that require proof of liability insurance as a prerequisite to auto registration.

Consumer choice plan   A health plan that includes financial incentives for preventive care and cost reduction.

Consumer credit   Credit used for personal needs other than home purchases.

Consumer finance company   A nondepository institution that makes loans to risky consumers.

Consumer price index (CPI)   A U.S. government index that tracks prices of a representative basket of goods and services.

Contributory negligence   A defense to a claim of negligence that is available when the injured party contributed to his or her own injury.

Contributory plan   An employee benefit plan for which the employee pays some or all of the costs.

Convenience check   A check supplied by a credit card lender for the purpose of making a cash advance.

Conventional mortgage   A fixed-rate, fixed term, fixed-payment mortgage loan.

Convertible   A type of term life insurance policy that allows the insured person to convert a term insurance policy to a permanent life insurance policy without additional proof of insurability.

Copay   Dollar amount of medical costs paid by the insured under a coinsurance provision, after meeting the annual deductible.

Corporation   A form of business organization that exists as a legal entity separate from its owners, that has limited liability for corporate losses.

Cosigner   A person who agrees to take responsibility for repayment of a loan if the primary borrower defaults.

Coupon payment   The annual dollar interest payment on a bond, equal to the coupon rate multiplied by the face value, usually paid to investors in two equal installments.

Credit   An arrangement to receive cash, goods, or services now and pay later.

Credit bureau   A company that collects credit information on individuals and provides reports to interested lenders.

Credit limit   The preapproved maximum amount of borrowing for an open-end credit account. Also known as a credit line.

Credit union   A nonprofit depository institution that is owned by its depositors.

Current-assumption whole life insurance   A type of permanent life insurance with premiums that depend on the insurer's actual mortality, expense, and investment experience.

Cyclical stock   A stock exhibiting above-average sensitivity to the business cycle.

Day trader   An active investor who buys and sells many times during the day in an attempt to make quick profits.

Dealer's invoice price   The price that a dealer pays to purchase a new vehicle from a manufacturer.

Debentures   Unsecured bonds.

Debt investor   An investor who lends money to an individual, a government entity, a financial institution, or another business.

Debt payment ratio   A financial ratio that measures the percentage of disposable income required to make debt payments.

Debt ratio   Total debt divided by total assets.

Debts   Everything you owe to others, including unpaid bills, credit card balances, car loans, student loans, and mortgages. Also known as liabilities.

Decreasing term life insurance   A type of term life insurance that features a level premium and decreasing protection.

Deductible   The amount of a loss that must be paid by an insured before the insurance company will pay any insurance benefit.

Default   Failure to meet the terms of a loan agreement, such as when payments are not made in a timely fashion.

Default risk   The risk of not receiving promised cash flows from an investment.

Defensive stock   Stock that is relatively insensitive to the business cycle.

Demand deposit accounts   Deposit accounts, such as checking accounts, from which money can be withdrawn with little or no notice to the financial institution.

Dependent   A member of a household who receives at least half of his or her support from the head of the household.

Depository institutions   Financial institutions that obtain funds from customer deposits.

Depreciation   The decline in value of an asset over time due to wear and tear, obsolescence, and competitive factors.

Derivative securities   Investments that derive their value from some underlying security's changes in price over time.

Direct investment program   A program offered by a publicly traded company to allow investors to automatically purchase shares of the company's stock on a regular basis without incurring brokerage fees.

Disability income insurance   Insurance that replaces the policyholder's lost income during a period of disability.

Discount bonds   Bonds that sell for less than their face value.

Discount points   Interest paid up front to a lender in return for a reduction in annual rate on a mortgage.

Diversification   An investment strategy that involves spreading money across a range of investments in order to reduce the overall risk of the portfolio.

Dividend reinvestment plan (DRIP)   Program that allows investors to receive dividends in the form of additional shares of stock instead of cash.

Dividend yield   The component of a stock investor's total return that is equal to the ratio of annual dividends to the market price of a stock.

Dividends   Periodic distributions of profits to equity investors.

Dollar cost averaging   An investment strategy in which you invest equal dollar amounts at regular intervals, regardless of fluctuations in price.

Due date   The date by which payment must be received by the lender if the account holder is to avoid late penalties and, in some cases, interest on new transactions.

Durable power of attorney   A legal document in which a person designates another to make decisions on his or her behalf if the person is incapacitated.

Earned income   Income from salaries, wages, tips, bonuses, commissions, and other sources.

Earnings per share (EPS)   A measure of company profitability equal to annual earnings divided by the number of shares outstanding.

Economic cycle   A pattern of ups and downs experienced by the U.S. economy.

Electronic cash   Money in digitized format.

Equity investor   An investor who has an ownership interest in a business.

Escheat   The legal process by which the state government acquires the estate of a person who dies without a will and has no living relatives.

Escrow account   A reserve account held by a mortgage lender in which it collects a monthly prepayment of property taxes and insurance and then pays those bills as they come due.

Estate   A person's net worth at death.

Estate planning   The development of a plan for what will happen to your wealth and dependents when you die.

Exchange-traded fund (ETF)   An investment company that has professionally, but not actively, managed assets, often intended to track a market index, and shares that trade in the secondary market.

Exclusion   A potential loss that is expressly excluded from coverage by an insurance policy.

Exclusive agent   An insurance agent who sells products for only one insurer. Also called a captive agent.

Exclusive provider organization (EPO)   Health-care plan that only covers medical costs from participating providers.

Executor/executrix   A person designated to carry out the provisions of a will.

Exemption   The dollar amount per household member that is subtracted from adjusted gross income in calculating taxable income.

Expansion   Periods characterized by increased business investment and employment opportunities.

Expense ratio   The ratio of annual mutual fund expense charges to fund assets.

Face amount   The value of assets insured under a policy.

Face value   1. The dollar value of protection payable to beneficiaries under the terms of a life insurance policy.

2. The dollar amount the bondholder will receive at the bond's maturity date.

Federal Deposit Insurance Corporation (FDIC)   A government-sponsored agency that insures customer accounts in banks and savings institutions.

Federal funds rate   The rate banks charge each other for short-term loans.

Federal Reserve Bank   The central bank that controls the money supply in the United States.

Fee-for-service plan   A health insurance plan that reimburses the insured for medical expenses incurred or pays the provider directly.

FICA tax   A payroll tax levied on earned income by the U.S. government to fund Social Security and Medicare. Stands for Federal Insurance Contributions Act tax.

Filing status   The household type, for tax filing purposes.

Finance charge   The dollar amount of periodic interest charged by a lender on a credit account.

Financial needs method   A method for estimating life insurance needs based on expected capital and income replacement needs.

Financial responsibility laws   State laws that require proof of ability to cover the cost of injury to persons or property caused by an auto accident.

Fixed expenses   Expenses that are a constant dollar amount each period.

Fixed-income investment   A debt investment that provides a fixed interest payment to the investor over the term of the investment.

Fixed-rate loan   A loan for which the rate of interest remains the same throughout the term of the loan.

Flexible spending account (FSA)   An account maintained by an employer in which the pretax earnings of an employee are set aside and can be used for reimbursement of qualified medical and child-care expenses.

Front-end load   A commission or sales charge paid by mutual fund investors at the time they purchase shares.

Fund family   An arrangement in which a single company operates several separately managed mutual funds with different investment objectives.

Futures contract   A contract to buy or sell financial securities in the future.

Global fund   A mutual fund that invests in U.S. and foreign securities.

Good faith estimate   An estimate of loan costs provided by the lender to the borrower.

Grace period   The time before interest begins to accrue on new transactions.

Grantor   A person or an entity who legally passes ownership to another person or entity.

Gross income   Income from all sources, including earned income, investment income, alimony, unemployment compensation, and retirement benefits.

Gross taxable income   Income from all sources, less allowed exclusions.

Group insurance   Insurance purchased by an employer for the benefit of employees.

Group underwriting   Underwriting in which the premium is based on the risk of the group as a whole rather than on characteristics of individual group members.

Growth fund   A mutual fund that focuses on capital appreciation.

Growth stock   Stock that compensates investors primarily through increases in value of the shares over time.

Guaranteed renewability   A feature of term life insurance that gives the insured person the right to renew the policy without additional proof of insurability.

Health maintenance organization (HMO)   A managed-care plan that attempts to control health care costs by encouraging preventive care and limiting participants to providers with whom the plan has contracted.

Health savings account (HSA)   An investment account in which an employer deposits pretax dollars allocated for payment of an employee's health-related expenses.

Heir   A person or an entity designated to receive something from your estate after your death.

Home equity   The market value of a home minus the remaining mortgage balance.

Homeowner's insurance   Insurance purchased by a homeowner to cover property and liability losses associated with a home.

Income fund   A mutual fund that focuses on providing stable dividend and interest income.

Income stock   Stock that compensates investors primarily through the regular payment of dividends.

Income-multiple method   A method for estimating life insurance needs as a multiple of income.

Incontestable clause   An insurance contract clause which states that the insurer cannot contest a claim for misrepresentation after a policy has been in force for a specified period of time.

Indenture   A legal document that details the rights and obligations of the bondholders and bond issuer.

Independent agent   An insurance agent who sells products for multiple insurers.

Individual retirement account (IRA)   A retirement account that allows the holder to subtract current contributions from taxable income and to defer income tax until withdrawal at retirement.

Inflation   The change in general price levels over time.

Inflation risk   The risk that inflation will erode the purchasing power of investment returns.

Initial public offering (IPO)   A company's first stock offering to the public.

Insolvency   The inability to pay debts as they come due.

Installment loan   A loan that requires repayment in equal periodic installments that include both interest and principal.

Interest rate   A cost of money, expressed as a percentage.

Interest rate caps   Caps on annual and lifetime increases in an adjustable rate mortgage's interest rate.

Interest-rate risk   The risk of price changes due to changes in interest rates.

Internal Revenue Code   A compilation of all statutes, regulations, and court decisions relating to U.S. income tax.

Internal Revenue Service (IRS)   The U.S. government agency that is responsible for collecting federal income taxes and enforcing tax laws and regulations.

International fund   A mutual fund that invests primarily in securities from countries other than the United States.

Intestate   Without a valid will.

Investment company   A financial intermediary that invests its funds in securities or other assets.

Investment-grade bonds   Medium- and high-grade bonds with low risk of default on interest or principal.

Irrevocable trust   A trust that the grantor cannot revoke. An irrevocable trust is not subject to probate or estate taxes.

IRS e-file   A system that enables the electronic filing of federal tax returns.

Itemized deductions   An alternative to the standard deduction in which the taxpayer reports and deducts actual expenses in certain allowed categories to arrive at taxable income.

Joint and survivor annuity   An annuity that provides a stream of equal payments until the death of the second spouse.

Joint tenancy with right of survivorship   A form of property ownership in which, after the death of one owner, the property passes to the surviving owner without going through probate.

Junk bonds   Bonds with a high risk of default.

Late payment penalty   A penalty fee charged to an account for making a payment after the due date.

Law of large numbers   A principle which holds that, for large pools of identical risks, the risk that actual losses per person will be greater than predicted decreases as the size of the pool increases.

Lease   A rental agreement between a lessor (i.e., the owner of a car or real property) and a lessee, in which the lessee agrees to pay money for the right to use the lessor's property for the period of the contract.

Lemon laws   State laws that protect consumers against chronically defective vehicles.

Lessee   A person who pays money for the privilege of using someone else's vehicle or real property for a period of time.

Lessor   An owner of an asset, commonly a vehicle or real property, who charges money for the use of that asset for a period of time.

Letter of last instruction   A nonbinding document that provides helpful information to survivors after the writer's death.

Lien   Public notice of a right to real property.

Life insurance company   A nondepository financial institution that obtains funds from premiums paid for life insurance, invests in stocks and bonds, and makes mortgage loans.

Life-cycle fund   A mutual fund that designs its asset allocation to meet the needs of individuals in a particular life stage.

Limit order   A request to buy stock at any price up to a specified maximum or to sell stock at any price above a specified minimum.

Limited liability   A statutory right of corporate shareholders that limits their potential losses to the value of the shares they hold.

Limited-payment life insurance   Whole life insurance that is paid up after a specified period.

Liquid assets   Cash and near-cash assets that can be easily converted to cash without loss of value.

Liquidity ratio   A financial ratio that measures the ability to pay household expenses out of liquid assets in the absence of regular income.

Liquidity risk   The risk of not being able to convert an asset to cash without losing value.

Listed security   A security that is approved to be bought or sold on a particular exchange.

Living trust   A trust established during the grantor's lifetime.

Living will   A legal document that specifies a person's preferences as to medical care in the event that he or she becomes unable to make decisions due to illness or disability.

Lock-in   Agreement with a lender that guarantees a particular mortgage interest rate at closing.

Major medical insurance   Insurance that covers the costs of most medical services prescribed by a doctor, subject to deductibles and coinsurance.

Managed-care plan   A health insurance plan that attempts to reduce costs through contractual arrangements with providers and financial incentives for low-cost alternatives.

Margin call   A request from a brokerage firm that the holder of a margin account add money to the account to maintain the required minimum.

Marginal reasoning   A strategy that takes into account the change in outcome or additional benefit resulting from a decision.

Marginal tax effect   The change in taxes owed as a result of a financial decision.

Marginal tax rate   Tax rate imposed on a taxpayer's next dollar of income.

Market capitalization   The total outstanding value of a company's stock at current market prices. It is calculated as the current stock price multiplied by the number of shares outstanding.

Market efficiency   A theory which suggests that prices immediately adjust to reflect all publicly available information.

Market order   An offer to buy stock at the market price.

Market risk   The risk of portfolio fluctuations caused by common market factors.

Market value   The price that something can be sold for today.

Maturity date   For a CD, the date on which the depositor can withdraw the invested amount and receive the stated interest.

Maximum limit   Lifetime maximum paid by the insurer to an insured person.

Medicaid   State-run program providing health-care coverage for the poor.

Medicare   Federal health insurance program for people age 65 and over.

Medigap policies   Insurance policies designed to pay deductibles and other costs that are not covered by Medicare.

Minimum payment   The minimum amount that must be paid by the due date to maintain good credit standing and avoid late payment penalties.

Money market account   A savings account which pays interest that fluctuates with market rates on money market securities.

Money market mutual fund   A mutual fund that holds a portfolio of short-term, low-risk securities issued by the federal government, its agencies, and large corporations and pays investors a rate of return that fluctuates with the interest earned on the portfolio.

Mortgage   A long-term amortized loan that is secured by real property.

Mortgage debt service   The total dollar amount of monthly mortgage principal, interest, property taxes, and homeowner's insurance.

Mortgage debt service ratio   The ratio of mortgage debt service to gross income.

Municipal bond   A long-term debt security issued by a state or local government entity.

Mutual fund   1. An open-end investment company that sells shares to investors and uses its investors' funds to purchase stocks, bonds, or other financial assets.

2. A collection of investments, managed by a professional investment firm, in which investors can buy shares.

Mutual fund company   A nondepository financial institution that sells shares to investors and invests the money in financial assets.

Mutual savings institution   A savings institution that is owned by its depositors.

NASDAQ   An electronic reporting system for frequently traded over-the-counter stocks. Stands for National Association of Securities Dealers Automated Quotation System.

Needs analysis   The process of determining the potential financial impact of a person's death on others.

Negative amortization   An addition to a loan balance that occurs when the monthly payment is insufficient to cover the monthly interest cost.

Negligence   A failure to fulfill a legal duty to another that causes injury to that person or to his or her property.

Negotiated order of withdrawal (NOW) account   A type of checking account that pays interest.

Net asset value   The market value of a mutual fund's assets less the market value of its liabilities, per share.

Net worth   The amount of wealth you would have left after paying all your outstanding debts.

No-fault automobile insurance   A type of automobile insurance system in which each insured driver in an accident collects his or her claim from his or her own insurer, regardless of who is at fault.

No-load fund   A mutual fund that doesn't charge a front-end or back-end load.

Nondepository institutions   Financial institutions that get funds from sources other than deposits.

Open-end credit   Preapproved continuous loans that can cover many purchases and usually require monthly partial payments. Also known as revolving credit.

Open-end fund   An investment company that sells its shares directly to investors and buys them back on request.

Opportunity cost   What you have to give up in order to do something.

Option contract   A contract that gives the holder the right, but not the obligation, to purchase or sell a specified investment at a set price on or before a specified date.

Ordinary life insurance   Whole life insurance with premiums payable to the time of death.

Overdraft protection   An arrangement by which a financial institution places funds in a depositor's checking account to cover overdrafts.

Overlimit charge   A penalty fee charged to an account for exceeding the credit limit.

Over-the-counter (OTC) market   An electronic network for trading securities through securities dealers.

Participating policies   Life insurance policies issued by mutual insurers that pay dividends to policyholders.

Passive investor   An investor who invests to make long-run returns and doesn't actively engage in buying or selling.

Payroll withholding   Money regularly withheld from employees' pay by employers for payment of the employees' taxes.

Periodic rate   The stated rate divided by the number of billing periods per year.

Permanent life insurance   A type of life insurance that provides both death protection and a savings vehicle.

Personal balance sheet   A statement that details the value of what you own and what you owe to others to arrive at an estimate of your net worth.

Personal cash flow statement   A summary of income and expenditures over a period of time.

Personal finance   A specialized area of study that focuses on individual and household financial decisions, such as budgeting, saving, spending, insurance, and investments.

Personal financial planning   The process of developing and implementing an integrated, comprehensive plan designed to meet financial goals, to improve financial well-being, and to prepare for financial emergencies.

Personal financial statement   A statement that summarizes your financial information.

Point of service (POS) plan   Health-care plan in which participating providers are affiliated with an HMO, but participants can still use nonparticipating providers if they are willing to pay a bigger share of the cost.

Pourover will   A will that leaves a person's remaining assets to a trust.

Preemptive right   The right of a stockholder to maintain his or her proportionate ownership when the company issues additional shares of stock.

Preferred provider organization (PPO)   A managed-care plan that provides participants with financial incentives to use certain providers.

Preferred stock   A type of stock that pays a fixed dividend.

Premium   The price an insurer charges a policyholder for insurance protection.

Prepayment penalty   A fee charged to a borrower when he or she pays a loan balance before the end of the loan term. Not all loans are subject to prepayment penalties.

Price-to-earnings (P/E) ratio   Measure of a company's future earnings potential calculated as market price divided by earnings per share.

Primary insurance amount (PIA)   The Social Security benefit payable to a program participant who retires at the normal retirement age.

Primary market   The market in which securities are sold by corporations to the public for the first time.

Prime rate   The interest rate that banks charge on loans to their most favored business customers.

Principal   1. A person who has delegated responsibility to an agent and to whom the agent has a duty.

2. The original amount borrowed or invested.

Principle of indemnity   The principle that insurance reimburse a policyholder only for actual losses.

Probate   The legal process of settling an estate.

Progressive tax   A tax that requires higher-income taxpayers to pay proportionately more in taxes than other taxpayers, through either higher tax rates or other rules.

Property tax   Local tax assessed on real estate that is proportional to value.

Prospectus   A document that gives potential investors financial information about a stock issue and the issuing company.

Proxy   A written agreement in which a shareholder gives another person the right to vote in his or her place.

Qualified terminable interest property (Q-TIP) trust   A trust for married couples in which the grantor retains control over the ultimate beneficiaries of the estate.

Rate of return   The total income earned on an investment over a period of time, including interest or dividends and capital gains, divided by the original amount invested. Also known as yield.

Real estate investment trust (REIT)   A closed-end fund that invests primarily in real estate or mortgages.

Real property   Land and anything attached to it, such as a home or commercial building.

Recession   A low point in the business cycle.

Refinancing   Obtaining a new mortgage to pay off a previous, usually higher-rate, mortgage.

Regressive tax   A tax that places a disproportionate financial burden on low-income taxpayers.

Regular checking account   A checking account that does not pay interest and requires the payment of a monthly service charge unless a minimum balance is maintained in the account.

Reinvestment risk   The risk that short-term investments will have to be reinvested at lower rates when they come due.

Renter's insurance   Insurance purchased by a renter to cover personal property and liability losses but not damage to the building itself.

Replacement ratio method   A method for estimating after-tax retirement income needs in current dollars by multiplying current expenses by a factor of 70 to 80 percent.

Residual claim   A common shareholder's right to the firm's assets and income after all the other claimholders are paid.

Retail credit card   A credit card that can be used only at the sponsoring retailer's outlets.

Revocable trust   A trust whose terms the grantor can change during his or her lifetime. A revocable trust bypasses probate but is still subject to estate taxes.

Rider   An addendum to an insurance policy that requires payment of an additional premium in return for additional specified insurance coverage.

Risk classification   The categorization of policyholders by characteristics that affect their expected losses; insurers use risk classification to price policies fairly.

Risk-averse person   A person who has a tendency to dislike risk and to be unwilling to invest in risky securities unless they earn higher investment returns than lower-risk securities.

Roth IRA   An individual retirement account to which contributions are made with after-tax dollars but in which investment earnings and withdrawals at retirement are tax free.

Round lot   A group of 100 shares of stock; stock is normally traded in round lots.

Rule of 72   A method of calculating the time it will take a sum of money to double that involves dividing 72 by the rate of interest earned on the funds.

Sales finance company   A nondepository institution that makes consumer loans to buyers of products offered through its parent company.

Savings and loan (S&L) association   A depository institution that receives funds primarily from household deposits and uses most of its funds to make home mortgage loans.

Savings ratio   A financial ratio that measures the percentage of after-tax income going to savings.

Schedule   A list of otherwise excluded valuables that are to be covered under a homeowner's or renter's policy for an additional premium.

Secondary market   The market in which previously issued securities are traded between investors.

Sector fund   A mutual fund that invests primarily in securities from a particular industry or sector.

Secured bond   A bond for which interest and principal payments are backed by assets or future cash flows pledged as collateral.

Secured loan   A loan that includes a pledge of collateral.

Securities   Investments in which the investor contributes a sum of money to a common enterprise, with the intention of making a profit through the efforts of others.

Securities exchange   A physical location at which securities are traded; the largest securities exchange is the New York Stock Exchange.

Selling short   A strategy in which an investor borrows stock from a broker, sells the stock, and later buys stock on the market to replace the borrowed stock.

Sensitivity analysis   Consideration of how an outcome changes with changes in other variables.

Single life annuity   An annuity that provides a stream of equal payments until death.

Single-payment loan   A loan that requires the repayment of interest and principal in a single payment at a specified date in the future.

Single-premium whole life insurance   Whole life insurance that is paid up with a one-time payment.

Sinking fund   A fund accumulated to pay an amount due at a specific time in the future, such as when a bond issue comes due.

Smart card   A card that stores identification and electronic cash in a computer chip.

Socially responsible fund   A mutual fund that limits its holdings to securities issued by companies that meet certain ethical and moral standards.

Specialist   A person responsible for matching a particular stock's buy and sell orders at a specific securities exchange.

Speculative investments   High-risk investments made in the hope of making a short-term profit.

Standard deduction   A dollar amount based on filing status that is subtracted from adjusted gross income in calculating taxable income.

Standard family trust   A trust for married couples that is designed to avoid estate taxes on the estate of the surviving spouse.

Sticker price   The manufacturer's suggested retail price (MSRP) for a new vehicle, including manufacturer-installed accessories and options.

Stock   An investment security that represents a proportionate ownership interest in a corporation.

Stock dividend   A dividend given to shareholders in the form of shares of stock instead of cash.

Stock market index   An indicator that shows the average price movements of a particular group of stocks representing the market or some market segment.

Stockbroker   A licensed professional who buys and sells securities on behalf of clients.

Stock-held savings institution   A savings institution that is owned by stockholders.

Stop order   An order to buy or sell stock holdings when the market price reaches a certain level.

Stop payment order   An order by which a financial institution promises not to honor a check that a depositor has written.

Stop-loss limit   The maximum out-of-pocket cost to be paid by an insured in a given year, after which the insurer pays 100 percent of covered charges.

Strict liability   A rule of law that holds a person liable for damages without proof of negligence.

Subsidized loans   Student loans awarded on the basis of need that do not require the payment of interest or repayment of principal until six months after graduation.

Tax avoidance   Strategic use of knowledge of tax rules to avoid overpayment of taxes.

Tax bracket   The range of income to which a particular marginal tax rate applies.

Tax credit   A reduction applied directly to taxes owed rather than to income that is subject to taxes.

Tax evasion   Deliberate nonpayment of taxes legally owed.

Taxable income   The amount of income that is subject to taxes under the law.

Teaser rate   A short-term below-market interest rate intended to encourage new customers to apply for a credit card.

Tenancy in common   A type of ownership in which each person owns his or her share independently and retains the right to transfer that share by sale or will.

Term life insurance   A type of life insurance that provides death protection for a specified term, often one or five years, and no cash value.

Testamentary trust   A trust established by the terms of a will.

Testator   The writer of a will.

Time deposit account   A savings account from which the depositor may not withdraw money, without penalty, until after a certain amount of time has passed.

Timing   An investment strategy in which you attempt to shift your asset allocation to capture upturns and avoid downturns in specific markets.

Tombstone ad   A formal advertisement of a stock issue in the financial press.

Total income   Gross income less certain exclusions allowed by the IRS.

Transaction date   The date on which you make a credit card purchase.

Travel and entertainment (T&E) card   A credit card that requires payment of the full balance each billing cycle.

Trust   A legal entity that holds and manages assets on behalf of someone else.

Trustee   A person or an entity who manages assets on behalf of another.

U.S. savings bonds   Bonds issued by the U.S. Treasury that pay interest that fluctuates with current Treasury security rates and that are exempt from state and local taxes.

Umbrella policy   A supplemental personal liability insurance policy.

Unearned income   Income from investments, interest, dividends, capital gains, net business income, rents, and royalties.

Unit investment trust (UIT)   An investment company that buys and holds a fixed portfolio of securities for a period of time determined by the life of the investments in the trust.

Universal life insurance   A type of permanent life insurance that allows policyholders to benefit from the investment experience of the insurer and provides a flexible premium option.

Unsubsidized loans   Student loans that accrue interest from the time they are awarded, although it is sometimes possible to defer the repayment until after graduation.

Value fund   A mutual fund that invests in companies that the market perceives to be undervalued.

Values   Fundamental beliefs about what is important in life.

Variable expenses   Expenses that vary in amount from period to period.

Variable life insurance   Permanent life insurance that has a fixed premium and allows policyholders to choose from different investment alternatives.

Variable universal life insurance   Permanent life insurance that involves a flexible premium feature and allows policyholders to choose from different investment alternatives.

Variable-rate loan   A loan for which the rate of interest varies periodically with a changing market rate, such as the prime rate.

Waiver of premium   An insurance option that allows the insured to waive premium payments under certain conditions, such as permanent disability.

Warranty   A legal promise made by a seller, such as with respect to the qualities of a vehicle being sold.

Web-only financial institutions   Financial institutions that do not have physical locations but offer a menu of cash management accounts, loans, and investments.

Whole life insurance   Permanent life insurance that provides death protection for the policyholder's whole life and includes a savings component.

Will   A legal document that transfers property upon the death of the property owner.

Wire transfer   Electronic transmittal of cash from an account in another location. A wire transfer requires payment of a fee.

Workers' compensation insurance   State-run program requiring employers to pay lost wages and medical costs associated with job related illness or injury.

Yield   The annual return on investment, including current yield and capital gains yield.

Yield to maturity (YTM)   Annualized return on a bond, if it is held to maturity and all interest payments are reinvested at the same rate.

Zero-coupon bond   A bond that doesn't make interest payments but instead is discounted at the time of sale.

INDEX